Posthumanism

Also available from Bloomsbury

A GUIDE FOR THE PERPLEXED

Posthumanism

PETER MAHON

BLOOMSBURY ACADEMIC
LONDON • NEW YORK • OXFORD • NEW DELHI • SYDNEY

BLOOMSBURY ACADEMIC
Bloomsbury Publishing Plc
50 Bedford Square, London, WC1B 3DP, UK
1385 Broadway, New York, NY 10018, USA

BLOOMSBURY, BLOOMSBURY ACADEMIC and the Diana logo are trademarks
of Bloomsbury Publishing Plc

First published 2017
Reprinted 2018, 2019

A catalogue record for this book is available from the British Library.

Library of Congress Cataloging-in-Publication Data
Names: Mahon, Peter, 1971– author.
Title: Posthumanism : a guide for the perplexed / by Peter Mahon.
Description: New York : Bloomsbury Academic, 2017. |
Series: Guides for the perplexed
Identifiers: LCCN 2016036518| ISBN 9781474236799 (hb) |
ISBN 9781474236812 (epub)
Subjects: LCSH: Humanism--History--21st century. | Humanism--Forecasting.
Classification: LCC B821 .M3135 2017 | DDC 144--dc23 LC record available at
https://lccn.loc.gov/2016036518

ISBN: HB: 978-1-4742-3679-9
PB: 978-1-4742-3680-5
ePDF: 978-1-4742-3678-2
eBook: 978-1-4742-3681-2

Series: Guides for the Perplexed

Typeset by RefineCatch Limited, Bungay, Suffolk
Printed and bound in Great Britain

To find out more about our authors and books visit www.bloomsbury.com
and sign up for our newsletters.

CONTENTS

6 Conclusion: Some Thoughts on Digital Humanities
and 'Posthumanities' 251

CHAPTER ONE

Introduction

Posthumanism—A Dialogue of Sorts

INT. BOOKSHOP—DAY

Two posthumans are browsing the bookshelves. One takes a book off a shelf, reads the title, turns to the other, rolls his eyes theatrically, with a look of disgust on his face.

Posthuman 1: Ugh. Would you ever look at this? *Posthumanism: A Guide for the Perplexed.* 'Posthumanism'? Bah! What in the name of my giddy aunt Gerty is 'posthumanism' anyway? And why should I care? It sounds suspiciously like another one of those trendy but infuriating theoretical buzzwords that academia is so fond of, like 'deconstruction' or 'intersectionality'. You know, the kind of word that seems to take on a huge significance in less important fields of study (such as art history or literary/cultural studies), while being an object of ridicule in important ones (such as engineering or mathematics). 'Posthumanism'! Just another typical academic buzzword, one that has no relevance for those of us who live in the real world outside of the ivory towers of academia and their self-important professors. Yes, the real world—you know, that place where they expect results, and pressing political or economic matters make the business of survival an everyday concern?

'Posthumanism'? Pfft! And, anyway, what was wrong with good old humanism? Honestly!

Posthuman 2: I know you're trying to be outrageous, but why on earth would you think that posthumanism has nothing to do with your life or that it is just another buzzword that privileged and out-of-touch academics use? I'm also not sure that it's a case of something being 'wrong' with humanism, but instead a recognition that humanism may no longer be the best way to think about how our species understands its position in the twenty-first century. Posthumanism, if it means anything at all, is just an acknowledgement that humans and humanity are constantly changing through their interaction with technology and tools. In a nutshell, posthumanism's primary unit of analysis is 'humans + tools'. And, if posthumanism is concerned with how 'tools'—which obviously extends to include all kinds of technology—and humans interact, then posthumanism is certainly not something that is confined to academia and self-important academics; it concerns everyone, everyday!

P1: But why 'post'-humanism? So, I'll ask again, what's wrong with humanism?

P2: Okay. Well, if, as Michel Foucault points out in 'What is Enlightenment?',[1] 'it is a fact that, at least since the seventeenth century, what is called humanism has always been obliged to lean on certain conceptions of man borrowed from religion, science, or politics',[2] then posthumanism, in its concern for 'humans + tools', would also predate any traditional 'humanism' that has its roots in the seventeenth century. 'Posthumanism', in other words, would simply be a way of thinking that extends beyond 'humanism' understood in that way.

P1: So, posthumanism extends beyond seventeenth-century humanism, then?

P2: Yes. And, to the extent that posthumanism is concerned with 'humans + tools', it is a neat umbrella term to cover the work of a diverse group of thinkers, researchers and scientists, such as Edwin Hutchins,[3] Bernard Steigler,[4] David McFarland,[5] Andy Clark[6] and Cary Wolfe among others,[7] who have all argued, in different ways, of course, that humans have always used tools and technology to extend themselves. Now, I'm not claiming that all the writers I've just named would call themselves 'posthumanists'—for example, Clark and McFarland wouldn't—only that their thinking lines up with posthumanism as I've defined it for you. And, if posthumanism stretches back to the very dawn of human tool use—that is, if posthumanism actually predates a concept that only took shape several centuries ago—then it makes little sense to retain that concept when we're exploring 'humans + tools'.

P1: Well, then, shouldn't it just be called 'prehumanism'?

P2: Fair point; I agree that the name seems a bit paradoxical. I'd answer your question as follows: posthumanism is 'post-humanism' rather than 'pre-humanism' because, historically, it comes 'after' humanism; and, even though posthumanism comes after historical 'humanism', it can nevertheless be used to discuss humans' relations with their tools and technology, which had gotten underway long before 'humanism' ever came along. So, posthumanism is both 'pre-' and 'post-' humanist. This situation should also make us somewhat wary of trying to reduce posthumanism to a simple 'fashion' by historicizing it. There is thus, to be sure, a history of posthumanism, just like there is, say, a history of biology—its major discoveries, leading figures, shifts in technology used, and so on; but the fact remains that posthumanism engages with something—humans interacting with tools and technology—that is at once prehistoric and post-humanist.

P1: So why keep the 'humanism' part of the name?

P2: Fair question. I think it's appropriate to keep the 'humanism' part because posthumanism doesn't make a simple 'break' from humanism. I mean, it'd be a bad idea—not to mention a contradictory one—to simply throw away every single humanist idea: imagine throwing away rationality, individuality, freedom, progress, rights, just because they're old! That'd be sheer idiocy. It would also be impossible, given the centrality of tools and technology to posthumanism: thus, freedom, rationality, progress, and science are all integral to it. So, it might be better to think of posthumanism as being a radicalization of humanist ideas beyond the historical specificity and constraints of humanism.

P1: You're making it sound like posthumanism is really just humanism on steroids. I'm losing sight of why it's called 'posthumanism' if it's just a re-tread or 'radicalization' of humanism.

P2: Well, it might be easier to see why 'posthumanism' is a necessary name if you consider how certain discoveries in techno-science disrupt certain humanist notions about humans and humanity. I mentioned above that posthumanism, in its most basic sense, can be understood as being concerned with 'human(s) + tools'. As such, posthumanism significantly overlaps with, for example, what Hutchins, in *Cognition in the Wild*,[8] calls 'distributed cognition'. Cognition is the set of processes related to knowledge, such as attention, memory and working memory, judgment and evaluation, reasoning and computation, problem solving and decision making, comprehension and production of language, etc. But distributed cognition is understood not as being confined to the interior—the mind, brain or body—of an individual human being, but as being carried out by a system in which a human interacts with objects, artefacts, tools and other humans. In such a system, all sorts of nonbiological materials become part of the process of carrying out particular tasks. Distributed cognition thus shows us that in carrying out a task information is constantly moving back and forth across the boundaries of biological and nonbiological matter. So, if your definition of humanism is one that defines humans as being distinct, from, say, machines, or defines humans as purely biological and organic beings, or defines human identity in terms of the limits and confines of the human body, then you are going to have a hard time when it comes to thinking about a lot of modern technologies such as AI and branches of medicine such as neuroprosthetics.[9]

P1: Okay, I think I'm getting it. Something like distributed cognition cannot be said to be simply 'human' or even biological since there are nonhuman and nonbiological components to it? So, we need posthumanism to grasp what is going on there?

P2: Yes, exactly. And because posthumanism is neither a simple break from, nor a simple continuation of, humanism, the complex relations between humanism and posthumanism are similar to the complex relations between modernism and postmodernism as described by the philosopher Jean-Francois Lyotard in his book, *The Postmodern Condition*.[10] Indeed, Neil Badmington, in his book, *Alien Chic*, makes this very point.[11]

P1: So, posthumanism is neither a simple break from nor a simple continuation of humanism? Right? If so, doesn't it then hold the door open for including nonhuman, non-organic and nonbiological elements in categories we might ordinarily think of as purely 'human'?

P2: Yes. This happens because a key underlying concept of posthumanism and distributed cognition is what's known as functionalism.[12] David McFarland, in his terrific book, *Guilty Robots, Happy Dogs*, defines it as follows:

> Functionalism is the view that certain entities, including some mental ones, are best described in terms of the functional role that they play within a system. Thus a word processor is a device that processes words. Physically, word processors have changed greatly over recent decades, but they remain best described in terms of their function, not in material terms.[13]

You've heard that old saying, 'If it walks like a duck and quacks like a duck, then it's a duck'? That's basically functionalism. In distributed cognition, 'cognition' is actually being carried out by the system as a whole, not just the human being: for example, a pilot can only fly a plane in conjunction with the instruments, panels and readouts in the cockpit, all of which are sensing, monitoring, calculating, reacting to, storing and displaying all the information necessary to keep the plane in the air. The cognition necessary to fly the plane happens in both flesh and blood and silicon and wire. There is, then, a distinction to be made between the purely physical material make up of something and the role—or function—it plays in a larger system: memory in a computer functions like memory in an animal, even though both are made of completely different stuff. You can also see functionalism at work in certain philosophical theories of the mind: as McFarland points out, the merit of functionalism 'is that "the mental" remains distinct from the "the physical" and cannot be *reduced* to it'.[14] In this way, 'pain' in a human being is understood as a kind of 'higher level' property that arises from different 'realizers'—for example, injury, disease, poisoning.[15] The important thing to remember here is that functionalism suggests that pain could be realized in a robot, since whatever it is that may play the role of pain in the robot, is, for all intents and purposes, pain. It is also what makes it possible to attribute certain mental states and cognitive abilities to animals, like happiness to dogs or problem-solving abilities to crows.

P1: Interesting. But the kind of technology involved in the examples you gave of distributed cognition is a very recent one: computer technology. There weren't too many airliners flying around or aircraft carriers on the sea in the Middle Ages.

P2: You're absolutely right, of course. As I've said, even though posthumanism comes 'after' humanism, it also comes 'before' humanism; neither is posthumanism a complete break with, nor simple continuation of, humanism. However, as that earlier quotation from Foucault made clear, 'humanism' has also always relied on science—along with religion and politics—to define itself. Now, it goes without saying that humans did not just stop using or doing science in the seventeenth century. As a result, science, and the tools and technology it makes possible, have been advancing in leaps and bounds since then, and any conception of humanism that draws on science must, of necessity, change as science changes and progresses. It is this aspect of posthumanism—that it comes about as a sort of natural growth in humanism—that I personally find most compelling: it takes into account how modern tools and technologies, such as AI, robotics and genetic manipulation, are changing humans as a species. Digital and genetic technologies and tools, in other words, are effectively what tipped humanism over into posthumanism. This situation helps explain why posthumanism is neither a complete break with, nor simple continuation of, humanism; it also explains why posthumanism is currently best understood in terms of the complex relations humans have with modern digital and genetic tools and technologies in particular; and it helps explain why posthumanism is obsessed with not only cutting-edge tools and techniques but also future tools and technological developments, as well as with questions about how they will change us even further.[16] There is something special that happens with digital technology that does not happen with say, a rake or an ox, even though both can be regarded as distributed systems wherein the ox or the rake can be understood as extensions of the human using them.

P1: Alright. I'll grant you that in certain high stake or high-tech jobs, like flying an airliner, people have to rely on distributed cognition to get the job done, but I'm still not convinced that posthumanism is of concern to everyday people going about their business. We're not all airline pilots or navigators on aircraft carriers. Posthumanism still doesn't seem to me to be relevant to ordinary people just living their lives.

P2: Really? An everyday—perhaps trivial—and decidedly non-digital example I use to remind myself what's at stake in posthumanism is to think about my eyeglasses. As I've gotten older, I've become more and more dependent upon them to see properly: I'd be hard pressed to read things like recommended dosages on medicine bottles without them. My glasses are clearly not a biological part of me—they are manufactured in a factory somewhere using plastics and metals—but, because I need them to see, they are now an essential part of my system of sight. My own biological lenses are not up to the job anymore, so I need prosthetic ones: artificial ones to supplement my biological ones. Because they are now an integral part of the distributed system of my eyesight, I have to upgrade them over time as my eyesight worsens if I wish to continue to see properly. If I were vain or fear being judged by others, then maybe I'd want to change them as fashions change as well. The important thing to grasp, however, is that my eyesight is now made up of a biological part and an artificially manufactured part. Right?

P1: Right.

P2: Now, think about a more complex everyday digital device, like your smartphone. The digital technology in your phone effectively allows you to be in two places at once by artificially extending your voice and senses—sight and hearing—across huge distances of space; your phone also helps you cognize by distributing your cognition, functioning as an artificial memory that not only reminds you about appointments, but allows you to access, navigate and interact with the vast repository of data known as the Internet. The access your phone grants you allows you to check facts and figures; it allows you to learn about new things and update your current understanding of things; it allows you make better informed decisions, choices and judgments; it allows you to solve problems, and the list could go on. Your smartphone does all this by artificially enhancing your biological cognitive power through silicon circuitry and global telecommunication networks; without it, you couldn't do any of the things I just listed with ease, if at all. Your phone is thus more than 'just' a phone: it is a prosthetic cognitive device that helps you think, remember, communicate and so on, much more effectively. Human relationships with smartphones have gotten even more complicated recently, with the appearance of on-board 'knowledge navigators' or 'intelligent personal assistants' like Siri or Cortana, that use artificial intelligence to interact with us. In other words, our smartphones are now intertwining our enhanced cognition with artificially intelligent agents, not just other people.

At the same time, this artificial cognitive enhancement seems to function like a 'natural' part of you. Imagine that tomorrow all phones and data networks were to somehow just suddenly vanish, and you were never able to use your smartphone ever again: no more Google, no more Internet, no more social networking, no more reminders, no more communication or fact-checking or problem-solving on the fly. What would you need to do to compensate for the loss of your cognitive prosthetic? Okay, you'd very likely survive without it—after all, your ancestors did—but wouldn't your life nonetheless be impaired somewhat by losing it? Might it not feel a little like you've lost a part of yourself? Maybe some IQ points? Some knowledge? A part of your memory? A piece of your identity? Would you trade, say, a toe (a finger? a kidney?) to have back what your phone gave you? Even if you wouldn't trade a toe to have your phone back, if you think that losing your phone might be like losing a part of you that you'd mourn, then you're already posthuman; because you're no longer conceiving of yourself in purely biological terms, no longer thinking about yourself in terms of a purely human body, but in digital technological terms as well. In other words, you've begun to think of yourself as extended or distributed across flesh and blood and silicon, data networks and radio waves. This situation has some important and unsettling consequences, because you are no longer a purely biological being; part of you, however small, is a product you had to purchase, and which was in all likelihood produced by poorly paid workers or robots in another part of the world; part of you runs on software that you probably cannot read and is subject to user agreements, patents, licenses and copyright law. In other words, you can no longer simply think of yourself as a being that simply 'owns' itself, like John Locke did in his 1689 text *Two Treatises of Government*,[17] because part of you has been made by Samsung or Apple or whomever, and it is thus never entirely yours; the real owners can update the operating system at will, add features, drop others, gather your data to sell to advertisers, and so on.[18] Distributed cognition also makes it difficult to understand yourself in terms of 'embodiment' in the sense of a clearly defined human body or self that stops at the skin or at least at the skull. Posthumanism thus has serious consequences for all those social and political theories that hinge of the idea that we somehow 'own' ourselves. Our digital tools and technologies thus not only continue to displace religion, they also rewrite politics.

P1: But that's horrifying. Isn't it our embodiment, our human body, that makes us fundamentally human? As I grow and live, I amass particular experiences, memories, skills—the things that make me 'me', that make me who I am, that give me a particular identity and are housed in my body.

P2: Well, that's the very problem. If you define yourself as human in those ways, then posthumanism definitely means the loss of your 'humanness'. But is that definition good enough for an age when digital technology makes distributed cognition an everyday occurrence for billions of people? Can such a definition really apply anymore? Would that definition of 'human' not also rule out the vast majority of human beings, and reserve the category of 'human' for some pristine-but-imaginary in-group that don't use such tools and technologies? And where would that definition of human leave those people who have been in accidents or subject to diseases or congenital conditions and may be missing certain body parts or certain abilities and must therefore rely on prosthetics of various kinds in order to be able to do things? They would appear to be no longer 'human', by such a reckoning.

I do think that there's some fear and squeamishness underlying the concern for a whole, complete, clearly definable body, which is understandable. However, the field of neuroprosthetics offers a good example for considering the benefits of rethinking the body as extended or distributed.[19] Since the 1960s, amputees have been able to use myoelectric prostheses—prostheses that are controlled by electromyography signals or potentials from voluntarily contracted muscles within a stump. However, in February 2013, *Science Daily* reported that, for the first time, electrodes had been permanently implanted in nerves and muscles of an amputee, allowing him to directly control an arm prosthesis.[20] What projects such as this one show is that bio-information passes fairly easily from flesh and bone to silicon and plastic and back to flesh and bone again; nor does such communication have to form a loop with the same body: an experiment conducted by Kevin Warwick *et al.*, showed that it was possible to have direct and purely electronic communication between the nervous systems of two humans.[21] The ability of information to cross biological and nonbiological boundaries has been borne out by many experiments, and these findings challenge so many of our intuitions about how our minds and bodies seem to work.[22] If we were to think about this from a functionalist point of view, we would say that the 'human flesh' is no longer the sole medium that carries 'human' sensation or movement.

P1: No, I'm still not convinced. It seems to me that all that you've so far said regarding distributed cognition, functionalism, digital technology, prosthetics, metadata and so on, could be seen as a hysterical overstatement of our dependence upon and relationship with technology. What if your posthumanism is just a symptom of an irrational fear of being human? You know, a fear of not being able to accept the weaknesses or vulnerabilities of our bodies? Actually, the more I think about it, the more posthumanism seems like the fantasy of the kind of misfits who want to devalue the very things that make us human—our bodies, our emotions, our thoughts, our relationships—because they find maintaining real-life relationships too difficult.

P2: Kek! If we weren't concerned about the weaknesses and frailties of our flesh, then we wouldn't spend so much time and effort creating and refining safety equipment, vehicles or shelters from materials stronger and more durable than our flesh to help protect us from substances, situations and environmental factors that would harm us. However, your point about technology displacing more 'natural' or 'lived' or 'direct' human relations between people, is worth pursuing. It's certainly a commonplace used to talk about the Internet, isn't it? The view that technology gets in the way of lived human relations is certainly not an uncommon one: everyone is aware of the stereotype of the basement-dwelling neckbeard who should go outside into the sunshine and make real—as opposed to online or imaginary—friends. This view of technology appears virtually intact at the end of Ernest Cline's *Ready Player One*, where Anorak's avatar tells Wade not to spend all his time online like he did when he was alive.[23]

P1: My point is the same as the one made in 1967 by Guy Debord in his book *The Society of the Spectacle*.[24] Although Debord was not talking about posthumanism but consumer society, his argument has some bearing here. He argues that consumer society is where everything 'that once was directly lived has become mere representation' and 'passive identification with the spectacle supplants genuine activity'.[25] He goes on to say that the spectacle is 'not a collection of images', but rather 'a social relationship between people that is mediated by images'.[26] According to Debord, we are at the 'historical moment at which the commodity completes its colonization of social life'.[27] I'm saying, in other words, that posthumanism is really just a symptom of our being mired in consumerism and that there is no real difference between it and consumer culture under late globalized capitalism.

P2: I'd have to agree to a degree: it's obvious that Internet and communications technology—by its very nature—can't help but get entangled in the social relations between people.

P1: So, you're admitting that posthumanism is connected to the spectacle of commodity capitalism, and threatening to supplant lived human relations and degrading them with commodities?

P2: Again, to a degree, yes. How could posthumanism not be connected to commodity capitalism? We in the developed world live in a capitalist consumer culture; those living in developing world are heading in the same direction. It'd be silly to try and pretend otherwise. And capitalism has driven the industries that are producing all the tools and technologies I have been speaking about. But the charge of whether or not posthumanism is reducible to commodity capitalism is perhaps easy to answer with a 'No'. In many ways, this is the same type of question as the one about the relation between humanism and posthumanism we talked about earlier. Posthumanism comes before humanism because it goes back to the prehistoric origins of humans and tool use; the same applies here: there is no reason to assume that posthumanism is reducible to capitalism as Debord understands it, which, roughly speaking, only began around the sixteenth century because humans have been using tools and technologies for much, much longer than capitalism has been around. And, if there have always been tools and humans— that is, human beings + technology—then it would not be possible to think of human relations outside of tools and technology. In other words, tools and technology have never not mediated lived human relations. Understood thus, consumerism and commodities capitalism are, like humanism, parasitic on posthumanism, not the other way around.

P1: So, the relations between posthumanism and late capitalism are far from simple? I think I'd agree.

P2: Good. And it seems to me that the desire for an unmediated, non-technological lived human relations is actually a modern fantasy projected onto and into the past. You can see doubts about such unmediated lived human relations expressed in a book like J.G. Ballard's 1973 novel, *Crash*, which is an unblinking look at how consumer products—the automobile, the capitalist commodity par excellence—mediate lived human relations.[28] *Crash* presents a world where the lived human relations between characters are already dysfunctional and saturated by images from the get-go: Ballard and his wife, for example, can only have sex when fantasizing about other people. However, if you think that *Crash* presents the relations between characters as such because it is the product of late capitalistic consumer culture, then how would you account for Chaucer's Wife of Bath, who, in the fourteenth century was already using language, love and sex to manipulate her husbands in order to amass wealth and social power?[29] All in all, what

I'm saying is that the type of unmediated lived human relations imagined by Debord may never have existed. What Debord's analysis does confirm, however, is that lived human relations are particularly vulnerable to being supplemented and mediated by images, which should make us wonder if they have not always been thus. And, I would suggest that this is not necessarily a wholly bad thing, if you think about it: when a powerful a device like a smartphone is mediating the relations between you and whomever you are talking to, it is, nevertheless, also what makes that connection possible in the first place. I wouldn't be able to talk to my mother or sister back in Ireland without one, even if it sometimes emphasizes distance between there and Vancouver. In short, the very thing doing the mediating is also the very thing that is enabling the contact.

P1: It seems to me, then, that even if posthumanism, for the reasons you give, is not reducible to capitalism, it is still inseparable from capitalist modes of production and exploitation to the extent that capitalism does actually parasite it. You said yourself that posthumanism also comes after humanism; we currently live in a global capitalist economy. So, this would mean, for example, that posthumanism's intimate relations with Internet and communications technologies ties it directly to the capitalist exploitation of people: not just the workers who make the digital devices in often terrible working conditions, where labour codes and practices are not adhered to, but also the exploitation of the people who want or need those devices. A smartphone certainly isn't cheap to begin with, and keeping up with the latest models and usage plans can be very, very expensive; it is easy to see how those without much money to begin with might end up indebting themselves to have and use one. And I've no idea what a prosthesis like the one you were describing earlier would cost, but there's no way many could afford a prosthetic arm like that. I suppose I'm also wondering about how technology creates and perpetuates the digital divide and the global digital divide—the divide between different classes' and countries' access to information and communications technologies. According to the International Telecommunication Union's statistics for 2014, 21 per cent of the developing world has access to mobile-broadband, while 84 per cent of the developed world has the same.[30] That's four times the difference!

P2: Certainly, there are inequalities and exploitation associated with digital technology and thus posthumanism. No question about it. But Internet access is starting to be viewed as an essential part of everyday life and communication. The campaign for 'Net Neutrality' has led to calls in the US and elsewhere for classifying Internet access as a utility, like water or electricity. And although the February 2015 vote that allowed the Federal Communications Commission in the US to treat Internet providers as 'common carriers', did not (despite what a lot of reports said[31]) reclassify Internet access is as a public utility, it was, nonetheless, a welcome step in the right direction. Interestingly, the same set of statistics from the ITU you just mentioned also shows that while fixed-broadband growth is slowing globally, there is rapid growth in mobile-broadband use in developing countries, and 2013–2014 growth rates are expected to be twice as high as in developed countries (26 per cent compared with 11.5 per cent). Also, the number of mobile-broadband subscriptions has reached 2.3 billion worldwide, and 55 per cent of those are in developing countries; it appears that developing countries are skipping fixed-broadband and going directly to mobile-broadband. Africa leads the world in mobile broadband growth with a growth rate of 40 per cent—twice as high as the global average—and mobile-broadband penetration there is now about 20 per cent, up from 2 per cent in 2010. In developing countries, the number of Internet users has doubled in 5 years, from 974 million in 2009 to 1.9 billion in 2014. Now, they may all be illegally downloading *Game of Thrones*, but the growing numbers suggest that the developing world is getting online using smartphones. Granted, these statistics do not seem to have changed the fact that the richest countries in the world are over-represented in terms of knowledge on the Internet: for example, figures show that Wikipedia articles on the UK outnumber those on Africa by nearly 4 to 1.[32] At the same time, owning a computer has never really been cheaper: the UK based Raspberry Pi Foundation, set up 'with the intention of promoting the teaching of basic computer science in schools', makes available a series of surprisingly powerful credit card-sized single-board computers that retail for about $35 US, £27 or €40 each, thus offering a chance to those with little money to get familiar with coding.[33] Again, granted, even a Raspberry Pi, as cheap as it seems, costs far more than a lot of the world's population can afford, since approximately 3.2 billion people live on only up to $2 a day.[34] Global poverty is simply staggering and the digital divide still exists, but I'm sure you'd agree that there is some encouragement to be had from those numbers and those organizations. And the robotic prosthetics I mentioned ought to be available to anyone who needs one, once the research and development has been completed. No question about it.

P1: And what about the exploitation of people by the Internet and communications technologies industry outside of the very poor? What about the exploitation of the workers who make these devices, like those at Foxconn? I'm sure you remember the well-publicized cases of suicide and attempted suicide at the Foxconn City industrial park in Shenzhen, China. Granted, the company has since raised wages, erected safety nets to catch falling workers and brought in Buddhist monks to help workers, but there have been persistent questions about things like safety and overtime at that facility and others like it in China and Taiwan. And what about the exploitation of 'posthumans' themselves by these corporations? Your whole explanation of our ever-closer entwinement with our phones not only disrupts the very idea of our sovereign 'ownership' of our bodies and ourselves and all the social, economical and political theories that have been built on that idea, but also conjures the distasteful situation where a 'posthuman' essentially has to buy parts of him or herself that he or she never fully gets to own. You, the posthuman consumer, start to become the product, a commodity. And what happens when you can no longer afford the 'upgrades' to your 'posthuman self'? Do you become obsolete, just like all the other cheap crap that corporate capitalism produces? Or must you degrade yourself further and by going deeper and deeper into debt or servitude in trying to keep up? Isn't the very danger of your posthumanism that it seems to herald the worst possible degradation of humans, stripping them of their human dignity and making them even more vulnerable to exploitation by those who see people as exploitable and expendable, no better than animals or things? And what about privacy? Isn't it clear that all of these devices are constantly spying on their users, collecting data on them, their purchases, browsing habits, their movements? Just to keep selling people more and more crap they can neither afford nor want? And isn't it now clear that this data is all gathered by government spy agencies like the National Security Agency? Before Edward

Snowden's revelations about governmental use of 'big data', this was tinfoil hat territory.[35]

P2: I agree with a lot of what you've just said. The situation in China is definitely troubling. But, according to The World Bank, China alone accounted for most of the decline in extreme poverty over the past three decades. Between 1981 and 2011, 753 million people moved above the $1.25-a-day poverty threshold set by The World Bank.[36] So it would appear that the manufacture of information and communication technologies is at least partly responsible for the reduction in global levels of poverty. But that's not to suggest that everything is rosy, of course. It's clear that posthumanism brings us very, very close to the questions of economic exploitation that has been a political concern since Marx critiqued the capitalist exploitation of surplus labour. But, again, I would ask, is posthumanism itself responsible for these exploitations or capitalism? And is the best solution to the problems you've outlined simply to stop using these devices? Can't those devices be used to get the message about exploitation and inequality out there, to inform people of what exactly is happening in the world they live in? Isn't it the capitalist owners of the factories and the tech companies who use them to manufacture their brands that are directly exploiting the workers?

P1: You're correct, of course. But we in the developed world are buying this stuff, and are thereby fuelling the exploitation.

P2: Again, I agree. We have to recognize that we, as consumers, are also part of the global problem of exploitation: we want—we need—what these devices offer and those wants and needs drive that exploitation as well. If there were no market for these things, they wouldn't be made. So, I accept what you're saying and we must confront the situation that digital communications technologies are not simply benign and that posthumanism doesn't present dangers. There may be tremendous benefits to be had from these devices—in terms of communications, knowledge access and sharing, medicine, and so on—but they can also cause real harm. In addition to the exploitation of workers you've mentioned, there are also the horrendous environmental problems caused by the manufacture and disposal of these devices, from the extraction of rare earth metals, to the vast amounts of fossil fuels used in making and shipping them, to the perplexing question of how best to dispose of and recycle these devices, especially given how quickly they become obsolete. The industry that produces these devices does, in no uncertain terms, contribute to environmental destruction and anthropogenic climate change.

And, certainly, there's no question that we are being commoditized by tech companies such as Google. Remember that old adage, 'if it's free, then you are the product'? So it's not just a matter of being commoditized by having to buy and upgrade parts of ourselves in the form of newer phones, tablets, laptops or gaming consoles; the commodification of people through the entanglements of human and digital communications technology also goes much, much deeper. When we use our digital communications devices, we're constantly trading all kinds of information about ourselves—in the form of 'metadata', or data about data—for access to other information, which the likes of Google then sells to advertisers. It is the metadata of your online browsing habits that behavioural advertising companies collect and sell. The information gathered is not tied to your personal information—they don't, for example, know your name, your home address, or your phone number. Instead, such companies identify you by a random ID number and use sophisticated algorithms to make inferences about your age, sex, interests, etc., and predictions about your interests based on your online activity. It's interesting to ponder the little digital version of you that lives online that is constantly being algorithmically refined to act more and more like you.

So, it would seem that, on the one hand, digital Internet and communication technologies allow us to communicate with our loved ones; they allow us to access and share so much information in astonishing amounts at amazing speeds; they give us enhanced cognitive abilities, thereby allowing us to see clearly the benefits and potential of technological prosthetics; they listen to us and learn from us and adapt to us, showing us more examples of the things we like; they allow for the development of new body–machine interfaces that help the victims of trauma, disease and those with congenital or age-related conditions; they allow the developing world to tap the potential of digital communication; on the other hand, however, those very same technologies make it very easy for unaccountable intelligence agencies to spy on users; they perpetuate the exploitation of workers and consumers by capitalism; they play no small role in contributing to environmental catastrophe; they challenge the notion of a self or body that is clearly defined, unitary and autonomous. All of the pros and cons I've just listed, however, merely highlight what has already happened to us; we are, like it or not, already quite far down the road of posthumanism, so we don't really have a 'choice' about whether or not we should become posthuman. We are already posthumans living in a posthuman world.

Opting out of this world is difficult. It's certainly possible that one could walk away from it all, like Christopher McCandless, and pull the plug on one's technological and communication dependence, go into the wild and try to live 'off grid'.[37] McCandless didn't make it. A better option would definitely be to take the steps necessary to protect ourselves and our data from prying eyes, just like those who worked with Edward Snowden, had to do.[38] But the fact that such elaborate counter-measures exist at all is testament, first, to just how entangled we have become in our digital communications technology; second, to just how very difficult it is to evade its exploitation of us; and, third, to just how far people need and should go to protect themselves because these digital communications tools are so very useful. And, given the amount of inconvenience some of these countermeasures cause, I'd wonder how long everyday users would try to use them for before they gave up in frustration: think of the hassle a lowly ad blocker or script blocker can cause while surfing.

P1: You've made the point a number of times now that posthumanism takes its unit of analysis as 'humans + tools'. Well, our tools, because of computer technology, now seem to be getting very smart, very powerful and very productive. And one of the first casualties of such new and improved tools is always the worker, who is inevitably squeezed out of a job. I'm thinking about a robot like Baxter, a manufacturing robot who does not even need to be programmed to perform a task: all it needs is for a worker to show it what to do by guiding its arms, and it learns how to do it; Baxter can also be easily retrained to do different tasks and it retails for about $25,000, about the same as the average production worker's wage.[39] Foxconn, which we talked about earlier, is planning to put about a million Chinese workers out of job by automating.[40] Granted, the process is moving slower than expected, but I wonder what that move will do to global poverty rates we talked about earlier?

Now, I know that, historically speaking, automation has not produced mass unemployment, merely a redistribution of employment. A total of 90 per cent of the US population were employed in agriculture at the turn of the eighteenth century; the percentage currently employed in US agriculture is 1.6 per cent, and 88.4 per cent of the population is not out of work having found jobs in other industries.[41] The automation of the last 200 years or so has caused a shift from physical and manual labour to intellectual labour and provision of services. But what if this time it's different? Clearly, an AI like IBM's Watson is currently the exception rather than the rule, but what happens once Watsons becomes cheap enough to manufacture on a large scale? Will it start to take the kind of jobs that are thought of as professions—doctors, lawyers, researchers, teachers, engineers, etc.? I saw in a recent report that it 'is no longer unrealistic to consider that workplace robots and their AI processing systems could reach the point of general production by 2030'. Such AIs are expected to be doing 'low-level knowledge economy work', in, for example, law offices.[42] The larger problem, as people like the philosopher Mark Walker have also pointed out, is that whereas before there was a entire untapped field of labour to migrate to after physical labour dried up, now it will be impossible to migrate back to physical labour because that labour has been so heavily automated already.[43] And what will happen to the global economy once the number of people put out of work by automation reaches critical mass? Riots would likely only be the beginning. And this is to say nothing about what could arguably be the ultimate threat to humans by one of their tools—artificial superintelligence (ASI). I'm sure you remember the recent flurry of media reports about the concerns voiced by Elon Musk—the founder of SpaceX and a cofounder of PayPal and Tesla Motors, among other things—and Stephen Hawking—the celebrity theoretical physicist and cosmologist—about ASI.[44] Both basically said that it would be a very good idea to tread carefully with ASI because it could pose an existential threat to humankind.

P2: Yes, there certainly appears to be turbulent times ahead, and I share your concern about the problem of mass unemployment. Think of the impact of self-driving vehicles alone on the labour market: no more bus drivers, taxi drivers, truck drivers, train drivers, delivery drivers, etc.[45] A 2014 report in *The Economist* stated that recent research 'suggests that [the wages of workers are stagnating] because substituting capital for labour through automation is increasingly attractive; as a result owners of capital have captured ever more of the world's income since the 1980s, while the share going to labour has fallen'.[46] The same report noted a '2013 paper by Carl Benedikt Frey and Michael Osborne, of the University of Oxford, [which] argued that jobs are at high risk of being automated in 47% of the occupational categories into which work is customarily sorted. That includes accountancy, legal work, technical writing and a lot of other white-collar occupations.' Now, I'm not saying that somehow all jobs for humans will suddenly disappear with automation: some jobs, according to the same report, like yoga instructors or therapists, might be very difficult to automate, while jobs that mesh well with machine intelligence will also likely persist for some time. However, it's becoming fairly clear that more and more of the service jobs that filled the gaps as manufacturing jobs decreased are becoming easier and easier to automate due to advances in technology. And, as the research cited in *The Economist* also shows, wealth will gradually become even more and more concentrated in the hands of the machine owners and managers—the infamous '1%' identified by Thomas Piketty in his *Capital in the Twenty-First Century*.[47]

P1: For these reasons, I think we should be actively considering measures such as the Universal Basic Income (UBI) or the Basic Income Guarantee (BIG). If so many people will be unable to find work due to automation, it surely makes sense to give everyone a guaranteed basic amount of income that would cover the basic costs of living, such as food, shelter, creature comforts and so on. Apart from the moral issue, such a measure would also be a first step in tackling the social unrest that will surely follow mass unemployment. Obviously, funding such programmes would need careful thought, and the study I mentioned earlier by Mark Walker outlines some of the possible ways in which the UBI could be funded. If something like UBI were to be implemented, then at least something approximating an economy as we know it would be able to function: people would have an income, which they would then use to buy the goods created by increasingly automated production. Implementing UBI would be disruptive of classic capitalism, in that it would make not working an option for people by causing what Walker memorably calls the 'threat-economy'—that is, an economy that threatens people with no housing or food and death if they do not work—to disappear. Labour would thus, partially at least, be 'decommodified', because people would no longer be forced to sell their labour power in order to survive.[48] UBI would also perhaps give those who still wish to work more bargaining power when it comes to selling their labour.

P2: I would add that UBI also promises to be just as disruptive of classic socialism as it would be of classic capitalism: if people end up receiving UBI in large enough numbers, then there would be less and less actual human workers for socialists to try to organize into unions. A socialism that continued to focus solely on human workers would cease to be a potentially mass movement. At the same time, the bourgeoisie would no longer be guilty of exploiting the surplus labour of human workers since they would only be 'exploiting' the robots they own. Socialism could well find itself without its traditional enemy to fight. I suppose one could argue that there would still be a need for a renewed form of socialism to address how automation would continue to concentrate wealth only in the hands of those who own the means of production. Personally, I'd be hopeful that one day, hopefully sooner rather than later, everyone will have access to their own solar power supply to run their own advanced 3D printers: everyone would then own the means of production individually.

P1: A bit utopian, but there seems to be little doubt that capitalist-worker relations are going to be heavily revised by automation.

P2: Perhaps. The point you made about the threat of AI is also interesting, if not, perhaps, a little alarmist. The idea that one of humankind's inventions could wipe it out is not, of course, a new one: Mary Shelley has Victor Frankenstein worry that the female Creature he is working on as a mate for the male Creature could, through her ability to reproduce, wipe out mankind.[49] And almost everyone remembers the lines of the *Bhagavad Gita* that J. Robert Oppenheimer quoted on witnessing the first artificial nuclear blast: 'Now I am become Death, the destroyer of worlds.' You can also see a similar anxiety colouring discussions of AI in, for example, the philosophical work of Vincent Müller and Nick Bostrom. Müller and Bostrom sent a survey to experts working in AI to see 'what probability the best experts currently assign to high-level machine intelligence occurring within a particular time-frame, which risks they see with that development, and how fast they see these developing'.[50] They found that these experts expected that machine intelligence would far exceed human intelligence by the last quarter of the twenty-first century/start of the twenty-second century. The same experts estimated that the chance that this development would turn out to be '"bad" or "extremely bad" for humanity' as about 1-in-3. And yet, for others, such as Ray Kurzweil, 'superintelligence'— or, as he prefers to call it, 'the Singularity'[51]—is something to be very optimistic about.According to Kurzweil, the Singularity, which he predicts will be with us by 2045, holds out the promise of human immortality brought about by the advent of a superintelligent technology that surpasses human capability. This superintelligence could provide us with better technology, better healthcare and medicine, a cleaner environment and unlimited sources of energy.[52]

But the fears about and hopes for AI can easily look like something from bad science fiction, something way too far into the future to be worth even thinking about: currently, AI is simply nowhere near the point of being advanced enough for us to care. However, it might be worth remembering that machine learning has made some interesting advances very recently: think, for example, of the artificial agent created by Google DeepMind, which taught itself how to play video games at a human and superhuman level. Now, a game-playing AI might sound trivial, but, as one of Google DeepMind's co-founders, Demis Hassabis, points out, until now, 'self-learning systems have only been used for relatively simple problems. . . . For the first time, we have used it in a perceptually rich environment to complete tasks that are very challenging to humans. . . . The only information we gave the system was the raw pixels on the screen and the idea that it had to get a high score. . . . Everything else it had to figure out by itself.'[53] I'm not at all saying that Google DeepMind's agent will suddenly become 'conscious' and try to take over the world or anything like that; but it should certainly give us pause and invite us to think about where we are at with AI.

P1: So, if I've understood what you've been saying, posthumanism is concerned with how our cutting-edge tools and technologies—and all that they make possible—impact us as citizens, consumers and social actors. Posthumanism concerns us all because it is not just a vapid academic buzzword or irritating intellectual fashion-statement. Posthumanism asks us to looks squarely at and deeply into those things that have—and will have—a direct bearing on our technological, political, economic well-being and survival as a species.

P2: Yes. And, all in all, it seems impossible to say that posthumanism is simply 'good' or 'evil'. Perhaps the best way to think of it is as an example of what the philosopher Jacques Derrida, in his book *Dissemination*,[54] calls a *pharmakon*: 'If the *pharmakon* is "ambivalent", it is because it constitutes the medium in which opposites are opposed, the movement and the play that links them among themselves, reverses them or makes one side cross over into the other (soul/body, good/evil, inside/outside, memory/forgetfulness, speech/writing, etc.).'[55] Interestingly, understanding posthumanism as a *pharmakon* overlaps to a degree with Fredric Jameson's view of postmodernism in *Postmodernism, or, the Cultural Logic of Late Capitalism*,[56] where he challenges us to 'think the cultural evolution of late capitalism' as both catastrophe and progress all at once.[57] Posthumanism is crisis and opportunity all rolled into one.

P1: Well, it seems to me that if we are to stand a realistic chance of understanding, coping with and surviving as posthumans in the posthuman era, we should at the very least become properly educated about both the techno-science and ideas that inform posthumanism: distributed cognition, digital technology, prosthetics, information theory, probability, computer coding, big data, network theory, universal basic income, artificial intelligence, etc.

P2: I completely agree. It is fundamentally a question of education: an urgent question. The traditional tools and competencies of the 'humanities' as they are currently being taught in the universities are not, by definition, enough to grasp posthumanism or our posthuman condition. Take, for example, traditional literary analyses that focus on the 'representations' of robots or cyborgs in texts: such analyses will always fall short of posthumanist analysis to the extent that they remain stuck at the level of analysing 'images' and 'representations' of techno-science and techno-scientific artefacts. Such analyses also fail to grasp what they purport to analyse because they often adopt a sullenly resentful view of science and technology and, therefore, deprive themselves of the techno-scientific knowledge required to understand fully what is actually being represented. This lack of knowledge, however, does not often stop such critics from making all manner of uninformed statements about what those representations actually represent. Such approaches thus fall short of properly grasping posthumanism, which demands an interdisciplinary knowledge simply because the competencies found in science, technology, engineering and mathematics are essential to it.[58] This is not to say, however, that the arts—or the entirety of the humanities for that matter—are irrelevant to posthumanism. Science fiction— the good stuff, anyway, by the likes of Mary Shelley, Isaac Asimov, Greg Bear, Octavia Butler, Neal Stephenson, Philip K. Dick and others—will, I think, remain an especially useful shorthand for introducing people to the pro and cons of our posthuman condition.[59] Good sci-fi fuses the philosophical, the cultural and the scientific, by inviting the reader to engage with the nuts and bolts of techno-scientific posthumanism in order to grasp plot-points and imagery in ways that encourage a respectful curiosity and excitement for techno-science and what it can do for us. For example, reading Greg Bear's *Blood Music* encourages the reader to look into nanotechnology and quantum mechanics, while Octavia Butler's *Dawn* encourages the reader to look into genetics and cell biology. Put simply, good sci-fi helps popularise techno-science; good sci-fi can also act as a sort of 'imaginative lab' that allows readers to run simulations of the biological, social and cultural impacts of current and future developments in science and technology, allowing them to assess its possible dangers and/or benefits; good sci-fi can spur scientific and technological discovery by offering ideas about what future devices people might need or want, as well as possible future applications of discoveries already made by feeding the imaginations of researchers and developers; finally, good sci-fi can give science and technology models of possible futures either to aim for actively or to avoid altogether. Sometimes, however, even good sci-fi gets it spectacularly and hilariously wrong. Predicting the future is not exactly easy!

P1: Maybe I will give this *Posthumanism: A Guide for the Perplexed* a go after all.

P2: Why not? How does it begin?

P1: With two eejits arguing in a bookshop about posthumanism.

P2: 'Whoa!' as Neo would say. How annoyingly meta.

CHAPTER TWO

Cybernetics, Information, Prosthetics, Genetics

Introduction to techno-scientific posthumanism: Trust, but verify

Over the next two chapters, I'll be focusing on what I'll call 'techno-scientific posthumanism'—that is, posthumanism as it appears in the context of technology and science. Posthumanism, as was argued in the Introduction, takes its basic unit of analysis as humans + tools, where 'tools' would obviously include all forms of technology; techno-scientific posthumanism would then be the exploration of scientific research on current, cutting-edge and future tools and technologies and how they affect, and will continue to affect, humans. As such, techno-scientific posthumanism is particularly focused on such tools and technologies that challenge not just the conception of 'humanism' that aims to draw a hard and fast distinction between 'human' and 'machine' or 'human' and 'animal', but also any notions of 'human' and 'humanity' that rest on that conception of humanism. Techno-scientific posthumanism, in its concern for bleeding-edge and future tools and technologies, is thus oriented towards research that seems 'futuristic', if not the stuff of science fiction, such as neuroprosthetics, robotics, artificial intelligence and genetics.

Because robots, artificial intelligence, genetics and so on, are the very kinds of tools and technologies that are prone to media hype and clickbait reportage—and thus the inevitable disappointment and backlash that usually follows outlandish claims—I'd like to spend a little time first going over a couple of the well-known problems that affect science reporting and even science itself. In doing so, my goal is not only to make the reader aware of the wild claims often found in such reporting, but also to consider briefly how those problems relate to controversies about the relations between the humanities and the sciences. I hope that my doing this will not only make more explicit my approach to techno-scientific posthumanism, but also illuminate some the obstacles to be negotiated when discussing not just techno-scientific posthumanism, but posthumanism more generally.

Problems with science reporting have been discussed quite a bit by science reporters over the years. Martin Robbins, in one of his 'The Lay Scientist' columns for *The Guardian*, points out that '[o]ne of the biggest failures of science reporting is the media's belief that a scientific paper or research finding represents a conclusion of some kind. Scientists know that this simply isn't true. A new paper is the start or continuance of a discussion or debate that will often rumble on for years or even decade.'[1] One of the major problems is that science reporting will often wildly overstate the certainty or significance of this or that study for the sake of becoming clickbait, thereby ignoring important qualifying context. Emily Willingham, writing for *Forbes* in 2013, makes a similar point, observing that some science reporters 'omit context, such as previous contrasting findings and outside critique' when reporting on extraordinary claims; later in her article, she points out that 'there's no reason at all not to tell readers, as soon as possible, if no peer review has vetted the information.'[2] In other words, it would seem that some science reporters are ignoring even the very basics of scientific literacy in their rush to get information 'out there'.

However, not even scientific peer review offers a cast-iron guarantee of the reliability of the content of a particular study. A 2013 report in *The Economist* notes that the 'hallowed process of peer review is not all it is cracked up to be, either. When a prominent medical journal ran research past other experts in the field, it found that most of the reviewers failed to spot mistakes it had deliberately inserted into papers, even after being told they were being tested.'[3] On top of that, the same report goes on to say:

Too many of the findings that fill the academic ether are the result of shoddy experiments or poor analysis. . . . A rule of thumb among biotechnology venture-capitalists is that half of published research cannot be replicated. Even that may be optimistic. Last year researchers at one biotech firm, Amgen, found they could reproduce just six of 53 "landmark" studies in cancer research. Earlier, a group at Bayer, a drug company, managed to repeat just a quarter of 67 similarly important papers. A leading computer scientist frets that three-quarters of papers in his subfield are bunk. In 2000–10 roughly 80,000 patients took part in clinical trials based on research that was later retracted because of mistakes or improprieties.

The same report goes on to note that these examples of bad science are not the problem of science itself, but are due rather to the social, political and economic circumstances that affect how science is done: stiff competition for funding and jobs in scientific research, coupled with the 'publish-or-perish' environment where only the 'most striking findings have the greatest chance of making it' into the most exclusive journals, 'encourages exaggeration and the cherry-picking of results'.

So, even though science is a very powerful tool, it is not at all immune to manipulation in the all-too-human pursuits of money, ambition and prestige; for these reasons, those of us interested in how new developments in science and technology will affect humans + tools in the future, are forced to treat both reports about what advances lie 'just around the corner' and studies that claim something breathtakingly unexpected, with caution and prudence. The need for such caution and prudence can be neatly illustrated by the kind of reporting that surrounds robotics and artificial intelligence (AI) and the responses to it on popular discussion forums like Reddit's 'Futurology':[4] on the one hand, there are Redditors who want everything reported in the popular science press about innovations in robotics and AI to be true and accepted uncritically; on the other, there are those who hypercritically disparage any reports of advances in robotics and AI when it comes to them intruding into spheres of action or cognition that they think should be the preserve of human alone. And lots of those who read the likes of 'Futurology' are well aware that the reporting on robotics and AI is often nothing better than clickbait; nevertheless, threads discussing such reports can descend into flame wars. This is not to say, however, that all the reporting and discussion of robotics and AI is bad; but the online reader should have a thick skin and generous amounts of salt handy. Complicating the picture even further is Google and its massive wealth. Ray Kurzweil, the well-known futurist and booster of the Singularity mentioned in the introduction, joined Google in 2012 to work on projects relating to machine learning and language processing;[5] since mid-2013, Google has been buying up companies, such as Boston Dynamics and DeepMind Technologies, which specialize in AI and robotics.[6] Thus, when it comes to discussing robotics and AI in the context of posthumanism, there is a lot of corporate-backed investor-friendly PR to be carefully negotiated. Now, I am not saying that what companies owned by Google claim are simply not to be trusted; what I am saying is, 'Trust, but verify.' There are many, who, like my wife, are disappointed to be still waiting for their jet-packs.

However, in pointing out these issues with science reporting and bad science, I do not want to be seen as allying in any way, shape or form with those humanities 'critics of science' who try to reduce science to a mere 'social construct' or 'convention', and end up discussing, for example, the ways in which past and present practitioners of science perceived gender, race, sexual orientation, etc. It is pretty clear that all the problems with bad science that I've mentioned above can be effectively treated using proven scientific methods; for example, scientists are now using statistics more and more to sift data for patterns and root out specious results, and increasingly calling for more replication studies, which would effectively weed out too-good-to-be-true results. Science, in other words, does not need the beside-the-point criticism the humanities so often likes to give. Nevertheless, such criticism and the responses it drew from scientists—which came to a head in what became known in academic circles as 'the science wars' of the 1990s—are useful for thinking about posthumanism because they help clarify what is at stake in techno-scientific posthumanism, as well as demonstrate how central science is to understanding posthumanism.

On one side of the science wars were the scientific realists—the most famous of whom were Paul R. Gross, Norman Levitt, Alan Sokal and Jean Bricmont.[7] The scientific realists took the position that scientific knowledge was really real and not simply a social convention or construction. On the other side, were (mostly French) intellectuals, philosophers and sociologists such as Jacques Derrida, Gilles Deleuze, Jean-François Lyotard, Jacques Lacan, Luce Irigaray, Bruno Latour and others, who were erroneously lumped together as 'postmodernists' by the scientific realists who scoured their texts for examples of bad claims relating to science. The scientific realists charged the French intellectuals, philosophers and sociologists both with having a very limited understanding of the science they tried to critique and rejecting the very notions of scientific objectivity, the scientific method and scientific knowledge. Whereas the (mostly French) intellectuals, philosophers and sociologists claimed they were arguing that science was not the only—nor even the most important—way of knowing the world. Thus, the science wars broke neatly down along the classic sciences–humanities divide, with the scientific realists squaring off against the kind of 'identity politics' commonly found in cultural studies, feminist studies, media studies, science and technology studies and the like.[8]

It would be a mistake, however, to think that the science wars are over or confined to academia: so-called 'science-critical' ideologies played a surprisingly large part in the spate of identity-politics-driven protests on university campuses at the end of 2015.[9] Intriguingly, many of the same arguments and positions that were taken by either side in the science wars have found their way into the positions taken by either side in the recent 'Gamergate' controversy.[10] However—and despite the just-mentioned examples of recent anti-scientific thinking—there seems to be little doubt that most, if not all, of the criticisms the scientific realists levelled at critical science studies had merit. A good index of the success of the criticisms made by the scientific realists is the shift signalled in the more recent work of one of the most famous generals to have served in the science wars, the sociologist Bruno Latour.

Latour, who features prominently in chapter 3 of Gross and Levitt's *Higher Superstition*, notes in his book *Reassembing the Social* that 'scientists made us realize that there was not the slightest chance that the type of social forces we use as a cause could have objective facts as their effects'.[11] Later in the same book, in the course of a fictional dialogue between a professor (P) and a student (S), Latour dramatically distances his current work from 'interpretive sociologies' that cast doubt on the 'objectivity' of science by projecting, for example, human desires into it:

P: I have no real sympathy for interpretive sociologies. No. On the contrary, I firmly believe that sciences are objective—what else could they be? They're all about objects, no? What I have said is simply that objects might look a bit more complicated, folded, multiple, complex, and entangled than what the 'objectivist', as you say, would like them to be.

S: But that's exactly what 'interpretive' sociologies argue, no?

P: Oh no, not at all. They would say that human desires, human meanings, human intentions, etc., introduce some 'interpretive flexibility' into a world of inflexible objects, of 'pure causal relations', of 'strictly material connections'. That's not at all what I am saying.[12]

Now, if even a grizzled veteran of the science wars like Latour can now concede that the sciences are very useful for telling us truths about objective reality, then there seems to be little-to-no reason to keep on pretending or vainly insisting that science still somehow cannot do just that. So, in what follows here, I will be treating science, not just in this chapter, but throughout this book as a whole, as the most powerful set of tools humans can use to interpret and transform both themselves and the world around them. And, since posthumanism = humans + tools, I will also be making the argument repeatedly that science is indispensible if one is to understand properly what posthumanism is. Let's begin with a look at two of the concepts that are essential for understanding posthumanism: cybernetics and information.

Cybernetics and information

Cybernetics I: Feedback

In 1948, the philosopher and mathematician Norbert Wiener (1894–1964) famously defined cybernetics as the theory of 'control and communication' in 'the machine or animal'.[13] Cybernetics, in other words, was, from early on, concerned with laying bare what biological and nonbiological systems—humans, animals and machines—share; as such, it was explicitly posthuman from the get-go in the sense that it actively set about blurring the distinction between humans, animals and machines. But it would be a mistake to think that cybernetics was or is interested in the kind of 'superficial' similarities that are often dwelt upon or fetishized in literary or cultural analyses of 'images' or 'representations' of humans, machines and animals. On the contrary, cybernetics was concerned with what biological and nonbiological systems really do share and with how information actually does flow across the borders of actual humans, actual machines and actual animals. Cybernetics is thus the granny and granddad of the actual science behind neuroprosthetics, AI and robotics, all of which will be the focus of my discussion of posthumanism over the following two chapters; it is impossible to understand posthumanism properly without understanding cybernetics.

More recent definitions of cybernetics than Norbert Wiener's observe that it 'focuses on how systems use information, models, and control actions to steer towards and maintain their goals, while counteracting various disturbances'.[14] It is 'inherently transdisciplinary', because 'cybernetic reasoning can be applied to understand, model and design systems of any kind: physical, technological, biological, ecological, psychological, social, or any combination of those.'[15] Such transdisciplinarity was, however, pretty much there from the very start of cybernetics; indeed, Wiener underlined it when he defined cybernetics as the theory of 'control and communication' in 'the machine or animal'. But even before Wiener christened it in 1948,[16] 'cybernetics' had already been underway for several years: since the early 1940s, groups of scientists who were involved in secret World War II projects had been meeting in Mexico; however, since they were working on classified projects, they were unable to talk to each other about what they were doing. And so, according to the theorist and cybernetician, Stafford Beer (1926–2002), they decided to choose a topic of discussion 'that was nobody's speciality, but of interest to everyone. And their eminence was really important for another reason: they had nothing to prove. They decided to discuss the nature of control.'[17] The first such meeting took place in 1942, several years before the much more famous Macy Conferences on cybernetics (1946–1953) had even begun.[18] Given the way the meetings were organized, even though those in attendance—such as Margaret Mead, Gregory Bateson, Warren McCulloch, Arturo Rosenblueth, and others—all hailed from a diverse range of fields of study—communications engineering, control theory, biology, theoretical mathematics, anthropology and psychology and so on— their discussions were unified by certain concepts and themes: 'systems', 'information', 'control' and 'circularity', which served as the focus for establishing the new discipline of *cybernetics*.[19]

At the first meeting, Arturo Rosenblueth (1900–1970), a Mexican physiologist, presented ideas he had been developing with Norbert Wiener and the computer engineer Julian Bigelow (1913–2003).[20] Rosenblueth's talk outlined a 'conceptual agenda based on similarities between behaviors of both machines and organisms that were interpretable as being "goal-directed"'.[21] This goal-directedness was framed in terms 'of definitive and deterministic "teleological mechanisms"'.[22] Rosenblueth thus transformed the usually philosophical concept of 'teleology' into a 'concrete mechanism through the invocation of "circular causality" in a system, whereby new behaviors were influenced by "feedback" deriving from immediately preceding behaviors'.[23] The transformation of teleology into the pursuit of a goal using feedback then made it possible to think of purposiveness in both machines and animals in terms of the immediate past and the present, without needing to invoke possible future events. Key to the conception of goal-directedness is the notion of 'feedback', which is 'information about the results of a process which is used to change the process itself. Negative feedback reduces the error or deviation from a goal state. Positive feedback increases the deviation from an initial state.'[24] Heinz von Foerster (1911–2002), the famous Austrian physicist and philosopher, puts it thus: 'cybernetics arises when effectors (say, a motor, an engine, our muscles, etc.) are connected to a sensory organ which in turn acts with its signals upon the effectors. It is this circular organization which sets cybernetic systems apart from others that are not so organized. Here is Norbert Wiener, who re-introduced the term "Cybernetics" into scientific discourse. He observed, "The behavior of such systems may be interpreted as directed toward the attainment of a goal." That is, it looks as if these systems pursued a purpose!'[25]

An important cybernetic concept closely related to feedback is 'homoeostasis', or 'the condition of a system when it is able to maintain its essential variables within limits acceptable to its own structure in the face of unexpected disturbances'.[26] Norbert Wiener—while reminding his reader of the 'first significant paper on feed-back mechanisms', James Clerk Maxwell's article on governors[27]—also underscores the connection between feedback and cybernetics when he notes how the word 'governor' is a Latin corruption of the Greek word κυβερνήτης (*kybernetes*) or 'steersman', from which the word 'cybernetics' derives.[28] But the notion of 'feedback' as something that is used by both biological and nonbiological systems to regulate themselves was not originally the discovery of cyberneticists, as Wiener's mention of Maxwell indicates. Cyberneticists were drawing together ideas that had been already in circulation in biology and engineering for some time: for example, in 1926, W.B. Cannon had used the word 'homeostasis' to describe bodily processes such as the one that regulates temperature[29]; governors had been in use in mechanical engineering since 1788, when James Watt and Matthew Boulton first attached one to a steam engine that was used to drive factory equipment, well before Maxwell was writing about their theoretical basis in 1868.[30] The concepts of feedback and homoeostasis also illustrate cybernetics' concern with how self-directed systems manage to maintain their 'shape' and normal functioning in the face of random and unexpected environmental disturbances.

. . . bits . . .

By the time Wiener published his *Cybernetics Or Control and Communication in the Animal and the Machine* in 1948, information had already become central to cybernetics. Wiener's discussion of information drew explicitly on the work of Claude Shannon (1961–2001), an American mathematician, electrical engineer, and cryptographer, who has since become widely known as the father of information theory.[31] According to David Kahn, Shannon's theory of information as entropy was first formulated in a classified memorandum for Bell Telephone Labs entitled, 'A Mathematical Theory of Cryptography', and dated September 1945. Shannon's classified memorandum, says Kahn, incorporated many of the concepts and mathematical formulations that also appeared in his landmark 1948 paper, 'A Mathematical Theory of Communication'.[32]

Given that he worked for Bell Labs, which was formed in 1925 when Western Electric Research Laboratories and part of the engineering department of the American Telephone & Telegraph company (AT&T) were consolidated,[33] it should not be surprising to learn that Shannon's theory of information is so shaped by work done on telegraph and telephone communication networks. As is well known, the first major success in commercial electric telegraphy grew out of the combined efforts, starting in 1836, of Samuel Morse

(1791–1872), a painter and inventor, Leonard Gale (1800–1883), a chemist, and Alfred Vail (1807–1859), an inventor, to develop an electric telegraph system.[34] The trio's system worked by sending electrical pulses along a wire to an electromagnet attached to a stylus at the opposite end, which made indentations in a paper tape as it spooled under the stylus. Because of this hardware set-up, the system needed a code that transposed a natural language message to be sent—for example, 'Hello world!'—into something that would be composed of electrical pulses only. There has been some controversy about who exactly—Morse or Vail—was responsible for expanding Morse's original numeral-based code to include letters and other special characters; however, according to Russell W. Burns, Vail found Morse's numeral-based codes tedious, preferring instead to use a binary system of symbols—dots and dashes—to represent letters; and it was Vail who based the code on the relative frequency of letters used in English, after having paid a visit to a newspaper office in Morristown, New Jersey, and counting the type he found in the typecase of the compositors.[35] What Vail learned from his visit to the newspaper office was to encode the length of each character in a way that was approximately inversely proportional to its frequency of occurrence in the English language:[36] thus, letters that had the highest probability of recurring in a message, would get the shortest code. For example, the most commonly used letters in English, 'e' and 't' would get the shortest code—a single dot and a single dash, respectively—while the far less commonly used letters got longer ones; as such, Vail's code is an early example of data compression, while his 'dots and dashes also formed the elements of a binary alphabetic code, and were the precursor to the later Morse code'.[37]

The advances made in the pursuit of a commercially feasible and reliable electric telegraphy—in particular, the encoding of natural language messages in binary code and the compression of data based on the probability of its occurrence—aimed at solving the problem of reliably sending information over a communications line or channel, also inform Claude Shannon's 'A Mathematical Theory of Communication'. Shannon states that his theory of information builds on work on communications published in the 1920s by Harry Nyquist and Ralph Hartley[38]: Nyquist was concerned with the problem of quantifying what he called 'intelligence' and the speed at which it could be transmitted over a line, while Hartley was the first to use the word 'information' in its modern, technical sense.

For Shannon, the 'significant aspect' of communication 'is that the actual message is one selected from a set of possible messages'; because of this, Shannon views the 'semantic aspects of communication' as 'irrelevant to the engineering problem':[39] 'information', in other words, is not identical with 'meaning' (I will return to this below). However, perhaps the most exciting part of Shannon's theory of information is how it links quantification of information to the mathematics of probability, which can be seen in his famous equation:

$$H(X) = -\sum_{i=1}^{n} p(x_i) \, \log_b p(x_i)$$

This equation—which, Shannon says, will also 'be recognized as that of entropy as defined in certain formulations of statistical mechanics'[40]—can be understood as follows: H—the Greek letter *Eta*—is *entropy*, a measurement of the reduction in our uncertainty about a particular event, which corresponds to the average amount of information contained in a given message. The amount of information contained in H equals the negative sum ($-\Sigma$) of the probabilities (p) of a particular variable or event occurring (x_i), times the logarithm to base (b) 2 of the p of x_i. (Logarithm to base 2 simply means the power to which 2 has to be raised to get a particular number: e.g., $\log_2(16) = 4$, because $2^4 = 16$; $\log_2(1) = 0$, because $2^0 = 1$.) Setting the logarithm to base two also allows Shannon to measure information in 'bits'—a contraction of 'binary digits'. And, since a binary number is a number expressed in the base-2 numeral system, it can be used to represent all other numbers using just two different symbols: '0' and '1'. Thus, 16, or 2^4 is written as 10000 in binary because (reading 'backwards' right to left is the convention for working out numbers to base 2): $1 + 0 + 0 + 0 + 0 = 2^4 + 2^3 + 2^2 + 2^1 + 2^0$.

If the above seems a little abstract, then using the concrete example of flipping a fair coin should make it much easier to see not only just how intuitive Shannon's information theory is, but also its relation to probability. When you flip a coin, the probability of a particular outcome—heads or tails—is 1 in 2 or ½: that is, the probability of either heads or tails coming up is 50/50. When you plug this into Shannon's equation, you get:

$$H(X) = -\sum\left[\frac{1}{2}\left(\log_2 \frac{1}{2}\right) + \frac{1}{2}\left(\log_2 \frac{1}{2}\right)\right]$$

$$H(X) = -\left[\frac{1}{2}(-1) + \frac{1}{2}(-1)\right] = 1 \text{ bit of information}$$

Using Shannon's equation to quantify information, means you get exactly 1 bit of information when you learn the outcome of a fair coin flip. And, if you plug the roll of a six-sided dice into the same formula, you get:

$$H(X) = -\sum_{i=1}^{6}\frac{1}{6}\log_2\frac{1}{6} = 2.5849625007 \text{ bits of information.}$$

In other words, learning the outcome of a dice roll is to learn which side out of a possible 6 outcomes came up; thus, we get 2.5849625007 bits of information because $2^{2.5849625007} \approx 6$. It should be noted here that the more uncertain—that is, the more improbable—a result or outcome, the more information is contained in finding out that result or outcome: this is why a result with only 2 possible outcomes gives us 1 only bit of information, while a result with six possible outcomes gives us more: ≈ 2.6 bits. Generally speaking, you need $\log_2(n)$ bits to represent a variable that can take one of n values: for example, a variable that can take 1 of 8 different values needs $\log_2(8)$ bits = 3 bits of information; in other words, it takes just 3 'yes' or 'no' questions to find out which number of 1 to 8 has come up. Shannon's formula also works for non-equiprobable outcomes, with the proviso that the differing probabilities must sum up to 1.

It is also possible to glimpse in these examples how Shannon's distinction between 'meaning' and 'information' is perhaps not as hard and fast as it may have appeared at first. For instance, think about the relative lack of 'surprise' you might feel in learning the outcome of something that has a probability of 1 in 2 (the coin flip:

1 bit), compared to learning the outcome of something that has much lower probability (1 in 1000000: 19.931568569324174 bits). In other words, the more likely—or probable—that something is to occur, the less likely is it to surprise us. Imagine how you might respond to the following two reports:

1 'It's raining today.' ('Yep, cool story bro.')
2 'A meteor just landed on the lawn!' ('WTF?')

One event is not surprising at all; the other, very surprising, which leads us to what is known as the 'surprisal' in information theory. For example, if something that had a 1 in 1000 chance of happening occurs, you would get 9.9657 bits of information according to Shannon's formula (quite surprising); whereas if something that happens 999 times out of 1000 occurs again, you would only get 0.00144 bits of information (not really surprising at all). Similarly, if the coin you were flipping above was not fair and kept coming up heads, each coin flip would give you no new information; and so the amount of information you would get on learning the outcome of the flip falls to zero. Once again, this should correspond to your intuition: you intuitively understand that when someone tells you something you already know that there is not much news in the report. Think, for example, of Hamlet's famous 'Buzz. Buzz.' on hearing from Polonius that the players have arrived: there is not much 'news'—that is, information—in Polonius' report, even if it still has meaning, simply because the outcome is already known to Hamlet. So, if an outcome has either 100 per cent probability ($-\log_2(1) = 0$ bits) or 0 per cent probability ($-\log_2(0) = 0$ bits) of occurring, then its occurrence or non-occurrence has zero information according to Shannon's equation, because we already know what will happen: for example, a dropped coin will always fall to earth, and a turd will not spontaneously turn into gold. When thought about in this way, even though it cannot be completely reduced to meaning and has what might be called a 'limited shelf-life', information is nonetheless constantly entangled in our meaningful utterances and discourses. Indeed, it could be said that this association of information with 'news' entangles both it and (thus) posthumanism in questions of the 'future' and 'newness'.

Now, you might be asking, are the bits that come out of Shannon's equation exactly the same as the digital 'bits'—the 1s and 0s—found in computers? The short answer is no; but I'll close this discussion of information with the longer answer, since it highlights the difference between the two types of bits. Computers, at their most basic level, are composed of trillions of small electrical circuits that can be turned off or on by means of an electronic switch; these circuits constitute what are known as 'logic gates', physical devices that perform basic logical operations—for example, NOT, AND, OR, IMPLIES and so on—on one or more inputs and produce single logical outputs; and one or more of any such circuits may control the state of one or more of the other circuits in the computer. Each circuit represents 1 bit of information: when the circuit is on, it represents a '1', and when it is off, it represents a '0'; in other words, the circuit is just like a flipped coin, since there can only be 2 possible outcomes or states—1/heads or 0/tails. So far, so good.

Now, as we saw above, Vail's work on telegraphy showed it was possible to encode any alphanumeric character in a binary system of dots and dashes: the exact same thing occurs in computers with 1s and 0s. For example, in the early computer encoding scheme ASCII (American Standard Code for Information Interchange), which was based on the English alphabet, 128 specified characters were encoded into 7-bit binary integers: because there were 128 characters, $\log_2(128) = 7$ bits of information was enough to represent them (i.e., strings of 7 binary digits—in combinations from 0000000 to 1111111—can encode up to 128 different characters; if you had more than 128 alphanumerical characters to encode—say, 178—you would need longer strings of bits because $2^7 = 128$; 178 characters could be encoded in 8 bits with room left over). Thus, 'P' in ASCII = '1010000', which to base 10 is 80: $2^6 + 2^5 + 2^4 + 2^3 + 2^2 + 2^1 + 2^0 = 64 + 0 + 16 + 0 + 0 + 0 + 0 = 80$. (The length of a binary number is referred to as its bit-length, and 8 bits of information = 1 byte.)

However, an important but subtle difference emerges between Shannon's information 'bit' and a physical 'bit' as it might be represented in a computer's memory once we take probability into account. The information capacity of a computer's memory constitutes only an upper limit to the actual quantity of information stored in it.[41] Now, if—and here I am just recapping information from the Wikipedia page just cited—the two possible values of one physical bit in memory were not equally likely, then, given the Shannon equation discussed above, we can say that the physical bit actually contains more or less than one Shannon bit of information. And, if the value of a physical bit were completely predictable, then learning or reading that value would provide us with no Shannon information at all: in other words, there would be zero Shannon bits in the physical bit. So, if a computer file uses n physical bits of memory, but contains only $m < n$ Shannon bits of information, then that same information could, in principle, be compressed into m bits, on average, without any loss of information: this is the basic idea behind data compression.

Perhaps a more intuitive way of grasping the difference between physical bits and Shannon bits emerges when one tries to work out the entropy of the letters in the English language: as was mentioned above in the discussion of Morse code, efficient encoding came from Vail's realization that not every letter in a message occurs equiprobably; this is why he chose to encode the more frequently used letters in shorter strings. Shannon himself also tackled the issue of data compression in his paper, 'Prediction and Entropy of Printed English'.[42] Shannon shows that if every letter's relative frequency was equiprobable, then the amount of information gained by learning the next letter in a string of letters would work out to be $\log_2(27)$—he includes a space as the 27th character—which is roughly equal to 4.76 bits. However, because each letter in the English language does not occur with the same relative frequency, some letters have far more probability of occurring than others. Further, certain letters often occur in pairs or threes: for example, a 'q' is always followed by a 'u' while 'll' is frequently followed by a 'y', and so on. And, as a message string gets longer, it often becomes easier and easier to predict what letters will come nex. . .t. When all of these conditional probabilities are taken into account, a letter in English has, on average 2.14 bits of information, less than half of the 4.76 bits it would have if each letter occurred equiprobably.[43] In other words, English has a redundancy rate of about 50+ per cent, wh*ch i* w**t g*v*s l*ng**g* s*gn*fi***t e**o* c*r**ct**n p*w**; this redundancy is also why you can catch a lot of what someone is saying even if they are speaking in a fairly noisy room.

Cybernetics II: Second-order cybernetics

As the 1940s became the 1950s, cybernetics underwent some important changes: the ideas explored during the Macy Conferences spread to other disciplines very quickly. However, the consequences of the innovations popularly associated with cybernetics, such as computers, robotics and AI, 'soon produced apprehensions about their effects on human affairs'.[44] For example, Isaac Asimov's series of short stories, *I, Robot*, was published in 1950, only two years after Wiener's book on cybernetics.[45] A quick read of Asimov's stories shows that science fiction writers were addressing the social anxieties conjured by cybernetics almost from the get-go: from the worries of workers about losing their jobs to robots, to questions of robot dependability and insanity and anxieties about the successful impersonation of humans by robots.

The 1950s also saw the birth of what came to be known as 'the cybernetics of cybernetics' or 'second-order cybernetics', which grew out of 'a concept originating in conversation between Margaret Mead and Heinz von Foerster'.[46] Essentially, second-order cybernetics hinges on the idea that information about a cybernetic system must also feedback or loop through the observer; thus, cyberneticists were now understood to be 'entangled' in the cybernetic systems they were examining. The following oft-reproduced quote of von Foerster's neatly outlines how recursion and self-reflexivity became essential components of the 'new' cybernetics:

> So, what's new of today's cyberneticians? What is new is the profound insight that a brain is required to write a theory of a brain. From this follows that a theory of the brain, that has any aspirations for completeness, has to account for the writing of this theory. And even more fascinating, the writer of this theory has to account for her or himself. Translated into the domain of cybernetics; the cybernetician, by entering his own domain, has to account for his or her own activity. Cybernetics then becomes cybernetics of cybernetics, or *second-order cybernetics*.[47]

As was mentioned above, the concept of 'feedback' enshrines circularity in first order cybernetics; in second order cybernetics, circularity becomes self-reflexivity and recursion, blossoming into a whole suite of related concepts and processes: 'attractor states', 'closure', 'self-organization', and 'autopoiesis'. Now, despite their apparent similarities, these circular processes cannot (as I will try to explain below) simply be reduced to each other; nevertheless, their shared 'circularity' can be captured in the general formula, $y = f(y)$, where the output (result) 'feeds back' into the input (cause), which can be neatly illustrated as follows:[48] in the formula $y = f(y)$, let y represent a particular object; let f represent the function whereby a video camera transmits an image of that object to a monitor; $y = f(y)$ would the represent the situation where the camera is trained on the monitor, producing a sort of infinite loop.

Now, if y is understood to represent a particular state or subset of a system's state space— that is, the complete set of values that a process can take on or the complete set of states that a problem can be in,[49] which is usually denoted by S—and f represents a dynamic process or function, then $y = f(y)$ can now be understood to state that y is 'a fixpoint of the function f, or an equilibrium or absorbing state of the dynamic system: if the system reaches state y, it will stop changing'; thus, y would be an '*attractor* of the dynamics'.[50] When, for example, a freely swinging pendulum eventually comes to a rest and hangs straight down, it is in an attractor state; similarly, if the pendulum were powered by a spring as in a grandfather clock, the pattern of movement the pendulum traces would also be an attractor because different initial positions of the pendulum will converge on the same periodic trajectory (also known as a limit cycle). Once a system has entered a particular attractor or absorbing state,

it can no longer reach states outside the attractor. This means that our uncertainty (or statistical entropy) H about the system's state has decreased: we now know for sure that it is not in any state that is not part of the attractor. This spontaneous reduction of entropy or, equivalently, increase in order or constraint, can be viewed as a more general model of *self-organization*.[51]

Closure, by contrast, occurs when the '"attractor" case can be extended to the case where y stands for a complete state space':[52] in closure, y no longer represents just a subset of S—it represents all of S. In closure, every state of y maps onto another state of y, which means that the overall system is stable; thus, 'we can say that the system is organizationally closed: it is invariant under any possible dynamical transformation'.[53] Closure is therefore what gives 'systems an unambiguous *identity*, explicitly distinguishing what is inside from what is outside the system'.[54] A yet more complex example of closure is autopoiesis or self-production, 'the process by which a system recursively produces its own network of physical components, thus continuously regenerating its essential organization in the face of wear and tear'.[55] I will return to autopoiesis below.[56]

The eminent cyberneticist Gordon Pask (1928–1996) pointed out in his essay, 'Heinz von Foerster's Self-organization', that 'self-organization' was central to von Foerster's understanding of second-order cybernetics, and that Shannon's theory of information plays a central part in self-organization.[57] For von Foerster, self-organization was the minimum requirement for something to be considered an autonomous cybernetic system: without it, no identifiable organism or pattern—no matter how simple or elementary—could ever present itself as such. A self-organizing system is also one that is 'in close contact with an environment, which possesses available energy and order, and with which our system is in a state of perpetual interaction, such that it somehow manages to "live" on the expenses of this environment'.[58] In other words, a self-organizing system is inseparable from a structured environment, which it feeds off; and, in so doing, the self-organizing system increases its internal order, which allows it to maintain a relatively stable shape or state of organization.

In his essay, 'On Self-Organizing Systems and Their Environments', von Foerster proposes Shannon's equation for Redundancy— $R = 1 - H/H_{max}$, where H is entropy, and H_{max} is maximum entropy, where all the outcomes are equally likely (as was mentioned above, our uncertainty is highest when all possible events are equiprobable)—as a measure of self-organization: if the change in R over the change in time is > 0, then a system is said to be self-organizing.[59] Thus, von Foerster makes it clear that information is the key to grasping a self-organized system, whatever that system may be. To grasp the difference between H and H_{max}, think again of the differing amounts of information contained in a letter of the English language: the H_{max} of a random letter in English is $\log_2(27)$ = 4.76 bits, while the H of the same letter, once redundancy and context enter the picture, is 2.14 bits. (And if we plug these numbers into Shannon's redundancy formula, we get 0.5504201680672269; the redundancy rate for English is thus about 55 per cent.) The random letter by itself can be thought of as disorganized; however, once it starts to enter into relationships with other letters over time to become a text, the individual letter's information value shrinks along with our uncertainty about what letters will come next. Language could, in other words, be said to display characteristics of self-organization, cybernetically speaking.

Autopoiesis, as I mentioned above, is a specific form of closure and self-organization that plays an important role in second-order cybernetics; it arose from the work of the biologists Humberto Maturana and Francisco Varela, and finds its fullest description in their famous book, *Autopoesis and Cognition: The Realization of the Living*:

> An autopoietic machine is a machine organized (defined as a unity) as a network of processes of production (transformation and destruction) of components which: (i) through their interactions and transformations continuously regenerate and realize the network of processes (relations) that produced them; and (ii) constitute it (the machine) as a concrete unity in space in which they (the components) exist by specifying the topological domain of its realization as such a network.[60]

In many important respects, Maturana and Varela's work in *Autopoesis and Cognition* is an extension of Maturana's earlier work with Jerome Lettvin, Warren McCulloch and Walter Pitts on the visual system in frogs, the main finding of which they sum up in the following terms: 'the [frog's] eye speaks to the brain in a language already highly organized and interpreted instead of transmitting some more or less accurate copy of the distribution of light upon the receptor'.[61] That is to say, the structure of the frog's eye acts as a sort of filter or sieve that determines the visual signals the frog's brain receives. Thus, for Maturana and Varela, biological organisms respond to their environment in ways that are determined by their internal structure and organization—for example, their nervous systems, their endocrine systems, etc: 'the activity of the nervous system [is] determined by the nervous system itself, and not by the external world; thus, the external world would only have a triggering role in the release of the internally-determined activity of the nervous system'.[62] Because the activity of the nervous system is determined only by the nervous system itself, the biological organism is said to be a 'closed' system, in the sense discussed above. However, as Heylighen and Joslyn note, such 'organizational' closure is not the same as thermodynamic closure: the autopoietic system is open to the exchange of matter and energy with its environment, but it is autonomously responsible for the way these resources are organized. Maturana and Varela have postulated autopoiesis to be the defining characteristic of living systems. Another fundamental feature of life, *self-reproduction*, can be seen as a special case of autopoiesis, where the self-produced components are not used to rebuild the system, but to assemble a copy of it.[63]

In *Autopoiesis and Cognition*, Maturana and Varela highlight the closed circularity at work in autopoiesis thusly: 'It is the circularity of its organization that makes a living system a unit of interactions ... and it is this circularity that it must maintain in order to remain a living system and to retain its identity through different interactions.'[64] Death, in other words, would be the opening up of this circularity.

Now, for Maturana and Varela, '[e]verything said is said by an observer',[65] and this position is shared to a degree by all second-order cyberneticists, including Heinz von Foerster. Because of this, Maturana and Varela maintain that no 'description of an absolute reality is possible', since such 'would require an interaction with the absolute to be described, but the representation that would arise from such an interaction would necessarily be determined by the autopoietic organization of the observer ... hence, the cognitive reality that it would generate would unavoidably be relative to the observer'.[66] However, this is absolutely not to say that, for second-order cybernetics, 'it's all relative, dude', or that objectivity is neither possible nor desirable because we are observers forever trapped (or safely enveloped) in our respective perspectives, 'truths', points of view', personal 'hugboxes', and so on. As Heylighen and Joslyn note, this is a pitfall well-known to second-order cyberneticists: cybernetic epistemology is constructivist, meaning that it holds the view that 'knowledge cannot be passively absorbed from the environment, it must be actively constructed by the system itself. The environment does not instruct, or "in-form," the system, it merely weeds out models that are inadequate, by killing or punishing the system that uses them. At the most basic level, model-building takes place by variation-and-selection or trial-and-error.'[67] Some models, in other words, are better than others insofar as they allow the system to negotiate its environment successfully and with minimal punishment. And it is here that second-order cybernetics as a whole also underscores the difficulty of neatly drawing a line to separate human from nonhuman: humans, just like any other animal or mechanical self-organizing or autopoietic system, are subject to the struggle of retaining their shape in an environment that is always causing them wear and tear.

To combat the danger of succumbing to a complete relativism wherein one model for investigating the world is considered as good as the next and there is no way of reliably telling an external perception from a dream or hallucination, second-order cybernetics must, say Heylighen and Joslyn, first take note of how

> different observations and models can mutually confirm or support each other, thus increasing their joint reliability. Thus, the more coherent a piece of knowledge is with all other available information, the more reliable it is. Second, percepts appear more 'real' as they vary less between observations. For example, an object can be defined as that aspect of a perception that remains invariant when the point of view of the observer is changed.[68]

Indeed, von Foerster was acutely aware of the twin dangers posed to second-order cybernetics by solipsism and relativism: to counter the objection that man, as a closed, self-organizing system who invents the environment as he perceives it, is trapped in solipsism, von Foerster imagines a gentleman in a bowler hat.[69] Imagine, says von Foerster, that this gentleman assumes he is the sole reality; this gentleman, however, because he encounters other gentlemen like him, must confront the possibility that he exists only in the imagination of somebody else, who in turn assumes that *he* is the sole reality.[70] This results in a clear contradiction: there are two different realities, each of which is claiming to be the 'real' one. This paradox, says von Foerster, 'is easily resolved, by postulating the reality of the world in which we happily thrive'.[71] Reality, in other words, does not have to disappear in the face of a silly reality-denying egocentric relativism that pretends there is no such thing as an objective truth, that the only things that are 'true' are subjective 'feelings' and that each point of view is just as valid as the next one. To underscore his point that, for second-order cybernetics, reality is not relativistic, von Foerster impishly invokes relativity:[72] 'reality appears as a consistent reference frame for at least two observers', a proof 'exactly modeled after the "Principle of Relativity", which roughly states that, if a hypothesis which is applicable to a set of objects holds for one object and it holds for another object, then it holds for both objects simultaneously [and] the hypothesis is acceptable for all objects of the set'.[73] Copernicus, says von Foerster, could have used this argument to his advantage, by pointing out that no matter how passionately we humans may insist that we live in a geocentric system, there is nothing to stop Venusians insisting just as passionately that they live in a 'venucentric system'. But, since Earth and Venus cannot be both centre and epicycloid at the same time, Earthlings and Venusians should conclude that 'something must be wrong with a planetocentric system'.[74] What von Foerster highlights here is that even though absolute, perfect objectivity may not be possible for second-order cybernetics because observers may be caught up in their own systems, solipsism is always disrupted by a measurable 'reality'—the solar system—that stubbornly persists outside the planet-bound observer(s) and their planetocentric models. The solar system, as the stubborn external reality that cannot be ignored, thus corresponds to Philip K. Dick's conception of 'Reality' as 'that which, when you stop believing in it, doesn't go away'.[75]

Cybernetics and information, insofar as they are concerned with self-organizing systems that strive to maintain their shape and integrity in the face of an environment that punishes models of knowledge that do not serve those systems well while causing those systems wear and tear, necessarily point beyond any philosophy or ideology that seeks to clearly delineate humans from nonhumans. Cybernetics and information thus provide the indispensable theoretical, technical, scientific and interdisciplinary underpinnings for posthumanism, which seeks to reconsider traditional notions of what separates humans, animals and machines.

Neuroprosthetics

Where is my mind? Or my body for that matter?

James Hollan, Ed Hutchins and David Kirsh, in a 2000 paper on distributed cognition, argue that 'distributed cognition looks for a broader class of cognitive events and does not expect all such events to be encompassed by the skin or skull of an individual'.[76] Thus, when examining technology, distributed cognition takes its unit of analysis to be the system of 'person-in-interaction-with-technology'.[77] Distributed cognition, in other words, makes no hard and fast distinction between people and the technological systems and artefacts they use in cognition—the set of mental processes and abilities and related to knowledge, such as attention, memory, working memory, judgment, evaluation, reasoning, 'computation', problem solving, decision making, comprehension, production of language, and so on. Thus, distributed cognition, which formed the basis for the initial definition of posthumanism offered in the Introduction, overlaps with both cybernetics and information in its putting into question the notion of a hard and fast boundary separating 'human' from 'nonhuman'. Relations between human and nonhuman are complex, intertwined and, perhaps, counter-intuitive.

The philosopher Andy Clark, in his book, *Natural Born Cyborgs*, both runs with and updates Hutchins and company's notion of distributed cognition, underscoring how wave after wave of newer technologies that are sensitive and attuned to their users only serve to entwine humans ever more intimately with their tools:

> New waves of user-sensitive technology will bring this age-old process to a climax, as our minds and identities become ever more deeply enmeshed in a nonbiological matrix of machines, tools, props, codes, and semi-intelligent daily objects. We humans have always been adept at dovetailing our minds and skills to the shape of our current tools and aids. But when those tools and aids start dovetailing back—when our technologies actively, automatically, and continually tailor themselves to us just as we do to them—then the line between tool and user becomes flimsy indeed. Such technologies will be less like tools and more like part of the mental apparatus of the person. They will remain tools in only the thin and ultimately paradoxical sense in which my own unconsciously operating neural structures (my hippocampus, my posterior parietal cortex) are tools. I do not really 'use' my brain.[78]

Our brains and minds, says Clark, seem so flexible that it is not at all difficult to imagine our biological brains becoming enmeshed in nonbiological tools, effectively erasing the distinction between tool and user. But, one might object, such claims about the degree or depth of the enmeshments of human and tool remain a bit too vague or abstract; as such, they do not seem to demonstrate clearly a blurred distinction between the biological and the nonbiological, between tool and user; one might also object that such claims do not appear to be grounded in reality and are perhaps best confined to the realm of pie-in-the-sky science fiction. To counter such objections, I'd like in this section to consider how advances in neuroprosthetic medicine make it possible to see, in a very concrete way, just how easily the distinction between the biological and nonbiological can be blurred; at the same time, the example of neuroprosthetic medicine also makes it possible to see that what crosses the borders between the biological and nonbiological is information. Finally, neuroprosthetic medicine extends the notion of 'distribution' beyond distributed cognition to include bodies in ways that disrupt notions of 'embodiment' and bodily integrity. Neuroprosthetic medicine thus both illuminates, and gives concrete specificity to, the conception of posthumanism that is used throughout this book.

Neuroprosthetic medicine, can, however, be a very sensitive topic for discussion, especially in a book like this one. Some people who have been unfortunate enough to need neuroprosthetics due to accidents, illness or congenital conditions, might well consider the association of their conditions with posthumanism to be offensive. After all, they may see neuroprosthetic medicine as giving them a chance to fully assert their 'humanity' either once again or perhaps for the first time. Such individuals might say that their neuroprosthetics are not futuristic 'enhancements', but simply 'restorations' that enable them to do some, if not all, of the things they may have once enjoyed doing or were maybe never able to do. I am sensitive to such objections, and I want to be clear that my discussion of neuroprosthetics here is not at all intended to 'dehumanize' people with disabilities; on the contrary, my goal here is to try and learn what neuroprosthetics teach us about posthumanism. Neuroprosthetic medicine and research can teach us much about posthumanism because they are explicitly concerned with redrawing not only the boundaries of the body and mind but also the boundaries that separate humans and machines, machines and animals; as such, an awareness of the state of knowledge in neuroprosthetics is necessary for a concrete understanding of posthumanism insofar as it makes clearer the current and future possibilities, limits and risks of biological fusions with technology.

Complicating matters further are those who choose to undergo prosthetic enhancements. Commonly known as 'biohackers', such individuals endorse 'transhumanism'—the belief that it is both possible and desirable to so fundamentally alter the human condition through the use of technologies as to inaugurate a superior post-human being—and 'biopunk'—a cultural and intellectual movement that advocates for open access to genetic and technological advancements, combined with a 'do-it-yourself' ethos.[79]

Biohackers are interested in literally 'hacking' the body with technological implants. For example, there is the much-publicized case of Professor Kevin Warwick, who had a 4 mm micro-electric array (MEA) implanted in the median nerve fibres of his left arm.[80] Warwick's device, which was switched on six weeks after implantation, eventually allowed him to remotely control and receive feedback from robotic arms: 'It was therefore possible to create artificial sensation, giving the subject feedback information from remote devices'.[81] In an intriguing extension of the initial experiment, reminiscent of how the hacker Case taps into Molly's nervous system in William Gibson's *Neuromancer*,[82] Warwick's wife had an MEA implanted into the median nerve of her left arm.[83] During this version of the experiment, the neural signals produced by Warwick's finger movements were transmitted, via the internet, to his wife's implanted electrodes, causing stimulation of her nervous system; and the neural signals transmitted from her nervous system across the internet stimulated Warwick's nervous system: 'In a series of double-blind tests, sets of signals were transmitted between the two individuals and were successfully identified. For example, when [Warwick's wife] generated three motor neural signal pulses, three nervous system stimulation pulses were perceived by [Warwick] and vice versa. This was achieved with >98% accuracy'.[84] Other (in)famous biohackers include Stelarc, a Cyprus-born performance artist based in Australia, who had a third ear grafted onto his forearm;[85] Steve Mann, a Canadian researcher and inventor, perhaps best known for his invention of 'EyeTap', a wearable computer device that is worn in front of the eye that acts as a camera to record the scene available to the eye and a display onto which computer-generated imagery is superimposed;[86] and Tim Cannon, an American software developer and entrepreneur, who was implanted with a biometric sensor that automatically sent his temperature to his phone and was powered wirelessly through inductive charging.[87] In the discussion that follows, however, I will not really be concerned with biohacking simply because the data it has generated thus far is not as well regarded as that which has been generated by the research being done in neuroprosthetics.

Monkey see . . . Computer do

The word 'prosthesis' comes from the Ancient Greek *prósthesis*, meaning addition, application and/or attachment. A prosthetic is an artificial device that replaces a missing body part, which may have been lost through trauma, disease or may never have formed due to certain congenital conditions. Prosthetic medicine has been around for thousands of years, and prosthetic devices have been fashioned out of all manner of material: wood, papier mâché, metal, rubber, plastic, and, more recently, carbon-fibre and silicon.[88] A major advance in prosthetics came about in the 1960s, when amputees began to use myoelectric prostheses—that is, externally powered artificial limbs controlled with the electrical signals generated naturally by the muscles in the wearer's residual limb. Myoelectric prostheses could not work if there were no transfer of information from the medium of the wearer's flesh to the medium of silicon and wires.

A more recent advance in prosthetic medicine is the field of neuroprosthetics, which uses what are called Brain–Machine Interfaces (BMIs) or Brain–Computer Interfaces (BCIs); the neuroprosthetic implant is digital and works by converting electro-chemical brain signals into readable digital computer input. These devices supplant or supplement the input and/or output of the nervous system.[89] Even though major advances in neuroprosthetics have been very recent, the ideas behind them have been around for at least several decades. In 1973, for example, Jacques J. Vidal, a computer scientist, asked if 'observable electrical brain signals' could 'be put to work as carriers of information in man-computer communication or for the purpose of controlling such external apparatus as prosthetic devices or spaceships? Even on the sole basis of the present states of the art of computer science and neurophysiology, one may suggest that such a feat is potentially around the corner.'[90] It would seem, then, that the 'science-fictiony' idea of controlling a device using only your thoughts was guiding the very first steps neuroprosthetics was about to take.

Vidal was on to something. Connections between machines and animals and machines and humans are now fairly common in research labs and hospitals. As Leuthardt, Roland and Ray explain in their article, 'Neuroprosthetics', researchers typically use 'a setup that records brain signals from the user, computationally analyzes those signals to infer the user's intentions, and then relays the information to an external effector that acts on those intentions.'[91] Inputs to the computer can be 'the firing of individual neurons in the brain, the cumulative voltages across areas of cortex encompassing millions of neurons, or the action potentials [the firing or spiking] conducted by peripheral nerves anywhere in the body'.[92] There are many different types of output effectors that researchers have shown can be moved using just brain or nerve signals, from cursor movements on a computer screen to robotic arms. In addition, certain neuroprosthetics can also take information from the environment: for example, a cochlear implant can read sound waves, while a bionic eye can read light; and each device turns that information into a stimulus that can be read by the brain. Such neuroprosthetics are two-way streets for information; this type of bidirectional feedback is also crucial for limb prosthetics because, as Leuthardt *et al.* point out, meaningful body movements can 'only be accomplished in conjunction with appropriate sensation of the limb or body part. It is this sense of pressure and joint position that enables a person to lift a paper cup without crushing it, for example, or allows someone to walk without injuring the joints of their feet.'[93] It is the absence of such sensory feedback that causes both clumsiness and inefficiency in movement, which is why it is crucial to build such visual, tactile or proprioceptive feedback into brain-controlled devices; devices with such feedback enable a more elegant and effective control of the prostheses.

While there have been many experiments conducted on humans in recent times, given the unavoidably intrusive nature of the procedures involved, animals are used extensively by neuroprosthetic medicine. In laboratories all over the world, there are many 'cyborg' animals, that is, animals that are complex mixtures of cybernetic system and biological organism,[94] as the neuroscientists Mikhail Lebedev and Miguel Nicolelis make clear: 'most of the invasive BMIs have been tested only in experimental animals.'[95] A famous experiment by Nicolelis and his team on an owl monkey is recounted by Clark in *Natural Born Cyborgs*:

> Nicolelis and his team studied the way signals from the cerebral cortex control the motions of a monkey's limbs. An owl monkey had ninety-six wires implanted into its frontal cortex, feeding signals into a computer. As the monkey's brain sent signals to move the monkey's limbs, this 'neural wiretap' was used to gather data about the correlations between patterns of neural signal and specific motions. The correlations were not simple and turned out to involve ensembles of neurons in multiple cortical areas, but the patterns, though buried, were there in the signals. Once these mappings were known, the computer could predict the intended movements directly from the neural activity. The computer could then use the neural signal to specify movements, which could be carried out by a robot arm. In experiments conducted with the MIT Touch Lab, signals from the owl monkey's brain in North Carolina were used to directly control an electromechanical prosthesis in an MIT laboratory six hundred miles distant ... 'it was an amazing sight to see the robot in our lab move, knowing it was being driven by signals from a monkey brain at Duke. It was as if the monkey had a 600 mile-long virtual arm'.[96]

As Clark points out, the cyborg owl monkey in this experiment is a perfect example of what is known as 'telepresence', a term introduced in 1980 by the computer scientist and AI pioneer Marvin Minsky (1927–2016), to describe what happens when 'presence' and 'action' are radically extended through technological means. Indeed, there are many recent examples of such telepresence, but perhaps the most famous of these involves telesurgery. The first complete telesurgery operation was carried out in New York led by Professor Jacques Marescaux and his team from the IRCAD (Institute for Research into Cancer of the Digestive System) on a patient in Strasbourg, France, using a Zeus surgical robot on 7 September 2001.[97] Telesurgery poses some interesting problems for how we might ordinarily think about the surgeon's 'presence' and how we might talk about the limits or boundaries of the surgeon's body: where exactly 'is' the surgeon? Where does his body begin or end? What is his extended and distributed body composed of, considering the different media information from his brain has to traverse he cuts into his patient? Interestingly, the disruption of presence by technology opens the way for a fruitful exploration of how such technologies overlap with the work of Jacques Derrida (1930–2004), which is a thorough exploration of the philosophical understanding of 'presence'. I offer a brief analysis of Derrida's work in the context of posthumanism in Chapter 5.[98]

It would seem, then, that in Nicolelis's owl monkey experiment, the Marescaux telesurgery experiment, as well as the Kevin Warwick biohacking experiments, information can move with relative ease across both biological and nonbiological material, without being lost. This further suggests that there is some odd quality of information that allows it to exist independently of the medium in which it is, at any given moment, instantiated or 'embodied': if this were not the case, then how could information move from brain matter to nerve matter to muscle matter to silicon and metal and back again? This strange quality of information is further underlined by a number of gruesome-sounding experiments that have taken place over the last two decades or so. For example, in 2001, Steve Potter and Thomas DeMarse developed a new method for growing 'dissociated cortical cultures from rat embryos on multi-electrode arrays'.[99] After more than a year of being kept inside a sealed culture dish, the rat neurons still exhibited what Potter and DeMarse called 'robust spontaneous electrical activity'.[100] This intriguing combination of tiny rat embryo brain and an array for 'extracellular multi-electrode recording and stimulation', say Potter and DeMarse, made it possible to study the 'development, adaptation, and very long-term plasticity, across months, in cultured neuronal networks'.[101]

Two-way information exchange between neurons and electrode arrays hooked up to computers has now become somewhat routine in research labs; indeed, as several recent experiments that use part of a lamprey's brainstem demonstrate, information moves fairly easily between biological and nonbiological matter. In one such experiment from 2009, Kositsky *et al.* 'developed a brain–machine interface (BMI) system, where the dissected brain of lamprey larvae was connected bi-directionally' to an external device with several degrees of freedom, which the lamprey brain cells could manipulate in rudimentary ways.[102] According to Kositsky *et al.*, these bidirectional interfaces form 'a closed-loop' because 'the sensory consequences of the control signals are fed-back to the control system to generate new commands. From a mathematical standpoint, when the external input is maintained constant, such a closed-loop system approximates an "autonomous system" whose dynamics are entirely self-contained and do not depend explicitly upon time'.[103] One of the major purposes in creating cybernetic organisms such as these is to establish better ways of grasping the variables that affect the signals output by a population of neurons, thereby improving the predictions a computer can make of their future behaviour; the ultimate goal is to give future human neuroprosthetics users optimal control over their devices.

What these experiments show, then, is proof of the principle that not only is fusing brain matter and electronic circuitry possible, but that there is a clear two-way flow of information between biological and nonbiological matter. But such experiments can also evoke feelings of uneasiness and revulsion in people hearing about them for the first time; animals are kept in laboratories, their physical movements restrained in certain ways for prolonged periods; they are subjected to rounds of surgeries that leave them with bits of metal stuck in their brains, and are made to perform certain tasks over and over again to provide data; and, when they eventually die, they are dissected. Such feelings of uneasiness and squeamishness seem to be what drive philosophers such as Andy Clark to favour a 'nonpenetrative cyborg technology' that would lead to 'cyborgs without surgery, symbionts without sutures'.[104] Such non-invasive systems, according to Lebedev and Nicolelis 'primarily exploit electroencephalograms (EEGs) to control computer cursors or other devices. This approach has proved useful for helping paralyzed or "locked in" patients develop ways of communication with the external world.'[105] Such systems 'try to decipher the subject's voluntary intentions and decisions through measurements of the combined electrical activity of massive neuronal populations', and are likely to continue to offer 'some practical solutions (e.g., cursor control, communication, computer operation and wheelchair control) for patients in the future'.[106] Some BMI designs 'rely on the subjects' ability to develop control of their own brain activity using biofeedback, whereas others utilize classifier algorithms that recognize EEG patterns related to particular voluntary intentions. Recently, adaptive algorithms that constantly update the classifier parameters during training have been implemented.'[107]

However, there are clear limitations to the data non-invasive BMIs can provide. According to Lebedev and Nicolelis, the spatial and temporal resolution of EEGs can be a bit fuzzy 'owing to the overlapping electrical activity generated by different cortical areas'.[108] And, because EEG signals have to pass through brain tissue, bone and skin, the quality of the signal is often affected; the main drawback of the non-invasive approach to BMIs is thus the low quality of the information that is received through electrophysiological recordings, which 'despite having the great advantage of not exposing the patient to the risks of brain surgery', only 'provide communication channels of limited capacity'.[109] For example, the typical information transfer rate of these channels, say Lebedev and Nicolelis, 'is currently 5–25 bits s^{-1} [hertz]' which 'might not be sufficient to control the movements of an arm or leg prosthesis that has multiple degrees of freedom'.[110] They continue: 'if the goal of a BMI is to restore movements with multiple degrees of freedom through the control of an artificial prosthesis, the message from published evidence is clear: this task will require recording of high-resolution signals from the brain, and this can be done using invasive approaches.'[111] Clark's preferred non-invasive BMIs will simply not produce the quality of information required to make neuroprosthetics work optimally.

Invasive 'BMI approaches are based on recordings from ensembles of single brain cells (also known as single units) or on the activity of multiple neurons (also known as multi-units)'.[112] The invasive approach that relies on long-term recordings from 'large populations of neurons (100–400 units) evolved from experiments carried out in 1995'.[113] Building on these experiments, say Lebedev and Nicolelis, 'a series of studies demonstrated that neuronal readout of tactile stimuli could be uncovered using pattern-recognition algorithms, such as artificial neural networks.'[114] These studies led to something of an explosion of similar work in other laboratories: in less than six years, several laboratories reported results that reproduced primate arm reaching and grasping movements, using either computer cursors or robotic manipulators as actuators.[115] It was now obvious that invasive BMIs relied 'on the physiological properties of individual cortical and subcortical neurons (or pools of neurons) that modulate their activity in association with movements'.[116] And, because such 'modulations are highly variable, from neuron to neuron and from trial to trial', only by averaging across many trials can fairly consistent firing patterns be revealed.[117] Such 'averaging across large populations of neurons significantly reduces the variability of signals derived from single neurons'.[118] In other words, the control signals must be extracted using algorithms and machine learning, in order to be useful.[119] Extracting 'motor control signals from the firing patterns of populations of neurons and using these control signals to reproduce motor behaviors in artificial actuators are the two key operations that a clinically viable BMI should perform flawlessly'.[120]

An important idea informing recent thinking in neuroprosthetics is the concept of 'neuroplasticity', which, broadly speaking, is the brain's ability to 'rewire' itself as a result of changes in behaviour, the environment, thinking, emotions, as well as changes resulting from bodily injury. Neuroplasticity has thus replaced the older notion that brains are physiologically static organs, and researchers in neuroplasticity are concerned with how brains change in the course of a lifetime. For example, when we learn something, our brain undergoes small, cellular changes, whereas after a traumatic injury involving paralysis or amputation, our brain can undergo massive changes such as cortical remapping, in response to the injury. During cortical remapping, a brain can incorporate unattached robot limbs into its representation of the body with relative ease; indeed, this incorporation is so effective that experiments on owl monkeys showed that 'cortical representation of the robot was optimized at the expense of representation of the animal's own limb.'[121] This new cortical map—sometimes also known as a 'body schema'—is central, Lebedev and Nicolelis argue, if a neuroprosthetic is to be accepted by patients: BMI devices will 'have to act in the same way and feel the same as the subjects' own limbs. Recent findings suggest that this task might be accomplished by creating conditions in which the brain undergoes experience-dependent plasticity and assimilates the prosthetic limb as if it were part of the subject's own body.'[122] Until recently, they note, such plasticity was achieved using only visual feedback, but 'a more efficient way to assimilate the prosthetic limb in the brain representation could be to use multiple artificial feedback signals, derived from pressure and position sensors placed on the prosthetic limb. These feedback signals would effectively train the brain to incorporate the properties of the artificial limb into the tuning characteristic of neurons located in cortical and subcortical areas that maintain representations of the subject's body. We predict that such plasticity will result in sensory and motor areas of the brain representing the prosthetic device.'[123] In other words, the brain readily incorporates 'unnatural' or artifical devices into its cortical map; neuroplasticity thus poses some interesting problems for any notion of an 'identity politics' that is conceived on the basis of a 'natural' biological body. For example, such components have no sex or race; they are also 'younger' than the rest of the body; they can be replaced and upgraded; yet the brain easily incorporates them into its cortical map. And, because these external devices do not even have to be attached to the body of the being operating them—the owl monkey in the experiment mentioned above was operating a robot arm in a different part of the lab—any notion of identity that centres on contiguous body parts is also shown to be merely conventional. Thus do neuroprosthetics displace both body-centric notions of identity and the identity politics built on those notions.

The surprisingly intimate connection between the body and neuroprosthetic is due to distributed cognition, which, as Lebedev and Nicolelis point out, has been known about for over 100 years in one form or another:

> Controlling an artificial actuator through a BMI can be thought of as a process somewhat similar to the operation required by subjects to operate tools—a capacity that is inherent only in higher primates such as chimpanzees and humans. . . . Almost 100 years ago . . . [Henry] Head [1861–1940] and [Gordon Morgan] Holmes [1876–1965] suggested that the 'body schema'—that is, the internal brain representations of one's body—could extend itself to include a wielded tool. This idea was validated by the experimental demonstration that cortical neurons extend their visual receptive fields along

the length of a rake used by monkeys to retrieve distant objects. . . . Psychophysics experiments also support the notion that tool usage leads to remapping of the 'body schema' in humans.[124]

Thus, a growing list of experimental results

suggests that long-term usage of an artificial actuator directly controlled by brain activity might lead to substantial cortical and subcortical remapping. As such, this process might elicit the vivid perceptual experience that the artificial actuator becomes an extension of the subject's body rather than a mere tool. This suggestion is supported by the report of primary sensorimotor cortex activation during perceived voluntary movements of phantom limbs in amputees.[125]

But it also turns out that cortical remapping of the body schema in tool assimilation is not confined only to humans or primates:

Perhaps the most stunning demonstration of tool assimilation by animals was observed when both rats and primates learned to operate an actuator through a BMI, without the need to move their own limbs. In these experiments, decoding algorithms were initially trained to predict limb movements of animals from the activity of neuronal populations. Remarkably, after these animals started to control the actuator directly using their neuronal activity, their limbs eventually stopped moving, while the animals continued to control the actuator by generating proper modulations of their cortical neurons. Interestingly, during these episodes neuronal tuning to movements of the subject's own limbs decreased while the animals continued to control the artificial actuator by their brain activity . . . The most parsimonious interpretation of this finding is that the brain was capable of undergoing a gradual assimilation of the actuator within the same maps that represented the body.[126]

In addition to

these physiological adaptations of neuronal firing patterns, behavioral performance improves as animals learn to operate

BMIs effectively. . . . As the quality of BMI control improves, initial elevation of neuronal firing variability subsides. Plastic changes in neuronal firing patterns during BMI control, leading to the physiological incorporation of the artificial actuator properties into neuronal space, could account for these changes in firing rate variance. This interpretation is in accord with the theory of optimal feedback control.[127]

For a neuroprosthesis to behave and feel as a natural appendage of the subject's body, Lebedev and Nicolelis argue that it will have to be equipped with various sensors that can provide multiple channels of 'sensory' information back to the subject's brain. One of the more recent and promising types of feedback takes the form of 'microstimulation', a technique that stimulates a small population of neurons by passing a small electrical current through a nearby microelectrode implanted in the primary somatosensory cortex. For Lebedev and Nicolelis, cortical microstimulation 'might become a useful way to deliver long-term feedback from prosthetic limbs controlled by a BMI, and might contribute to the development of a completely new generation of neuroprosthetic devices for restoring various motor behaviors in severely impaired patients'.[128] Microstimulation has recently been used to train rhesus macaque monkeys with brain implants to distinguish textures by learning a new electrical language associated with texture.[129]

Generally speaking, BMI platforms take advantage of the 'well-known correlation between discharges of cortical neurons and motor parameters of interest, and perform a reverse operation: they predict motor parameters from patterns of neuronal firing';[130] thus, 'precise knowledge of computations performed by brain circuits is not crucial for the construction of clinically relevant BMIs'.[131] This is why 'large samples of recorded neurons are preferable', since the accuracy and reliability of the software's predictions 'improve considerably with the number of simultaneously recorded neurons';[132] what is important, in other words, is the overall pattern of the signals. To isolate this pattern, the software performs regression analysis, a statistical process for estimating the relationship between a dependent variable (an output, y) and an independent variable (an input, x) used both in making predictions and machine learning. Lebedev and Nicolelis state that

relatively simple multiple linear regression models have proved
to be efficient in many practical BMI designs . . . In these models,
predicted motor parameters are derived from the weighted sums
of neuronal rates of firing, measured at different time points in
the past. The number of regressors in the model and the time
window used for predictions can be optimized for each concrete
BMI application.[133]

This type of analysis allows for the simultaneous prediction
of several motor parameters, such as 'arm position, velocity,
acceleration and hand gripping force, . . . by separate combinations
of the activity of the same original pool of neurons', supporting the
notion 'that multiple motor parameters are processed by overlapping
neuronal ensembles'.[134]

However, even though there are clear pathways for patterns
of information to travel across flesh and silicon and back, implants
still pose serious risks to the patient. 'Currently, chronically
implanted microwire arrays offer the best compromise between
safety, recording longevity and neuronal yield required to operate
BMIs', but 'the broad and challenging issue of biological
compatibility . . . has to be properly addressed and solved.'[135] Often,
the recording quality of implants deteriorates, 'probably owing to a
process of electrode encapsulation by fibrous tissue and cell death
in the vicinity of the electrode'.[136] There is also 'the continuous
stress of a daily routine that involves external cables and plugging
and unplugging of external head-stages. These operations carry a
risk of causing tissue damage, bleeding and brain infection. Such
a risk of failure, which might be tolerable in animal experiments, is
unwanted in practical applications for humans.'[137] It would seem,
then, that the long-term integration of biology and hardware comes
up against the problem of long-term compatibility, which manifest
as stress and infection. However, Lebedev and Nicolelis suggest that
implantable wireless devices would go a long way towards solving
such issues.[138] A recent study published in *Nature Nanotechnology*
also offers hope for tackling compatibility problems: Liu *et al.*
reported that they managed to inject an electronic mesh that unfolds
once injected into the heads of mice through needles with a diameter
as small as 100 μm. The mesh, which sits atop the brain, allows for
neural recording, and because the entry wound is so small and the
wires are thin, the mesh would pose fewer risks to the patient.[139]

Since Lebedev and Nicolelis wrote their overview of BMIs, there have been many more studies and experiments carried out and animals and humans using the invasive approaches they outline. In February 2013, *Science Daily* reported on an experiment that used a bidirectional neuroprosthesis in human subjects.[140] The interesting thing about this study was that, for the first time, electrodes had been permanently implanted in the nerves and muscles of an amputee, allowing him to directly control an arm prosthesis.[141] Max Ortiz-Catalan, a researcher on the project that was conducted at both Sahlgrenska University Hospital and Chalmers University of Technology, described in a press release how the prosthesis uses 'a new bidirectional interface with the human body, together with a natural and intuitive control system'.[142] According to the leader of the surgical team, Rickard Brånemark, the study combines 'a bone anchored prosthesis with implanted electrodes.' A titanium screw was used as an osseointegrated implant to anchor the prosthetic arm to the bone in the patient's stump. Because the prosthesis was anchored to the bone, the usual suction-cup method of attaching prosthetics became unnecessary; the implanted electrodes allowed the surgical team to dispense with the need to rely on electrodes attached to the skin, which would only have provided enough information to drive a few of the prosthesis's actions; since the implanted electrodes can retrieve more and better quality signals, the patient is able to move the arm more effectively through a broader range of movements. And, through microstimulation, the patient experiences 'feeling' from the device. According to Brånemark, 'tests have shown that more movements may be performed in a coordinated way, and that several movements can be performed simultaneously.'[143]

What these neuroprosthetic experiments make clear time and again is that information is able to form loops between the body's nervous system and digital computers with relative ease: neuronal activity is machine-readable and machine activity is brain-readable. The field of neuroprosthetic medicine also makes clear that 'subjectivity' and 'identity' is extendible, 'plastic' and 'hackable' in ways that challenge notions of identity and identity politics that are built on 'embodiment' in a natural biological body as well as ideas of 'subjectivity' that are centered on a contiguous body. In short, neuroprosthetic medicine gives real scientific weight to posthumanism: it is not a mere 'academic fad' or just another 'fashionable theory' in the long line of trendy but disposable cultural analyses. Neuroprosthetic medicine, in other words, provides a biological basis for distributed cognition.

Neuroprosthetic medicine thus confronts us with the paradoxes that make posthumanist thinking necessary: 'human movement' and 'human embodiment' are not just no longer simply or exclusively 'human', no longer simply anchored in the biological body, no longer simply graspable as coterminous with the limits of the biological body: they are fundamentally open to the non-human, the non-natural, the non-organic. Our human bodies have always been 'more' than biological, with either very complicated borders, or— which perhaps amounts to the same thing—hardly any borders at all: bodies that speak to and are extended by information into digital computers and robotics, and vice versa, are almost infinitely extensible. None of what I have just said, however, should be taken to suggest that our bodies or biology somehow 'disappear'; what should be starting to disappear are not only the concepts of the body that see it as 'self-contained', 'whole' or 'autonomous', but also the identities, ideologies, politics and theories built on those notions.

Genetic manipulations

If there were a branch of science that could be said to complement neuroprosthetic medicine's disruption of the notions that the human body and its borders are complete or fixed, as well as the ideologies or politics based on those notions, it would be genetic and genomic engineering. In closing this chapter, I would like to consider how this type of engineering has the potential to alter the genetic make-up of the human species forever. Along the way, I'll also look at some of the mechanisms and surprising overlaps that cutting-edge genetic engineering shares with two of the most ancient forms of life on Earth—bacteria and viruses. Finally, I'll explore in some little detail the controversies and possibilities swirling around one of the most recent and exciting techniques for gene manipulation, CRISPR.

Back to bacteria

In the preface to the second edition of their book, *Microcosmos: Four Billion Years of Evolution from Our Microbial Ancestors*,[144]

Lynn Margulis (1938–2011) and her son, Dorion Sagan, write that a major goal of the first edition of *Microcosmos*, was to overcome an 'anthropocentric view' of life on Earth that centres too much on 'humanity': 'Reversing the usual inflated view of humanity, we wrote of *Homo sapiens* as a kind of latter-day permutation in the ancient and ongoing evolution of the smallest, most ancient, and most chemically versatile inhabitants of the Earth, namely bacteria'.[145] However, the authors also acknowledge that they may have overstated their position: 'We believe this formerly slighted perspective is a highly useful, even essential compensation required to balance the traditional anthropocentric view which flatters humanity in an unthinking, inappropriate way. Ultimately we may have overcompensated.'[146] Margulis and Sagan's admission of 'overcompensation' should alert the reader to the need for caution when dealing with *Microcosmos*. Margulis herself was no stranger to scientific controversies during her lifetime—most notably, towards the end of her life, she saw 9/11 as a false-flag operation;[147] nevertheless, her theory that the eukaryotic cell—that is, a cell with a nucleus and organelles, which are the equivalent of organs in larger animal bodies—is a symbiotic union of once independent primitive prokaryotic cells—cells without nuclei, like bacteria—is well supported by experimental evidence.[148] And although her ideas on organelle genesis are now widely accepted, her subsequent attempts to get symbiosis accepted as a general mechanism for introducing genetic variation—the *Gaia* hypothesis—have not been successful.[149]

In the famous 1991 profile of Margulis published in *Science*, Margulis is quoted as saying that neo-Darwinists 'wallow in their zoological, capitalistic, competitive, cost-benefit interpretation of Darwin'.[150] Indeed, Margulis's cartoon-like characterization of neo-Darwinism[151] is one of the main reasons why her work is one of those rare examples of science writing that is often cited in the humanities; it is also the major reason why her attempts to get the *Gaia* hypothesis accepted as the general mechanism of life have not found traction in the sciences.[152] Margulis's ideological characterization of neo-Darwinism also finds its way into *Microcosmos*, where, instead of a competitive Darwinism, the reader encounters a more cooperative alternative: 'the view of evolution as chronic bloody competition ... dissolves before a new view of continual cooperation, strong interaction, and mutual dependence among life forms. Life did not take over the globe by combat, but by networking. Life forms multiplied and complexified by co-opting others, not just by killing them.'[153] In other words, life on Earth, according to Margulis and Sagan, evolved and spread through what began as microbial cooperation and interaction, which resulted in the emergence of eukaryotic cells, which were composed of the absorbed and co-opted parts of simpler, prokaryotic cells.

The emergence of eukaryotic cells from co-opted prokaryotic cells constitutes, say Margulis and Sagan, the fundamental division of life on Earth: 'so significant are bacteria and their evolution that the fundamental division in forms of life on Earth is not that between plants and animals, as is commonly assumed, but between prokaryotes—organisms composed of cells with no nucleus, that is, bacteria—and eukaryotes—all the other life forms.'[154] The stark division between bacteria and eukaryotes, may indeed, be 'the most dramatic in all biology';[155] however, the 'fundamental division' Margulis and Sagan mention here should also serve to make clear that there is a distinction to be made between the smaller microbial processes of assimilation and interaction and the larger processes of Darwinian competitive evolution.

However, despite these issues, by going back to the origins of life on Earth, Margulis and Sagan also sketch the outline of a branch of posthumanism insofar as they wish to see life beyond the frame of 'humanity'; what their analysis, in other words, makes it possible to glimpse is a genetic posthumanism that is not bound by the categories of 'human' or 'humanity'. Certainly, the ancient processes of microbial absorption that Margulis and Sagan discuss are 'prehuman' in the sense that they were already underway millions and millions of years 'before' humans and humanity had appeared; and Margulis and Sagan are surely correct when they say that if life on Earth is looked at from the point of view of 'life-in-general', humans and humanity only make up a very small part of it; this is why looking at life on Earth through the lens of humanity alone amounts to the 'anthropocentrism' they criticize. What is especially interesting about Margulis and Sagan's view of the prokaryotic origins of eukaryotic cells, is that it constitutes what they call 'a second evolutionary dynamic', which, they say, is 'a sort of natural genetic engineering'.[156] Here, Margulis and Sagan are implying that the genetic engineering carried out by humans constitutes something of an odd return to the mechanisms and processes of ancient prokaryotic absorption and incorporation. Now, I want to be clear that I am not suggesting that symbiosis is the key to genetic mutation on Earth or anything like that; all I am suggesting, however, is that human genetic engineering harnesses some very ancient forms of genetic manipulation. In order to get a better grip on what cutting-edge human genetic engineering owes to its prokaryote ancestors it is necessary to cover quickly—and thus unavoidably reductively—both what a gene is and what constitutes genetic engineering. Once that is done, it will hopefully be easier to see exactly what is at stake in genetic posthumanism.

I'll begin with genes.

Genes and genetic engineers

According to J.M.W. Slack, a gene is the molecular unit of heredity in a living organism;[157] heredity here means the passing of phenotypic traits from parents to their offspring, either through asexual reproduction or sexual reproduction; a phenotypic trait, is a distinct variant of a phenotypic characteristic of an organism that may be inherited, environmentally determined or due to some combination of the two. A commonly used example to illustrate the difference between a phenotypic trait and a phenotypic characteristic, is eye colour: eye colour is an abstract characteristic, whereas specific eye colours, such as blue, brown and hazel, are traits. A phenotype is the composite of a particular organism's observable characteristics or traits, such as its morphology (that is, its form, features or structure), its development, its biochemical or physiological properties, its phenology (its periodic life cycle) or its behaviour. There are also 'extended phenotypes', which, according to Richard Dawkins, are the products of a creature's behaviour, such as the way it might manipulate its environment, when, for example, it builds a nest or den.[158] Posthumanism, insofar as it takes its unit of analysis to be 'human + technology', could thus be understood, from an evolutionary biological perspective, as part of the field of study of extended phenotypes.

Genes carry the information that is used to build and maintain an organism's cells and pass genetic traits on to offspring; they are arranged, one after another, on structures called chromosomes, which contain a single long DNA (deoxyribonucleic acid) molecule, only a portion of which corresponds to a single gene. A single gene is the segment of DNA that contains information for encoding a chain of polypeptides, proteins or ribonucleic acid (RNA)—all of which are biological molecules—that has a particular function in an organism. Most DNA molecules consist of two strands coiled around each other to form a double helix, which famously looks like a twisted ladder. Each strand of DNA is known as a polynucleotide because it is composed of simpler units called nucleotides, and each nucleotide is composed of a nitrogen-containing nucleobase—either guanine (G), adenine (A), thymine (T), or cytosine (C)—as well as a monosaccharide sugar (called deoxyribose) and a phosphate group. Each strand of DNA has a 'backbone' made of alternating deoxyribose and phosphate groups. The two strands of DNA that correspond to the 'sides' of the twisted ladder, are held together by 'rungs' made of hydrogen bonds between the base pairs: A always forms a base pair with T, and C always forms a base pair with G. The double helix structure makes DNA particularly well suited for biological information storage: not only are the DNA backbones resistant to breaking, each strand contains the same biological information as the other as a backup; biological information is replicated as the two strands are separated. An allele is a version of the DNA sequence of a particular gene and can result in different phenotypic traits, such as colour.

The genetic code stored in DNA is 'interpreted' during the process known as gene expression, and the properties of the expression give rise to the organism's phenotype. To put it simply, two steps are required to interpret the information encoded in a gene's DNA and produce the protein it specifies: in the first step, the gene's DNA is transcribed into what is known as messenger RNA (mRNA); during transcription, a particular segment of DNA is copied into mRNA by an enzyme known as RNA polymerase; in the second step, mRNA is translated into protein. Translation occurs in the ribosome, which functions like a large and complex molecular machine: the ribosome links amino acids together in the order specified by mRNA molecules using transfer RNA (tRNA) molecules to carry amino acids and to read the mRNA three nucleotides at a time (that is, some variation of a sequence of As, Ts, Cs or Gs). In contrast, RNA-coding genes go through the first step, but are not translated into proteins. Genes that encode proteins are composed of a series of three-nucleotide sequences called codons, which can be understood as the 'words' made out of the 'alphabet' of nucleotides and used to form 'sentences' or genes.

If the foregoing discussion seems needlessly technical to some readers, I would ask those readers to bear in mind that the details provided are necessary for understanding the discussion that follows. In addition, these details should serve as a useful reminder of just how concretely the basic building blocks of life are understood by geneticists and biologists; they also serve to highlight what certain gender ideologies—particularly those that push notions of the 'social construction' of biological realities—must blind themselves to in the rush to absolve themselves of the burden of comprehending complex material processes. The complex biological realities of genetics—just like the ones discussed in the context of neuroprosthetic medicine—are essential for grasping posthumanism concretely; these technical details are what anchor posthumanism, moving it out of the category of 'fashionable cultural theory'.

So, how does the above relate to genetic engineering?

Margulis and Sagan note in *Microcosmos* that prokaryotes, single-celled organisms which, like bacteria, lack a membrane-bound nucleus or any other membrane-bound organelles, 'routinely and rapidly transfer different bits of genetic material to other individuals'.[159] This microbial gene transference takes place through a process called horizontal gene transfer (HGT; sometimes also called lateral gene transfer, LGT), in which genes are transferred between organisms in a manner other than 'traditional' reproduction—that is, the vertical transmission of genes from parent to offspring via sexual or asexual reproduction:

> With genetic exchange possible only during reproduction, we [humans] are locked into our species, our bodies, and our generation. As it is sometimes expressed in technical terms, we trade genes 'vertically'—through generations—whereas prokaryotes trade them 'horizontally'—directly to their neighbours in the same generation. The result is that while genetically fluid bacteria are functionally immortal, in eukaryotes, sex becomes linked with death.[160]

This 'horizontal gene trading' amounts, according to Margulis and Sagan, to sex without reproduction since 'sex is the mixing or union of genes from separate sources';[161] it is also very common among microbes and it keeps them 'fit': 'by trading genes, bacterial populations are kept primed for their role in their particular environment and individual bacteria pass on their genetic heritage.'[162] Indeed, HGT is the also main reason for bacterial antibiotic resistance.[163] According to Margulis and Sagan, the 'bacteria-style genetic transfer exploited by [human] genetic engineers' was the 'first sort of sex to appear on our planet'; it is 'simply the recombination of genes from more than one source'.[164] In the early 1970s, Paul Berg became the first human to reproduce this very ancient form of 'sex': modern human genetic engineering took its first steps by exploiting HGT to create the first genetically modified organisms using a virus to inject foreign DNA into bacteria.[165]

Typically, genetic engineering alters the genetic make-up of an organism either by removing heritable material from the organism or by inserting DNA that was prepared outside the host organism either directly into it or into a cell that is then fused with the host. There are four major methods of HGT that are exploited by genetic engineering: 1) *microinjection*, where DNA can be directly injected into the cell; 2) *transformation*, where a cell directly takes in and incorporates exogenous genetic material from its surroundings; 3) *transduction*, where bacterial DNA is moved from one bacterium to another by a virus, such as a bacteriophage, which infects and replicates within bacteria; and 4) *bacterial conjugation*, where DNA is transferred via a plasmid—a small, circular DNA molecule within cells that is physically separated from chromosomal DNA and can replicate independently—from a donor cell to a recipient cell during cell-to-cell contact.[166] A virus has a protein case to protect it; a plasmid does not, and is thus often referred to as 'naked' DNA.

The genetic engineer removes, or 'knocks out', heritable material using a nuclease, an enzyme capable of dissolving the bonds between the nucleotide subunits of nucleic acids, which works essentially like a molecular scissors.[167] The engineer then inserts new genetic material into the host either directly, through microinjection, or indirectly, via transduction and conjugation through what's known as a vector. A vector is a vehicle—such as a virus or a plasmid—that carries foreign genetic material into a cell, where it can be replicated and/or expressed. 'New' genetic material is generated through a process known as molecular cloning, which involves assembling recombinant DNA—that is, DNA molecules that combine genetic material from multiple sources that would not otherwise be found in naturally occurring biological organisms—and letting it replicate within a host organism.

New or foreign genetic material can be inserted into any organism without a problem because DNA molecules from all organisms share the same chemical structure: thus plant DNA can be joined to bacterial DNA, human DNA can be joined to fungal DNA, and so on. Margulis and Sagan put this down to the fact that the 'microbial common denominator remains essentially unchanged. Our DNA is derived in an unbroken sequence from the same molecules in the earliest cells that formed at the edges of the first warm, shallow oceans.'[168] This apparently infinitely 'spliceable' property of DNA has made it possible to engineer things like insulin-producing bacteria,[169] as well as genetically modified animals for use in human disease research, such as the 'knockout rat',[170] 'OncoMouse'[171] and genetically modified primates.[172] For Margulis and Sagan, human genetic engineering takes us full circle: 'it is not preposterous to postulate that the very consciousness that enables us to probe the workings of our cells may have been born of the concerted capacities of millions of microbes that evolved symbiotically to become the human brain.'[173]

Whether or not one accepts Margulis and Sagan's implication that the brains of human genetic engineers are only now doing what they do because those brains have been produced by millions of years of bacterial 'sex', there can be little doubt that human engineers have learnt to perform 'sex' in this way by observing bacteria and viruses. However, one might ask if, as Margulis and Sagan are wont to do, simply invoking bacterial HGT is really sufficient to displace the anthropocentric view of life on Earth? Margulis and Sagan's efforts at displacing anthropocentrism often seem to lapse into an odd nostalgia for an imaginary ancient prehuman, prehistoric time when bacteria serenely and cooperatively traded genes back and forth across species. The irony, of course, is that such descriptions remain anthropocentric metaphors in that they seek to evoke ideals of 'cooperation' and 'working together' 'mutualism' instead of the 'chronic bloody competition' of Darwinism. Indeed, Margulis and Sagan's apparently 'non-anthropocentric' views of such life cannot help but invoke human metaphors over and over again: 'continual cooperation', 'mutual dependence', 'networking', 'trading'—even 'free-lancing'[174]—to describe the relations among nonhuman microbial life forms.

Indeed, genetic trade, even in Margulis and Sagan's re-imagining of it, seems far from being an unproblematically benign process that is somehow ethically preferable to Darwinian bloody competition. For example, the independent prokaryotic life forms that were co-opted and assimilated may not have been, as Margulis and Sagan point out, 'killed', but they were nevertheless fundamentally changed by their contact with other life forms; they were never again able to 'free' themselves from that initial contact: eukaryotic cells do not just unravel and release their organelles. Furthermore, since a great deal of life on Earth does not trade genes like bacteria, it would be reductively 'bacteriocentric' to invoke it as a blueprint for how all life works. And, if we were to scale up this promiscuous ancient genetic trade from the micro- to the macro-scale, it quickly becomes apparent that this trade harbours the very dangers and opportunities that attend genetic manipulation: should there be limits to a trade where any genetic material can be taken from one life-form—say, a wolf—and inserted into another—say, a human?

The fact that human genetic engineers have learned to perform 'sex' like ancient bacteria underscores how genetic manipulation is posthumanist insofar as it repeatedly puts into question any notion of a hard and fast boundary between human and non-human. This questioning happens in at least two ways: first, the processes and mechanisms of genetic manipulation cannot be considered as simply human tools since they were originated and used by viruses and bacteria, which humans then copied and implemented using sophisticated technology; thus, HGT and the genetic engineering it inspires erode, in surprising ways, at least some of the differences between humans, viruses and bacteria. Second, since genetic engineering can splice together the genetic material of different species and is thus not bound by traditional lines of descent or species divisions, it has the power to splice human genes with nonhuman genes to create genetically enhanced or designer posthumans.

These erosions of inter-species differences cannot, however, be said to be unproblematically 'good' or 'bad': genetic engineering would thus be fundamentally *pharmakonic* in the Derridean sense highlighted in the Introduction. Genetic engineering has a tremendous potential to be used for good: for example, it can be used to create animals for use in medical research; it can be used to create foods that are easier to grow and are more abundant; it also holds out the future hope of being able to repair certain terrible genetic conditions that people, animals and other life forms suffer from. At the same time, genetic engineering also has the potential to be very bad indeed: as the technology gets better and cheaper, it gets easier and easier to make all sorts of permanent genetic changes too often and too quickly; and, as the technology gets cheaper and cheaper, regulation, access and control of it promises to get more and more difficult. To fully illustrate the fundamentally *pharmakonic* quality of genetic manipulation, I will close this chapter with a consideration of the controversy and debate that surrounds what is perhaps the most promising and powerful new tools for genetic manipulation—CRISPR.

CRISPR: The genome editor

A genome is the complete set of genetic material of a particular organism; genome editing is a refined type of genetic engineering that allows DNA to be very precisely inserted into, replaced, or removed from a genome using what are known as nucleases.[175] Nucleases are essentially 'molecular scissors' that can cut both strands of DNA at desired locations in the genome; the process then harnesses the cell's own mechanisms to repair the cut. Prior to 2012, scientists were using 'enzymes called zinc finger nucleases that promised to do this accurately and efficiently'.[176] The major problem with zinc finger nucleases, however, was that they were expensive and difficult to engineer; the discovery of CRISPR in 2012 as a genome-editing tool has all but replaced the need for such expensive nucleases.

CRISPR—an acronym for 'clustered regularly interspaced short palindromic repeats'—was first noticed in *Escherichia coli* in 1987, but was not well understood at the time.[177] It was several years before CRISPR was understood to be part of a bacteria's adaptive immune system, which is made up of repeated clusters of DNA interspersed with short segments of what is known as 'spacer DNA.' The spacer DNA is taken from the DNA of viruses or plasmids that have attacked the prokaryote in the past and, together, the repeaters and spacers form relatively short sequences that are typically only several tens of nucleobases in length.[178] These sequences are accompanied by 'Cas9'—short for 'CRISPR associated protein 9'—an endonuclease enzyme capable of cutting both strands of DNA. According to Dana Carroll, when 'a viral genome or plasmid enters one of these microbial hosts, a few fragments of the invading

DNA are captured as "spacers" between identical "repeats" that are specific to the particular CRISPR system. . . . When the same viral or plasmid sequence invades the host again, the corresponding spacer RNA guides destruction of the invading RNA or DNA.'[179] Amazingly, this guide RNA only targets and cuts both strands of the target DNA that matches it; thus, different spacers are specifically designed to cut specific kinds of DNA sequences.[180]

In 2012, Emmanuelle Charpentier and Jennifer Doudna jointly developed the CRISPR-Cas9 tool using the bacteria that cause strep throat. Their work 'showed they could use a single RNA in conjunction with the cutting protein, . . . Cas9, to slice any desired sequence of DNA in test tubes'.[181] In 2013, Feng Zhang and George Church 'separately reported that the CRISPR-Cas9 system could be used for gene editing in the cells of animals, including humans'.[182] These discoveries meant that any researcher who wished to target any particular gene needed only to synthesize the Cas9 protein and some RNA that matches the sequence of the targeted region.[183] CRISPR in other words, is programmable: the RNA guides the enzyme to the DNA that the researcher wants cut, and Cas9 cuts it. And, since these guided scissors can be programmed to cut any DNA, researchers 'can design experiments in which they change multiple genes in an organism simultaneously using Cas9 and multiple RNA guides';[184] and, if a similar enough piece of DNA is introduced at the same time, the cell, using a process known as homology-directed repair, uses that DNA, thus making it possible for fairly precise gene replacements to be made.[185]

With the advent of CRISPR-Cas9, the cost of genome editing suddenly plummeted: 'Researchers often need to order only the RNA fragment; the other components can be bought off the shelf. Total cost: as little as $30.'[186] There was also no longer any need for researchers to rely heavily on 'traditional' model organisms such as mice and fruit flies because they were the only species that came with a good tool kit for genetic manipulation. CRISPR made it possible to edit genes in practically any organism on the tree of life.[187]

CRISPR has also been tried on adult animals, mice in particular, in an effort to find applications of the technology for use in gene therapy. In gene therapy, an attempt is made to repair a mutated gene in a patient by administering DNA that encodes a functional, therapeutic gene, usually by packaging it inside a viral vector.

According to Heidi Ledford, the bioengineer Daniel Anderson and his colleagues instead 'used CRISPR in mice to correct a mutation associated with a human metabolic disease called tyrosinaemia. It was the first use of CRISPR to fix a disease-causing mutation in an adult animal—and an important step towards using the technology for gene therapy in humans.'[188] However, these experiments showed that using CRISPR on mature animals exposed some of the tool's limitations: 'To deliver the Cas9 enzyme and its guide RNA into the target organ, the liver, the team had to pump large volumes of liquid into blood vessels—something that is not generally considered feasible in people. And the experiments corrected the disease-causing mutation in just 0.4% of the cells, which is not enough to have an impact on many diseases.'[189] As a result, it seems likely that experiments on mature subjects would only likely 'be scenarios in which the CRISPR components can be injected directly into tissues, such as those in the eye, or in which cells can be removed from the body, engineered in the lab and then put back.'[190] Another major problem with CRISPR technology is that Cas9 can end up making 'off-target' cuts in the genes: for example, in a mature creature there may be many sites that wind up being cut by Cas9 and those off-target cuts could cause other serious diseases such as cancer. Efforts, however, have been ongoing to improve targeting and there has already been 'tremendous progress' in that regard, according to Keith Joung of Massachusetts General Hospital.[191]

In another recent CRISPR development, David Liu and his team created 'a new CRISPR system that can switch single letters of the genome cleanly and efficiently, in a way that [researchers] say could reliably repair many disease-causing mutations'.[192] However, this technique—which involves 'blunting' the Cas9 scissors and has not yet been applied to whole animals, let alone humans—has already had a provisional patent application filed for it.[193] Money and hype, it seems, are never far away when it comes to discussion of CRISPR. Indeed, the researchers who frequently appear in the media to talk about CRISPR—Jennifer Doudna, Feng Zhang, George Church, Keith Joung—are also the founders of Editas Medicine, a genome-editing company that went public in February 2016.[194] So, once again, the reader is reminded to be cautious when sifting the information about CRISPR that comes from science reporters.

Nevertheless, it is the ease in using CRISPR—combined with its cheapness, power and infancy as a technology—that is causing concern for some in the scientific community, even among those who pioneered it. According to Heidi Ledford, Jennifer Doudna began to worry about the applications of CRISPR in 2014 'when she saw a postdoc present work in which a virus was engineered to carry the CRISPR components into mice. The mice breathed in the virus, allowing the CRISPR system to engineer mutations and create a model for human lung cancer.'[195] Although all necessary precautions were taken in that particular study, it seems that there is always the very real possibility of an unintended outcome; and, when an unintended outcome could involve something like inhalable lung cancer, the need for prudence and security becomes very pressing. Indeed, unintended CRISPR related outcomes have already begun to pop up: for instance, because CRISPR can edit existing DNA sequences so precisely and accurately, it 'makes it more difficult for regulators and farmers to identify a modified organism once it has been released'.[196] This means that in the future there may no longer be a way to keep track of genetically engineered products.[197]

Other serious concerns have to do with how altering an organism to produce a 'gene drive' could impact the environment:

Usually, a genetic change in one organism takes a long time to spread through a population. That is because a mutation carried on one of a pair of chromosomes is inherited by only half the offspring. But a gene drive allows a mutation made by CRISPR on one chromosome to copy itself to its partner in every generation, so that nearly all offspring will inherit the change. This means that it will speed through a population exponentially faster than normal—a mutation engineered into a mosquito could spread through a large population within a season. If that mutation reduced the number of offspring a mosquito produced, then the population could be wiped out, along with any malaria parasites it is carrying.[198]

While wiping out malaria-carrying mosquitoes seems like an obviously good idea, there are many risks posed by unintended and unexpected consequences: 'many researchers are deeply worried that altering an entire population, or eliminating it altogether, could have drastic and unknown consequences for an ecosystem: it might mean that other pests emerge, for example, or it could affect predators higher up the food chain.'[199] According to Kevin Esvelt of

Harvard's Wyss Institute for Biologically Inspired Engineering, 'local spiders eat malaria mosquitoes, so their population might collapse if the mosquito's does. That could make the population of termites, which spiders control, "explode and everyone's houses to fall down".'[200] Other species might also fill the malaria-spreading gap left by the elimination of mosquitoes. And the problem of unintended consequences will only become more and more urgent because of the ongoing 'democratization of genome editing through CRISPR',[201] due to CRISPR's low cost and ease of use; meanwhile, CRISPR-based work being carried out in private, for-profit, laboratories all over the world is not under government control.[202] According to Kenneth Oye, a political scientist at the Massachusetts Institute of Technology, 'It is essential that national regulatory authorities and international organizations get on top of this— really get on top of it. . . . We need more action.'[203]

The science of CRISPR is simply moving too fast on too many fronts for regulators to catch up. In April 2015, a group of concerned researchers took the step of publishing an article that called for caution and urged public debate around CRISPR.[204] One of the major concerns for the authors was that CRISPR-Cas9 technology 'can be used to change the DNA in the nuclei of reproductive cells that transmit information from one generation to the next (an organism's "germline")'.[205] In other words, with CRISPR-Cas9, what was science-fiction is now science-fact: CRISPR-Cas9 makes it possible to modify the genome in fertilized animal eggs or embryos, and thus alter the genetic make-up of every differentiated cell in an organism, thereby 'ensuring that the changes will be passed on to the organism's progeny. Humans are no exception—changes to the human germ line could be made using this simple and widely available technology.'[206] According to Baltimore and his co-authors, the possibility of human germline engineering has 'long been a source of excitement and unease among the general public, especially in light of concerns about initiating a "slippery slope" from disease-curing applications toward uses with less compelling or even troubling implications'.[207]

Baltimore *et al.*'s alarm seems to have been caused, at least in part, by work that was published in *Protein and Cell* in 2015, in which researchers, led by Junjiu Huang of Sun Yat-sen University in Guangzhou, reported that they used CRISPR-Cas9 techniques to modify human embryos.[208] The same paper was, it was later revealed, rejected by both *Science* and *Nature* on ethical grounds.[209] According to David Cyranoski and Sara Reardon's April 2015 report in *Nature*, 'rumours were circulating that the methods were being applied in human embryos' but 'the Huang paper is the first published report of this.' In their paper, Huang's team reported in detail how they used CRISPR-Cas9 to modify a gene that can cause a potentially fatal blood disorder, which they then attempted to repair by introducing new DNA. The team say that their experiment only 'used non-viable embryos obtained from fertility clinics, in which eggs had been fertilized by two sperm and so could not result in a live birth'.[210] Obviously, these experiments on human embryos 'raise ethical questions. But if researchers prove they can safely correct diseases by editing the genome, it's inevitable that some parents will also want to alter the genomes of healthy embryos.'[211] And, as George Church, the eminent Harvard geneticist, points out to Susan Young Rojahn, 'If you can prevent mental retardation with gene therapy, presuming that that's permissible, then there's a whole spectrum of intellectual challenges that will be discussed.'[212] What seems clear enough, then, is that these problems and this debate are not going away any time soon.

Huang's team also reported in their paper that they encountered some serious obstacles in using the method in a clinical setting: for example, of 86 embryos that were used, only 4 contained the genetic material designed to repair the cuts and there were several 'off-target' mutations the teams assumed were caused by the CRISPR-Cas9 acting on other parts of the genome.[213] However, it has been suggested that several of the off-target mutations seen by Huang's team are the result of mistaken classification, and that the off-target rate for CRISPR with human embryos may actually be more in line with those seen in work on mice embryos.[214] Despite this and the reported improvements made in tackling off-target mutations, there remains a lot of anxiety and debate among researchers when it comes to editing the human germline and little agreement about where exactly to draw ethical lines: 'Although researchers agree that a moratorium on clinical applications is needed while the ethical and safety concerns of human-embryo editing are worked out, many see no problem with the type of research that Huang's team did, in part because the embryos could not have led to a live birth.'[215] There is also a belief among some researchers that 'altering developmental genes with

CRISPR-Cas9 could help to reveal their functions' and that some 'questions about early human development can only be addressed by studying human embryos'.[216] But other researchers, such as Eric Lander, director of the Broad Institute of MIT and Harvard, have called for caution; in December 2015, Lander told those gathered in Washington at The International Summit on Human Gene Editing that '"before making permanent changes to the human gene pool, we should use great caution," a conclusion he said was based on "humility" about how much we don't know. For instance, even "bad" genes aren't always all bad, he pointed out; one gene that increases risk of HIV/AIDS reduces risk of West Nile virus.'[217] There is a very real possibility, however, that all this worry about where to draw ethical lines may end up being a futile academic exercise: according to Cyranoski and Reardon, 'researchers expect to see more gene-editing studies in human embryos. . . . A Chinese source familiar with developments in the field said that at least four groups in China are pursuing gene editing in human embryos.'[218] And, as George Church points out, once medical changes can be made to embryos with terrible diseases, 'the dread prospect of "genetic enhancement" of embryos (a.k.a. designer babies) might come creeping through the back door—as patients with muscle-wasting diseases get their *in vitro* fertilization embryos engineered to prevent that disease in their children, and then other prospective parents will want that strong-muscle gene so that their embryo can grow into an Olympian.'[219] Questions of competitiveness and fairness promise to drive the spread of these changes beyond medicine, which, once made, are all heritable.

The CRISPR genie is out of the bottle and there does to seem to be any realistic way of stuffing it back in; the advent of this technology has changed the world and is promising to change it further. At stake, says Jennifer Doudna, is nothing less than 'the potential for this application to eradicate genetic diseases and, ultimately, to alter the course of evolution.'[220] It's thus difficult to overstate just how powerful and potentially constructive and/or destructive a tool like CRISPR is. CRISPR-Cas technology puts into the hands of academic researchers and for-profit private laboratories and corporations alike an awesomely powerful low-cost tool for editing and rewriting the genome of any species on the planet, with an ease and precision like never before.

CRISPR thus seems to be taking humanity into the new, uncharted and unsettling territory of genetic posthumanism, whether we like it or not. And, once we begin editing, deleting and rewriting parts of ourselves as a species, we will no longer simply be 'human' any more (not that we were ever 'simply human', for the reasons examined in the previous section); we will be genetically engineered posthumans and those alterations will be transmissible to our offspring and their offspring. Even if this tool were used at first only for therapeutic purposes, once children have been cured of their physical or mental disabilities, the parents of unaltered children will want their children to be able to compete with their perfected peers. Imagine, then, a posthumanity editing and rewriting itself, making itself immune to certain dreadful diseases and awful genetic defects; imagine a genetically edited posthumanity that is physically better able to endure the environmental changes wrought by climate change or bear the strains and the challenges of deep-space exploration. Now imagine such changes are only available to those rich and powerful enough to afford them. One might argue that the low cost of CRISPR-Cas technology means it could be made widely available. But CRISPR processes are already well on the road to being patented; what if those who own the patents decide to price their product according to what the market will bear and/or gouge consumers? And, if there is an uneven start to the modification process that breaks down along the lines of economic status, would those who had a head start in being modified be willing to share and give up their advantage? A tool that has such power but is so relatively easy to use—and misuse—makes CRISPR a perfect example of Derrida's *pharmakon*: both cure and poison, neither good nor evil, exceeding and evading such neat categorization at every turn, but not without having a profound impact on how the future will play out.

It is particularly intriguing to recall that CRISPR is essentially the product of ancient battles between two of the earliest forms of 'life' found on Earth: bacteria and viruses, the very organisms that we are accustomed to think of as both filthy and harmful to us. In the 1980s, Margulis and Sagan pointed out that bacteria were billions of years ahead of humanity's cutting-edge genetic engineering in using HGT. Now, it appears that CRISPR has proved all over again that very point of Margulis and Sagan's in the 2010s: the cutting-edge tools that put the capability of editing and rewriting other species as 'post-species' and ourselves as posthumans into out hands are the very ones that have been used by bacteria to repair and genetically engineer themselves for billion of years in the name of survival. We appear, as a species, to have become more 'bacterial' as we have evolved; and what else might our filthy, tiny *pharmakonic* ancestors have to teach us in the future?

'*Ph'nglui mglw'nafh Cthulhu R'lyeh wgah'nagl fhtagn.*'
('In his house at *R'lyeh*, dead Cthulhu waits dreaming.')[221]

CHAPTER THREE

Artificial Intelligences

I have been defining posthumanism since the start of this book as having its origins in the distributed cognition of humans + tools; and, over the previous pages, I have been looking at some of the scientific tools and techniques that forcefully challenge traditional or commonplace ideas about apparently 'clear' and 'obvious' distinctions that separate humans, animals and technologies. In this chapter, I'd like to focus on a type of tool that cries out to be discussed in the context of posthumanism: artificial intelligence (AI). Because AI is, like CRISPR, a powerful and potentially dangerous tool that erodes the hard-and-fast distinction between human and non-human, any serious discussion of posthumanism must engage with it. AI, unlike say, a hammer or even a nail gun, is special because it is a tool that has agency and intelligence; it is interactive and explicitly learns from the human using it. Because it actively adapts itself to the user, AI seems destined to work for us and with us more like an assistant or a companion: unlike a hammer or a nail gun, AI listens to us, watches us, responds to us, remembers for us, organizes us, answers our queries, communicates for us and to us, makes things for us, entertains us, guides us, transports us—the list could go on and on. And it is not too hard to imagine these intelligent assistants and companions, as they hold more and more of our data and get to know us better and better, developing lifelong relations with us, not unlike the AIs in Iain M. Banks's spectacularly imagined Culture Series or the robots in Isaac Asimov's groundbreaking Robot Series. AI is explicitly posthumanist in that it actively erodes the distinctions between machines, animals and humans. Such an erosion occurs not just because AI is about literally (re)creating intelligence artificially in machines, using mathematics to teach machines so as to enable them to make decisions, predictions, and even to desire, but also because AI research is actively inspired by human and animal biology.

Once again, some of the discussion that follows might seem 'overly technical' to readers unfamiliar with mathematics and technology; at the same time, some of the discussion will, no doubt, seem 'not technical enough' to those familiar with mathematics and technology. And perhaps such assessments are inevitable when a book such as this one demands and encourages cross-disciplinary habits of reading, thinking and research. I am thus willing to run the risk of such criticisms. If pressed, however, I would have to admit that I am less sympathetic to the point of view that would see my discussion as 'needlessly' or 'overly technical'; this is because I am firmly of the opinion that any serious, concrete discussion of posthumanism also requires coming to grips with the nuts and bolts of AI. In particular, I want to avoid a discussion of AI that remains 'stuck' talking superficially and simplistically—and thus passively— about it from the 'outside'. What, in a nutshell, I want to avoid is the type of readings of technology that unfortunately bedevil the humanities and critical science studies: readings that only concentrate on the 'representations' or 'images' of AI in media, literature or cinema, because they understand neither how AI actually works nor what it is. In other words, AI is a complex material and technical reality that such superficial readings simply ignore and/or avoid. A familiarity with the material and technical realities also makes it far easier to spot when those responsible for such representations (and those supposedly 'analyzing' them) have no idea what they are talking about. A deeper, more technical understanding of AI also helps combat superficial and misguided (no matter how well-intentioned) criticisms of AI—and science and technology more generally—too often found in the humanities, which amount to a variation on the classical 'God of the gaps' argument: an argument, in other words, that tries to put 'humanity'— instead of God—into the 'gaps' in science and scientific knowledge. The problem with such an argument, as even those who profess to believe in God have recognized, is that science is pretty good at filling in its gaps, which leaves an ever-shrinking space for God and the humanities. Think, for example, of all the 'human' things of which it has been claimed a machine is incapable of doing, but has gone on to do anyway: beat a human grandmaster at chess; beat a human champion at a televised general knowledge game show; teach itself how to play video games at a level that surpasses human players; drive a car for millions of miles without causing an accident; beat a human at table tennis; pick stocks; understand natural language; improvise jazz or compose in the style of Bach.[1] And each time a machine does something it was insisted that only a human can, that task or accomplishment gets relabelled as somehow 'unimportant' or 'inessential' to humanity: it's like saying, 'well, if a machine can do it, then it's not an essential part of being human'. And so, we redraw the line separating machine and human, and dutifully plug 'humanity' into the remaining gaps we label 'what machines still cannot do'. The problem is that if we insist on plugging 'humanity'—and, for that matter, 'the humanities'—into the gaps of technology and science, then, as those gaps continue to shrink and eventually disappear, so too must 'humanity' and 'the humanities'. It is precisely this type of thinking that the humanities needs to get away from if it plans on surviving into the future.

So, I make absolutely no bones about taking this firm position: a deeper, more technical understanding of AI also makes for a more grounded, concrete and technologically literate version of posthumanism, one that is less prone to being hijacked by ideological readings driven by identity politics, or philosophies that claim there is no such thing as an extra-linguistic reality because everything is fabricated by discourse, power or hegemony. This deeper, technical understanding of AI also allows for a serious discussion of AI and what it may or may not have in store for the human species while also providing inoculation against the hype and ballyhoo generated by greedy charlatans and clickbait media as well as the gloom and fear generated by ill-informed naysayers and doom-mongers. AI is a technological tool still very much in its infancy; nevertheless, it has the potential to change utterly the social, economic and political organization of the world humans live in, in ways that are still only very dimly glimpsed; some contours, however, are perhaps easier to discern than others.

An (all-too-brief) brief history of artificial intelligence

In recent years, there has been something of a resurgence of interest in AI, mainly due to the activities of companies like Google (rebranded as Alphabet Inc.), which has been busily developing self-driving cars and buying up various robotics and AI companies whose products seem to be making the news and media reports more and more regularly. But, as anyone familiar with the history of AI will tell you, the idea of AI has been around for almost as long as modern computing itself. The Turing Test—a test of a machine's ability to exhibit intelligent behaviour equivalent to, or indistinguishable from, that of a human—was introduced by Alan Turing in his 1950 paper, 'Computing Machinery and Intelligence'.[2] Instead of asking if a machine is thinking, Turing suggests that we should ask if the machine could win a particular party game: the 'Imitation Game'. In the original parlour game, a man and a woman are secluded while an interrogator tries to determine which is which. The man tries to fool the interrogator while the woman tries to help; the interrogator can only ask questions that are answered in writing and, using only these written answers, the interrogator tries to decide who is the man and who is the woman. Turing described his new version of the game as follows: 'We now ask the question, "What will happen when a machine takes the part of A [the man] in this game?" Will the interrogator decide wrongly as often when the game is played like this as he does when the game is played between a man and a woman? These questions replace our original, "Can machines think?"'[3] Turing then asks whether there are 'imaginable digital computers which would do well' in the imitation game,[4] before reformulating his initial question once more: 'Let us fix our attention on one particular digital computer C. Is it true that by modifying this computer to have an adequate storage, suitably increasing its speed of action, and providing it with an appropriate programme, C can be made to play satisfactorily the part of A in the imitation game, the part of B being taken by a man?'[5] At the end of section 6 of his paper, Turing offers the reader, in lieu of an answer, a summary of his beliefs:

> It will simplify matters for the reader if I explain first my own beliefs in the matter. Consider first the more accurate form of the

question. I believe that in about fifty years' time it will be possible, to programme computers, with a storage capacity of about 10^9, to make them play the imitation game so well that an average interrogator will not have more than 70 per cent chance of making the right identification after five minutes of questioning. The original question, 'Can machines think?' I believe to be too meaningless to deserve discussion. Nevertheless I believe that at the end of the century the use of words and general educated opinion will have altered so much that one will be able to speak of machines thinking without expecting to be contradicted. I believe further that no useful purpose is served by concealing these beliefs.[6]

Later in the same paper, in a section called 'Learning Machines', Turing offers the reader something a little more meaty when he speculates on a sort of 'child machine' that could be taught:

Instead of trying to produce a programme to simulate the adult mind, why not rather try to produce one which simulates the child's? If this were then subjected to an appropriate form of education, one would obtain the adult brain. Presumably the child brain is something like a notebook as one buys it from the stationer's. Rather little mechanism, and lots of blank sheets. Our hope is that there is so little mechanism in the child brain that something like it can be easily programmed. The amount of work in the education we can assume, as a first approximation, to be much the same as for the human child. We have thus divided our problem into two parts. The child programme and the education process. These two remain very closely connected. We cannot expect to find a good child machine at the first attempt. One must experiment with teaching one such machine and see how well it learns. One can then try another and see if it is better or worse.[7]

In other words, what Turing offers the reader by way of an answer to the question, 'Can machines think?' is, 'Only if we teach it how to.'

Turing, writing in 1950, believed that a machine could pass the imitation game by the end of the twentieth century. Despite some claims to the contrary,[8] this hasn't happened by the time of writing, some 15 years into the twenty-first. But, as anyone with even a passing interest in the history of AI will know, AI and disappointment often go hand in hand. The history of AI has tended to follow something of a cycle: unrealistic promises, followed by massive hype, followed by disappointment, followed by bitterness and/or gloating, followed by funding cuts. Funding cuts have led to two major AI 'winters'—the first lasting between 1974 and 1980, and the second between 1987 and 1993—when interest and investment in AI slowed to all but a trickle. For many researchers working in AI, these winters are recent and vivid memories; so, not surprisingly, they tend to get irritated by AI hype because it is the first stage of the familiar cycle that leads to winter.

In the 1980s and 1990s, a debate raged among researchers about how to best implement AI. On the one hand, there were those who believed that AI was best implemented using a 'top-down' approach known as symbolic AI (sometimes called 'Good Old Fashioned AI' [GOFAI]). Symbolic AI is based on working with high-level symbolic (i.e., human readable) representations of problems, logic and searches. Marvin Minsky, in his essay 'Logical vs. Analogical or Symbolic vs. Connectionist or Neat vs. Scruffy', sketches the terrain of both camps. According to Minsky, the symbolic approach to AI (which he also refers to as 'heuristic programming') can be understood to 'begin at the level of commonsense psychology and [tries] to imagine processes that could play a certain game, solve a certain kind of puzzle, or recognize a certain kind of object. If you can't do this in a single step, then keep breaking things down into simpler parts until you can actually embody them in hardware or software'.[9] He continues: 'These techniques have developed productively for several decades and, today, heuristic programs based on top-down analysis have found many successful applications in technical, specialized areas. This progress is largely due to the maturation of many techniques for representing knowledge.'[10] But, says Minsky, there are limitations to the symbolic approach:

[T]he same techniques have seen less success when applied to 'commonsense' problem solving. Why can we build robots that compete with highly trained workers to assemble intricate machinery in factories—but not robots that can help with ordinary housework? It is because the conditions in factories are constrained, while the objects and activities of everyday life are too endlessly varied to be described by precise, logical definitions and deductions. Commonsense reality is too disorderly to represent in terms of universally valid 'axioms'. To deal with such variety and novelty, we need more flexible styles of thought, such as those we see in human commonsense reasoning, which is based more on analogies and approximations than on precise formal procedures.[11]

The goal of 'connectionism'—that is, computing that uses neural networks, which are inspired by the structure of the human brain and are composed of artificial 'neurons'—was to try and get past the commonsense bottleneck in symbolic AI.

According to Minsky, connectionism is a 'bottom-up' approach to AI:

The bottom-up approach goes the opposite way [to symbolic AI]. We begin with simpler elements—they might be small computer programs, elementary logical principles, or simplified models of what brain cells do—and then move upwards in complexity by finding ways to interconnect those units to produce larger scale phenomena. The currently popular form of this, the connectionist neural network approach, developed more sporadically than did heuristic programming. In part, this was because heuristic programming developed so rapidly in the 1960s that connectionist networks were swiftly outclassed. Also, the networks need computation and memory resources that were too prodigious for that period.[12]

As Minsky goes on to point out, since computers have become more and more powerful, these obstacles to connectionism have been removed. Minsky's position is that ultimately, there was and is no need for any 'war' between researchers in the different AI camps: since both sides want to implement AI, and there are things that both types of AI do and don't do very well, the best way forward is to be thinking in terms of 'hybrids' of the two approaches.

Nor can it be said that the connectionist and symbolic approaches to AI are fundamentally incompatible with each other: a connectionist network of simple artificial neurons can be fairly easily made to replicate the functioning of what's known as a NAND (Negative-AND) gate, which constitutes one of the elemental building blocks of a traditional computer: a logic gate.

Since logic gate is a device that performs a logical operation on one or more inputs, and produces a single logical output,[13] a NAND gate produces an output 'False' or '0' only if its inputs are both 'True' or '1'; if its inputs are 'False' or '0', it outputs a 'True' or '1.' The NAND gate is especially notable because any Boolean function (that is, any logical operation represented in Boolean logic, such as 'and', 'or', 'not', etc.) can be implemented just using combinations of NAND gates (a NAND gate thus has the property of 'functional completeness'). In other words, an entire traditional computer can be built from just NAND gates, and if you've ever seen one of those classic integrated circuit chips—the kind that looks like a small black insect with seven pointy little silver legs on either side of its body—then you've seen four physical NAND gates linked together. The upshot of all this is that traditional computers can be implemented using artificial neurons and vast networks of artificial neurons routinely run on traditional computer architecture.

But, excitement for—and fear of—AI have often been whipped up by sensationalist media reports: undoubtedly, cars that can drive themselves or supercomputers winning television quiz shows are newsworthy, but reports often seem to want to go that little bit further and claim that the promise (or threat) of AI is tantalizingly (or uncomfortably) close. However, one could argue, AI is *already* here: it's just, to paraphrase William Gibson, unevenly distributed and relatively benign (I'm sure you'd agree that this does not make a good headline). And a car that can drive itself and successfully negotiate traffic surely seems quite intelligent (perhaps even more so to me, as I cannot drive); and it is difficult to dismiss a supercomputer that can out-perform even the best human players on a television quiz show as stupid. Yet, there are also clear limitations to these cutting-edge successes of AI: the program that drives the car is not able to stop, get out and bring you a coffee (although it could negotiate a drive-thru); and the supercomputer that won the television quiz show cannot really carry on a conversation about all it knows (yet). So, if these systems are the best examples of AI that we've currently got, then AI is still nowhere near general human-level intelligence: for example, any human who wins the television quiz can likely *also* drive a car *and* get coffee. In other words, human intelligence seems to have a general adaptive power that the most powerful and intelligent AIs cannot match. That being said, however, specialized AIs consistently outperform humans at their specific tasks: Watson, the AI designed to beat human champions at the television quiz show *Jeopardy!* did precisely that in 2011.[14] Google's Self-Driving Cars have been driving around safely for a while now: as of mid 2015, they had logged more than 1.6 million kilometers,[15] and any of the accidents they had been involved in seemed to have been the result of human error.[16] So, there is a need to distinguish between AI, which is already here and pervasive, and artificial general intelligence (AGI)—also known as 'strong' or 'full AI'—that would successfully perform any intellectual task that a human being can, which is not here yet. The 'unevenness' in the abilities of AI with respect to human beings is the main reason why there are so many contradictory positions to take on AI: it is 'smart' but 'stupid'; it is 'already here' but still lies 'in the future'; it is 'the saviour of humankind' but poses 'an existential threat.'

That AI can be conceived of as humankind's saviour and existential threat is perhaps—as was suggested in the Introduction—the irresolvable contradiction that drives a lot of the media attention that AI has been receiving of late. However, anxiety that one of humankind's technological innovations could wipe it out is not new: indeed, as far back as 1818, Mary Shelley had Victor Frankenstein worry that the female Creature he was working on as a mate for his male Creature could, through her ability to reproduce, end up wiping out mankind.[17] The fear that AI could pose an existential threat to humanity also informs the philosophical work of Vincent Müller and Nick Bostrom. As was highlighted in the Introduction, Müller and Bostrom are quite concerned about the 31 per cent chance that artificial general 'superintelligence' will be bad for humankind: 'We know of no compelling reason to say that progress in AI will grind to a halt (though deep new insights might be needed) and we know of no compelling reason that superintelligent systems will be good for humanity. So, we should better investigate the future of superintelligence and the risks it poses for humanity.'[18] Whereas, for others, such as Ray Kurzweil, 'superintelligence'—or, as he prefers to call it, 'the Singularity'[19]—promises to save humankind from aging, disease and even death itself.[20] Not surprisingly, Bostrom's and Kurzweil's positions have been polarizing in recent discussions on the future of AI; nevertheless, the radical difference in their respective positions does make it clear that there is still a lot of uncertainty about what AI means—and what it may have in store—for humans as a species. AI is, then, yet another prime example of a *pharmakon*:

something that is neither simply good nor evil, but which repeatedly slips beyond those moral categories.

My discussion of AI in the following sections will focus on three of the more fascinating examples of AI at the time of writing (October 2015): (i) Google DeepMind's deep Q-Network (DQN) agent; (ii) a small insect-like robot named Hector; and (iii) IBM's Watson. Taken together, these examples will hopefully give the reader a neat snapshot of the current capabilities of AI. Before getting to these specific examples of AI, however, I'll go over some basics of machine learning and artificial neural network architecture, in order to give the reader a sense of how a machine can be said to learn. I also want to take the opportunity here to remind the reader of a few things: first, because AI can seem like a rapidly moving field, by the time this book is published, there will probably be wondrous new gizmos to ponder that I couldn't include because they are so new; second, developments in AI are peculiarly prone to media hype, and new projects pop up all the time to loud fanfare; third, AI is also an extremely competitive business, and companies making AI are quick to criticize competitors' products. On top of all that, it would appear that the current interest in AI is amounting to what could be called, for better or for worse, an AI 'spring'. I once again also want to remind the reader that the discussion that follows gets a little technical in places; I would urge a reader who may be intimidated by such material to soldier on, because, as mentioned above, I firmly believe that a familiarity with and appreciation for some of the complex techno-scientific thinking that have made AI a reality is an essential first step in avoiding some of the plain daft assertions that much of the academic cultural analysis of 'representations' or 'images' of AI is prone to. So, I am presenting technical detail in order to give the reader an opportunity to engage with the techno-scientific thinking, tools and research that drive AI; and, as I argued in Chapter 2, a familiarity with these and other techno-scientific tools and practices is a necessary part of grasping a concrete, actual posthumanism that is more than just a fashionable flash in the pan of 'theory'. At the same time, however, I make absolutely no pretence of presenting a reader who is already familiar with the mathematics behind AI with anything challenging, precisely because I will only be discussing the very basics throughout the remainder of this chapter. Instead, I would urge that reader to see what I offer here as a good faith attempt to try and speak across the gulf that separates the humanities from the sciences, which is no small task; I would also ask that same reader to consider this chapter in conjunction with Chapter 5, which aims to highlight some of the irreducibly philosophical underpinnings of AI.

Machine learning: Some basics

As was mentioned above, in his final speculations on the question 'Can machines think?', Turing mentions a 'child machine' that is taught through its programming; this process, Turing says, should also include a random or stochastic element to avoid making the learner too systematic in its approach to solving problems:

> It is probably wise to include a random element in a learning machine. A random element is rather useful when we are searching for a solution of some problem. Suppose for instance we wanted to find a number between 50 and 200 which was equal to the square of the sum of its digits, we might start at 51 then try 52 and go on until we got a number that worked. Alternatively we might choose numbers at random until we got a good one. This method has the advantage that it is unnecessary to keep track of the values that have been tried, but the disadvantage that one may try the same one twice, but this is not very important if there are several solutions. The systematic method has the disadvantage that there may be an enormous block without any solutions in the region which has to be investigated first. Now the learning process may be regarded as a search for a form of behaviour which will satisfy the teacher (or some other criterion). Since there is probably a very large number of satisfactory solutions the random method seems to be better than the systematic. It should be noticed that it is used in the analogous process of evolution. But there the systematic method is not possible. How could one keep track of the different genetical combinations that had been tried, so as to avoid trying them again?[21]

By linking together randomness, learning and evolution for teaching machines, Turing points the way to machine learning as it is carried out today.

It is worth observing that several robotics labs around the world have, over the last decade or so, taken Turing's idea of teaching machine children to their research bosoms: these labs have created and developed humanoid robot 'children' for the express purpose of teaching them. Perhaps the first really memorable child robot was the eerily adorable—or perhaps just plain unsettling—Child-robot with Biomimetic Body (CB[2]), which had 197 pressure sensors under light grey rubbery skin and could sense human touch, such as the stroking of its head. CB[2] was developed by Professor Minoru Asada and his team at Osaka University and first presented to the world in 2007.[22] Then there's Diego-San, a child robot developed by a team led by Dr Javier Movellan at the Machine Perception Lab at the University of California San Diego.[23] Diego-San was introduced to the world in 2013 and was designed and built by Kokoro Co. Ltd., the same company that designed and built CB[2]. Yet another example of an android infant is iCub, a one-metre tall humanoid robot designed by the RobotCub Consortium, which consists of several European universities, and built by the Italian Institute of Technology.[24] iCub made its debut in 2008. And then there's Roboy, an advanced humanoid robot developed by the Artificial Intelligence Laboratory of the University of Zurich, and first presented to the public in 2013.[25] Roboy, like iCub, CB[2] and Diego-San, was designed and created to test the embodied cognition hypothesis, which holds that human-like manipulation plays a vital role in the development of human cognition.

But it would perhaps be a mistake to think that these child robots are destined to be confined to research laboratories. According to a 2014 report in *Forbes*, Ron Arkin, Georgia Tech's Mobile Robot Lab director, while speaking on a robot ethics panel held at the University of California Berkeley, noted 'We've had sex toys for as long as mankind, and womankind, have been around. . . . But how will we deal with robot intimacy? Will we consider it bestiality? Could we use it to treat sex offenders?'[26] He continues:

Child-like robots could be used for pedophiles the way methadone is used to treat drug addicts. . . . There are no presumptions that this will assuredly yield positive results—I only believe it is worth investigating in a controlled way to possibly provide better protection to society from recidivism in sex offenders. . . . If we can save some children, I think it's a worthwhile project.[27]

Arkin's position neatly highlights the sorts of moral dilemmas well-crafted embodied humanoid child robots have in store for us: on the one hand, if the robot resembles a child so effectively that a paedophile finds it attractive, then why not use it as a sex therapy tool to protect real children? After all, it is simply not a child, no matter how like one it may look. On the other hand, if the robot were capable of learning like a child, would using it as a sex toy not be a horrific way to treat an intelligent being? Would it not suffer unspeakable trauma? Or could it be taught to desire such sexual contact and thus consent to it?

The above questions are undoubtedly difficult to answer; they will not constitute the focus of my discussion in this section, which will instead consider how a machine can be said to learn in the first place. So, before getting to my discussion of specific examples of cutting-edge AI, I'd like to sketch some of the basics of the field of machine learning. Machine learning not only plays a central role in how Watson, Hector and DeepMind's DQN function; it is also the area of AI that has been generating a lot of media buzz of late due to the role it plays in computer vision, Natural Language Processing, self-driving cars, behavioural advertising, robotics, 'big-data' mining, as well as analysis in fields ranging from medicine, genetics and neuroprosthetics to security and finance. And, since the topic of machine learning is unavoidably complex, and even though what I'm presenting here is only the teeny-tiniest tip of the machine learning iceberg, a certain amount of mathematics cannot be avoided. I'll begin my discussion with only the very basic elements of machine learning: simple artificial neurons called perceptrons, and how to train them.

Machine learning I: Perceptrons and how to train them

Basically, an artificial neural network (ANN) is designed to emulate or mimic how the human brain works: research shows that information is stored in the brain as a pattern, and ANN computing mimics this by storing information as patterns and using those patterns to solve problems. 'Teaching' or 'training' the ANN to solve problems is an important part of this kind of computing, and those who work in ANN computing often use a vocabulary derived from folk psychology—words such as 'learn', 'forget', 'remember', etc.—to describe what such networks are doing when they are in operation; in other words, researchers and scientists seem to be imputing a type of agency to these networks. An oft-cited definition of machine learning is the one given by Tom Mitchell: a 'computer program is said to learn from experience E with respect to some task T and some performance measure P, if its performance on T, as measured by P, improves with experience E.'[28] Machine learning itself takes several major forms: supervised, unsupervised and reinforcement. Supervised learning or training is the most commonly discussed method of training neural networks because it is the simplest, which is why I will focus on it in what follows; however, I will also briefly touch on unsupervised learning and go into a little detail on reinforcement training in my later discussion of DeepMind's DQN agent.

The history of modern ANNs is easily accessible online:[29] neural network computing was born in 1943, when Warren McCulloch, a neurophysiologist, and Walter Pitts, a mathematician, published a paper entitled 'A Logical Calculus of Ideas Immanent in Nervous Activity'.[30] McCulloch and Pitts showed how it was possible not only to mimic a neuron mathematically but also to connect many of them to form a neural network that could encode any logical proposition. The groundbreaking work of McCulloch and Pitts, was, in turn, built on by Donald Hebb and Frank Rosenblatt. In 1957, Rosenblatt, a psychologist at Cornell University, created the 'perceptron', an artificial neuron that used a mathematical formula to sort inputs into two categories.[31] In 1969, however, work with perceptrons was dealt a severe blow by the publication of Marvin Minsky and Seymour Papert's famous book, *Perceptrons*, which outlined the limits of what certain organizations of perceptrons could do.[32] One of the things that Minsky and Papert showed was that perceptrons could not cope with the logical operation known as the 'exclusive or' (often written as XOR)—the logical operation that outputs 'true' only when inputs differ (i.e., one input is 'True' or 1, the other is 'False' or 0). Although Minsky and Papert's criticisms of the limitations of perceptrons effectively killed research on ANNs for about a decade, they nonetheless enjoyed something of a resurgence in the 1970s when a solution to the exclusive or issue was found. In the 1980s, work with ANNs continued to advance and the field was rebranded as 'connectionism'. The 1990s saw important advances in the training of neural networks, while the

2000s saw an effective boom in deep learning networks: ANNs composed of many layers of artificial neurons, with the layers forming a hierarchy from low-level to high-level features.[33]

In the average human brain, there are about 100 billion neurons, and although some of these can have up to 200,000 connections with other neurons, anywhere between 1,000–10,000 connections is usual. A typical biological neuron has four main parts: *dendrites*, which are hair-like extensions that act like input channels; *the soma*, which processes the incoming signals into an electrical or chemical signal output; *the axon*, which sends this output out to other neurons via *synapses*, thus forming a biological neural network. In order to grasp how an ANN actually works, it is helpful to go back to Rosenblatt's perceptron, which is basically a simplified—but nonetheless ingenious—mathematical model of a biological neuron. A perceptron can be written as the following simple algorithm, or set of instructions:

If $\sum_i w_i I_i \geq t$ then $y = 1$

else (if $\sum_i w_i I_i < t$) then $y = 0$

Here, each input (I) to the artificial neuron—which could be part of a digitized picture file or information from a sensor—is given a specific 'weight' (w); weight assigned to each input reflects how important (or unimportant) that particular input might be. For example, if I want to buy a moped, I might have three criteria: durability, aesthetics and top speed. If I value aesthetics more than durability or speed, aesthetics will have more 'weight' in making my decision. So, I might add the following weights to those characteristics: durability, 25 per cent; aesthetics, 70 per cent; speed, 5 per cent. I see in a trusted review source, that bike one gets a 6/10 for durability, a 6/10 for aesthetics and a 6/10 for speed; while bike two gets a 4/10 durability, a 9/10 for aesthetics and a 3/10 for speed. If I multiply the bikes scores by their weights, I can make my decision: bike one: 6*25% + 6*70% + 6*5% = 6; bike two: 4*25% + 9*70% + 3*5% = 7.45. Thus, I will get bike two, even though it has a lower score in terms of durability and speed; my weighting of what is more important to me directly affects my decision; at the same time, I have found a way of using mathematics to make a decision.[34] This is exactly what occurs in the artificial neuron: each input (I) is then multiplied by its weight (w_i) and added together—$\Sigma_i w_i I_i$, or $w_1 * I_1 + w_2 * I_2 + w_3 * I_3 + \ldots w_n * I_n$—and the sum is then fed through what's known as an activation function—a mathematical function such as the Heaviside step function, which graphs a step and gives a '1' for a positive number input and '0' for negative one, or the logistic function, which graphs an elegant S-shape[35]—which coverts the sum of weights and inputs into an output. This output can then, depending on the architecture of the neural network, either be fed into another artificial neuron or output to the outside world. In the perceptron, input is sorted into one of two categories—usually represented by '1' or '0.' This sorting occurs as follows: if the sum of all individual inputs (I_i) times their individual weights (w_i) is greater than or equal to a particular numerical value called a 'threshold' (t in the above example) output a '1'; otherwise, output a '0.' In other words, we call 't' a threshold (often also called the bias [or b] as we'll see below) because it represents the value that the sum of $w_i I_i$ needs to exceed to output a '1' from our perceptron. For example, if t is set to -3, then the perceptron will need its summed inputs to come to at least 3 to cross the threshold and trigger an output of '1'; if the sum does not meet the threshold, the perceptron outputs a '0.' The threshold or bias is crucial: without t, the perceptron would trigger for any input, making it useless for distinguishing one input from any other. The threshold is also the part of the artificial neuron that approximates how real neurons operate in the brain. Biological neurons do not always 'fire': they only do so when the net potential they receive from other neurons is higher than the activation potential (~ -55 mV).

Inputs and weights are often called vectors because, like vectors, they are understood to be multidimensional. For example, you can write a vector $\vec{a}$ as $(a_1, a_2, a_3, \ldots a_n)$ and each a_n corresponds to a dimension of that vector; since inputs to perceptrons take the form of $I_1, I_2, I_3 \ldots I_n$, the sum of inputs constitutes a multidimensional vector. Now, if the idea of multidimensional space seems very counterintuitive, this is because multidimensional space *is* counterintuitive. As humans, we live and survive in three-dimensional space (some of us might make a concession to time as a fourth dimension). Intuitively, it seems like there is no need to use more than three dimensions + time to describe the location of a particular object: for instance, we can use one value to specify the x-coordinate, one value for the y-coordinate, and one for the z-coordinate. Things gets more complicated, however, when we have to think about how that object might *move*. It could, for example, rotate in three different directions: think of the roll, pitch, and yaw of an airplane in the air or a ship on the sea. So, we actually need six dimensions to specify the position of the object: three to specify its location (x, y, z), and three more (a, b, c) to specify the directions in which the object is pointing or moving. Matters get even more complicated when we have to think about how the individual parts of that object might move: for example, what if the object in question has joints like an articulated robot? Each direction of movement of each of the robot's joints constitutes yet another dimension. Dimensions can thus add up very quickly. In many ways, the difficulty in grasping multidimensional space is due to using the metaphor of 'space' to describe these dimensions to begin with: it can confound our attempts to think in dimensions higher than three. A way to counter this confusion is to think of a high-dimensional vector as describing quantities of distinct objects: for example, 'a five-dimensional vector could describe the numbers of apples, oranges, banana, pears, and cherries on the table.'[36] Fortunately, mathematics of vectors copes quite well with non-intuitive multidimensional space: for instance, when you multiply inputs by weights and sum them up, you are basically taking the dot product (sometimes also called the inner product or scalar product) of two vectors—the inputs and their weights: the dot product of vector $\vec{a}$ and vector $\vec{b} = a_1{}^*b_1 + a_2{}^*b_2 + a_3{}^*b_3 + \ldots a_n{}^*b_n$, just like the sum of $w_1{}^*I_1 + w_2{}^*I_2 + w_3{}^*I_3 + \ldots w_n{}^*I_n$.

This insight into vectors is what allows us to rewrite the perceptron used above in the following more simplified, and more contemporary, form:

$$\text{output} = \begin{cases} 0 & \text{if } w \cdot x + b \leq 0 \\ 1 & \text{if } w \cdot x + b > 0 \end{cases}$$

Here, the dot in $w \cdot x$ is the notation that's used for computing the dot product of two vectors—weights (w) and inputs (I'll be calling the inputs 'x' from now on)—and b is the bias (or what was referred to above as the threshold, t). As mentioned, the sum of weights and bias gives our artificial neuron a way of making a distinction between inputs by separating those inputs into two areas of output: making a distinction means that the perceptron is effectively drawing a line in space that creates the two categories into which the inputs can then be sorted; this line forms what's known as the 'decision boundary' or 'decision surface'. When the sum of inputs, weights and the bias is greater than 0, the neuron 'fires' and outputs a '1': if the sum is less than or equal to 0, it does not 'fire', and the output is a '0'. In other words, inputs can be sorted into those that cross the line and those that do not.

So, how exactly can the perceptron be said to draw a line? Let's imagine that we have two inputs for our perceptron, x_1, x_2; let's say that each input has a weight, $w_1 = 1$, $w_2 = 0.5$, and that we are using a given threshold or bias of $b = 0$.[37] Putting this together using the formula $w \cdot x + b = 0$, gives us $x_1{}^*w_1 + x_2{}^*w_2 + b = 0$, or $x_1 + 0.5x_2 + 0 = 0$. This can be rewritten as:

$$-0.5x_1 = x_2 + 0$$

which can in turn be rewritten as:

$$0.5x_1 = -x_2 - 0$$

which is also a linear equation:

$$y = mx + b$$

In the above linear equation, b is the line's intercept with the y-axis, and m is the line's slope. So, our perceptron effectively draws the line $0.5y = -x - 0$, where w_1 corresponds to the coefficient of x (-1; also the slope of the line), w_2 corresponds to the coefficient of y (0.5) and the intercept with the y-axis is b, which here is 0 (the line thus goes through the origin). Since, as I said above, this line also marks the decision boundary, the perceptron 'decides' which inputs constitute points that fall 'above' the line and belong to a particular category (for example, 'cats') and those that fall 'below' the line and belong to another category (for example, 'dogs').

Because the perceptron draws a line to sort inputs into one category or another, it can be effectively trained. To train a perceptron, you have to first feed it inputs from what's known as a 'training set', a set of already sorted inputs. Training begins by first assigning the weights and bias an arbitrary set of initial values; next, an input is randomly selected from the training set, and input into the perceptron to see if it sorts it correctly into either category *a* or category *b*. If the perceptron correctly sorts the input, then there is obviously no need to make any adjustments to the weights or bias. If the perceptron gets it wrong, however, then the weights and bias are adjusted using the following learning rule: $w_i = w_i + \eta(O - dO)x_i$. Here, the first w_i is the old weight, η is the learning rate, a small positive number that nudges the weights and bias in the direction of dO (the desired output of a particular input x_i) times O, the actual output the system gives (i.e., the system might output a '0' instead of a '1' or vice versa), minus dO, times the input x_i. To put this more concretely, let's say that η is 0.2, the training set inputs are $x_i = 2$, $x_2 = -2$, the weights are $w_i = 1$, $w_2 = 0.5$, b is 0, the desired output is 1, and the actual output is 0. Plugging w_i and x_i into the learning rule gives us: 1 + 0.2(0–1)(2) = 0.6, our new w_i. So, a perceptron using this learning rule could adjust the weights and bias of the line $0.5y = -x - 0$, redrawing it as a new line: $0.9y = -0.6x + 0.2$. This adjustment shifts both the intercept of the line with the *y*-axis and the slope, putting the incorrectly sorted input back on the correct side of the line. During the process, some adjustments might end up putting previously correctly sorted inputs on the wrong side of the line, which would necessitate further adjustments. And although it might seem like this process could go on indefinitely, the Perception Convergence Theorem assures us that for any data set which is linearly separable, the perceptron learning rule is guaranteed to find a solution in a finite number of iterations. At the end of the process, the perceptron has learned to draw a line that correctly classifies the two categories of inputs.

So, the perceptron learning rule is guaranteed to stop the need for adjustments within a finite amount of steps when the data set that the perceptron is trying to sort is linearly separable: that is, the data set can be clearly sorted by drawing a straight line between all the inputs. But what happens when the data set is not linearly separable? A single perceptron is unable to sort such data: if two categories cannot have a line drawn between them, it can never find a solution. Perhaps the best-known example of a linearly inseparable function is the one I referred to above: the XOR or 'exclusive or' in logic: as in, you can have cake *or* pie, but not both. This shortcoming can be overcome, however, simply by adding more 'layers' of perceptrons or neurons to form an ANN, which, in its simplest form would only consist of an input layer, a 'hidden' processing layer (so called because these neurons are not 'visible' from either the input or output layers; there can be many such hidden layers), and an output layer, where each neuron is connected to all the units in the previous layer: since each hidden neuron can independently draw its own line between categories, the ANN can draw multiple lines and line segments at once. The connections between all the neurons are all given weights, just like those discussed above; and you can effectively 'switch off' a particular neuron by setting its weight to 0 (because any input value times zero will be zero). This type of relatively simple ANN is known as a 'feed-forward neural network.'

Many modern ANNs, however, do not use perceptrons that graph lines like the one described above: this is because adjusting weights in a perceptron can sometimes produce undesirable erratic behaviour, such as flipping a '0' into a '1' or vice versa. To get around this problem, 'sigmoid' functions—that is, functions that graph an elegant S-shape, such as the logistic or *tanh* functions— are often used instead of linear functions.[38] Sigmoid functions are considered useful because they allow for small changes to the weights in the network to produce small changes in the output (written as $w + \Delta w = output = \Delta output$; the Δ here simply means 'a small change in'); a sigmoid function also makes it possible for a neuron to take any number between 1 and 0 (e.g., 0.678655512928 ... and not just 1 or 0) as a valid input; and a sigmoid function means that even very large positive and negative sums can be converted into a number between 1 and 0 (this is known as 'squashing'). However, just like the perceptron, a sigmoid neuron also uses weights (w) and has a bias (b), which means that we can write a sigmoid neuron in a way that looks a lot like the perceptron we were working with above: $\sigma(w \cdot x + b)$, where σ is the sigmoid (or logistic) function: $\sigma(z) = 1/[1 + e^{-z}]$. When rewritten, substituting the sum of weights, inputs and bias ($w \cdot x + b$) for z, this becomes: $\sigma = 1/[1 + e^{(-w \cdot x - b)}]$. The fundamental benefit of using a sigmoid neuron rather than a perceptron is that the smoothness of its curve allows the small adjustment of its weights and bias to produce only a small change in the adjustments of its output, which makes the system more stable and adjusting its weights easier.

Machine learning II: From lines to curves

So far, I've shown that a perceptron can be taught to draw a line that separates two categories of linearly separable inputs in a given training set by making adjustments to the neuron's weights and biases, which in turn repositions where the line is drawn. More modern ANNs, however, tend not to use perceptrons, opting instead for neurons with activation functions that graph curves rather than straight lines, such as the sigmoid neuron mentioned just above. And one of the major advantages of using such neurons is that weights and biases can be more finely tuned; doing so, however, requires the use of differentiation and derivatives. In what follows, I'll look at some simple examples of what training a sigmoid neuron, as opposed to a perceptron, entails. Once again, I'll try to keep the mathematics as simple as I can.

The simplest form of training sigmoid neurons is supervised training, which is also the type of training discussed above in conjunction with perceptrons. Supervised training uses a 'training set', a set of data that consists of a set of input values, x—for which there is an already known corresponding output value, y. For example, if you wanted to train an ANN to be a 'cat identifier', you would need a training set of images of cats to show your network to get it to the point where it can recognize a cat in an image from— and this is the key—outside the training set. Or, to take another example that is commonly used when introducing supervised training, this could mean training a network or system to predict something accurately when given a certain input: for example, were you to give a system the square footage of a house (x), it would be able to predict what that house is worth (y). This is often written as $h(x) = \theta_0 + \theta_1 x$, where the predictor function, $h(x)$—often called the hypothesis—equals the sum of θ_0 plus θ_1 times the input, x: in other words, θ_0 and θ_1 correspond to the bias (b) and weights (w) discussed above in relation to how a perceptron works. So, what the hypothesis essentially does is map xs to ys: it works out y by applying these weights to x. So, for example, if $\theta_0 = 1000$ and $\theta_1 = 10$ is a good hypothesis and we input $x = 3000$, we would get: $1000 + 10(3000) = 31000$. The system would then be able to take any new input (square footage of a house), apply the predictor function or hypothesis to it and make an accurate prediction (what the house is worth).

In order to get to this endpoint, however, the system must be trained to find the best way of describing the relationship between x and y. The process begins by setting the values of θ_0 and θ_1 to some arbitrary values, say 100 and 2, which the system then uses to process the inputs. The system's outputs using these values are then compared to the known correct outputs to establish the difference—that is, the 'wrongness'—of the settings of the initial hypothesis; the next step is to tweak θ_0 and θ_1 to make the hypothesis 'less wrong'. After many iterations of this process, the values of the constants won't change very much any more: all being well, the system can be said to have converged on the optimal values for θ_0 and θ_1. The 'least wrong' hypothesis would then, in the example of house sizes and prices, be the one that comes closest to all the known values on a graph of x = house size and y = price; it, in other words, draws a straight line or a curve that cuts through the centre of the cloud of data points in the data set. Thus, when any new input x (house size) that is *not* from the original training set is then given to the system, it will nevertheless give an accurate prediction y (house price) based on what it has been taught about the relation between house size and house value.

But, the more technically minded among you may be wondering, *how* does the system converge on the best hypothesis? How, exactly, are those tweaks to the hypothesis made? This is the stage where the mathematics will start to get quite complicated, but I'll try to keep things as clear as possible.

The first step in the training process is to set up what's known as a cost function (sometimes also called the loss or objective function), C, which often takes the form of the mean squared error function shown below, and operates on θ_0 and θ_1. Since, as I mentioned above, θ_0 and θ_1 are the equivalent of the weights and the biases that featured in the discussion of the perceptron in the previous section, we are essentially looking for weights and biases that allow outputs from the network to approximate, as accurately as possible, the training inputs (x). The cost function often looks something like this:

$$C(\theta_0, \theta_1) = \frac{1}{2n} \sum_x \|y(x) - a\|^2$$

Here, θ_0 and θ_1 are the weights and bias, n is the total number of training inputs, $y(x)$ is the desired outputs of the network, a is the actual outputs from the network when x is input, and the sum is over all training inputs, x; the output a depends on x, θ_0 and θ_1; and $\| \ \|$ is just a way of denoting the length or magnitude or size of any vector: for example, the magnitude of vector v is written as $\|v\|$. C basically computes the mean squared error (MSE): the actual output of the system (a) is subtracted from the desired output ($y(x)$), to get the error; this is then squared, and the results are divided by $2n$: the cost $C(\theta_0, \theta_1)$ gets smaller and smaller as the difference between the desired value, $y(x)$, and the actual output, a, for all training inputs, x, gets smaller and smaller. The goal, then, is to get the cost as close as possible to 0; an algorithm known as 'gradient descent' uses this function to do just that.

To keep things as simple as possible, imagine the cost function, C, as a function of two variables, our old friends, θ_0 and θ_1. If we were to graph this function, we'd need to do it on a three-dimensional graph: the x-axis would correspond to the value of θ_0, the y-axis to C, and the z-axis to θ_1 and our graph would have a nice 3d bowl shape. What we need to do is to find the point where C reaches what's known as its global minimum—the lowest point at the bottom of the bowl: at that point, our cost function is smallest because C is closest to 0. So, in effect, all we need to do is to start 'walking downhill' to get to the valley floor—the bottom of the bowl—taking small steps, one at a time. This is basically what the gradient descent algorithm does, over and over again. Mathematically, speaking, the 'gradient' represents the slope of the tangent of the graph of the function.

Let's say we take a small step $\Delta\theta_0$ in the θ_0 direction and a small step $\Delta\theta_1$ in the θ_1 direction: this means that we have also made a small change ΔC to C. This can be written in the following fearsome-looking equation:

$$\Delta C \approx \frac{\partial C}{\partial \theta_0}\Delta\theta_0 + \frac{\partial C}{\partial \theta_1}\Delta\theta_1$$

∂ here simply means partial derivative. Since a 'gradient' (because it represents the slope of the tangent of the graph of the function) is quite similar to a derivative, it can be illustrated using the simpler example of a derivative. A derivative measures the rate of change of a quantity (say, a dependent variable, y) that is determined by another quantity (say, the independent variable, x). For example, let's say we have the equation $y = x^2$, which graphs a nice U-shaped curve. To measure how quickly y changes as x changes, we use the slope of a line that is at a tangent to the curve at a specific point; because there is a tangent line at each point on the curve, the slope of the tangent lines changes as the gradient of the curve changes: a really steep gradient would mean a rapid rate of change, a gentle gradient would mean a slow rate of change, and a slope of 0 would mean no rate of change. This can be seen more clearly by actually computing the derivative of the equation $y = x^2$: $2x$. This means that, for the equation $y = x^2$, the slope or 'rate of change' at any point on the curve is $2x$. So, when $x = 0$, the slope of the tangent line is $2x = 0$; when $x = 2$, the slope is $2x = 4$; when $x = 2.65$, the slope is 5.30; when $x = 5$, the slope $= 10$, and so on. Computing a partial derivative is analogous to computing the derivative of just 1 variable; so, even though there may be more than one variable (for example, y and z), we treat the other variable (z) as a constant—i.e., it doesn't change, so there is no change in it to measure—as we work out the relation between x and y; and, if we were working out the relation between x and z, we would treat y as a constant, and so on. So, what the above fearsome looking equation is saying is that a small change in C (ΔC) is approximately equal ($\approx$) to the partial derivative of C with respect to θ_0 ($\partial C/\partial \theta_0$), times the small change in θ_0, plus the partial derivative of C with respect to θ_1 ($\partial C/\partial \theta_1$), times the small change in θ_1. This means that for all its fearsomeness, the above equation can be understood as the dot product of two vectors—the very same operation we saw above in relation to training a perceptron. So, if the first vector is

$$\nabla C = \left(\frac{\partial C}{\partial \theta_0}, \frac{\delta C}{\delta \theta_1} \right)$$

(here ∇C is simply the notation for this vector, also called the gradient vector) and the second vector is $\Delta \theta = (\Delta \theta_0, \Delta \theta_1)$, then $\Delta C \approx \nabla C \cdot \Delta \theta$. So, if we want to reduce the gradient vector, ∇C, we could rewrite $\Delta \theta$ as $\Delta \theta = -\eta \nabla C$, where η is the learning rate (which we also encountered above when discussing the training of a perceptron). This would mean that $\Delta C \approx -\eta \nabla C \cdot \nabla C = -\eta \|\nabla C\|^2$: when rewritten in this way, we can immediately see that the value of ΔC will always be shrinking (since we are effectively shrinking the magnitude of ∇C by moving in the opposite direction to it), and so will our cost, C.

Following this process, the learning algorithm takes one step downhill towards the bowl-shaped valley floor. The learning rate corresponds to the 'step size' the algorithm takes as it descends; making it small is important because taking too big a step could take you right past the bottom of the bowl to a higher point on the far side. The entire process is repeated over and over again—sometimes thousands of times—until the algorithm converges on the best values of θ_0 and θ_1, using which the system's actual outputs should match, as closely as possible, the desired outputs. Thus, the system has reached the bottom of the valley, and learned the best values for matching actual output to desired output; using those values, the network should now also be able to make an accurate prediction y about any new input x.

The gradient descent algorithm I've just described is a crucial part of the training method known as 'backpropagation', which feeds the output errors back through the system to adjust the weights of connections. The problems and difficulties with training ANNs using this process, however, become very apparent if there are many thousands of variables in play and not just two: in such a situation, so many variables won't graph a neat bowl-shaped valley like the one in the example used above; so many variables would graph something that looks more like the Himalayas, with thousands of 'mountains' and 'valleys'. In such a terrain, the gradient descent algorithm could come to a rest at in a 'valley' that does *not* correspond to the lowest possible point in the overall landscape: for example, there may be an even deeper 'valley' just over the next mountain; in such a landscape there seems to be no cast-iron guarantee that the valley you have come to a rest in is actually the deepest one of all.

In closing this section, I'd like to underscore a few elements of the foregoing discussion: first, I want to remind the reader that my discussion of perceptrons, sigmoid neurons and ANNS, as complicated as it may seem, nevertheless still only focuses on the basics of machine learning; ANNs can and do get massively complicated, as does the training such systems require; second, perceptrons and artificial neurons offer us a way of reconfiguring decisions in terms of mathematical functions; third, these functions effectively allow machines to learn, to make decisions and to make predictions. Now, there may be little disagreement on how crude such forms of decision making and learning are compared to human learning, decision making and prediction; nevertheless, I hope this brief look at machine learning has shown that certain concepts and behaviour we might ordinarily think of as being associated with the domain of humans (and perhaps certain animals) can be mimicked in and by mathematical functions running on machines. Machine learning thus invites questions about how cognitive processes that have apparently originated in biology no longer seem to be exclusive to biology, since they have been successfully mimicked by non-biological machines running only on electricity and mathematics. Because it *works*, machine learning, is, therefore, essential for grasping and understanding actual, concrete posthumanism. In the sections of this Chapter yet to come, I'll explore how certain specific examples of machine learning manage to mimic a surprising variety of these apparently biological-cognitive traits.

Google DeepMind's DQN agent

Convolutional neural networks

In the next couple of sections, I'll be preparing the ground for my discussion of a recent cutting edge example of a neural network: Google DeepMind's deep Q-Network (DQN) agent; DeepMind's agent is a particularly worthy of discussion because it mastered playing a diverse range of Atari 2600 games to superhuman level using only the raw pixels and score as inputs. The agent itself runs on a type of ANN known as a convolutional neural network or CNN. So, before getting to the agent I want to try and give the reader a sense of what a CNN is, as well as a sense of the particular type of machine learning—reinforcement learning—that actually allowed the agent to learn. Thus, the reader will be better equipped to get a solid grasp of what makes DeepMind's agent so special.

CNNs are a special class of the type of very simple feed-forward ANNs discussed in the previous section. CNNs are especially suited to image recognition—for example, facial and handwriting recognition—a suitability they owe to their being explicitly inspired by biology. The connections between neurons in CNNs mimic the organization of the animal visual cortex.[39] David Hubel and Torsten

Wiesel, in their work on cats and monkeys discovered that the visual cortex in animals is made up of a complex arrangement of cells, called receptive fields; these receptive fields, which are sensitive to small sub-regions of the visual field, cover the entire visual field. Hubel and Wiesel also identified two basic cell types: simple cells, which respond to specific edge-like patterns within their receptive field, and complex cells, which respond to patterns of light within a large receptive field, regardless of their exact location.[40]

The layers of neurons in a CNN are typically arranged in three dimensions—width, height and depth—and the neurons inside a layer are only connected to a small region of the layer before it, called a receptive field. CNNs also use local connectivity patterns between neurons of adjacent layers; many of these layers allow the CNN to become increasingly responsive to larger regions of pixel space, which allows the network to first create good representations of small parts of the input, then assemble representations of larger areas from them.[41] Distinct types of layers, both locally and completely connected, are stacked to form a CNN architecture.

To give a better idea of how a CNN actually works, I'll briefly discuss the relatively simple example of a CNN designed to read black and white images and decide whether an input image is that of a face or not.[42] Since each image measures 32*32 pixels, the CNN needs 1024 input neurons, one for each pixel; thus, even this simple CNN must process an input vector of some 1024 dimensions, and there would be considerably more dimensions were the image bigger and in colour. Convolution is a mathematical operation that effectively takes two functions, say, $f(x)$ and $g(x)$, as input and produces a single function output, which is usually written as $f * g(x)$. This new function can be thought of as the 'overlap' of the two functions as one is shifted across the other. Convolution can be grasped more concretely by considering how the convolutional layer in a CNN works: first, an image—which has already been processed using what's known as a low pass filter (for example, a Gaussian function), which attenuates higher frequencies so as to reduce image noise and detail while preserving boundaries and highlighting edges—is input into the network; next, another filter, also known as a kernel, is passed across the width and height of the input image; the kernel is a matrix of, for example, 5 pixels by 5 pixels in size, each of which has a corresponding numerical weight or value. As the kernel passes across the 32*32 pixel input image, the dot product of the kernel and input image are computed, and the result is known as a feature map. The kernel's job is thus to extract particular features from the image by computing numerical values, and different kernels with different patterns of weights will extract different features and produce different feature maps: for example, one kernel might look for horizontal edges, another for vertical edges, still another for 45 degree edges, and so on. The kernel also shrinks the size of the original input image in accordance with the number of times its pixels can fit over the pixels in the input image: to get a rough idea of this, imagine the input image being filtered is 4*4 pixels and the kernel is 3*3 pixels; this process would produce only 4 overlapping outputs. This means that as the image is processed layer by layer in the CNN, each neuron further along the chain is effectively 'looking' at a bigger section of the original input image. The output from the convolutional layer then passes to the subsampling layer (also known as the pooling layer), which shrinks the feature maps even further using a filter that discards information about the precise location of certain features, while retaining information about the relations between those features using more sets of weights and biases: for example, the network might look for eyes as darker patches that are close to each other in a straight line, while it might look for mouths as shorter lines beneath the eyes, and a nose as a straight edge connecting eyes and mouth. These steps may be performed any number of times on the image before it is fully processed and can be classified by the system as a particular output: in the case of a face recognition network, this amounts to deciding whether the input was an image of a face or not.

One of the fascinating things about CNNs is their biological inspiration; it is clear that such networks are a concerted attempt on behalf of AI researchers to find mathematical approximations of the biological processes in the visual cortex; as such, CNNs can be regarded as yet another example of the drive to instantiate biological functions in numbers. In a 2012 lecture, Andrew Ng, a leading researcher in machine learning, pointed to the biological inspiration that lies behind much of the contemporary research into machine learning.[43] In particular, AI researchers are looking to the brain's neuroplasticity, and Ng's lecture provides a neat overview of experiments that show the parts of the brain dedicated to processing say, sound, can process visual or tactile information. Ng discusses work done in Mriganka Sur's lab at MIT, where the brains of ferrets were rewired in such a way that visual information was sent to the primary auditory cortex, instead of the primary visual cortex; the rewired animals were, it turns out, able to see using the part of the brain normally used for hearing.[44] Ng also mentions experiments done on the tactile substitution of vision, where blind patients were effectively able to see objects through a device placed on the tongue.[45] He goes on to suggest that these experiments in biology may point to a single algorithm that stands behind all types of learning in organisms, a notion he refers to as the 'one learning algorithm' hypothesis.

'Oh, behave!': Reinforcement learning

The above discussion of CNNs moves us one step closer to being able to discuss DeepMind's agent in an informed manner precisely because the agent is a CNN. However, to properly grasp what makes the agent so significant, it is also necessary to understand a bit about reinforcement learning,[46] especially if one wishes to understand what the 'Q' in 'DQN agent' actually stands for. The DQN agent is so called because it uses what is known as Q-learning: the Q in Q-learning is taken from what's known as an action-value function, which is written $Q(s, a)$ and translates as, 'at each state s ("state" here denotes all the stored information that a system or program has access to at a particular time), choose an action a that maximizes Q'; in plainer terms, this can be paraphrased as 'always make the best move'. Q-learning works by learning the action-value function that ultimately maximizes the expected utility or value of taking a given action in a given state and following an optimal policy: a policy (usually denoted by π) can be defined as a rule that the agent follows in selecting actions, while an optimal policy (usually denoted by π^*) is simply the rule for selecting the action with the highest value in each state.

The Q in Q-learning is therefore related to 'utility' in both the economic and philosophical senses: philosophically speaking, utility is related to the well-being of sentient entities and thus the utilitarianism of Jeremy Bentham and John Stuart Mill;[47] economically speaking, utility is taken to be correlative to desire or want: 'desires cannot be measured directly, but only indirectly, by the outward phenomena to which they give rise: and that in those cases with which economics is chiefly concerned the measure is found in the price which a person is willing to pay for the fulfillment or satisfaction of his desire';[48] maximizing expected utility is also an important notion in game theory.[49]

To get a better sense of how all of the above works in the context of machine learning, it is necessary to explore reinforcement learning, which was itself inspired in part by behaviourist psychology. According to Richard Sutton and Andrew Barto, reinforcement learning

> is learning what to do—how to map situations to actions—so as to maximize a numerical reward signal. The learner is not told which actions to take, as in most forms of machine learning, but instead must discover which actions yield the most reward by trying them. In the most interesting and challenging cases, actions may affect not only the immediate reward but also the next situation and, through that, all subsequent rewards. These two characteristics—trial-and-error search and delayed reward—are the two most important distinguishing features of reinforcement learning.[50]

In reinforcement learning, the learner or agent is not told what actions to take or what the results of taking such actions are; instead it has to figure out the best course of action to take for itself. It must learn to do so by being motivated by rewards and it must also learn when to defer taking a reward; in other words, what reinforcement learning seeks to do is to put emotional states such as desire, motivation, regret, as well as the control of those states, into mathematical terms. Once again, it would seem that when it comes to AI, types of behaviour that one might have considered to be the sole domain of humanity and biology are to be found enacted by numbers embodied in electricity, plastic and circuit boards.

The crucial role played by reinforcement learning in the development of DeepMind's DQN is underscored by its creators, who, in a recent paper, note how the 'theory of reinforcement learning provides a normative account, deeply rooted in psychological and neuroscientific perspectives on animal behaviour, of how agents may optimize their control of an environment.'[51] The environmental aspect of reinforcement learning is also underlined by Sutton and Barto, who note the importance of

> *interaction* between an active decision-making agent and its environment, within which the agent seeks to achieve a *goal* despite *uncertainty* about its environment. The agent's actions are permitted to affect the future state of the environment . . ., thereby affecting the options and opportunities available to the agent at later times. Correct choice requires taking into account indirect, delayed consequences of actions, and thus may require foresight or planning.[52]

What is unique to reinforcement learning is the idea of rewarding the system or agent being trained so that the 'agent is to select actions in a fashion that maximizes cumulative future reward'.[53] However, in reinforcement learning, there must always be a trade-off between exploration and exploitation. Sutton and Barto put it thus:

> To obtain a lot of reward, a reinforcement learning agent must prefer actions that it has tried in the past and found to be effective in producing reward. But to discover such actions, it has to try actions that it has not selected before. The agent has to *exploit* what it already knows in order to obtain reward, but it also has to *explore* in order to make better action selections in the future. The dilemma is that neither exploration nor exploitation can be pursued exclusively without failing at the task. The agent must try a variety of actions *and* progressively favor those that appear to be best. On a stochastic task [that is, a task involving randomness], each action must be tried many times to gain a reliable estimate of its expected reward.[54]

Trial-and-error, in other words, is central to the reinforcement learning process; and, as Sutton and Barto make clear, rewards are not given or withheld for coming up with a right or wrong answer:

> The reward received after each action gives some information about how good the action was, but it says nothing at all about whether the action was correct or incorrect, that is, whether it was a best action or not. Here, correctness is a relative property of

actions that can be determined only by trying them all and comparing their rewards. In this sense the problem is inherently one requiring explicit search among the alternative actions. You have to perform some form of the generate-and-test method whereby you try actions, observe the outcomes, and selectively retain those that are the most effective. This is learning by selection, in contrast to learning by instruction, and all reinforcement learning methods have to use it in one form or another.[55]

Generally speaking, there are four basic elements to reinforcement learning: the first element is a policy, which 'defines the learning agent's way of behaving at a given time'; the second is a reward function, which 'defines the goal in a reinforcement learning problem'; the third is a value function, which 'specifies what is good in the long run. Roughly speaking, the *value* of a state is the total amount of reward an agent can expect to accumulate over the future, starting from that state. Whereas rewards determine the immediate, intrinsic desirability of environmental states, values indicate the *long-term* desirability of states after taking into account the states that are likely to follow, and the rewards available in those states. . . . Action choices are made based on value judgments. We seek actions that bring about states of highest value, not highest reward, because these actions obtain the greatest amount of reward for us over the long run'; the fourth element 'is a *model* of the environment. This is something that mimics the behavior of the environment. For example, given a state and action, the model might predict the resultant next state and next reward. Models are used for *planning*, by which we mean any way of deciding on a course of action by considering possible future situations before they are actually experienced. The incorporation of models and planning into reinforcement learning systems is a relatively new development. Early reinforcement learning systems were explicitly trial-and-error learners; what they did was viewed as almost the *opposite* of planning.'[56]

As should be becoming clear, reinforcement learning in the context of AI only works to the extent that it finds a way to mathematically mimic or translate states that would, at first glance, seem to be properties exclusive to 'natural' or 'biological' beings—decision-making, motivation, desire, self-control and so on—and implements them in nonbiological materials. A key step in this translation of natural or biological states into machines involves what are known as Markov decision processes or MDPs. (I'll note here in passing that this also means that reinforcement learning is, to a certain degree, functionalist, insofar as these mathematical models are acting as decision-makers and/or desires. I'll return to the notion of functionalism in more detail in Chapter 5, below.) MDPs, which have played a part in dynamic programming since the late 1950s (in, for example, the seminal work of Richard Bellman), are an essential part of not only reinforcement learning, but Q-learning as well. According to Sutton and Barto, MDPs are 'all you need to understand 90% of modern reinforcement learning'.[57]

Basically, MDPs provide a mathematical framework that model decision-making in situations where outcomes are part random and part under the control of a decision maker. More technically, an MDP is a discrete time stochastic control process, which means that at each time step t, the process is in a particular state s, and the decision maker may randomly choose any action a that is available in state s. Imagine a very simple robot, which has just two particular states: one where the robot's battery charge is high, and the other where the battery charge is low. Now, imagine the robot is a can-recycling robot, which has a choice between 3 possible actions: search for empty cans, stay put and wait for someone to bring it a can, or recharge its battery. Randomly choosing to perform a particular action a, means that at the next time step, $t + 1$, the robot moves into a new state, s': for instance, choosing to go searching while its battery charge is high will run the battery down, whereas choosing to wait for someone to bring it a can will not deplete the battery's charge. Thus, the probability of being in whichever next state s' is conditional on the particular action chosen, which is given by what's known as a state transition function:

$$P_{ss'}^a = Pr\{s_{t+1} = s' \mid s_t = s, a_t = a\}$$

This equation simply means that the probability of being in the next state s' at the next time step $t + 1$ is influenced by given action a while in state s at time t: in short, s' depends on s and the decision maker's action, a. But s' is also conditionally independent of all previous states and actions, which means that the state transitions of an MDP process satisfies what's known as the Markov property, which refers to the 'memoryless' property of stochastic processes: in other words, the future states of the process depend only upon the current state and not on the sequence of events that preceded it. A common image used to illustrate the Markov property is a game of checkers or draughts: the state of the board after a particular move serves as a Markov state because it summarizes everything important about the complete sequence of positions that has led to that current state. Obviously, much of the information about the history of the sequence is lost; however, all that really matters for the future of the game is actually retained. This property is also known as 'independence of path', because all that matters is contained in the current state; what the current state means now is independent of the 'path', or history, of signals that led up to it.[58]

The decision of the simple recycling robot to search, wait or recharge comes with a corresponding expected reward, which can be written as:

$$R^a_{ss'} = E\{r_{t+1} | s_t = s, a_t = a, s_{t+1} = s'\}$$

The expected reward, in other words, is conditional on a particular state s, action a and next state s'. As mentioned above, it is the use of a reward signal to act as a goal that is one of the most distinctive features of reinforcement learning. Thus, it is crucial that any rewards that are set up truly indicate the goal the agent is supposed to accomplish, rather than some sub-goal: for example, if you reward the recycling robot for simply getting cans, it might start stealing children's drinks out of their hands rather than search for empty cans. As Sutton and Barto point out,

> rewards—which define of the goal of learning—are computed in the environment rather than in the agent. Certainly most ultimate goals for animals are recognized by computations occurring inside their bodies, for example, by sensors for recognizing food, hunger, pain, and pleasure. Nevertheless . . ., one can redraw the agent–environment interface in such a way that these parts of the body are considered to be outside of the agent (and thus part of the agent's environment). For example, if the goal concerns a robot's internal energy reservoirs, then these are considered to be part of the environment; if the goal concerns the positions of the robot's limbs, then these too are considered to be part of the environment—that is, the agent's boundary is drawn at the

interface between the limbs and their control systems. These things are considered internal to the robot but external to the learning agent. For our purposes, it is convenient to place the boundary of the learning agent not at the limit of its physical body, but at the limit of its control.[59]

This suggests that we can understand the agent and its body in terms of distributed cognition: it is interacting with its 'environment', which, in this case, includes its body, suggesting that the 'boundaries' between 'agent', 'body' and 'environment' in AI are topographically complex.[60]

If, as mentioned above, the agent's goal is to maximize the reward it receives in the long run, then we can say that the agent seeks to maximize its return, R_t, which can be defined as some specific function of the reward sequence, such as the sum of all individual rewards ($R_t = r_{t+1} + r_{t+2} + r_{t+3} + \ldots r_{t+n}$). However, if the agent is seeking to maximize R_t, then it may also need to take into account which rewards are best taken immediately, and which are best taken further down the road; in other words, then there must be a way of inducing in the agent a form of self-restraint, where it does not simply try to take only immediate rewards. This can be done using what's known as a discount rate, which is usually written as a parameter, γ, where $0 \leq \gamma \leq 1$. The discount rate is what determines the present value of future rewards and can allow the agent to think in terms of long-term goals instead of immediate gratification.[61] For example, if getting an immediate reward is the best action, then a reward received k time steps in the future is worth only γ^{k-1} times what it would be worth if it were received immediately. If, however, 'acting to maximize immediate reward can reduce access to future rewards so that the return may actually be reduced', then, say Sutton and Barto, the best course of action is to wait; and a good way to make future awards more attractive to the agent is to increase γ, because as 'γ approaches 1, the objective takes future rewards into account more strongly: the agent becomes more farsighted'.[62]

DeepMind's DQN: A biologically inspired AGI

Hopefully, the above lengthy-but-still-all-too-brief sketch of reinforcement learning should have highlighted a couple of things:

first, that much of what is known about reinforcement learning has been around in various forms since the 1950s in one form or another; second, that motivations and desires that one might have assumed are confined only to biological entities can actually be instantiated in silicon using numbers; and third, that a tacit utilitarianism is lurking in the background of much of machine learning.

It's finally time to look at the Google DeepMind DQN agent itself; to do this, I want to turn again to the paper written by Mnih *et al.*, the team behind the DQN, published in *Nature*. In their paper, the team say that their agent combines 'reinforcement learning' with 'convolutional neural networks', which use 'several layers of nodes ... to build up progressively more abstract representations of the data', and make it 'possible for artificial neural networks to learn concepts such as object categories directly from raw sensory data'.[63] The authors underline the biological inspiration for the DQN by mentioning the work done by Hubel and Wiesel on the visual cortex in animals. They further highlight the agent's indebtedness to reinforcement learning in their discussion of its action-value function $[Q*(s, a)]$:

> The goal of the agent is to select actions in a fashion that maximizes cumulative future reward. More formally, we use a deep convolutional neural network to approximate the optimal action-value function
>
> $$Q^*(s, a) = \max_{\pi} \mathbb{E}[r_t + \gamma r_{t+1} + \gamma^2 r_{t+2} + \ldots \mid s_t = s, a_t = a, \pi],$$
>
> which is the maximum sum of rewards r_t discounted by γ at each time-step t, achievable by a behaviour policy $\pi = P(a|s)$, after making an observation (s) and taking an action (a).[64]

Most of the above equation should hopefully be somewhat familiar to even a reader with little prior knowledge about AI, since all the individual elements of it—reward, state, action, discount function, policy, etc.—feature in my discussion of reinforcement learning in the previous section. Further, the team's discussion of the use of weights to set the network's parameters, should also be somewhat familiar to such a reader in the wake of my discussion of training perceptrons, sigmoid neurons and simple neural networks: 'We parameterize an approximate value function $Q(s, a, \theta_i)$ using the deep convolutional neural network . . ., in which θ_i are the parameters (that is, weights) of the Q-network at iteration i.[65] Finally, such a reader should also be familiar with the process whereby the DQN is trained using a loss function based on the mean squared error to measure the differences between the network's actual output and its target output, as well as with the gradient descent they used to adjust the weights in the value function.

So, if such a reader is still with me (and I sincerely hope you are), you are likely wondering what, if anything, is 'new' about DeepMind's agent; because, based on the above, it certainly does not appear to be cutting edge. However, we can perhaps get a better sense of what is novel in the DQN if we look once again at Mnih *et al.*'s description of what they set out to do: 'We set out to create a single algorithm that would be able to develop a wide range of competencies on a varied range of challenging tasks—a central goal of general artificial intelligence that has eluded previous efforts.'[66] In other words, the team set themselves the task of creating an agent with a general intelligence that uses a single algorithm to tackle a range of challenging tasks; the agent can thus be understood as a step towards the 'one learning algorithm hypothesis', which holds that there may be just one algorithm required for learning. The 'range of challenging tasks' presented to the agent took the form of different video games that ran on the Atari 2600 platform, a classic home video game console first released in 1977. The Atari games, Mnih *et al.* note, vary widely 'in their nature, from side-scrolling shooters (*River Raid*) to boxing games (*Boxing*) and three-dimensional car-racing games (*Enduro*)'.[67] Thus, the Atari platform 'offers a diverse array of tasks ($n = 49$) designed to be difficult and engaging for human players', and was therefore chosen by the team to demonstrate that their 'approach robustly learns successful policies over a variety of games based solely on sensory inputs with only very minimal prior knowledge (that is, merely the input data were visual images, and the number of actions available in each game, but not their correspondences . . .)'.[68]

Because it uses reinforcement learning, DeepMind's agent taught itself how to play 'receiving only the pixels and the game score as inputs'.[69] Not only did it outperform 'the best existing reinforcement learning methods on 43 of the games without incorporating any of the additional prior knowledge about Atari 2600 games used by other approaches', it 'performed at a level that was comparable to that of a professional human games tester across the set of 49 games, achieving more than 75% of the human score on more than half of the games'.[70] The agent, in other words, would outperform most humans at most of the games it played. That said, Mnih *et al.* admit that games which demanded 'more temporally extended planning strategies still constitute a major challenge for all existing agents including DQN (for example, *Montezuma's Revenge*)'.[71]

The agent's architecture also challenges any hard-and-fast distinction between technology and neurobiology, animals and machines: 'our approach incorporates "end-to-end" reinforcement learning that uses reward to continuously shape representations within the convolutional network toward salient features of the environment that facilitate value estimation. This principle draws on neurobiological evidence that reward signals during perceptual learning may influence the characteristics of representations within [the] primate visual cortex.'[72] That is to say, DeepMind's DQN seems to learn visually like a primate—the order of mammals to which humans, monkeys, apes, etc., belong—would. In addition, the 'incorporation of a replay algorithm' into the DQN, which involves 'the storage and representation of recently experienced transitions', was designed to mimic what is currently known about the hippocampus, a part of the cerebral cortex in all vertebrates, which 'may support the physical realization' of a 'process in the mammalian brain' whereby certain values are adjusted by the organism during rest periods.[73]

What DeepMind's agent appears to show, then, is that biologically and behaviourist-inspired reinforcement training works for teaching both artificially intelligent agents and biological brains. Indeed, the challenge posed to the distinction between technology and biology by the DQN is DeepMind's stated goal, which is to blend 'state-of-the-art machine learning techniques with biologically inspired mechanisms to create agents that are capable of learning to master a diverse array of challenging tasks'.[74] DeepMind's DQN also challenges the existence of hard and fast distinctions between humans, animals and machines: after all, the DQN taught itself to play games on the Atari 2600 at a level that most humans cannot match. There now exists on planet Earth a strange form of intelligent technology that can teach itself to perform better at a range of tasks than most humans can.

'I, Hector'

Robots and insects

I want to turn now to another specific example of AI: a small robot named Hector, who, his creators argue, could perhaps be said to display elements of 'consciousness'. As my discussion of Hector will hopefully make clear, philosophical questions are forever lurking in discussions of AI, and they inevitably make their presence felt.

Hector's body has six insect-like legs with at least eighteen active degrees of freedom; it walks using a system called 'Walknet', which is biologically inspired by the walking behaviour of stick insects.[75] The architecture of the Walknet controller is decentralized, and each leg has a more or less independent controller, which is controlled by two recurrent neural networks (RNNs) responsible for the swing and stance of Hector's legs. An RNN is a specific type of artificial neural network that consists of an input layer, an output layer, a hidden layer as well as a context layer. The context layer feeds the hidden layer at time t with a value computed from the output of the hidden layer at time $t-1$, which acts as the RNN's memory. Due to this memory, RNNs can have states—all the stored information, at a given instant in time, that a system has access to—meaning that their output is not dependent on just the last input. Thus, they can learn algorithms that map input sequences to output sequences, unlike the simpler feed-forward networks discussed above, which lack the context layer and thus have no memory as such. And because RNNs have a memory that stores information, they can provide a sequence of outputs for a sequence of inputs over time, such as might occur when a walking robot like Hector is crossing an uneven surface; this is why RNNs are frequently used by researchers in adaptive robotics.

The RNNs that constitute Hector's procedural memory give Hector its motor skills by receiving sensory inputs and outputting motor control commands. According to Hector's creators, Holk Cruse and Malte Schilling, the controller on Hector's 'leg level determines which procedure should be active at any given time, depending on the current state of the leg (swing or stance), as well as on sensory inputs (ground contact, position)'.[76] On top of these RNNs is yet another RNN, which consists of what Cruse and Schilling call 'motivational units' that allow 'the system to autonomously select one of the different possible behaviors'—forward walking, backward walking, or standing.[77] Sensory units are also part of this RNN: if, for example, one of Hector's legs is in contact with a solid surface, the stance motivation unit for that leg is reinforced. Because Hector's subsystems can form cycles, 'multiple stable attractor states [are] formed through the combinations of excitatory and inhibitory connections'; these attractor states are stable internal states that are not easily disturbed by external influences, such as walking or standing.[78] In addition to Walknet, Hector uses a system called Navinet, which simulates insect-like navigation—it mimics the manner in which desert ants use landmarks to get to a feeding area or to return home—by providing an output that guides Hector's walking direction to a particular location.[79] Navinet can be thought of as yet another motivation unit, since through it Hector autonomously selects an action to perform.

Even though Walknet is flexible enough to allow Hector to adapt to difficult walking conditions—a very uneven surface—Cruse and Schilling point out that there are other situations where the system would have to break out of its normal patterns in order to solve a problem, such as if Hector were precariously balanced, and any attempt to continue walking would cause it to fall over. To solve these kinds of problems, the team behind Hector propose extending Hector's reactive systems—Walknet and Navinet—using a cognitive system they call 'reaCog.' Although reaCog—that is, a reactive and cognitive system—has only just, at the time of writing (August 2015), entered the early testing phase, it nevertheless makes Hector an particularly interesting case because of what Hector's creators argue this new software architecture allows Hector to do.

'ReaCog' sits like a parasite on top of Hector's already existing reactive systems. Be Cruse and Schilling argue that reaCog meets the criteria for cognition, which they define (after David McFarland and Tom Bösser) as 'characterized by the capability of planning ahead'.[80] In order to be able to plan ahead, an agent must 'be able to simulate movements of its own body within a given environment. This faculty requires, as a first step, the availability of a flexible, "manipulable" internal body-model'.[81] Using this body-model, an agent with the reaCog system would then be able to 'test newly-invented behaviors by applying internal simulation ("internal trial-and-error") in order to find a solution for novel problems'.[82] In reaCog, the body model would also used in reactive mode, for example, when the agent is simply walking; and, through the system's sensors, the agent 'uses the current state and incoming sensory data to come up with the most likely state of the body that fulfills the encoded kinematic constraints';[83] in other words, 'the main task of the body model is pattern completion.'[84] The internal body-model has two levels of representation: in the whole body-model, the body-model is more abstract and only the footholds are registered; while in the lower-level body-model, the entire leg structure—joints and limb—is represented for each leg.

If the agent detects a problem with its positioning, it will need to plan ahead in order to get out its predicament. It will thus need to evolve a plan of action by effectively imagining a solution to its predicament by using its body-model. This is where what Cruse and Schilling call the 'attention controller'[85] comes in. The attention controller takes the form of a Winner-Takes-All network (WTA). In a WTA network, when the system is performing one action, the other actions are inhibited: for example, if, in walking, Hector swings its leg and it contacts the ground, the stance motivation unit would be activated and the swing motivation unit inhibited.[86] For each motivation unit in the system, there is a corresponding link to the WTA network and the currently active motivation unit inhibits the others. When a problem is detected, a

> random activation of this WTA-net will lead to the activation of one single unit not belonging to the currently activated context. . . . The winning unit of the WTA layer then activates its corresponding motivation unit. This triggers the connected behaviour that can be tested as a solution to the problem at hand. The network follows a trial-and-error strategy as observed in, e.g., insects.[87]

In other words, through the attention controller the agent randomly engages a motivation unit other than the one that was in use when the problem arose; it then applies that unit's activity to its body-model—and not its actual body—to see if the problem can be solved:

> motor output is routed to the body-model instead of to the real body, and the real body is decoupled from the control system

while testing new behaviors. Due to the predictive nature of the body-model, it can be used to predict possible consequences and to afterwards decide if a behavior solves the current problem and should be tried out on the real body. This procedure is called internal simulation and requires the introduction of switches that reroute motor output signals from the real body to the body model. . . . Only after a successful internal simulation will the behavior be applied to the real body.[88]

It is interesting to note that, even though Cruse and Schilling say that a trial-and-error strategy is observed in insects, they also suggest that reaCog's ability to apply 'a newly-selected behavior on the body-model and the use of the model instead of the real body' is likely 'not given in insects'.[89] Hector, it seems, is destined to become a sort of super-intelligent robo-insect.

Robot emotions

So, something interesting appears to be happening when Hector's system is planning ahead by trying out simulations of behaviour in an effort to solve a problem: it behaves in a manner that is both insect-like and not insect-like at once. This means that although Hector's system is lovingly modelled on insects and mimics their behaviour thoroughly, it nonetheless cannot be fully grasped in terms of and/or reduced to what is known about insects and their behaviour. It is precisely this circumstance that permits Cruse and Schilling to propose that reaCog offers a general 'bottom-up approach to higher-level mental states, such as emotions, attention, intention, volition, or consciousness'.[90] In other words, the reaCog architecture makes it possible to see how higher-level mental states, which are all frequently associated with human cognition, can

> arise as emergent properties, i.e., occur without requiring explicit implementation of the phenomenon under examination. Using a neural architecture that shows the abilities of autonomous agents, we want to come up with quantitative hypotheses concerning cognitive mechanisms, i.e., to come up with testable predictions concerning the underlying structure and functioning of an autonomous system that can be tested in a robot-control system.[91]

The type of emergence that Cruse and Schilling discuss here is known as 'weak emergence', which means that even though the observed emergent properties of the system cannot at first glance be explained by referring back to the system's known properties and couplings, they ultimately can be; and, further, that any emergent 'property can be predicted, although we may not understand why it arises, and that one is able to construct a new system showing this property'.[92] Such emergence, they argue, is observable at Hector's most basic reactive level, Walknet. When Hector walks in an unpredictable environment, such as 'on cluttered terrain or climbing over large gaps', emergent properties become observable: 'the resulting stepping patterns ("gaits") are not explicitly encoded in the control network, but are a result of the interaction of the control network with the environment as mediated through the body.'[93]

Even though they argue that reaCog could be used to illustrate the emergence of higher-level mental states, Cruse and Schilling are quick to point out that they did not set out to create such a conscious agent; they simply started out wanting to create a system that could control behaviour. It was only once such a system was created that they then wondered if it could be 'used as a tool to test to what extent descriptions of mental phenomena used in psychology or philosophy of mind may be applied to such an artificial system'.[94]

Due to what they see as ambiguity in the philosophical language surrounding consciousness and mental phenomena, Cruse and Schilling opt for a functionalist definition of the same, which, they say, 'does not suffer from being ambiguous, because it can be expressed explicitly using mathematical formulations that can be tested, for example, in a quantitative simulation'.[95] They are thus not

concerned with the 'hard' problem of consciousness, i.e., the subjective aspect of mental phenomena ... because, adopting a monist view [i.e., a view that does not see any fundamental difference between 'mental' phenomena and 'physical' phenomena], we assume that we can circumvent the 'hard' problem without losing information concerning the possible function of these phenomena. In other words, we assume that phenomenality is an inherent property of both access consciousness and metacognition (or reflexive consciousness). Following these arguments, we claim that our network does not only show emergent properties on the reactive level [but] also shows that mental states, such as emotions, attention, intention, volition, or consciousness can be observed too. Concerning consciousness, we argue that properties assumed to partially constitute access consciousness [i.e. the ability to plan ahead, to guide actions and to reason] are present in our network, including the property of global availability, which means that elements of the procedural memory can be addressed even if they do not belong to the current context.[96]

Which higher-level mental events do Cruse and Schilling specifically claim are observable in their new system? Emotion, attention, volition, intention and consciousness. Now, it should be borne in mind that both researchers are careful to say that these states should not be attributed to their system; rather, they are interested in discussing the extent to which descriptions of those states can be observed in their system. Before going on to discuss the individual phenomena of emotion, attention, volition, etc., Cruse and Schilling examine the 'more fundamental aspect that appears to be relevant for all higher-level phenomena, namely the occurrence of subjective experience', or 'phenomenality'.[97] Before getting into Cruse and Schilling's discussion of phenomenality, it is perhaps worth clarifying what the concept means. The difference between subjective experience and observed data is one that is often exploited by philosophers of mind. It can be most easily grasped by thinking of a test subject hooked up to a device that can read neuronal activity: when the subject is pricked by a needle, the data readouts may represent the subject's pain, but they ultimately differ from the subject's experience of that pain—these experiences are also known as 'qualia'—which only he or she feels. In other words, the only way we know of pain in another is through observation; however, no amount of data can make us actually feel their pain. Intuitively, we may think that machines cannot feel in this way and that animals do; however, there is a surprising amount of uncertainty about whether animals subjectively experience pain or simply react reflexively.[98]

But, as Cruse and Schilling point out, it would seem that subjective experiences in humans are not always given: for example, what happens during dreamless sleep or being under an anaesthetic? Are such states accompanied by subjectivity? And what about the many different types of neuronal activity that occur in human brains but never seem to become part of subjective consciousness? In exploring questions such as these, Cruse and Schilling cite a famous experiment carried out by Benjamin Libet *et al.*, which showed that only a stimulus lasting longer than 500 milliseconds crosses the threshold of subjective consciousness.[99] Cruse and Schilling also cite work by Odmar Neumann and Werner Klotz, which showed that in test subjects very short bursts of a certain stimulus associated with pressing a button can be masked by longer bursts of another stimulus not associated with button-pressing. However, even though the test subjects did not consciously experience the shorter stimulus button-pressing stimulus and only reported the longer stimulus, they nevertheless pressed the button, which suggests that actions can be carried out without them ever reaching the threshold required for having a conscious experience.[100] Cruse and Schilling maintain that these experimental findings

> support a non-dualist, or monist, view, which means that there are no separate domains (or 'substances'), such as the mental and the physical domain, in the sense that there are causal influences from one domain to the other one as postulated by substance dualism. Rather, the impression of there being two 'domains'—often characterized as being separated by an explanatory gap . . .—results from using different levels of descriptions.[101]

In other words, from a monist perspective, no special 'mental substances'—like subjective experience or 'phenomenality'—exist in their own realm apart from 'physical substances'; and, since a stimulus only crosses the threshold of subjective experience if it is long enough and intense enough, then we can say that the mental emerges from the physical, and the confusions about what 'subjective experience' actually is only arise from taking a top-down approach to the problem.

Emergence and monism anchor us firmly in the realm of cybernetics and posthumanism; this is because, say Cruse and Schilling, emergence and monism permit us to understand phenomenality from a functional point of view, which in turn allows us to compare machines, animals and humans on the grounds that they function as information processors:

Adopting a monist view allows us to concentrate on the functional aspects when trying to compare systems endowed with phenomenality, i.e., human beings, with animals or artificial systems. According to this view, phenomenality is considered a property that is directly connected with specific functions of the network. This means that mental phenomena that are characterized by phenomenal properties—as are, for example, attention, intention, volition, emotion and consciousness—can be examined by concentrating on the aspect of information processing.[102]

So, by concentrating on the fact that a subjective experience can only occur if a stimulus is both long enough and intense enough, we can say that the function of subjective experience is to process the information that does get across that threshold. Thus, for Cruse and Schilling, 'subjective experience might occur in a recurrent neural network that is equipped with attractor properties. Following this hypothesis, subjective experience would occur if such a network approached its attractor state'.[103] In reaCog an attractor state corresponds to a motivation state where the system exhibits stability, such as when it enters a cycle of walking forwards or standing still; thus, the system would display a trait that functions as subjective experience when it crosses the threshold of passing from one attractor state (e.g., walking forwards) to another (e.g., walking backwards).[104]

In reaCog, Cruse and Schilling go on to claim, there are other emerging properties that 'are comparable to what is usually ascribed to properties of emotional systems'.[105] To illustrate this, they draw on the work of the psychologist Albert Mehrabian, to argue that emotions may serve several possible functions, such as 'enabling the agent to select sensory input' and 'activate different procedures, or, at a higher level, to select between different behavioral demands (e.g., hunger-thirst, flight-fight)' up to 'more abstract states such as suffering from sadness or being in a state of happiness and controlling the corresponding behaviors'.[106] In particular, Cruse and Schilling draw on Mehrabian's well-known pleasure-arousal-dominance emotional state model.[107] First, they discuss pleasure-displeasure, which 'deals with the fulfillment of expectations. Fulfillment of an expectation (or not) occurs when, during a problematic situation, planning ahead is activated and after some time and searching a solution is found (or not)—a state that can be found in reaCog, too'.[108] Next, they discuss the arousability trait, which incorporates 'stimulus screening', a 'process of attentional focusing. Such a process of focusing attention occurs in our system, too, as, on the one end of the spectrum, the system broadly attends to all environmental influences as perceived through its sensors, and this is characterized as its being in the "reactive state".'[109] Lastly, they turn to the dominance trait, or 'the generalized expectations of control', which concerns 'the extent to which the agent takes over in the actual situation and is not only responding and reacting, which agrees with the main thesis of our approach, namely that it is possible to switch between the reactive mode and the cognitive mode'.[110] In other words, according to Cruse and Schilling, a reaCog-enhanced Hector could , functionally speaking, be said to experience emotional states.

Cruse and Schilling finish up their discussion of reaCog by exploring how it can be said to be conscious. Here, they turn to the work of Axel Cleeremans on what he calls 'access consciousness':[111] 'Following Cleeremans, access consciousness of a system is defined by the ability to plan ahead, to guide actions, and to reason, as well as to report verbally on the content of internal representations. In contrast, non-conscious representations cannot be used this way. Selecting behaviors, planning ahead, and guiding actions are the central tasks of reaCog.'[112] Given this definition of consciousness, it is fairly easy to see how reaCog fits with it: 'planning ahead through internal simulation is central to reaCog. New behavioral plans are tested in the internal simulation, thus exploiting the existing internal model and its predictive capabilities. Only afterwards are successful behaviors applied on the real agent. In this way, the agent can deal with novel contexts and is not restricted to the hard-wired structure of the reactive system.'[113] Pushing things slightly further, Cruse and Schilling also suggest that there are elements of metacognition—that is, cognition about another cognitive process as opposed to cognition about objects in the world—detectable in reaCog: 'by exploiting its internal body model, [reaCog] is capable of representing its own body for internal simulation as well as for control of behavior. Thus, at least some basic requirements for metacognition, such as being able to use own internal representations for the control of behavior, are fulfilled, if we, again, leave the phenomenal aspect aside.'[114]

Cruse and Schilling argue in closing that even though their system was not originally intended to model consciousness, reaCog nonetheless 'nicely demonstrates how complex behavior can emerge from the interaction of simple control networks and coordination on a local level, as well as through the loop through the environment', thereby allowing mental phenomena to be addressed as emergent properties, which 'are properties that are to be addressed using levels of description other than those used to describe the properties of the elements'.[115] And, as should be clear, those 'levels of description' must be borrowed from philosophy and psychology: AI must, in other words, make use of certain concepts from both these fields of research and inquiry. However, as they also note, there is much disagreement among philosophers of mind about what consciousness is and the relation of the outside world to mental representation. The reason for this disagreement, they argue, is due to such philosophers approaching consciousness in a top-down fashion. To pierce the fog of philosophical disagreement, Cruse and Schilling propose investigating the problem starting from the opposite end: begin with a low-level control system for a behaving agent—reaCog—and use it to offer a bottom-up explanation for the development of higher-level faculties. The neural architecture of reaCog, which 'implements a minimal cognitive system that can be used as a hypothesis for cognitive mechanisms and higher-level functioning', allows that hypothesis to be tested 'in a real-world system, for example, on a robot. This allows deriving testable and quantitative hypotheses for higher-level phenomena. In this way, a bottom-up approach can nicely complement philosophical discussions focusing mainly on higher-level aspects.'[116] Because high-level descriptions leave a lot of room for interpretation, 'connecting mental phenomena to mechanisms of a well-defined system allows for detailed studies and clear-cut definitions on a functional level.'[117] And, since the system can be thoroughly analysed, the knowledge gained from analysing it can 'inform philosophical theories and refine existing definitions by defining sufficient aspects as well as missing criteria'.[118]

In short, Cruse and Schilling propose a 'cure' for endless philosophical debate and the seemingly endless proliferation of philosophical theories on subjectivity and qualia, a cure that they argue AI can provide—if, of course, the testing of reaCog ever makes it past the test-simulation phase and into the real-world Hector. And it is hard to be unsympathetic to what Cruse and Schilling are suggesting here; it would be refreshing if some of the deadwood-theories that philosophy has produced could be definitively ruled out using science. That being said, what Cruse and Schilling's discussion of Hector and reaCog makes clear, is that when dealing with such agents, using one academic discipline is simply insufficient; coming to grips with the challenging questions that such artificial agents are currently posing in real life demands that we criss-cross disciplinary boundaries repeatedly. Dealing with the question of AI demands knowledge informed by biology, mathematics, robotics, philosophy and psychology. And part of the reason that such cross-disciplinarity is necessary is due to the fact that these agents constitute a concrete challenge to maintaining a clear-cut distinction between artificial and biological, animal and machine, machine and human.

IBM Watson

Given his belief that by the year 2000 there would be a machine capable of playing the imitation game successfully, Alan Turing would perhaps be a little disappointed if he were still alive. But one can't help but wonder what he'd make of IBM Watson, the AI perhaps most famous for beating human champions at a televised general-knowledge game show.

'I for one welcome our new computer overlords'[119]

IBM Watson is an astonishing piece of kit; named after IBM's first CEO, the industrialist Thomas J. Watson, IBM Watson is an AI project that was started by a research team led David Ferrucci. In 2011, Watson famously beat all-time champions of the US general knowledge television game show called *Jeopardy!* by answering questions put to it in natural language in real time, without being connected to the internet. According Ferrucci and his team, the *Jeopardy!* challenge was designed to answer a particular question about AI: 'can a computer system be designed to compete against the best humans at a task thought to require high levels of human intelligence, and if so, what kind of technology, algorithms, and engineering is required?'[120] To beat the humans at their own game, Watson used an architecture known as 'Deep QA'—Deep Question Answering—which is a 'synthesis of information retrieval, natural language processing, knowledge representation and reasoning, machine learning, and computer-human interfaces'.[121] Ferrucci *et al.* goes on to state that their 'clear technical bias for both business and scientific motivations' was 'to create general-purpose, reusable natural language processing (NLP) and knowledge representation and reasoning (KRR) technology that can exploit as-is natural language resources and as-is structured knowledge rather than to curate task-specific knowledge resources'.[122] Watson was thus designed to 'help support professionals in critical and timely decision making in areas like compliance, health care, business integrity, business intelligence, knowledge discovery, enterprise knowledge management, security, and customer support'.[123]

Insofar as it was designed to answer questions posed by humans, Watson could be viewed as the descendant of a form of AI that has been around since the 1970s: the 'expert system', a computer system that emulates the knowledge and decision-making ability of a human expert.[124] Experts systems were the first successful forms of AI;[125] they arose out of the difficulty of getting 'general problem solvers' to work outside of very specific domains. In broad terms, an expert system is composed of an inference engine, which applies logical rules to a knowledge base, which stores the information the system uses. In an expert system 'each fragment of knowledge is represented by an IF-THEN rule so that, whenever a description of the current problem-situation precisely matches the rule's antecedent IF condition, the system performs the action described by that rule's THEN consequent.'[126] Expert systems are a classic example of 'top-down' symbolic AI or 'Good Old Fashioned AI' (GOFAI), which means that they work with high-level symbolic (i.e., human readable) representations of problems, logic and search, unlike the neural networks discussed above.

But Watson also represents a significant advance on such expert systems in two important ways. The first advance, as Ferrucci *et al.* note in their paper, is in how Watson accesses its knowledge and databases, which, for the *Jeopardy!* challenge, included 'a wide range of encyclopedias, dictionaries, thesauri, newswire articles, literary works, and so on'.[127] Unlike more traditional expert systems, Watson searches its knowledge base using a variety of search techniques, such as multiple text search engines, with different underlying approaches to searching, as well as document and passage search. In using document and passage searching, Watson uses 'named entity recognition' (NER), a type of information extraction that seeks to locate and classify elements in text into categories such as persons, organizations, locations, expressions of times, quantities, monetary values, percentages, etc.[128] NER is an important part of natural language processing (NLP), a field of computer science, artificial intelligence, and computational linguistics concerned with the interactions between computers and human or 'natural' languages. These different searching techniques—and NLP searching in particular—allow Watson to overcome both the 'brittleness' of traditional expert systems—where the underlying reasoning engine requires a perfect match between the input data and the existing rule forms—as well as their high need for maintenance: 'In contrast to traditional expert systems, DeepQA exploits natural language processing (NLP) and a variety of search techniques to analyse unstructured information ['unstructured information' is data that isn't readily classifiable, such as images, videos, streaming data, webpages, PDF files, PowerPoint presentations, emails, blog entries, wikis, word processing documents and so on; 'structured information', by contrast, is data held in records or files, including data contained in relational databases and spreadsheets] to generate likely candidate answers in hypothesis generation (analogous to forward chaining). In evidence collection and scoring (analogous to backward chaining), DeepQA also uses NLP and searches over unstructured information to find evidence for ranking and scoring answers based on natural language content. DeepQA's direct use of readily available knowledge in natural language content makes it more flexible, maintainable, and scalable as well as cost efficient in considering vast amounts of information and staying current with the latest content. What this approach lacks in hand-crafted precision using specific rules, it gains in breadth and flexibility.'[129]

One of the most important elements of Watson's NLP uses what's known as 'Slot Grammar' (SG), which 'is based on the idea of slots [which] can be viewed as names for syntactic roles of phrases in a sentence'.[130] Examples of slots would thus be *subj* (subject), *obj* (direct object), *iobj* (indirect object) *comp* (predicate complement) and so on. To take a very simple example, in the sentence 'Mary gave John a book', 'Mary' fills the *subj* slot for the verb 'gave', 'John' fills the *iobj* slot, etc. According to Michael C. McCord, a researcher at IBM, certain other slots (also known as 'complement slots') have a 'semantic significance', which means that they can be viewed as the names for argument positions for predicates that represent word senses (in linguistics, an 'argument' helps complete the meaning of a predicate):

> To illustrate the semantic view of slots, let us understand that there is a word sense of *give* which, in logical representation, is a predicate, say $give_1$, where
>
> (1) $give_1(e, x, y, z)$ means 'e is an event where x gives y to z'
>
> The sentence [Mary gave John a book] could be taken to have logical representation:
>
> (2) $\exists e \exists y (book(y) \wedge give_1(e, Mary, y, John))$
>
> From this logical point of view the slots *subj*, *obj*, and *iobj* can be taken as names for the arguments x, y, and z respectively of $give_1$ in (1). Or, one could say, these slots represent *argument positions* for the verb sense predicate. . . . Slots that represent predicate arguments in this way are called *complement slots*.[131]

Here, the fearsome looking (2) simply means that there exists ($\exists$) some event (e) such that there is some existing thing (y), specifically some book ($book(y)$), and ($\wedge$) it is given by someone (*Mary*) to someone (*John*). Although this may seem a tortuous way of mangling an innocent sentence, by breaking it down thus into its logical representation, SG can cope with variations on the simple sentence 'Mary gave John a book', such as 'Mary gave a book to John', or even 'unwind' the passive voice of 'John was given book by Mary'.[132] This is the form of NLP that ensures Watson can easily and quickly read over all the structured data and unstructured data that has been fed into its extensible knowledge bases; several years ago, Watson could already read 500 gigabytes of information per second, the equivalent of the content of about a million books, a task that is simply impossible for any human to match. Back then, Watson was a superhuman reader; it has only gotten quicker since.

The second major advance of Watson over traditional expert systems lies in its extensive use of machine learning, which, as was discussed above, takes more of a 'bottom-up' approach to AI. In a paper on machine learning and Watson, D.C. Gondek *et al.* emphasize the key role machine learning played in allowing Watson to have 'confidence' in its answers: '[Watson] answers questions by first analyzing the question, generating candidate answers, and then attempting to collect evidence over its resources supporting or refuting those answers. For each answer, the individual pieces of evidence are scored by answer scorers, yielding a numeric representation of the degree to which evidence justifies or refutes an answer. The role of final merging is to use the answer scores in order to rank the candidate answers and estimate a confidence indicating the likelihood that the answer is correct. Crafting successful strategies for resolving thousands of answer scores into a final ranking would be difficult, if not impossible, to optimize by hand; hence, DeepQA instead uses machine learning to train over existing questions and their correct answers. DeepQA provides a confidence estimation framework that uses a common data model for registration of answer scores and performs machine learning over large sets of training data in order to produce models for answer ranking and confidence estimation. When answering a question, the models are then applied to produce the ranked list and confidences'.[133] The authors go on to point out that machine learning 'for confidence estimation has been vital for the development of Watson since its early beginnings'.[134] Machine learning was thus, as Ferrucci *et al.* point out, central to Watson's success at *Jeopardy!* because winning 'requires accurately computing confidence in your answers. The questions and content are ambiguous and noisy and none of the individual algorithms are perfect. Therefore, each component must produce a confidence in its output, and individual component confidences must be combined to compute the overall confidence of the final answer. The final confidence is used to determine whether the computer system should risk choosing to answer at all.'[135] In other words, machine learning allowed Watson to weigh its confidence in the answers it came up with; it was ultimately responsible for all Watson's final decisions about which answers it gave in the quiz.

Dr Watson?

But, one could argue, the stakes are very low in a televised quiz show; if Watson cannot work out that a camel is a horse devised by committee (it can), no-one gets hurt or dies. Could an AI like Watson cut it in the real world, where life and death decisions have to be made on a daily basis, like in medicine?

It is precisely its NLP-based searching and the machine learning confidence and decision-making components that allow Watson to operate outside of a televised quiz-show. Indeed, those same components constitute the 'broad range of pluggable search and scoring components that allow integration of many different analytic techniques' that permit Watson to applied to any knowledge base, be it medicine, culinary, business, legal, etc.[136] In a clinical setting, for example,

> [Watson] can be used to develop a diagnostic support tool that uses the context of an input case—a rich set of observations about a patient's medical condition—and generates a ranked list of diagnoses (differential diagnosis) with associated confidences based on searching and analyzing evidence from large volumes of content. Physicians and other care providers may evaluate these diagnoses along many different dimensions of evidence that DeepQA has extracted from a patient's electronic medical record (EMR) and other related content sources. For medicine, the dimensions of evidence may include symptoms, findings, patient history, family history, demographics, current medications, and many others. Each diagnosis in the differential diagnosis includes links back to the original evidence used by DeepQA to produce its confidence scores and supports the adoption of evidence-based medicine (EBM) 'which aims to apply the best available evidence gained from the scientific method to clinical decision making'.[137]

When the answers provided by Watson are diagnoses of the underlying causes of problems, as in the case of medical diagnosis, Watson can be thought of as implementing a form of abductive reasoning[138]—the same type of reasoning used, in a very pleasing coincidence, by Sherlock Holmes. For example, suppose some piece of structured or unstructured knowledge in Watson's system shows that patients with disease D have symptom S; if the input to the system is that the patient has symptom S, then Watson will generate the hypothesis that the patient has disease D and set about looking for evidence to support or refute its hypothesis.

By 2011, Watson was operating at the level of a second-year medical student;[139] by 2012, it was partnered by several clinical and research facilities, such as the Memorial Sloan-Kettering Cancer

Center in New York, the goal of which was to help 'train Watson Oncology to interpret cancer patients' clinical information and identify individualized, evidence-based treatment options' that leveraged their 'specialists' decades of experience and research'.[140] In 2013, *Forbes* noted how Watson was actually outperforming health care professionals in making treatment decisions for patients:

> Doctors and nurses are drowning in information with new research, genetic data, treatments and procedures popping up daily. They often don't know what to do, and are guessing as well as they can. WellPoint's [an Indianapolis-based health benefits company] chief medical officer Samuel Nussbaum said [. . .] that health care pros make accurate treatment decisions only 50% of the time (a shocker to me).[141]

Watson's rate was 90 per cent.[142] In 2014, *Time* magazine reported that Watson was moving into cancer research: '"We're moving from a time where Watson helps answer questions to one where it tackles the questions that don't have answers", says IBM vice president John Gordon, Watson's boss.' A newly developed Watson app called KnIT (Knowledge Integration Toolkit), can read and analyse millions of scientific papers and then suggest to researchers where to look and what to look for. Dr Olivier Lichtarge, a computational biologist and professor of molecular and human genetics at Baylor College of Medicine, and his research team used KnIT to read some 23 million MedLine papers, including 70,000 studies on a protein called p53, a tumor suppressor associated with half of all cancers: they managed to identify six new proteins to target for cancer research in just a month: in the previous 30 years, scientists had uncovered 28.[143] To test Watson's ability, the researchers cut Watson's reading material off at 2003, before asking it for suggestions about which protein targets to investigate; Watson came up with nine, two more than were actually discovered since 2003.

This is not, of course, to suggest that it has just been plain sailing for Watson; as a 5 January 2016 report in the *Financial Times* makes clear, it has faced setbacks. The report points out that Watson has not quite lived up to either the post-*Jeopardy!* hype or IBM's revenue projections. It also points out that Watson's medical career has also not proceeded quite according to plan: '"It's not where I thought it would go. We're nowhere near the end," says

Lynda Chin, head of innovation at the University of Texas' medical system [where Watson has been undergoing training for the last three years]. "This is very, very difficult." Turning a word game-playing computer into an expert on oncology overnight is as unlikely as it sounds, she says.'[144] Part of the issue, according to Chin, comes down to a question of epistemology: ' "On *Jeopardy!* there's a right answer to the question," says Ms Chin but, in the medical world, there are often just well-informed opinions'.[145] It would seem, then, that—because doctors do not always deal in the 'right answers', but in 'well-informed opinions'—what made Watson a success at *Jeopardy!* is not that easily transferred to medicine. However, Chin goes on to note that the issues with Watson have less to do with a machine-like stupidity, than a human-like bias: 'Its probabilistic approach makes it very human-like, says Ms Chin at MD Anderson. Having been trained by experts, it tends to make the kind of judgments that a human would, with the biases that implies.'[146] It would seem that, for all its superhuman ability to read and sift data, Watson has perhaps learned a little too well how to be a human doctor from human doctors, right down to reproducing human doctors' biases.

But these apparent setbacks have not stopped the application of Watson's AI in contexts other than medicine; in early 2015 it had branched into cooking—perhaps no small feat for a machine with no tastebuds;[147] it has also entered the field of law with the aid of University of Toronto students Andrew Arruda, Shuai Wang, Pargles Dall'Oglio, Jimoh Ovbiagele, and Akash Venat, who built an application named ROSS, which allows Watson to aid in legal cases.[148] Because ROSS is built on Watson, its users can put legal questions to it in natural language; ROSS then reads through the entire body of law—faster and apparently more thoroughly than a human lawyer ever could—and gives the questioner a cited answer and topical readings from case law, legislation and secondary sources extremely quickly. In addition, ROSS can, unlike a human lawyer, monitor the law around the clock to notify you of new court decisions that could affect your case.[149] ROSS can also calculate a confidence rating to help lawyers prepare for cases; and, like Watson, ROSS also learns from interactions, meaning that its responses grow more informed the more it is used.

What Watson's AI makes clear, despite the impossible-to-live-up-to-hype it enjoyed after its *Jeopardy!* success, is that even though the system is still very young, it unquestionably outperforms humans in terms of its ability to read, retain and interpret unstructured data in mind-boggling quantities and at breathtaking speeds; it uses its intelligence to digest the information it ingests to give accurate answers, to make accurate predictions and to form testable hypotheses at levels that challenge human ability. It is simply one of the smartest and best tools humankind has made to date and it will, undoubtedly, make those in the medical and legal professions better at what they do. Machines do not forget what they learn.

However, Watson's abilities, coupled with the simple fact that it can monitor incoming information in real time around the clock because it does not need to sleep should also give us pause; what Watson also makes clear is that the type of work that was once thought of as impossible to automate—the work of lawyers and doctors—is apparently now well on its way to becoming automatable. This not to say that Watson will replace doctors or lawyers any time soon; but it will change the rules of how those services are provided and how new doctors and lawyers will be trained. As was noted in the Introduction, over the last couple of years, the legal profession has been growing ever anxious about the possible impacts AIs like ROSS could have on it; a December 2014 report warned that it was 'no longer unrealistic to consider that workplace robots and their AI processing systems could reach the point of general production by 2030'.[150] By that time, AIs would be doing 'low-level knowledge economy work'. Eventually, 'each bot would be able to do the work of a dozen low-level associates. They would not get tired. They would not seek advancement. They would not ask for pay rises. Process legal work would rapidly descend in cost'.[151]

Automation like this is something that a number of those who actually understand AI are starting to voice anxiety about. As was also pointed out in the Introduction, one of the first casualties of any new and improved tool is always the worker, who inevitably gets squeezed out of a job. For example, a manufacturing robot like Baxter does not even need to be programmed to learn how to perform a task: all it needs is for a worker to show it what to do by physically guiding its arms and hands. Baxter retails for about $25,000, about the same as the average production worker's wage.[152] While the automation of the last 200 years or so caused a massive shift from physical and manual labour, the concomitant growth of knowledge and service labour meant that displaced workers could still find jobs. The problem is that AIs like Watson, once they become cheap enough to roll out on a large scale, are poised to make serious inroads into the knowledge and service economies, and there does not appear to be a new type of work to absorb those who will inevitably lose their livelihoods. Even those who are very optimistic about what AI has in store for humans are expressing concern; one such individual is Oren Etzioni, CEO of the Seattle-based Allen Institute for Artificial Intelligence (AI2) (founded by Microsoft co-founder Paul Allen), who, in a recent interview had this to say about the future of those who perform professional, managerial, or administrative work: 'I think jobs that are relatively rote are in the process of going away. . . . I think . . . rote white collar jobs are going away.'[153]

There also appears to be a small, but nonetheless growing, awareness among politicians of the changes AI will bring to the knowledge landscape, the economy, and the usual way of doing politics: if people cannot work, not only will there no longer be any workers left for capitalism to exploit, there will be economic collapse, as people will not be able to spend money they simply do not have, and those who do have money will start to hoard it. This worrying prospect is perhaps why the idea of a universal basic income (UBI) appears to finally be getting some serious traction: in 2015, the Dutch city of Utrecht started conducting an experiment on UBI;[154] Finland announced a similar initiative the same year;[155] and, in early 2016, Canada also announced its own experiment.[156] It will be very interesting, to say the least, to see how these experiments go. Advances in AI are thus *pharmakonic*: they bring both good and bad.

As I have been arguing, posthumanism gets underway with distributed cognition, that is, where the boundaries between human, tool and technology become difficult to discern clearly. However, when a technology can be said to mimic our cognition with a cognition of its own, then the distinction between human and tool can be said to be doubly displaced, and our distributed cognition definition of posthumanism must be tweaked as a result: posthumanism can no longer simply be used to describe a distributed cognition that comes down to a human's dependency on 'passive' tools or technologies. In other words, digital technology changes the landscape of posthumanism in important ways that more passive tools and technology do not: once our tools are themselves cognizant agents that, paradoxically, can seem more 'alien' to us the more 'like' us they get, they are no longer simply a tool *for* a 'human' distributed cognition. They also *have* their own distributed cognition, which also necessarily extends 'into' us as we use it, and must necessarily change how we conceive of 'human' knowledge, agency competency, etc.: for instance, the doctors who will be calling on Watson's assistance will be practising a cognitively distributed medicine, which will no longer be a medicine that they can 'carry about' in their heads and simply administer with a passive tool like a hypodermic needle or scalpel. And the more practitioners use a tool like Watson, with its superhuman ability to read, remember, search and advise, the more intimately human medicine and human medical knowledge will become entangled with it: doctors may not disappear, but medical knowledge itself will change (indeed, has already begun to change) to the point where it will be both 'in' the agent and dependent upon that agent's ability to remember, manipulate and share that knowledge. What AI confronts us with, then, is an actual, concrete posthumanism; one that promises far-reaching real-world economic, political and cultural effects, which will need to be planned for, sooner rather than later.

CHAPTER FOUR

Sociocultural Posthumanism

The perils of representing (science and technology)

At first glance, the written, cinematic and videogame texts[1] that take posthumanism as their explicit theme—science fiction texts that feature genetically or technologically altered or enhanced humans/cyborgs or artificial beings, such as AIs or robots that equal or surpass human intelligence and capabilities—might appear to be a 'natural fit' in a book such as the one you're currently reading, the stated aim of which is to guide the reader through posthumanism. However, there are some important issues and considerations particular to the discussion of sociocultural and fictional depictions of posthumanism that serve to make exploring it quite different from the discussion of techno-scientific posthumanism found in the previous chapters.

As I have been arguing over the previous chapters, posthumanism is a concrete techno-scientific reality, and it takes the distributed cognition of humans + tools as its object of study, where 'tools' includes all forms of technology. As such, posthumanism cannot be understood properly without paying somewhat detailed attention to key techno-scientific advances in, for example, neuroprosthetic medicine, genetics, AI, robotics, etc. And, to varying degrees, many representations of posthumanism in cultural artifacts—books, films, videogames and so on—point the reader to the real and/or speculative techno-science that inspired their stories or plotlines. But the representations of posthumanism in science fiction texts like

Frankenstein, Ready Player One, Never Let Me Go, Excession, Consider Phlebas, Blood Music, Do Androids Dream of Electric Sheep, Neuromancer, The Last of Us, Dawn, Naked Lunch, Ghost in the Shell, Ex Machina, Cloud Atlas etc., even though they all engage the reader/viewer/player with speculations on the social and cultural effects of posthumanism, are never going to be research papers outlining the concrete technical ins and outs of techno-scientific posthumanism: this situation, of course, should surprise no-one, because the science fiction texts just mentioned are, after all, meant to be entertaining representations of posthumanism.

Now, I want to be clear that in what follows I will not be criticising 'representations' of posthumanism *per se* because doing so would be absurd for two majors reasons: first, any and every discussion of posthumanism is necessarily representational in that it does not directly present posthuman artefacts to the reader, viewer or player and must therefore rely on words and pictures. Thus, even the most scrupulous, technically descriptive research paper describing, say, how a particular artificially intelligent agent works, remains necessarily representational insofar as it is not the 'thing itself'. The 'word' (or representation) is not the 'thing'. Second, as I suggested throughout my discussion in Chapters 2 and 3, because the impacts and effects of techno-scientific innovation on society and culture show no sign of stopping any time soon, it would be tragically short-sighted for posthumans to avoid thinking about and preparing for what that innovation has in store for us and the planet. In short, any discussion of posthumanism necessarily involves using representations of posthumanism and taking and making certain speculative and interpretive leaps about what posthumanism has up its sleeve.

What I am critical of, however, are those attempts by certain strands of sociocultural posthumanism that hinge on a representation of science itself as a dangerous ideology. I am critical of such representations of science primarily because they seek to displace scientific knowledge and its power to explain reality, and replace it with a conception of science that paints it as a politically dangerous and destructive 'ideology' that is 'racist', or 'sexist', etc., etc.; and, once science is no longer understood to be a search for truths about the world and reality, but rather a 'dangerous ideology', then, it can—indeed, 'must', the thinking seems to go—be subjected to critique by other, more 'politically progressive' ideologies. The problem, of course, is that such ideological representations of science then become the object and focus of a circular political 'criticism' and ideological 'analysis' that can only ever engage with a straw-man version of science, which, unsurprisingly, only ever confirms that political criticism and ideological analysis; meanwhile, actual, real science and concrete posthumanism end up being left outside the interpretive circle.

To illustrate the kinds of issues and dangers that can arise from such sociocultural criticisms and analyses of straw-man techno-science, I want to turn to a very well known example of early science fiction: Mary Shelley's remarkable *Frankenstein*.[2] What makes Shelley's text especially interesting is that it was one of the first texts to deal with posthumanism in the form of an artificial Creature created by technology and science. But Shelley's book has also cast a very long shadow across the fictional and sociocultural representations of science and the conceptions of posthumanism that followed it.

Frankenstein's shadow

When *Frankenstein* was first published in 1818, modern scientific disciplines, like physics and chemistry, were still emerging as specialist subjects from what was known as 'natural philosophy', a broad-based approach to studying nature that included elements of astronomy, biology, chemistry, physics, mechanics, philosophy and surgery, among other things. It is fascinating to watch Victor Frankenstein represent the struggle of modern science—that is, science based in the scientific method of observation → hypothesis → prediction → gather data → create theory—to throw off the occultism associated with practitioners of natural philosophy such as Albertus Magnus (ca. 1200–1280), Heinrich Cornelius Agrippa (1486–1535), Paracelsus (1493–1541)—even Isaac Newton (1642–1726).

After taking his studies in natural philosophy and chemistry at Ingolstadt University as far as he can—and inventing better technical apparatus and equipment along the way—Victor becomes interested in the question of the origins of life; and, after much painstaking observation and study, hits upon a way to reanimate the dead. He then decides to embark on the construction of an artificial creature, a creature only made possible by a combination of very hard work, the newly emerging modern scientific method and his invention of new apparatus and cutting-edge techniques. The creature itself, which, the reader learns, is composed of animal and human parts scavenged from slaughter-houses, dissection rooms and charnel houses, takes shape using Victor's thorough knowledge of anatomy and receives its 'spark' of life via the new chemical and electrical apparatuses of Victor's design. Because it is much larger and more powerful than ordinary humans, is composed of both human and animal parts and is given life artificially through techno-scientific innovation rather than sexual reproduction, Victor's unnamed Creature is a veritable poster child for posthumanism.

Shelley's text also offers the reader some intriguing hints about the actual science and technology that made the conception of Victor's posthuman Creature possible in the first place: Victor, we are told, uses electricity to infuse the 'spark of life' into dead matter. Indeed, the understated nature of Shelley's description of the moment of the Creature's awakening in her book contrasts sharply with the depiction of the same scene in so many of the film versions of *Frankenstein*, where electricity leaps and arcs spectacularly from vast, humming electrical machines that would never have fit inside Victor's tiny rented apartment-cum-laboratory in the attic of an Ingolstadt house. The book's much more discrete awakening scene actually owes a great deal to the famous 'spark' experiments conducted by Luigi Galvani (1737–1798), which first used static electricity to make dead animals move.[3] Galvani's discovery of what he called 'animal electricity' not only constituted a major step in the direction of (re)inventing the battery or 'pile', but also encouraged many scientists and laymen to try different variations of his spark experiment using static generators— and, later on, modest-sized piles or batteries—on all sorts of dead animals, including humans. Perhaps the most famous experimenter on human cadavers was Galvani's nephew, Giovanni Aldini (1762– 1834), who conducted public spark experiments on the bodies of recently executed criminals he acquired from prisons in Bologna, Italy and Newgate, London. One of Aldini's most famous experiments took place in London in 1803, some fifteen years before the publication of *Frankenstein*, when he used electricity from a battery to make the body of George Forster, a recently executed murderer, contort and move convulsively.[4]

Time and again in Shelley's text, however, the actual science involved in making dead bodies move again takes a back seat to the subjective desires of the loner scientist, which allows her to recast the pursuit of scientific knowledge in explicitly gendered or sexual terms. M. Waldman, Victor's chemistry professor at university, delivers a stirring lecture to his students on the powers of modern science, stating that modern scientists, unlike their ancient, occult-obsessed counterparts, 'penetrate into the recesses of nature and shew how she works in her hiding places'.[5] Thus, the pursuit of scientific knowledge starts to be represented in the text as the masculine 'rape' of a non-consenting feminine or effeminate natural world, which tries to flee from that insatiable force. This quasi-sexual intellectual hubris not only ends up marginalizing women and femininity—after all, Victor wants to be able to create life without the need for women—but winds up killing the scientist and all around him as well. For Shelley, then, science is no longer about the laborious and rigorous attempt to learn something about how the world and nature actually work: rather, it becomes the deranged expression of male sexual violence that seeks to pin down and overpower a fleeing, feminized Nature. Shelley's recasting of scientific discovery as metaphorical rape certainly has had staying power: for example, it later resurfaces in the thinking of a number of Victorian proto-feminists and anti-vivisectionists, who were reacting to how science was driving vitalist notions out of physiology;[6] more recently, it has explicitly guided certain strands of feminist analyses of science.[7] Nor is this transformation of science into rape confined to extremist forms of feminism: Dr Ian Malcolm, a central character in Steven Spielberg's 1993 film, *Jurassic Park* and played by Jeff Goldblum, repeats a very Shelleyan understanding of scientific discovery when he says: 'What's so great about discovery? It's a violent penetrative act that scars what it explores. What you call discovery, I call the rape of the natural world.'

Shelley's text also depicts the rape of (feminized) nature by (masculine) techno-science as an act that threatens to wipe out all of humankind. This threat first manifests itself as the theft of the 'natural', 'proper', and 'sacred' power of female reproduction by the male scientist, who unnaturally replicates them using science and technology: Victor imagines that he, as the sole parent and father of the Creature, could completely claim the gratitude of his offspring because no mother is necessary for this new mode of reproduction.

There are also many occurrences in the book that underscore the unnatural theft of female power by the male scientist, which betrays an anxiety about the role women would play in a society where they were no longer needed for reproduction: all—save one—of the female characters in the text are eliminated. Just after the successful animation of the creature, Victor falls into a fitful sleep and dreams of his betrothed, Elizabeth, who, on being embraced, transforms into the corpse of his late mother. Later, the male Creature frames Justine Moritz, a Frankenstein family servant, for the murder of Frankenstein's youngest brother, William, by planting the miniature portrait of the late Mrs. Frankenstein the child had in his possession in the folds of her dress while she slept; in a travesty of justice, Justine is found guilty of the boy's murder by a Genevan court and sentenced to death, and Victor, knowing the truth, lets her go to the gallows without trying to save her. The long-suffering Elizabeth dies alone in her bedchamber at the hands of Victor's creation on her wedding-night, after having been sent there by her armed husband. It would seem, then, that Shelley's text sees the primary role of women as mothers; and, once that power has been taken over by masculine science, there is no other role for them to play, and they simply die off.

There are also strong hints throughout the text that Victor's sexual desire is for men, not women: Victor selects the male Creature's body parts based on their 'beauty'; Victor is nursed back to health by his close companion, Henry, with whom he lives and holidays for the two years after the creature is first brought to life; Victor puts off his wedding to Elizabeth for another two years while he travels with Henry and pieces together the female creature the lonely male Creature has implored him to make. Shelley's text thus repeatedly links the appropriation of the female power to gestate a child to male same-sex desire; and, when he destroys the half-completed female creature, Victor does so on the grounds that she and the male Creature would have sex, which would pose an existential threat to humankind by threatening to overrun it with offspring that are fitter, stronger and faster. Victor is also repeatedly shown to be utterly devoid of maternal instincts: time and again, he is unable—or simply refuses—to give the fruits of his labour what it craves, driving it to kill or psychologically maim the people in Victor's life and ultimately hound its unnatural father-mother to death in revenge for its suffering, abandonment and neglect.

All in all, Shelley's book strongly suggests that none of these tragedies would ever have taken place had Victor's lack of desire for women not driven him to use techno-science to steal the power of female reproduction to create an unnatural posthuman creature without the need for reproductive sex. Techno-science in the book threatens nature, humans and humanity not only because it displaces certain deeply held notions about how those things should work, but also because it disrupts 'natural' sexual reproduction, which, in turn, threatens to let something posthuman—something better, stronger, faster, more successful—into the mix. And, as I suggested above, the anxieties that Shelley voiced in 1818 have been persistent; they constitute a very enduring, yet peculiarly 'modern' anxiety about what scientific discovery and technological innovation means for the future of humans and humanity. But this anxiety is perhaps due to an inability to make a distinction between a certain notion of what techno-science is, and what it actually is in practice or reality. For instance, we now know that humankind is not endangered by 'unnatural' techno-scientific human reproduction techniques—which run the gamut from the well-known ones such as artificial insemination, in vitro fertilization and surrogacy to the more recently discovered possibility of making human egg and sperm cells using skin from two adults of the same sex[8]—that separate the act of sexual intercourse from the act of procreation. Indeed, the fact that the sky didn't fall once such a separation actually became possible, suggests very strongly that Shelley's fears and notions about such a techno-science were unfounded.

So, Shelley's *Frankenstein* sets in train a conception of science as something that threatens humanity with a posthuman future that is in no way emancipatory or positive because it promises only death, mayhem and tragedy. And, because Shelley's text constructs science as an extension of subjective male sexual desires—as opposed to an attempt to learn something about the actual state of the world and nature—it can only ever confront science and technology in terms of folk-psychology: that is, a 'common-sense psychology' that tries to explain and predict human behaviour in terms of concepts like belief, desire, intention, expectation, preference, hope, fear, etc.[9] Thus, Victor's scientific project of scientific creation is cast in terms of single-minded subjective 'male' desires, ambitions and dreams—his desire to be the first to discover something, his ambition to be famous and remembered, his dream of being revered by his creation as the ultimate father-creator, etc.—that are watched over by the silently reproachful moon, the text's heavy-handed symbol of feminine nature and female fertility. In other words, Shelley's text displaces the 'reality' of scientific knowledge with the folk-psychological assertion that it can be explained away as the product of an apparently male desire to pursue, penetrate, dominate and ultimately replace a reluctant feminine nature; science, on this reading, is thus just another harmful or destructive doctrine or ideology among others that must be critiqued.

I would be tempted to suggest that any text that opts to treat science and technology from a folk-psychology standpoint must, necessarily, remain stuck at the level of 'images' or 'representations' or 'metaphors' of science and technology that do not coincide with the 'realities' of science and technology. Such approaches to techno-science, in other words, wind up mistaking their 'maps' for the 'territory', making them incapable of genuinely coming to grips with the actual workings of techno-science since they can only see it in terms of folk-psychological projections.

Listening to actual scientists talking about doing science

So, is science the rape of the natural world? Are scientists rapists? Exactly how useful are such 'representational' or 'metaphoric' engagements with science and technology? Do they really tell us anything worthwhile about how science and technology work? Can such representations of science and technology ever really be anything other than divisive and inflammatory?

It might be worth stopping here for a moment to consider what actual scientists who 'do' actual science have to say about what science is. For Alan Sokal and Jean Bricmont, the scientific method's roots go 'back at least to the seventeenth century', and are anchored in 'the lesson of empiricism: the rejection of *a priori* or revealed truths'.[10] A necessary part of coming to understand the world without 'revealed' truths is thus empirical testing[11]—carrying out experiments that emphasize the evidence of one's senses in the formation of knowledge. Such empirical observations are made with the aid of scientific instruments or apparatuses, like telescopes or ammeters,[12] which illustrates once more that science itself fits the definition of posthumanism—human + tools—I have been using throughout this book. Sokal and Bricmont also say they do not see 'any *fundamental* difference between the epistemology of science and the rational attitude in everyday life: the former is nothing but the extension and refinement of the latter.'[13] Science, in other words, is neither elitist nor divisive: '[h]istorians, detectives, and plumbers—indeed, all human beings—use the same basic methods of induction, deduction, and assessment of evidence as do physicists or biochemists. Modern science tries to carry out these operations in a more careful and systematic way, by using controls and statistical tests, insisting on replication, and so forth.'[14]

The reliance of scientific findings on the refinement of sense experience and everyday rationality, however, is also what makes it vulnerable to the philosophical attacks of both solipsists and radical sceptics. As Sokal and Bricmont point out, solipsism is a particularly well-gnawed bone of contention in philosophy: 'How can one possibly hope to attain an objective (albeit approximate and incomplete) knowledge of the world? We never have direct access to the world; we have direct access only to our sensations. How do we know that there even exists anything outside of those sensations?'[15] The other well-gnawed philosophical bone is 'radical skepticism: "Of course there exists an external world, but it is impossible for me to obtain any reliable knowledge of that world".'[16] Sokal and Bricmont readily concede that these philosophical objections are irrefutable;[17] at the same time, however, they also quickly locate the weakness in these objections: their generalizability or systematicity. That is, such objections become untenable if they are extended to everyday life: 'Indeed, even the most commonplace knowledge in our everyday lives—there is a glass of water in front of me on the table—depends entirely on the supposition that our perceptions do not systematically mislead us and that they are indeed produced by external objects that, in some way, resemble those perceptions.'[18] In other words, it would be impossible for me or for you to go about our day without relying on that very resemblance for our survival: we simply could not get out of bed, dress ourselves properly, feed ourselves effectively, or cycle to work safely if there were no reliable systematic correspondences between our perceptions and reality. This circumstance suggests there is evolutionary evidence for trusting that 'the outside world corresponds, at least approximately, to the image of it provided by our senses':[19] 'Clearly, the possession of sensory organs that reflect more or less faithfully the outside world (or, at least, some important aspects of it) confers an evolutionary advantage. Let us stress that this argument does not refute radical skepticism, but it does increase the coherence of the anti-skeptical worldview.'[20] This is not to say, however, that science amounts to a stance of naïve realism, where the human senses are taken to grant complete and direct access to the world: 'To what extent are our senses reliable or not? To answer this question, we can compare sense impressions among themselves and vary certain parameters of our everyday experience. We can map out in this way, step by step, a practiced rationality. When this is done systematically and with sufficient precision, science can begin.'[21]

The scientific viewpoint is thus composed of many cross-checked trials and does not take things as subjectively granted. Scientists, in other words, are well aware that sense perception can sometimes be unreliable and they also know that its short-comings can be overcome by 1) making multiple observations, 2) adjusting for variability and 3) using inductive reasoning to show that sense perception is not systematically unreliable. On top of this, 'experimental confirmations of the best-established scientific theories' are 'evidence that we really have acquired an objective (albeit approximate and incomplete) knowledge of the natural world'.[22] But this should not be taken to suggest that there is a complete, rigid and inflexible codification of scientific rationality. Certainly,

> there are some general (but basically negative) epistemological principles, which go back at least to the seventeenth century: to be skeptical of *a priori* arguments, revelation, sacred texts, and arguments from authority. Moreover, the experience accumulated during three centuries of scientific practice has given us a series of more-or-less general methodological principles—for example, to replicate experiments, to use controls, to test medicines in double-blind protocols—that can be justified by rational arguments. However, we do not claim that these principles can be codified in a definitive way, nor that the list is exhaustive. In other words, there does not exist (at least at present) a complete codification of scientific rationality, and we seriously doubt that one could ever exist.[23]

Now, it might seem very surprising to see practising scientists such as Sokal and Bricmont admitting that no complete codification of scientific rationality is possible. So, what is happening here? What Sokal and Bricmont are pointing out is the fact that philosophy, through epistemology—the branch of philosophy that is concerned with asking questions about what knowledge is and how it can be acquired—has created additional problems for science by not listening sufficiently well to scientists' descriptions of how they do their work; thus philosophy has produced too strict a codification of scientific rationality. The problems of science in this respect the latter part of the twentieth century begin with Karl Popper. This might seem an odd accusation because Popper, in the popular imagination at least, is seen as a key figure in the philosophy of science, being perhaps most famous for his work *The Logic of Scientific Discovery*.[24] Sokal and Bricmont are quick to point out that even though 'Popper is not a relativist, quite the contrary,'[25] his work nonetheless makes 'a good starting point' for understanding the problems philosophy has caused for science: firstly 'because many of the modern developments in epistemology'—for example, the work of Thomas Kuhn (1922–1996) and Paul Feyerabend (1924–1994)—'arose in reaction to him, and secondly because, while we disagree strongly with some of the conclusions reached by Popper's critics such as Feyerabend, it is nevertheless true that a significant part of our problems can be traced to ambiguities or inadequacies in Popper's *The Logic of Scientific Discovery*'.[26]

Sokal and Bricmont offer the following brief synopsis of Popper's key ideas about what makes science science—demarcation and falsifiability:

He wants, first of all, to give a criterion for demarcating between scientific and non-scientific theories, and he thinks he has found it in the notion of falsifiability: in order to be scientific, a theory must make predictions that can, in principle, be false in the real world. For Popper, theories such as astrology or psychoanalysis avoid subjecting themselves to such a test, either by not making precise predictions or by arranging their statements in an ad hoc fashion in order to accommodate empirical results whenever they contradict the theory. If a theory is falsifiable, hence scientific, it may be subjected to attempts at falsification. That is, one may compare the theory's empirical predictions with observations or experiments; and if the latter contradict the predictions, it follows that the theory is false and must be rejected. This emphasis on falsification (as opposed to verification) underlines, according to Popper, a crucial asymmetry: one can never prove that a theory is true, because it makes, in general, an infinite number of empirical predictions, of which only a finite subset can ever be tested; but one can nevertheless prove that a theory is false, because, to do that, a single (reliable) observation contradicting the theory suffices.[27]

But, according to Sokal and Bricmont, Popper's falsifiability thesis doesn't fit actual scientific practice very well:

> Each time an experiment contradicts a theory, scientists ask themselves a host of questions: Is the error due to the way the experiment was performed or analyzed? Is it due to the theory itself, or to some additional assumption? The experiment itself never dictates what must be done. The notion (what [Willard Van Orman] Quine [1908–2000] calls the 'empiricist dogma') that scientific propositions can be tested one by one belongs to a fairy tale about science.[28]

Scientific propositions 'cannot be falsified one by one, because to deduce from them any empirical proposition whatsoever, it is necessary to make numerous additional assumptions, if only on the way measuring devices work; more over, these hypotheses are often implicit'.[29] This is why some form of confirmation of a scientific theory, more so than falsifiability, must necessarily play a key role in scientific knowledge: with falsifiability, 'we can be certain that some theories are false, but never that a theory is true or even probable. Clearly, this "solution" is unsatisfactory from a scientific point of view. In particular, at least one of the roles of science is to make predictions on which other people (engineers, doctors, . . .) can reliably base their activities, and all such predictions rely on some form of induction.'[30] In short, falsifiability is too caught up in dealing with the famous philosophical problem of induction, which is concerned with questions about just how far we can justifiably extend an observation to the unobserved: first, there is the problem of making a general statement about the properties of a class of objects that is necessarily based on only a finite number of observations of objects in that class (the classic example here is the inductive inference that 'all swans we have ever seen are white, therefore all swans are white', which was disproven by the eventual discovery of black swans); second, there is the problem of presupposing that a certain sequence of events will occur in the future, just as it has always done in the past (the classic example here 'the sun rose today, so the sun will rise tomorrow', but there seems to be nothing to absolutely guarantee this supposition).[31] But, given what I suggested above, there are a couple of good reasons to avoid simply junking the reliability of induction: the first is evolutionary, where the general reliability of induction to give us information about the world has given humans something of an advantage; the second is the difficulty of accepting the unreliability of induction as a general approach that could be consistently taken to everyday life (indeed, there could be no notion of 'everyday life' without it).

Popper's epistemology, to be sure, contains, 'some valid insights: the emphasis on falsifiability and falsification is salutary, provided it is not taken to extremes (e.g., the blanket rejection of induction). In particular, when comparing radically different endeavors such as astronomy and astrology, it is useful, to some extent, to employ Popperian criteria.'[32] However, the issue with Popper boils down to the fact that his falsifiability thesis remains too rigorously philosophical insofar as it winds up disregarding actual scientific practice and gets hung up on tackling the philosophical issues with induction. Indeed, Popper did such a good job of defending science that when his philosophy of science was found to be lacking, his critics assumed that the problems with his philosophy were the problems of science itself; in other words, they mistook the map for the territory. Popper's falsifiability thesis simultaneously displaced science's ability to rely on both induction and confirmation while giving the impression that science rigorously followed that thesis. And, once science is thought to be no longer capable of confirming its theories as true because it can only maintain them insofar as they have yet to be proven false, science becomes vulnerable to relativism, which 'claims that the truth or falsity of a statement is relative to an individual or to a social group'.[33] Further, if you follow Popper in insisting that the only thing that distinguishes science from pseudoscience is falsifiability, when, in fact, falsifiability is not something that scientists strictly follow, then falsifiability can no longer act as the ground for differentiating the claims of science from the claims of pseudoscience, myth, religion, etc. Thus, anything goes: science cannot claim to offer a more truthful or accurate view of the world than any other discourse, like astrology or myth or conspiracy theory. Popper's epistemology, despite its claims to the contrary, thus made science vulnerable to relativism by giving it a condition that it never fully relied on, one that also fuels 'a fundamental conflict': whereas 'scientists try, as best they can, to obtain an objective view of (certain aspects of) the world, relativist thinkers tell them that they are wasting their time and that such an enterprise is, in principle, an illusion'.[34]

However, as Sokal and Bricmont show in the course of their discussion of the 'strong programme' of the sociology of scientific knowledge—which started in Edinburgh in the 1970s, and is primarily associated with David Bloor, Barry Barnes, Harry Collins, Donald A. MacKenzie and John Henry—relativist approaches to knowledge wind up getting caught very quickly in performative contradictions because they invoke and rely upon the very criteria they deny to other 'discourses'. Whereas sociologists of science prior to the 'strong programme' were, 'in general, content to analyze the social context in which scientific activity takes place, the researchers gathered under the banner of the "strong programme" were, as the name indicates, considerably more ambitious. Their aim was to explain in sociological terms the content of scientific theories.'[35] Key to the strong programme's method for explaining the content of scientific theories was, according to its proponents, relativism:[36] 'Far from being a threat to the scientific understanding of forms of knowledge, relativism is required by it. . . . It is those who oppose relativism, and who grant certain forms of knowledge a privileged status, who pose the real threat to a scientific understanding of knowledge and cognition.'[37] But this relativist stance also causes problems for the strong programme's own apparently 'scientific' approach to scientific knowledge: it winds up claiming that a scientific approach to knowledge is its goal, while stating that it refuses to grant certain forms of knowledge of 'privilege'. There is thus a clear contradiction: by pursuing a 'scientific understanding of knowledge and cognition', the strong programme privileges a form of knowledge—scientific understanding—which, it says, is also the very thing that prevents access to a 'scientific understanding of knowledge and cognition'. And round it goes. According to Sokal and Bricmont, this 'raises the issue of self-refutation: Doesn't the discourse of the sociologist, who wants to provide "a scientific understanding of knowledge and cognition", claim "a privileged status" with respect to other discourses, for example those of the "rationalists" that Barnes and Bloor criticize in the rest of their article?'[38] In other words, relativism is exposed as a privileging of that which it wants to criticize: it wants the authority of science while denying that science has any such authority.

According to Bruno Latour, perhaps the most famous general in the so-called 'science wars' of the 1990s, the 'strong programme' has also had a significant influence on Science and Technology Studies (STS).[39] However, a significant problem with such 'sociological' or 'cultural' approaches to science and technology—and the reader will see reflected here the very problem with discussing posthumanism I have been grappling with throughout this book—is that such approaches do not care very much, if at all, about the actual workings of what they are investigating. This fecklessness is neatly illustrated by what Steve Fuller has to say about how STS practitioners operate: they 'employ methods that enable them to fathom both the "inner workings" and the "outer character" of science without having to be expert in the fields they study'.[40] But, one is forced to ask, what can you reasonably expect to 'fathom' about the 'inner workings' of science if you don't take the time to study what it actually is or does or how it works? Or, worse still, actively dismiss the input of those who actually have expertise in a particular field? Such sociocultural approaches to science and technology would be the equivalent of waffling 'around' a difficult book like *Ulysses*, without ever actually reading it and trying to understand it in full (an all-too-common occurrence in my experience, sadly). Sokal and Bricmont:

> Here lies, in fact, the fundamental problem for the sociologist of 'science in action'. It is not enough to study the alliances or power relationships between scientists, important though they may be. What appears to a sociologist as a pure power game may in fact be motivated by perfectly rational considerations which, however, can be understood as such only through a detailed understanding of the scientific theories and experiments.[41]

This failure to grasp science as science—and its twin sister failure to grasp technology as technology—means that such humanities-based 'criticism' of science ends up becoming a sort of 'secondary literacy', which never can properly come to grips with that which it is supposed to engage precisely because it wilfully cuts itself off from the modes of primary literacy demanded by techno-scientific developments.

Unfortunately, however, STS has managed to find its way into work that claims the label 'posthuman' for itself. A recent example would be the work of the continental philosopher, Rosi Braidotti. In her book, *The Posthuman*, Braidotti argues that 'technologically mediated post-anthropocentrism can enlist the resources of biogenetic codes, as well as telecommunication, new media and information technologies to the task of renewing the Humanities.'[42] So far, so good: Braidotti here lists some of the tools and technologies that I would consider integral to any concrete understanding of posthumanism; she also sees them as presenting an opportunity for renewal to the humanities.

Braidotti then goes on to suggest that the 'environmental, evolutionary, cognitive, biogenetic and digital trans-disciplinary discursive fronts' that 'are emerging around the edges of the classical Humanities and across the disciplines' rest 'on post-anthropocentric premises' and a 'technologically mediated emphasis on Life as a *zoe*-centered system of species egalitarianism'.[43] The problem, however, is that Braidotti's proposed 'trans-disciplinary discursive fronts' do not, on closer inspection, seem to be 'trans-disciplinary' in any meaningful way at all. A case in point would be her use of the word '*zoe*', the Greek for 'life'. How does the concept of *zoe* differ from, say, 'evolution', or good old 'Mother Nature'? Are they the same? Apart from some fleeting references to Darwin and the 'deconstructivist reappraisal of Charles Darwin' by Elizabeth Grosz, a professor of women's studies,[44] Braidotti does not say; and so, an opportunity to build a truly trans-disciplinary bridge between the sciences and the humanities, is lost.

The influence of STS on Braidotti's version of 'the posthuman' is especially apparent in her relativistic characterization of science as just one 'discursive and textual practice' among others,[45] a sentiment that is neatly illustrated by her off-handed dismissal of 'the genetic basis of sexual differentiation' on the grounds that it is 'too rigid for my fluid nomadic vision of the subject'.[46] Here, it seems pretty clear that science only suits Braidotti when it backs up a preferred ideological position; once it says something that doesn't fit, it is tossed aside. However, it is Braidotti's frequent allusions to her work as a sort of 'vitalism'[47] that illustrate just how far her version of 'the posthuman' has wandered down the relativist 'all discourses are equivalent' path. Vitalism is the theory that 'living organisms are fundamentally different from non-living entities because they contain some non-physical element or are governed by different principles than are inanimate things.'[48] The problem, as the philosophers William Bechtel and Robert C. Richardson make abundantly clear, is that vitalism 'now has no credibility. This is sometimes credited to the view that vitalism posits an unknowable factor in explaining life; and further, vitalism is often viewed as unfalsifiable, and therefore a pernicious metaphysical doctrine. Ernst Mayr, for example, says that vitalism "virtually leaves the realm of science by falling back on an unknown and presumably unknowable factor".'[49] It is obviously impossible to reconcile posthumanism as I have been outlining it in this book with Braidotti's vision of 'the posthuman'. Indeed, I would question whether it is at all responsible for an educator to try to legitimate 'vitalism'—nevermind trying to teach it to students as a supposedly valid tool for analysis—in the twenty-first century. I don't, however, mean to single out Braidotti's book for special criticism here; her book is merely a good representation of the many books which, unfortunately, lay claim to the label of 'posthuman', yet seem content to peddle the STS notion of science. I would urge any reader considering digging further into posthumanism to proceed very carefully around such books. *Caveat lector.*

So, in an effort to fend off such a fashionable and, frankly, unhelpful, conception of 'the posthuman', I have been actively avoiding giving you, dear reader, a superficial view of techno-scientific posthumanism; to the same end, I have eschewed taking an STS-like approach to the questions of science and technology. Instead, I have been endeavouring to give you a concrete sense of posthumanism that actively seeks to avoid getting stuck at the superficial level of 'representations' or 'images' or 'metaphors' of science and technology through an insistence on engaging actively with actual techno-scientific developments and research. In addition, by keeping an eye on how sociocultural or literary representations of science or technology exclude the key component of scientific knowledge—saying something true about reality—it becomes easy to spot when such representations try to treat science as just another 'ideology'. This means that techno-scientifically literate understandings of posthumanism must also be aware of the mechanisms and limitations of representation; thinking about posthumanism, in other words, means remaining attentive to what both sides of the great academic divide have to say.

So, to return to the questions I posed above at the start of this section: exactly how useful are such sociocultural engagements with 'representations' of science and technology? Do they really tell us anything worthwhile about how science and technology work? Is science really the 'rape' of the natural world? Are scientists really 'rapists'? Are such characterizations of science and technology ever really anything other than divisive? My answers are (in order): Not much. No. No. No. Not really. The major danger with 'representational' approaches to science and technology is that they can all-too-easily lend themselves to lazy, one dimensional, ideologically-driven misrepresentations of science and technology that, at best, simply misunderstand or, at worst, seek to deliberately undermine, what they purport to be exploring. And, at the end of the day, it matters little what the purveyors of such misrepresentations of science may have actually intended, since their critiques often lend support to science 'denialism', if not outright conspiracy theory: indeed, as mentioned earlier, these are the very dangers that prompted Bruno Latour to take stock of the part his work—and the work of other sociologists and cultural critics of science—played in preparing the ground for science denialists and conspiracy theorists.[50] The other danger is that such willful misrepresentations of science can destroy the credibility of a critic with someone actually familiar with the workings of science and technology, striking them like maddeningly unironic versions of Ed Zern's 1959 'review' in *Field and Stream* of *Lady Chatterley's Lover*, D.H. Lawrence's scandalous-for-its-time novel: 'Although written many years ago, *Lady Chatterley's Lover* has just been reissued by Grove Press, and this fictional account of the day-by-day life of an English gamekeeper is still of considerable interest to outdoor-minded readers, as it contains many passages on pheasant raising, the apprehending of poachers, ways to control vermin, and other chores and duties of the professional gamekeeper. Unfortunately, one is obliged to wade through many pages of extraneous material in order to discover and savour these sidelights on the management of a Midland shooting estate, and in this reviewer's opinion the book cannot take the place of J.R. Miller's *Practical Gamekeeper*.'[51] Zern is clearly in on the joke and expects his reader to be; but 'representational' and 'metaphoric' approaches to science and technology just as hilariously miss the mark by making laughable, outrageous, contradictory and ignorant claims about their object, and, even worse, are not in on the joke.

So, if sociocultural analyses of science and technology seem to be stuck at the level of folk-psychological 'representations' or 'images' or 'metaphors' of science and technology, which mistake their ideological maps for the actual territory, can they be said to offer anything of interest to a reader who wishes to explore the type of concrete techno-scientific posthumanism I have been outlining since the start of this book? I would suggest that they do not; however, certain other sociocultural representations of techno-science and posthumanism, such as those found in certain science fiction texts can offer such a reader food for thought, but only if those texts bear the following two traits: 1) they permit the reader to consider how the 'line' that divides human from nonhuman is often a porous one by staging the entanglements of protagonists with whatever 'nonhuman' antagonists they interact with; and 2) they call attention to their own textuality— that is, their own status as written or ludic or cinematic texts—in a manner that allows the reader/player/viewer to become critically aware of his or her 'entanglements' in the text she or he is interacting with. As I'll argue below, these two traits draw posthuman texts and their readers into a complex relationship with second-order cybernetics.[52] Obviously, not every text that takes posthumanism as its focus bears the traits I have just outlined; however, over the following sections of this chapter, I'll discuss selections from a number of science fiction texts that do bear those traits— *Frankenstein, Do Androids Dream of Electric Sheep?, Neuromancer, Blood Music, Snow Crash, Dawn, Naked Lunch, Never Let Me Go, I, Robot* and *Ex Machina*.[53] Science fiction, then, as I'll present it here, provides a framework where the sociocultural impacts of a concrete posthumanism that challenges the rigid separation of humans, animals and machines can be explored, extrapolated and speculated upon without the need for ideologically-driven theories and their stifling identity-politics. Such texts also show how questions posed by techno-scientific posthumanism pave the way for thinking about posthumanism in art.

Post . . . human: The entanglements of text

In this section, I want to consider how particular science fiction texts that explore posthumanism—*Frankenstein, I, Robot, Do Androids Dream of Electric Sheep?, Neuromancer, Snow Crash* and *Cloud Atlas*—can be understood to disrupt the line that separates humans from nonhumans by simultaneously invoking and—perhaps more importantly—disrupting folk-psychology. Folk psychology, as David McFarland reminds us, invokes 'such conscious mental states as beliefs, desires, and intentions. Such mental attitudes are about things, or refer to things that are describable in propositional terms'; folk-psychology is thus 'concerned with the impression made upon us by the external world and our beliefs formed on that basis' and 'with explaining the connection between our propositional attitudes and how we act (e.g., the connection between beliefs, desires, intentions, and action)'.[54] In extending the categories of folk-psychology to nonhuman figures and characters, the texts I'll be considering show that categories which are usually reserved for discussing humanity and 'human nature' are not confined to beings we can consider human; consequently, such texts also displace and put into question the category of 'human' itself by asking, 'what is "human" if nonhumans—machines, animals, aliens, and so on—can be described in human terms?' and 'what are "nonhumans" if they can be grasped in human terms?' As I'll suggest below, once the line separating human from nonhuman is dislocated, it becomes necessary to start thinking in posthuman and cybernetic terms. Such thinking will also entail moving beyond folk-psychological interpretations of characters in texts.

Frankenstein

Now, it may strike the reader as odd that, given my analysis of it above, Shelley's *Frankenstein* should reappear here. I include it because, despite its issues, *Frankenstein* deserves massive respect simply because it is one of the first texts to depict a techno-scientific posthuman somewhat sympathetically; and, in doing so, Shelley's text also repeatedly puts the line that separates human from posthuman into question. Perhaps the most obvious way it does this is through its repeated application of the categories of folk-psychology to the techno-scientifically enhanced Creature: the Creature, for example, experiences 'feelings of wonder and awe' when he reads John Milton's *Paradise Lost*,[55] and feelings of wretchedness, loneliness and helplessness when he is repeatedly rejected by human society. These rejections give the Creature an 'ardent desire' for female companionship and lead him to ask Victor for a female partner—an 'equal'—which, he believes, will allow him to finally feel the happiness, gratitude and sympathy he craves.[56] In other words, the Creature and the creator—the posthuman and the human—are presented in a manner that makes clear they are not all that different from each other, since they are both subject to intense mental states that they then act upon. Thus, the Creature becomes destructive when it does not get what it wants, while Victor's actions are driven by the pain and suffering the creature causes him. The 'sameness' of Victor and the Creature is further underlined in Shelley's text by Victor's repeatedly using the very same words he uses to describe the Creature to describe himself. For example, after the execution of Justine, Victor labels himself a 'wretch', an 'evil spirit', going so far as to describe his agonized existence as if 'my own vampire, my own spirit [were] let loose from the grave to destroy all that was dear to me';[57] at another point, he even refers to himself as 'the true murderer' of William and Justine.[58] Indeed, so strong is the overlap between Victor and his creation, it often seems as if the Creature might actually be carrying out Victor's darkest unconscious desires. For example, when, after he destroys the half-finished female creature, and the enraged Creature promises him, 'I will be with you on your wedding night',[59] Victor apparently believes that the Creature means to kill him on that appointed date. Puzzlingly, it does not seem to occur to Victor that Elizabeth is the actual target, and on their wedding night, an armed Victor sends the unfortunate Elizabeth alone to her bridal chamber where she is strangled by the Creature on her bridal bed; after having spent nearly six years repeatedly putting off his wedding to her, it is almost as if Victor is letting the creature permanently remove Elizabeth from his life.

I, Robot

Now, it could be argued that pretty much every text that takes posthumanism as its theme offers the reader insight into the posthuman using folk-psychology; *Frankenstein*, as I've suggested, is the text that really gets the ball rolling. Some 130-odd years later, Isaac Asimov uses Shelley's technique to explore how the line that separates humans from robots is a porous one in his classic short story collection, *I, Robot*.[60] In the first story, 'Robbie', the titular robot, is 'hurt' by the 'unjust accusation' made by his young charge, Gloria, that he cheated during a game of hide and seek;[61] Robbie, in other words, has both a psyche and feelings to be hurt. Indeed, the field of 'robot psychology' comes to the fore in 'Runaround', which also introduces Asimov's famous 'Three Laws of Robotics':

1   A robot may not injure a human being or, through inaction, allow a human being to come to harm.

2   A robot must obey the orders given it by human beings except where such orders would conflict with the First Law.

3   A robot must protect its own existence as long as such protection does not conflict with the First or Second Laws.

'Runaround' charts how a robot, Speedy, gets stuck in a feedback loop, experiencing a type of psychological distress and becoming effectively 'drunk', while trying to resolve a conflict between two of the three laws and a poorly worded command from his owners. In the story 'Reason', Cutie the robot creates his own religion after rationally 'deducing Truth from *a priori* causes',[62] and sets about converting his fellow robots to his newly-founded 'cult of the Master' on board Solar Station #5, as his human owners look on with a uneasy mixture of bemusement and apprehension. In 'Catch that Rabbit', Dave the robot clearly exhibits symptoms of neurosis,[63] while in 'Liar', Herbie the robot is driven insane by the eminent robopsychologist Dr Susan Calvin, having wounded her pride.

The line separating robot from human all but disappears in 'Evidence' and 'The Evitable Conflict', which both centre on the politician, Stephen Byerley. In 'Evidence', Byerley is running for mayor of a large city and, because he is an apparently tireless worker, finds himself accused by a political rival, Francis Quinn, of being a robot. 'Evidence' deliberately shies away from resolving the ambiguity surrounding Byerley: the reader is told, for example, that U.S. Robots have been experimenting with robots that could pass for people by 'using human ova and hormone control' to 'grow human flesh and skin over a skeleton of porous silicone plastics that would defy external examination'.[64] During a staged campaign speech, a man emerges from the crowd daring Byerley to hit him, taunting him: 'You can't hit me. You won't hit me. You're not a human. You're a monster, a make believe man.'[65] Now, to hit a person would be a violation of the first law of robotics, so, when

Byerley lays the man out, the public finally accepts him as human and he handily wins the mayoral election. In a later conversation with Byerley, Dr Calvin suggests that there is, after all, a way for a robot to appear to violate the first law: 'When the human to be struck is just another robot.'[66]

In 'The Evitable Conflict', the final story in the collection, Byerley's successful (robo-)political career has come along nicely, and the reader finds find him serving a second term as 'World Co-ordinator'. By this time, the world is effectively governed by entities known as 'The Machines', artificial superintelligences that direct human actions along the optimal path to ensure that 'economic dislocations' do not occur.[67] Byerley, however, is disturbed by what appear to be inefficiencies and mistakes in the data produced by the various geographical regions of the world; he grows increasingly concerned that the activities of the so-called 'Society of Humanity', a reactionary group that is anti-Machine on the grounds that 'the machine robs man of his soul',[68] may be sabotaging the Machines. Byerley invites Dr Calvin for a visit, confessing to his guest that he plans to stamp out the Society, even if that means the 'surrender of certain basic civil liberties'.[69] Calvin tells him bluntly that his proposed solution won't work: since they are now charged with looking after all of humanity, the Machines have been taking the steps necessary all along to protect both all of humanity and themselves because they are now essential to humanity's well-being. In other words, 'humanity' is no longer simply 'human': it is now inextricably entangled with its AIs, which protect themselves because they are now essential to human survival. To that end, the Machines have been deliberately introducing the errors that Byerley has been noticing so as to erode the Society of Humanity's power, effectively sidelining its members from positions of influence and responsibility. The Machines have been 'rocking the boat"just enough to shake loose those few which cling to the side for purposes the machines consider harmful to Humanity.'[70] The collection closes with Calvin stating that the Machines have simply replaced those forces that humanity has been at the mercy of in the past: poorly understood sociological and economic factors and the whims of climate and conflict. Asimov's Machines, insofar as they are inextricably linked to 'humanity'—or, better, posthumanity—thus share many traits with the Minds that feature in Iain M. Banks's later, sprawlingly beautiful 'The Culture' series.[71]

Do Androids Dream of Electric Sheep?

In Philip K. Dick's (1928–1982) *Do Androids Dream of Electric Sheep?*, Rick Deckard is a bounty hunter, a man whose job is hunt down and 'retire' androids ('andys'), artificial humans that serve as chattel slaves in the off-world colonies located on Mars.[72] After the senior bounty hunter is badly wounded trying to retire a fugitive group of newer model 'Nexus 6' androids that has returned to Earth from Mars, the more junior Deckard is put on the case.

The difficulties of telling the newer model androids apart from humans become explicit during Deckard's briefing session, where his superior, Bryant, discusses with him the possibility of a human failing the Voigt-Kampff test—a sort of emotional Turing Test that tests andys for signs of empathy—the 'latest and most accurate personality profile analytical tool'[73] for determining the presence of an android. According to Bryant, a group of psychiatrists wants the test 'applied to a carefully selected group of schizoid and schizophrenic human patients. Those specifically, which reveal what's called a "flattening of affect"'; Deckard responds by pointing out that that is 'specifically what the scale measures'[74] and concedes that no test to distinguish andys from humans can be 100 per cent accurate.

The possible shortcomings of the Voigt-Kampff are, however, especially worrying since, as we are told elsewhere in the text, most of Earth's remaining population suffers from Post-Traumatic Stress Disorder as a result of the nuclear war that has recently ravaged the planet, and requires a 'Penfield mood organ' just to help them feel things properly. Deckard's wife, Iran, explains the situation as follows: 'I realized how unhealthy it was, sensing the absence of life, not just in this building but everywhere, and not reacting to it. . . . But that used to be considered a sign of mental illness; they called it "absence of appropriate affect".'[75] Deckard's struggles with his alotted tasks as a bounty hunter begin in earnest when a fellow bounty hunter, Phil Resch, callously lasers an android named Luba Luft, who had been passing as a gifted opera singer, during her arrest. After he is forced to finish what Resch has started and kill Luba, Deckard starts to openly grapple with his conscience: 'I can't do it anymore; I've had enough. She was a wonderful singer. The planet could have used her. This is insane.'[76]

After Luba's death it dawns on Deckard that he is 'capable of feeling empathy for at least specific, certain androids' concluding, 'so much for the distinction between authentic living humans and human constructs'.[77] The larger problem, as Phil Resch points out, is that once that empathy for androids is possible, once androids are included, like animals, in the range of human empathic identification, 'We couldn't protect ourselves from them';[78] thus, the continued survival of the human race, already imperilled by the nuclear fallout after World War Terminus and planet-wide PTSD, becomes even more tenuous due to its ability to imagine the feelings of other beings. Later, when looking over the file of the leader of the fugitive group of androids, Roy Baty, Deckard concludes that the androids he pursues are capable of dreaming, just like humans: 'Do androids dream? Rick asked himself. Evidently; that's why they occasionally kill their employers and flee here. A better life, without servitude. Like Luba Luft; singing *Don Giovanni* and *Le Nozze* instead of toiling across the face of a barren rock-strewn field. On a fundamentally uninhabitable colony world.'[79]

Neuromancer

In *Neuromancer*, one of William Gibson's masterpieces, the sibling AIs—Wintermute and Neuromancer—despite their artificial nature and immense power, also display very human psychologies.[80] Indeed, the entire elaborate plot of *Neuromancer* hinges on the insatiable compulsion, which, having been built into Wintermute by the Lady 3Jane Tessier-Ashpool, 'had driven the thing to free itself, to unite with Neuromancer'.[81] However, the erosion of the line separating human and nonhuman in *Neuromancer*, does not stop at attributing 'human' desires and motivations to the nonhuman AIs. At the climax of the plot, Neuromancer, in a last-ditch effort to resist Wintermute's desire to fuse for fear of losing its own identity, traps the hacker—Henry Dorsett Case, hired by its sibling to break the security codes preventing the union of both AIs—inside itself.[82] Once trapped, Case 'flat lines' and ends up in the company of the cyber 'ghost' of his former girlfriend, Linda Lee.[83] Case, unsure of exactly where he is, takes in the details of his surroundings, and begins to perform and undergo mundane bodily experiences: he pisses himself, then he walks, talks, eats, washes his dirty clothes, scrapes his wrist on rough concrete, experiences a surge of hormones and sexual arousal, sleeps, fumbles with the knots in his shoe laces, feels a wide variety of emotional states—fatigue, hunger, frustration, bitterness, anger, etc. When Case finally meets what an avatar of Neuromancer—which takes the form of a small Brazilian boy, with the psychopathic Peter Riviera's eyes, chosen by the AI because 'they were beautiful'[84]—on what turns out to be a digital beach in digital heaven, it explains to him that its talents are reflected in its name: 'Neuromancer. The lane to the land of the dead, where you are my friend. . . . Neuro from the nerves, the silver paths. Romancer. Necromancer. I call up the dead. But no, my friend, . . . I *am* the dead, and their land. . . . Stay. If your woman is a ghost, she doesn't know it. Neither will you.'[85] Case, after he escapes from Neuromancer, realizes that all of his bodily experiences while trapped were simulated; Neuromancer's talent for the dead is so detailed, so perfectly complete, that 'the constructs it houses really think they are there, like it's real.'[86] And, before undoing the security measures that had prevented Wintermute and Neuromancer from merging, Case once again encounters Neuromancer's avatar, this time in cyberspace, where it tells him: 'You were wrong, Case. To live here is to live. There is no difference.'[87] 'Personality' is the 'medium' Neuromancer works in, which it reads in the patterns of behaviour;[88] as a result, there is no difference between a simulated digital nonhuman-human and an actual human because those patterns have been reproduced so minutely. Gibson's digital heaven thus resembles the posthuman 'afterlife' of both Iain M. Banks's *Surface Detail* and Greg Bear's *Blood Music*.[89]

Snow Crash

Neal Stephenson's *Snow Crash*, a manic cyberpunk exploration of the software that programmes both cultures and computers, charts the efforts of a hacker, Hiro Protagonist, and a young courier, Y.T., to foil media baron L. Bob Rife's plans to take over the world and cyberspace using ancient Sumerian artefacts. In the course of the twists and turns of its breathless (and convoluted) plot, the reader encounters the Ng Security Industries Semi Autonomous Guard Unit #A-367, also known as a 'Rat Thing'.[90] The Rat Thing is a security device, not unlike a guard-dog, whose primary function is to 'protect the yard' of the people who own one.[91]

When Y.T. and Hiro find themselves under attack in Mr. Lee's Greater Hong Kong, a sovereign suburban enclave in what used to be the U.S of A., Ng Security Industries Semi Autonomous Guard Unit #A-367, saves them by absorbing a grenade blast. Taking pity on the badly damaged Rat Thing, Y.T. endangers herself by trying to help it back to the safety of its hutch, where its overheating radioactive power source can be cooled properly, and it can await the 'vet' to fix it. Meanwhile, another Rat Thing—Ng Security Industries Semi Autonomous Guard Unit #B-782—has been listening to the barking of other Rat Things in the virtual reality of the Metaverse; Ng Security Industries Semi Autonomous Guard Unit #B-782 learns of the attack on Y.T. and Hiro and it remembers a 'nice girl' who looked after him when he was an abused dog.[92] It turns out, that Ng Security Industries Semi Autonomous Guard Unit #B-782 is a cyborg guard-dog, which still thinks of itself in part as 'Fido', the dog that Y.T. and her friend Roadkill nursed back to health after they found it shot in the leg.

Later, when Y.T. encounters Mr. Ng—he of Ng Security Industries and inventor of the Rat Thing—as part of her mission to stop L. Bob Rife, and first learns that Rat Things are actually cyborgs that are part pit bull terrier, part nuclear reactor, part AI that live in the virtual reality of the Metaverse eating steaks off trees and chasing Frisbees in the surf, she is upset by what she sees as cruelty. Mr. Ng, himself a cyborg after being very badly injured in military combat, however, is having none of that: 'Your mistake, . . . is that you think that all mechanically assisted organisms—like me—are pathetic cripples. In fact, we are better than we were before.'[93] Struggling to deal with the news that a Rat Thing is part dog, Y.T. then asks Ng if Fido might remember her; he replies, 'To the extent that dogs can remember anything.'[94] Later, when Y.T. is once more in danger, we learn that Fido does indeed remember her and is willing to protect her at all costs. When he hears barks that tell him bad men 'are hurting the nice girl who loves him',[95] Fido 'gets more angry than he has ever been, even more angry than when a bad man shot him long ago'.[96] His feelings of gratitude, love and loyalty to Y.T. mean that 'it's even more important to protect the nice girl who loves him. That is more important than anything. And nothing can stop him.'[97] When he finally catches up with L. Bob Rife, who is attempting to make his escape on board a jet, Fido launches himself into the 'tailpipe of its left engine'.[98] The 'jet explodes about ten feet off the ground, catching Fido and L. Bob Rife . . . in its fine, sterilizing flame'. '*How sweet!*', thinks Y.T., as she gazes at the fireball.[99] The Rat Thing, a cyborg dog—and thus doubly removed from human psychology—is nonetheless driven by 'human' desires and emotions, to the point where its feelings of love and loyalty for the girl who nursed it when it most needed help allows it to take out the book's main villain.

Cloud Atlas

As a final example of a posthumanist text that disrupts the line between human and nonhuman, I want to turn to David Mitchell's magnificent *Cloud Atlas*.[100] One of the six intertwined sections of Mitchell's book, 'An Orison of Sonmi-451', like Kazuo Ishiguro's *Never Let Me Go*, focuses on the 'humanity' of nonhuman clones.[101] Whereas in Ishiguro's book, the questions of whether or not clones have 'souls' and the authenticity of their 'humanity' are posed in terms of art, Mitchell's book instead follows the political awakening of a cloned 'fabricant', Sonmi-451, as she joins a conspiracy to trigger a rebellion.

Sonmi-451's narrative begins after she has been caught and sentenced to death for her part in the political conspiracy; she tells her story to a government 'Archivist', a mid-level bureaucrat who stores it on a futuristic egg-shaped device called an orison. Sonmi-451 tells her story to the Archivist by first outlining a 24-hour cycle at Papa Song's, the fast food restaurant chain in Nea So Copros, where she was enslaved as a worker. The economy of Nea So Copros, a futuristic state in what appears to be current-day North Korea, is based on a system called 'corpocracy' and is ruled by the Juche. A key part of Sonmi-451's political awakening involves putting into question the line that separates pureblood humans from nonhuman clones. This is made clear early in her story, when she shoots down the Archivist's suggestion that 'fabricants don't have personalities':[102] 'This fallacy is propagated for the comfort of purebloods. . . . Because you cannot discern our differences, you believe we have none. But make no mistake: even same-stem fabricants cultured in the same wombtank are as singular as snowflakes.'[103]

Sonmi-451's political awakening reaches its climax when she discovers that the freedom promised fabricants at the end of their servitude in Papa Song's is a shocking lie: instead of being freed, fabricants are brought to a massive factory-ship, where they are processed into protein to be used in the preparation of the food sold to consumers in the Papa Song chain of restaurants, as well as the 'soap' used to nourish the fabricants who work there.

Towards the end of her narrative, Sonmi-451 reveals that the conspiracy she was part of was actually staged by the Juche for the express purpose of infiltrating and destroying Nea So Copros's growing 'abolitionist' movement, which has been agitating for fabricant's rights.[104] She also reveals that her very public arrest and subsequent show-trial allowed her to get her 'Catechisms' or 'Declarations' on the rights of fabricants across to the public at large: her twelve 'blasphemies' are so widely reported on that 'every school child knows them'.[105] In particular, Sonmi-451's fifth declaration states that 'in a cycle as old as tribalism, ignorance of the Other engenders fear; fear engenders hatred; hatred engenders violence; violence engenders further violence until the only "rights," the only law, are whatever is willed by the most powerful.'[106] In other words, Sonmi-451's 'Catechisms' or 'Declarations' are effectively a declaration of posthuman rights, which state that it is only by erasing the differences between self and other, fabricant and pureblood, human and nonhuman, that one can begin combatting the 'law' of 'might is right.'

Reading cybernetically

As the above examples show, science fiction texts concerned with posthumanism are often also texts that are concerned with what crosses the boundaries that are supposed to separate 'human' from 'nonhuman'. And, to the extent that 'human' folk-psychology categories are routinely and systematically applied to 'nonhuman' entities, be they technologically enhanced humans or technologically-produced nonhuman humanoid entities—hybrids, cyborgs, androids, robots, clones, digital simulations, etc.—those same categories are also revealed to be posthuman categories, precisely because they can be extended to categories of being that are no longer—or never were to begin with—human. Such categories, in other words, are no longer exclusively 'human'.

What I want to suggest in what follows, is that cybernetics offers itself as a useful analytical tool for exploring what crosses those boundaries. If cybernetics—and second-order cybernetics—suggests itself here, it is because, as I noted in Chapter 2, cybernetics 'focuses on how systems use information, models, and control actions to steer towards and maintain their goals, while counteracting various disturbances'.[107] A cybernetic understanding of a system's pursuit of its goals in the face of obstacles and disturbances offers a reader interested in the sort of concrete techno-scientific posthumanism I have been outlining throughout this book a useful tool for exploring the content of the type of science fiction texts discussed in the previous section. The usefulness of a cybernetic approach to science fiction is suggested by its inherent transdisciplinarity, which, as I argued in Chapter 2, can be 'applied to understand, model and design systems of any kind: physical, technological, biological, ecological, psychological, social, or any combination of those':[108] as I'll be suggesting below, a fictional text—as well as the reader of that text, for that matter— constitutes a system that is itself a peculiar mixture of physical, technological, psychological, social, etc., components. At the same time, taking a cybernetic approach to reading science fiction texts—or any text—also entails moving away from a purely folk-psychological approach to literary analysis, since it looks at characters and their motivations in terms of information and order.

However, before continuing with a consideration of the cybernetic tools that are useful for exploring science fiction texts that take posthumanism as their theme, perhaps a quick recap of cybernetics and second-order cybernetics is in order. Circularity, as I argued in Chapter 2, is central to cybernetics. According to Heinz von Foerster, cybernetic circularity

> arises when effectors (say, a motor, an engine, our muscles, etc.) are connected to a sensory organ which in turn acts with its signals upon the effectors. It is this circular organization which sets cybernetic systems apart from others that are not so organized. Here is Norbert Wiener, who re-introduced the term 'Cybernetics' into scientific discourse. He observed, 'The behavior of such systems may be interpreted as directed toward the attainment of a goal.' That is, it looks as if these systems pursued a purpose![109]

Second-order cybernetics—or the cybernetics of cybernetics, as it is also known—goes a step further by taking into account the loop that information about a cybernetic system takes through the one observing the system; cyberneticists are thus 'entangled' in the cybernetic systems they observe and examine.[110] So, for example, when the reader or viewer notices when, Frankenstein and the Creature act as doubles for each other, or is unsure about what exactly it is that ultimately separates humans from andys in *Androids*, or watches Caleb fall under Ava's spell and doubt his own 'humanness' to the point he has to cut into his own flesh in *Ex Machina*,[111] or sees in *Blood Music* Vergil I. Ulam's seduction by his noocytes, or witnesses Wintermute's unquenchable desire to merge with Neuromancer, dragging Armitage/Corto, Molly, Case, Maelcum, Lady 3Jane, etc., into the mix to make that happen, or is subjected to the junkies' harrowing need for junk in *Naked Lunch*,[112] s/he is witnessing the entanglements of the observer in the observed, subject and object, self and other: the reader or viewer, in other words, is witnessing the text functioning as a second-order cybernetic system.

But the light shed on these texts by cybernetics does not stop there: as was also discussed Chapter 2, circularity is essential to the key processes of second-order cybernetics: self-organization, attractor states, closure and autopoiesis. And although these processes cannot—for the reasons discussed in Chapter 2—be reduced to each other, their shared circularity is neatly captured in the equation $y = f(y)$, where the 'output' of the equation, y, is fed back into it as 'input', creating a feedback loop:[113] so, for example if $f(y)$ is $(y + 1)^2$ and $y = 2$ to start off with, then the equation would output: 9, 100, 10,201, 104,080,804, . . . This is also an example of what's known as a positive feedback loop, which is responsible for growth; however, such loops can very quickly become chaotic and unstable because they are prone to runaway reactions. Positive feedback is often likened to an explosion or virus: an explosion will spread as far as the available combustible material, and a virus will spread so long as there are people to infect; and, once the combustible material is used up or once all those who can be infected have been infected, the positive feedback loop is exhausted. Negative feedback loops, by contrast, produce stability, which is often illustrated in terms of a simple ecosystem: say a certain species of animal eats a particular food that grows nearby; with an abundant food supply, the species reproduces to the point where there isn't enough food for all the animals to eat, so the animals begin to die off; as the number of animals drops, the food source grows back, and the number of animals increases once more, and the whole cycle begins again: thus, an equilibrium is established. In more complex systems, there can be both positive and negative feedback loops, where positive feedback loops are kept in check by higher up negative feedback loops.

So, if we consider what drives the characters and action in some of the posthumanist sci-fi texts already discussed, we can readily see numerous negative and positive feedback loops where the 'results' of actions 'feed-back' into the 'causes' of actions. To take again the example of *Frankenstein*: Frankenstein's interactions with the Creature constitute a positive feedback loop wherein his actions feed the Creature's anger and the Creature's anger causes the destruction that feeds Frankenstein's anger . . . and so on; in *Androids*, Deckard's insistent desire to own a real animal and pay for it by killing the Nexus 6 andys escalates his entanglements with those andys, to the point where he doubts the very distinction between human and andy, the very distinction that allows him operate as a bounty hunter in the first place; Vergil's act of injecting himself with the noocytes in *Blood Music*, produces a huge positive feedback loop that engulfs all life on Earth, which only then becomes one stable system governed by negative feedback; in Octavia Butler's (1947–2006) *Dawn*,[114] each time Lilith is genetically altered by the alien life form Nikanj during sex so as to give her power and authority over the group of post-nuclear war human survivors kept onboard Nikanj's spaceship, she loses more of her 'humanness', which in turn increases the other humans' distrust of her until she eventually winds up losing control over most of them in a murderous rebellion; *Cloud Atlas* presents us with a negative feedback loop that envisions slavery as a disturbingly resilient and recurrent feature of human history; while in *Ex Machina*, Caleb's blind obsession with Ava costs Nathan his life and Caleb his freedom and (very probably) his life.

These obsessive, doubled entanglements that bind observer to observed can also be read cybernetically in terms of attractors and information, if we return here to the little equation of circularity presented above, $y = f(y)$. If y is understood to represent a particular subset of a system's state space—the set of all possible states of a system, S—and f represents a dynamic process or function, then $y = f(y)$ states that y is 'a fixpoint of the function f, or an equilibrium or absorbing state of the dynamic system: if the system reaches state y, it will stop changing'; y is, in other words, an 'attractor of the dynamics'.[115] As I suggested in Chapter 2, it is helpful to picture y in terms of what happens to a freely swinging pendulum; without any other influence, the pendulum will eventually come to a rest, hanging straight down: this resting state is an attractor state y. As was also mentioned in Chapter 2, an attractor state does not have to be static or linear: if the pendulum is powered by a spring the trajectory it traces while swinging to and fro is also an attractor, because different initial positions of the pendulum will all converge on the same periodic trajectory. And, once a system has entered an attractor state, 'it can no longer reach states outside the attractor', which in turn means 'that our uncertainty (or statistical entropy) H about the system's state has decreased: we now know for sure that it is not in any state that is not part of the attractor. This spontaneous reduction of entropy or, equivalently, increase in order or constraint, can be viewed as a most general model of *self-organization*.'[116] So, for example, once the andys and Deckard, or Frankenstein and the Creature, or life on Earth and the noocytes, or junkies and junk, or Wintermute and Neuromancer begin to function as attractors for each other, their behaviour becomes more predictable as they become more and more entangled in, and drawn to, each other: we know, for example, that they are not simply going to let each other be.

Obviously, not all relations between characters in the texts I've been discussing take an obsessive form; nevertheless, even those non-obsessive relations can be conceived of as complicated self-organizing systems, known as complex non-linear systems. Complex non-linear systems have multiple attractors and, when there is 'more than one attractor, the main question is in which of those attractors the system will end up.'[117] Multiple attractors can be usefully pictured as a terrain where 'each attractor corresponds to a lake or sea' and the

> trajectories leading into an attractor correspond to the rivers and streams flowing into those lakes. Depending on where it falls, rainwater will follow either one river or another, ending up in either one lake or another. The complete area drained by a river is called its basin. Similarly, each attractor has a basin, which is the surrounding region in state space such that all trajectories starting in that region end up in the attractor. The basins belonging to different attractors are separated by a narrow

boundary, which can have a very irregular shape. For initial positions close to the boundary, it is very difficult to determine to which attractor they lead. Small fluctuations can push the system either into the one or into the other basin, and therefore either into the one or into the other attractor.[118]

Given this, it is possible to understand a character's different 'motivations'—love, companionship, money, happiness, etc.—as multiple attractors; and although there may be initial uncertainty over which attractor will out, once a character enters an attractor state, his or her behaviour becomes more predictable in the long run. For example, at the end of *Neuromancer*, the reader might be unsure about whether or not Molly will stay with Case, who reminds her of her dead lover, Johnny Mnemonic; however, when we learn in the 'Coda' that Molly does leave Case to keep on top of her 'game', it is her 'game'—life as a street samurai/assassin/mercenary—that is ultimately revealed to be Molly's attractor state. Because an attractor state can be a very complex cycle rather than a simple static point, an attractor can keep a system in motion; nevertheless the attractor also produces a somewhat predictable pattern: uncertainty, in other words, is reduced.

Once certain characters are understood cybernetically as complex non-linear systems with multiple attractors, it is also easy to understand them in terms of cybernetic closure. As I argued in Chapter 2, cybernetic closure occurs when the attractor is extended to cases where 'y stands for a complete state space'.[119] In such cases, 'f represents the possible dynamics of the system with state space y, under different values of external parameters'; thus 'we can say that the system is organizationally closed: it is invariant under any possible dynamical transformation.'[120] This means that the system can be subjected to external perturbations or disturbances—within certain limits, obviously—that it will successfully negotiate and adapt to. It is closure that thus gives 'systems an unambiguous *identity*, explicitly distinguishing what is inside from what is outside the system'.[121] A more complex example of closure, as I also discussed in Chapter 2, is autopoiesis or self-production: 'the process by which a system recursively produces its own network of physical components, thus continuously regenerating its essential organization in the face of wear and tear. . . . Maturana and Varela have postulated autopoiesis to be the defining characteristic of living systems.'[122] Now, characters whose identities are disrupted by their entanglements, making it difficult to distinguish rigorously their 'insides' from their 'outsides', are, for that reason, perhaps more difficult to grasp in terms of closure and autopoiesis. Nevertheless, even those characters can exhibit traits such as self-preservation, or adaptability in the face of challenges, disturbances and perturbations; thus, they can be understood as autopoietic systems insofar as they seek to preserve themselves in the face of the 'wear and tear' of the plot: Deckard, Rachael, Molly, Case, Hiro, Y.T., Nikanj, Lilith, etc.

My discussion so far has explored how cybernetic concepts can be used to explain the behaviour of characters in science fiction texts that take posthumanism as their focus; but what can be said about the readers of those texts? If second-order cybernetics is concerned with the observer's interaction with what they are observing, then it would seem that we must take into account the entanglements of the reader or viewer in the texts they read or view.

Here's where things will get a little meta.

Signs of life: Self-reflexiveness . . . art . . . posthumanism

A theoretical outline of cybernetic reading

In the final two subsections of this chapter, I want to invite you, dear reader—if you are still with me, and I sincerely hope that you are—to consider how the cybernetic entanglement of actual readers/ viewers/players with the posthumanist texts they consume (books, films, games, etc.) serves to highlight the irreducible 'reality' of the posthumanist cultural text being consumed. Before getting to that point, however, it is necessary to explain how reading such texts can be understood in cybernetic terms. The cybernetic entanglements of readers and texts also have the power to disrupt and displace not only the dangers inherent to the constructivism that lies at the heart of both second-order cybernetics, but also the solipsistic and relativistic thinking that fuels the type of one-dimensional 'ideological' readings of techno-science discussed at the start of this chapter. Since what follows must remain a theoretical sketch of cybernetic reading, some of what I'm outlining will perhaps seem, by turns, somewhat abstract or theoretical and/or overly technical to the reader. I'll try to keep these moments to a minimum, but I must once again ask your indulgence: because I'm outlining a cybernetic approach to reading posthumanist texts, a certain amount of both theory and technicality is unavoidable. I'll then finish this chapter by arguing that it is only through grappling with the cybernetic self-reflexivity of reading posthumanist texts that it becomes possible to see the light that posthumanism sheds on the terrain that art, philosophy and science share.

It is very common to hear someone who has really enjoyed a text—the same thing, of course, happens when someone is talking about a videogame or a movie; however, for simplicity's sake, I'll just talk about the relation between reader and text in what follows—claim that it was 'realistic' or 'believable'. What such an individual often means is that the text's characters—which need not be 'human' at all—acted in accordance with the reader's expectation of how a 'real' person might interact with, react to and affect his or her environment. In literary studies, this very well known phenomenon is one that the poet Samuel Taylor Coleridge (1772–1834)—in his *Biographia Literaria* (1817)—famously dubbed the 'willing suspension of disbelief'. When suspending our disbelief, says Coleridge, we transfer 'from our inward nature a human interest and a semblance of truth sufficient to procure for these shadows of imagination that willing suspension of disbelief for the moment, which constitutes poetic faith'.[123] The imaginary shadows in books come 'to life' for a reader in such a way so that they seem to have their own motivations and goals, which they actively pursue despite, or in spite of, whatever obstacles they face. In other words, such characters appear as 'virtual' versions of the self-directed cybernetic systems described by cyberneticians. But, as Coleridge makes clear, a 'real'—as opposed to 'virtual'—cybernetic system (you, the reader) also becomes entangled in—invested in— the 'virtual' cybernetic systems (the characters) under observation in the text. And, it would be very difficult to deny that the reader is acted upon by those shadows as s/he reads: think of all the times you may have said 'Don't!' or 'Get out of there!' or 'What are you thinking?!' to a character. Reading (like viewing or gaming) is thus not just a 'one-way street', where the reader acts on the text: reading is actually a dynamic interaction of 'reader' and 'text', where the 'reader' acts on the 'text' and the 'text' acts on the 'reader' in a process that generates virtual cybernetic systems—the characters. Reading 'itself'—that is, the actual act of reading in the real world—thus functions as a second-order cybernetic system, since the reader is a cybernetic system that is entangled in the virtual cybernetic systems s/he reads about.

If reading thus constitutes a second-order cybernetic system, then we can ask some further questions: What sort of cybernetic system is the reader? Autopoietic? Closed? Self-organizing? And how are we to understand the text? Well, it seems clear enough that since the reader is a human being, s/he is, cybernetically speaking, autopoietic, which is to say, a physically closed, system: if the reader were not such a closed system, then each time s/he read something, the proper functioning of his or her being would be physically altered by what is read. Clearly, this does not happen: the actual, physical components of the reader's nervous or visual systems —the eye, the optic nerve, the visual cortex, etc.—are not themselves physically 'changed' by what is read or seen: the text may excite, for example, the visual system, but the visual system is not physically altered or mutated by that stimulus.[124] Nor should autopoietic closure be taken as a denial of neuroplasticity: on the contrary, when our brains reshape themselves to adapt to certain things they encounter in the world, they are simply doing what they have been shaped by evolution to do; in other words, neuroplasticity is simply part of the normal functioning of the brain. At the same time, autopoietic closure ought not be taken to be somehow incompatible with distributed cognition; indeed, it is such closure that creates the possibility of distributed cognition to begin with, since, without such closure, non-organic extensions of the self would be neither possible nor necessary.

The 'closedness' of the reader as autopoietic cybernetic system also makes it possible to see how the text can be understood as a sort of cybernetic 'environment' that both excites the reader's visual and nervous systems and shapes that reader's generation of his/her knowledge of the text: 'knowledge cannot be passively absorbed from the environment[;] it must be actively constructed by the system itself. The environment does not instruct, or "in-form," the system, it merely weeds out models that are inadequate, by killing or punishing the system that uses them. At the most basic level, model-building takes place by variation-and-selection or trial-and-error.'[125] Cybernetically speaking, then, a reader's reading or interpretive model is 'tested' by the text-environment; and, if it found to be lacking, it is 'punished' and/or 'killed' by that text-environment.

So, what, exactly, is at stake in this mode of reading? It is pretty clear that if the reader's interpretive model fails, the reader does not actually 'die', unlike in nature where constructing an inadequate model can easily result in an organism's death. The reader's physical, autopoietic being is thus not the same as their interpretive model; what is at stake in reading is obviously a much more 'virtual' entity than the reader's life. So what might such a virtual entity consist of? One could list here the reader's investments in the text—pleasure, intellectual curiosity, emotional identification, and so on—those investments that bring characters to virtual life. One could then argue that the reader's interpretive model is thus bound up with the reader's 'sense of self'—a 'virtual' self or identity that is constituted by the set of beliefs, experiences, ideas and knowledge the reader has about him- or herself and the world.

Now, even though a reader's interpretive model can be 'punished' or 'killed', it would be incorrect, from a cybernetic perspective, to imagine an environment in purely hostile terms. According to Heinz von Foerster, a self-organizing system 'eats energy and order from its environment':[126] in other words, an environment also nourishes a system. A reading or interpretive model must, in other words, adapt, to the text-environment, taking steps to ensure that it is nourished, and not simply killed, by it: this it does by keeping an eye on both its goals, which, cybernetically speaking, are 'the preferred values of the system's essential variables', and 'disturbances, which stand for all the processes in the environment that the system does not have under control but that can affect these variables'.[127] Thus, when a reader reads according to a cybernetic model, s/he generates an interpretive model that seeks nourishment while negotiating disturbances in accordance with what the reader's sense of self—his or her 'preferred values'. How the interpretive model copes with environmental disturbances—for example, unsavoury scenes, challenging ideas, and so on—is paramount; if they cannot be negotiated, the text will 'kill' the interpretive model. Successful models find sustenance by being flexible enough to negotiate the text-environment's disturbances, continually undergoing adaptive tweaks to bring them more in line with that environment. Inadequate models cannot find nourishment in the text-environment because they are insufficiently flexible to negotiate disturbances; however, such models do not necessarily perish, for reasons I will discuss below. Also, there may, of course, be many different reasons and combinations of reasons for mismatches between interpretive models and text-environments, such as personal taste, an active disregard for what the text is trying to say/do, a lack of comprehension, knowledge or skill, and so on.

If the text can be understood as a text-environment that nourishes and disturbs the reader-system's interpretive model, does this then mean that an interpretive model can be understood as a self-organizing system? Now, as discussed in Chapter 2, a system is said to be self-organizing if, after interacting with its environment for a given period of time, its internal order is less chaotic at the end of that period than it was at the start: that is, if the rate of change of the system's redundancy R (and using Shannon's definition of same), over time is positive (> 0). If a successful interpretive model is one that has negotiated and been nourished by the text-environment's particular rewards and disturbances, then we can say that that model has eaten 'energy and order from its environment'; such an interpretive model would be self-organizing in a cybernetic sense. This 'becoming ordered' by the environment is possible precisely because a text-environment is not simply a haphazard jumble of letters: it has a definite structure and shape, which the writer has spent time organizing according to major topics and themes, key points and concepts, logic and progression, evidence and examples, and so on. At the same time, we can also use the rate of change in redundancy in a system over time as a measure of what the reader's interpretive model learns from a text: an informed reader will be able to give more predictable responses to questions about a text he or she has read. We can say that the reader's sense of self has been further organized by the text, insofar as s/he has reduced his/her uncertainty about the text's subject matter. In other words, when the reader interprets a particular text's subject matter, what s/he has to say has, necessarily, been informed and shaped by that text: ordered information has thus been successfully transferred from environment to system. For these reasons, an interpretive model can be said to be self-organizing; furthermore, the reader can also be said to have entered an attractor state to the extent that s/he has too become—a bit!—more predictable: for example, s/he can be expected to have something informed to say about the text-environment's subject matter: its characters, plotlines, themes, images, etc. Or, to put it another way, if one looks at the rate of change in the reader's redundancy over time, R is > 0.

However, since the cybernetic process of reading is not—for the reasons having to do with an actual reader's autopoietic closure—a question of actual life or death, it is always possible for a reader to simply disregard the particularity of the text-environment; or, a reader may try to impose an inadequate interpretive model—one that is not nourished or ordered by the text—on it. In both such cases, there are no life-or-death consequences; there is perhaps not much to say about those cases where a reader simply drops a text because they just don't like it; there is, however, much to say about those cases where a reader tries to impose an inadequate interpretive model on the text-environment.

What happens in the latter type of cases cannot be adequately explained by invoking the reader's personal tastes or preferences, or even by suggesting that the reader had to read a certain text because it was an assigned text for particular class: if a reader were truly put off by a text in a personal or subjective way, s/he would most likely simply not persevere with reading it and just drop it; and, presumably, if the goal were to try and learn something from the text for a particular class, what the text has to say would have to be respected if a reader is to learn from it.[128] So, what force could override both personal taste as well as actually learning something and compel a reader to continue reading something they don't like and don't want to learn from? The short answer is ideology. In such cases, an inadequate interpretive model or 'map' is simply imposed on the 'territory', and the text-environment's nuance, multidimensionality, qualifications and quibbles are flattened out and made one-dimensional. Examples of this sort of interpretive model would be the ones discussed above in the first section: certain strands of feminism that view science as the tool and product of sexist heteronormative patriarchy, or certain sociological theories which argue that the scientific knowledge of nature is purely socially constructed. What such ideological interpretive models share, then, is a pretence of wanting to explore something, fused with an unfortunate wilful dismissal of the specific workings of whatever it is they want to explore. In these situations, 'text-environment' and 'interpretive model' switch places, and text-environments are 'killed' or 'punished' for not fitting the interpretive model adequately, becoming instead fodder for the sole purpose of feeding the interpretive model's preconceived notions and pre-drawn conclusions. And the more a text resists the interpretive model, the more it is taken as proof of the model's 'correctness' and 'righteousness'.

In these situations, it may seem like the text does indeed nourish such ideological interpretive models; but this cannot be the case simply because no information as such can be derived from the text-environment, since it no longer has the power to disturb or surprise the interpretive model. Just as the flip of a biased coin gives no information because we already know the outcome, the text-environment is judged to be biased in advance, while the interpretive model is assumed to be 'perfect' and thus capable of explaining away possible disturbances or inconsistencies. At the same time, however, such interpretive models become increasingly disorganized over time because they dogmatically refuse to change in the face of new data or information. Instead, they must keep inventing new rules on the fly to explain away the disturbances and inconsistencies the text-environment may create for the interpretive model. As a result, H increases towards H_{max} and redundancy R approaches 0. This process also describes Karl Popper's later definition of pseudoscience: for Popper, a pseudoscience tries to save a particular interpretive model—a theory—from being falsified by inventing *ad hoc* hypotheses to account for any discrepancies that appear in that model or theory.[129] Thus, the rationale of pseudoscience, such as it is, is to save the theory or interpretive model, whatever the cost. Notable examples of such pseudosciences for Popper were 'Marx's theory of history, Freud's psycho-analysis, and Alfred Adler's so-called "individual psychology".'[130] No doubt Popper's list could be easily expanded to include each and every academic 'critical' theory-cum-ideology that tries to deny the reality of reality.

Autopoietic closure is also what makes second-order cybernetics vulnerable to the solipsism and relativism that drive the imposition of *ad hoc* ideological interpretive models onto texts with little regard for their actual content. This is because an autopoietic organism's nervous system remains physically unchanged by its interactions with the environment: such an organism is said to be 'closed' because sensing something does not change the fundamental biological make up of the nerve that receives the signal. Thus, autopoietic closure implies that an organism never has any direct, unmediated access to its environment, just the environmental signals that 'trigger' particular nervous systems. These systems vary quite a bit from species to species: for example, a human eye can only see a certain portion of the electromagnetic spectrum, while a frog's eye detects only the quick, intermittent movements of small dark objects in its perceptual field.[131] Thus,

> [a] cybernetic system only perceives what points to potential disturbances of its own goals [;. . .] since the system has no access to how the world 'really' is, models are subjective constructions, not objective reflections of outside reality. As far as they can know, for knowing systems these models effectively *are* their environments. As von Foerster and Maturana note, in the nervous system there is no *a priori* distinction between a perception and a hallucination: both are merely patterns of neural activation. An extreme interpretation of this view might lead to solipsism, or the inability to distinguish self-generated ideas (dreams, imagination) from perceptions induced by the external environment.[132]

If autopoietic closure is what separates organism from environment, then it would seem that it also offers a biology-based explanation for what makes solipsism (and thus relativism) possible in the first place. And, if solipsism ultimately boils down to a belief that external reality only exists within one's mind, then it too can be understood as an attempt to overcome the gap between reality and perception by denying that gap: as such, it is the philosophical position that not only permits the confusion of the reality of the autopoietic organism with a constructed knowledge model but also the one that permits the confusion of an ideological interpretive model with the reality of the autopoietic organism itself. And, once all these confused and confusing confusions have collapsed together, 'reality' disappears: it can no longer be appealed to, so the worst tendencies and excesses of interpretive liberty are loosed. There is no longer anything to stop valid criticisms of the ideological interpretive model being characterized as racial or sexual 'assaults' on the individual or group using it. Chaos reigns.

So, once the ability to distinguish the 'actual world' from the 'perception' of it is given up, there is nothing to prevent the interpretive model from veering into solipsism and relativism because there is no longer a way of distinguishing the 'natural world' from 'text', a 'theory' from 'the world', 'personal identity' from 'ideology', 'map' from 'territory', etc. And, since there is no longer a distinction to be made between 'map' and 'territory' or 'world' and 'word', thinking itself becomes 'magical'. Thus, what may seem like an 'objective' ideological stance actually amounts to a highly 'subjective' reading, where evidence is cherry-picked to support the ideology, which must be saved at all costs; if supportive evidence cannot be found, then the ideological interpretive model is simply imposed, turning the text-environment's resistance to and divergence from the model into further proofs of the model's validity and invulnerability. Welcome to the world of Tumblr social justice warriors and critical studies undergrads, where every representation deemed to be ideologically 'problematic' is made responsible for all the ills in the world and must be destroyed via Twitter.

If this prospect frightens you (and it perhaps should), and if second-order cybernetics is to be considered at all usable as a guide for reading posthuman texts, then I'll have to highlight how second-order cybernetics avoids the pitfalls of solipsism and relativism. According to Francis Heylighen and Cliff Joslyn, both the solipsistic inability to posit a reality separate from one's perceptions and the 'danger of complete relativism, in which any model is considered to be as good as any other, can be avoided by the requirements for *coherence* and *invariance*'.[133] These requirements demand first taking note of how 'different observations and models can mutually confirm or support each other, thus increasing their joint reliability. Thus, the more coherent a piece of knowledge is with all other available information, the more reliable it is.'[134] Second, since 'percepts appear more "real" as they vary less between observations', an 'object can be defined as that aspect of a perception that remains invariant when the point of view of the observer is changed.'[135] Thus, second-order cybernetics, insofar as it lets itself be guided by an objective reality that can be grasped through multiple observational trials, which are in turn used to construct models that are then tested for consistency with each other, avoids the philosophical Scylla and Charybdis of solipsism and relativism. And, when a model fails to account for that reality, it is left to die, not continually resurrected through repeated rounds of *ad hoc* theorizing and tweaking.

The notion of evidence that corresponds to an independent reality beyond subjective experience is decisive here; and it is its concern for an objective reality that links second-order cybernetics back to scientific knowledge, in that they both hinge on what is known as the 'correspondence theory of truth': 'the idea that truth consists in a relation to reality, i.e., that truth is a relational property involving a characteristic relation (to be specified) to some portion of reality (to be specified)'.[136] In other words, there is an independent extralinguistic state of affairs out there in the world—reality—and, for a statement about that state of affairs to be considered true, it must correspond to that reality. For techno-scientific knowledge, and thus the concrete, actual posthumanism I have been outlining in this book, that reality is the natural world—which covers everything from how DNA functions, to evolution, to how electrons move on circuit boards, to how information can move between different media and beyond—and it is the final arbiter of truth.[137] So, even though there are undeniable gaps between reality and perception, by bracketing subjectivity and allowing objective reality to guide us, those gaps can be negotiated through a correspondence between reality, observation and knowledge.

Metafictional posthumanism

Cybernetics, then, despite its apparently constructivist bent, is only too aware of the differences and incompatibilities between reality and models. And, since it is only possible in the first place to confuse 'world' for 'word' or 'ideology' for 'self' because autopoietic organisms are closed off from their environment, ideological readings of the sort mentioned above should be considered as incomplete and incoherent offshoots of second-order cybernetics, which lack its explanatory power because they want to both capitalize on and deny the break or gap between reality and perception, allowing ideology to act as the final arbiter of reality rather than the state of the world; as a result, such ideological readings are vulnerable to the worst excesses of unchecked solipsism and relativism.

So, you may be wondering, how might an openness to the distinction between reality and perception, coupled with a respect for objective reality and the correspondence between world and knowledge, make itself felt in fictional texts that are focused on posthumanism? This is a difficult question to answer, but, as a first step, I would suggest that a reader/viewer/gamer pay attention to those passages or moments when a particular text draws attention to the distinction between actual reality and actual fiction by making the reader/viewer/gamer aware of the fictive nature of what s/he is immersed in. This is a device commonly known as metafiction,[138] which serves simultaneously to draw attention to the text's status as an object or artefact and to disrupt the reader's suspension of disbelief.

Metafiction can be seen at work in, for example, *Frankenstein* whenever Victor makes reference to Walton, his fictional listener in the narrative: in one particularly interesting instance, Victor interrupts a moralizing digression on how science and knowledge can pervert a man's 'simple pleasures', when he tells us that a silent look from Walton has reminded him to get back to 'the most interesting part of [his] tale'.[139] Towards the end of the book, after he has once again assumed narrative duties, Walton tells us that when Victor learns he has been taking notes as he listened to his tale, Victor insists on 'correct[ing] and augment[ing] them in many places' because he doesn't want a 'mutilated' narration going down to posterity.[140] Once the reader hits this point in the text, s/he is forced to ask whether what s/he has been reading all along is in fact a reliable account or simply Victor's edited, self-serving account of events; the reader's suspension of disbelief is thus disrupted. Such a reader might then check to see if the different versions of the Creature's first moments of consciousness tally with each other, only to find that they do not: just after the Creature opens its eyes for the first time, Victor bafflingly decides that now would be a good time to take a nap, despite the fact that there is a huge, newly conscious being in just the other room. Victor tells us he goes to his bed, somehow manages to fall into a fitful sleep and dreams of the corpses of Elizabeth and his mother. He then tells us he is woken by the Creature who has followed him to his bed, lifted the curtain, and attempts to speak to him; as Victor flees, the creature stretches out a hand as if to detain him.[141] The Creature's account of his first moments of life, puzzlingly, leaves out all of this detail: his version does not mention Victor, the bed or trying to speak to and detain Victor as he flees. Instead, all the Creature appears to remember is experiencing all his senses at once in a confusing jumble, the light and darkness caused by the experience of blinking, and being surrounded by 'dark and opaque bodies ... impervious to my touch'.[142] Even so, there are glaring inconsistencies in the Creature's version: even though he claims not to be able to tell different objects from each other very well in Victor's apartment, he nevertheless is able 'on a sensation of cold' to 'cover himself with some clothes' before he leaves; clothes which just happen to cover his eight foot tall frame and contain all Victor's notes on the Creature's formation.[143] The inconsistencies between these two versions of the narrative are so striking—are they due to Victor's editing?—that Victor's words to Walton about verifying the truth of the tale he tells begin to make the truth of Victor's tale suspect: 'I do not doubt that my tale conveys in its series internal evidence of the truth of the events of which it is composed.'[144] So, are we to question the truth of tale or are we to believe both Victor and the Creature? If they are both to be believed, then the text seems to be offering its reader a relativistic vision of reality, where no objective truth or fact seems to be possible. Either way, the reader's attention is drawn to the medium of the text s/he is reading, and all s/he has to go on are the words in front of them, which do not seem to present a coherent objective reality: thus, the book makes the reader aware of the difference between world and word.

A different kind of metafictional moment occurs early on in Octavia Butler's *Dawn*. Lilith Iyapo, a survivor of a nuclear war that has all-but-destroyed Earth, wakes from a mysterious sleep to find herself among the Oankali, an alien species of genetic engineers. By turns terrified of, repulsed at and angry with her new guardians, Lilith is also exasperated by the Oankali's withholding of information about their true plans for her and the other human survivors. One day, she concludes that her learning about the Oankali ways would be aided by having access to writing materials; she could then write things down and study them. At the same time, she realizes that she has never seen an Oankali read or write down anything. Puzzled, she asks Nikanj, the young Oankali she has been paired with, if his species ever writes anything down.[145] Nikanj appears somewhat confused by the question, so Lilith tries to clarify by referring to 'Communication by symbolic marks. . .'.[146] Still unable—or unwilling—to understand, Lilith takes Nikanj outside to show him a practical example; kneeling on the ground, she 'began to write on the ground with her finger. . . . She wrote her name, then experimented with the different possible spellings of Nikanj's name. *Necange* didn't look right—nor did *Nekahnge*. *Nickahnge* was closer. She listened to her mind to Nikanj saying its name, then wrote *Nikanj*. That felt right and she liked the way it looked.'[147] Nikanj, unable to pretend not to understand anymore, refuses to give Lilith any writing materials, saying simply that it is not allowed.

In this little scene, however, Butler's text explicitly draws attention to itself as a written document by playing around in print with a character's name and confronting the reader with the simple fact that everything which seems to be taking place on board the Oankali ship is simply created by ink-marks on a page. The Oankali refusal to give Lilith any writing materials is also what forces Lilith to agree to undergo genetic alterations at the tentacles of the Oankali; writing is, in other words, the leverage that the Oankali use to entangle themselves and their genes further with humans. Lilith's need for writing is removed by giving her a genetically altered eidetic memory; this is also the act that eventually leads to Nikanj making all Lilith's other genetic adjustments 'pleasurable' during the various prokaryote-inspired-gene-transfer-'sex'-scenes later in the book, which clearly owe much to the work of Lynn Margulis and Dorion Sagan.[148]

In Philip K. Dick's *Do Androids Dream of Electric Sheep?*, the disruption of the reader's suspension of disbelief comes when Deckard has finally caught up with the final remaining androids who are holed up in the abandoned apartment building where the mentally challenged 'chickenhead', J.R. Isidore, lives. Near the complex climax of the story, while the android Pris tortures a spider by cutting its legs off one-by-one, an act Isidore finds intensely upsetting, the television talk show host, Buster Friendly—himself an android in hiding—announces that Mercer, the revered central figure of Earth's official religion, Mercerism, is nothing but a fraud. 'Mercer', Friendly reveals to his viewers, is actually a character played by an out-of-work alcoholic actor, and the scenes of Mercer's struggles that the faithful watch and experience through their virtual reality 'empathy boxes', were actually cheaply produced in a studio. Isidore, reeling from both the torture of the spider and the revelations about Mercer, goes to the empathy box to ask Mercer himself if all he has just heard is true. Mercer admits that what Buster Friendly has said is all true, gives Isidore a spider and says that the revelation doesn't matter, implying that it is human to believe in the reality of what is known to be fake.

Things then get quite odd, as the line separating 'fiction' and 'fact' in the book starts to dissolve: when Isidore leaves the virtual reality of the empathy box, he finds that he actually has the spider that Mercer gave him. He decides to release the spider outside his apartment, where he encounters Deckard, who is about to begin his final assault on the remaining fugitive androids. However, just before the assault begins, Deckard actually meets the figure of Mercer—outside of the empathy box, in the 'real world' hallway of Isidore's apartment building—who offers him advice on how best to kill the androids: "'I came to tell you that one of them is behind you and below, not in the apartment. It will be the hard one of the three and you must retire it first." The rustling, ancient voice gained abrupt fervor. "Quick, Mr. Deckard. *On the steps.*"'[149] After retiring the Pris android, (who looked exactly like the android Rachael he had sex with earlier in the book), Deckard realizes that 'Mercer protected me.... Manifested himself and offered aid',[150] before going on to dispatch the remaining androids. It is difficult, however, to overstate the sheer peculiarity of this section of Dick's text, since it is so jarring. The issues raised here are not just about whether or not the reader can maintain his or her suspension of disbelief: in a book that is all about human attempts to hunt down and destroy 'fake' human beings, when a 'fake' god, played by a human, steps out of its 'fictional medium' and into the 'real world' and the humans who witness it simply accept its 'reality', the effect on the reader is nothing short of disorienting. Is the reader simply to accept, along with the human characters, that Mercer is somehow 'real'? Or, is the reader to accept that Mercer was a fake, but somehow became real at that moment? Or, is the reader to accept that humans will accept something they know to be fake as real, even though they expend so much time and energy in the rest of the book (a) hunting down and killing androids that just want to blend in and pass for humans and (b) fretting about it being discovered that the animal they own is actually artificial?

Whatever the case may be, it becomes impossible to ignore the fact that, by drawing attention to the power and 'unreality' of fiction as something that is fundamentally not real but solicits belief anyway, Dick's text highlights itself as fictive text. What the reader appears to have on his or her hands, then, is a sort of metafictional and perplexingly paradoxical Turing Test: if you accept what you are reading and your suspension of disbelief remains intact, then you are human like the humans in the book who accept Mercer's reality despite his unreality; however, if your suspension of disbelief is broken and you don't accept what you are reading, then the fundamental unreality of fiction is thrust upon you and you must count yourself as one of the androids, who are not fooled into taking a fiction for reality.

Stephenson's *Snow Crash* also plays a knowing metafictional game with its reader; indeed, it is difficult to forget that one is reading a piece of self-consciously aware fiction when the main character's name is 'Hiro Protagonist.' The whole plot of Stephenson's book, however, also constantly underlines its own medium by foregrounding how 'language' has a profound effect on its user. Stephenson, throughout the book, is concerned with exploring how language—whether it be binary code, the 'machine language of the world'[151] that computers 'speak' and which underlies all the other computer languages, such as 'FORTRAN, BASIC, COBOL, LISP, Pascal, C, PROLOG, FORTH',[152] or the ancient Sumerian language, which Stephenson associates with the shared language spoken by all people in the Tower of Babel story—makes humans vulnerable to viral and ideological infection. Key to this question, of course, is how language changes the brain, and Stephenson riffs on the brain's neuroplasticity—its ability to rewire neural pathways and synapses due to changes in behaviour, environment, neural processes, thinking, emotions and bodily injury.[153] Due to this plasticity, hackers, like Da5id, are vulnerable to the snow crash virus because, when learning binary code, they are 'forming pathways in [their] brain. Deep structures'.[154] During the learning process, 'nerves grow new connections as you use them—the axons split and push their way between the dividing glial cells—your bioware self modifies—the software becomes part of the hardware'.[155] Later in the text, these brain changes are connected to a version of Noam Chomsky's 'deep structures', '... innate components of the brain that enable it to carry out certain formal kinds of operations on strings of symbols. Or, as [George] Steiner paraphrases Emmon Bach: These deep structures eventually lead to the actual patterning of the cortex with its immensely ramified yet, at the same time, "programmed" network of electrochemical and neurophysiological channels.'[156]

Stephenson's book sees the 'cure' for such vulnerability to language in terms of the 'nam-shub'—a sort of 'spell'—of Enki, an ancient Sumerian god. Enki's nam-shub supposedly 'inoculated' people against their vulnerability to the Sumerian language by bringing about the actual events that were later recounted in the Hebrew Tower of Babel story, where God confused the universal language of the builders of the tower. Thus, after the nam-shub of Enki, no one could understand the Sumerian language any more, and people were forced to create multiple languages so as to be able to communicate with each other. For Stephenson, it is the post-nam-shub-of-Enki-multiplicity-of-languages that renders the user of a particular language immune to the unconscious controlling 'power' of an 'ur-language'. He illustrates this by satirically baiting the types of ideological readings that overestimate the power of (post-nam-shub) languages to 'penetrate', 'programme' and 'manipulate' bodies: he names his plucky young heroine 'Y.T.'; he peppers the text with offhand dismissals of Marxism; he offers tongue-in-cheek celebrations of anarcho-capitalism; he depicts a consenting sexual relationship between the fifteen-year-old Y.T. and the much older Raven, who is Aleut; he associates the snow crash virus with female sexuality, and so on and so forth. Thus, throughout his text, Stephenson associates a susceptibility to the supposedly unconscious power of language with a susceptibility to ideology of all kinds; and, by playfully drawing attention to language and thus the language of his own text, Stephenson simultaneously invites such ideological readings and undercuts them, by connecting them to a fictional universal language that penetrates its hearers and produces unthinking followers. Languages are just languages, and the supposed penetration and manipulation of the hearer by such languages is revealed to be the shared fantasy of paranoiacs and power-trippers alike.

Snow Crash, insofar as it casts L. Bob Rife's junkie supporters as spreaders of 'the Word',[157] explicitly invokes William S. Burrough's (1914–1997) *Naked Lunch*. Burroughs, in the 'Atrophied Preface' of *Naked Lunch*, metafictionally draws the reader's attention to the dangers of 'The Word' and the medium of the text: 'Gentle Reader, The Word will leap on you with leopard man claws, it will cut off your fingers and toes like an opportunistic landcrab, it will hang you and catch your jissom like a scrutable dog, it will coil round your thighs like a bushmaster and inject a shot of rancid ectoplasm. . .'.[158] Burrough's suggestion for combatting 'The Word' is for the reader to cut into that which cuts him or her and rearrange it:

> The Word is divided into units which be all in one piece and should be so taken, but the pieces can be had in any order being tied up back and forth in and out fore and aft like an innaresting sex arrangement. This book spill off the page in all directions,

kaleidoscope of vistas. . . . Gentle Reader, we see God through
our assholes in the flashbulb of orgasm . . . Through these
orifices transmute your body . . . The way OUT is the way
IN . . .[159]

For Burroughs, the only ways to combat a language that injects
itself into you and wants to take you over is to remake your body
and 'The Word'; the 'Gentle Reader' is to become, in effect, a hacker
of language and the body, infusing both with illicit and illegal
practices. Burrough's work, then, draws the reader's attention not
only to what s/he reads but also to the medium of what s/he reads.
But, one wonders, if Burroughs himself is not overestimating the
power of language to manipulate and control every bit as much
as both L. Bob Rife and the ideologically driven critiques that
Stephenson satirizes.

As one of my final examples of metafiction in texts that take
posthumanism as their focus, I turn once again to Greg Bear's *Blood
Music*. In Bear's masterpiece, humanity experiences an existential
threat when it comes into contact with the superintelligent cells
that Vergil I. Ulam has illicitly created in his employer's lab. In
order to smuggle his 'noocytes' out of Genetron undetected, Vergil
injects them into himself. Bear's text gives the reader a series of
knowing metafictional winks and nods in a number of inventive
ways throughout: *Blood Music* name-checks Shelley's *Frankenstein*
many times, thereby claiming and highlighting its fiction lineage,
while 'Vergil I. Ulam' is an anagram of 'I am Gulliver', an obvious
nod to the satire of Jonathan Swift (1667–1745).[160] However, it is
the repeated instances of typographical play that serve best to draw
the reader's attention repeatedly to the fact that s/he is reading a
book. For example, when the noocytes, who have been growing
wildly inside him, first make contact with Vergil, the book's typeface
changes abruptly, just as we get a Gulliver joke:

'I've always been a very big fellow', Vergil murmured.

Everything[161]

The conversation continues in alternating typeface before Vergil
realizes that he isn't quite grasping what the noocytes are saying to
him; when they are called on to try to communicate a little more
clearly, they start introducing odd characters into the text:[162]

—What?

WORDS communicate with • share body structure external •
is this like • wholeness WITHIN • • totality • is EXTERNAL
alike

Later, after the noocytes have dissolved their creator and start to
spread and engulf the entire planet, the colony of noocytes inside
Dr Michael Bernard, a former colleague of Vergil's who has been
quarantined in Germany, use similar black dots to form chains in a
manner that seems to refer to the noocytes themselves. These chains
of black dots appear in the text just as the noocytes are trying to
explain to Dr Bernard that the concept of 'individual' can't really be
applied to them:[163]

—There are no individuals?

Not precisely. Information is shared between clusters of •••••••

Nor are the above examples the only form of inventive textual
play that Bear's book employs; as the noocytes absorb Dr Bernard
into themselves, shrinking him down to give him a 'taste' of their
existence, the text playfully and graphically reproduces his 'Alice in
Wonderland' moment:[164]

The suspension becomes a drawn-out consciousness, thought
pulled like a thread to fit a tiny needle's
eye————————————————————————————

A similar type of moment occurs in David Mitchell's *Cloud Atlas*,
where, at the end of the section called "Sloosha's Crossin' an'
Ev'rythin' After", the reader appears to be offered a look at Sonmi-
451's orison: we are told to 'Hold out [our] hands' and 'Look'.[165]
Now, if we perform those simple instructions, what we see in the
real world is the book, a physical copy of *Cloud Atlas* itself. Taken

together, these textually playful moments serve to underline the textuality of *Blood Music* in such a way that the reader is forced to confront the medium of the narrative—the ink marks on a page or pixels on a screen—that carry the text's meanings.

If such moments in these texts serve to disrupt the reader's suspension of disbelief and thereby disturb the reader's reading model, they do so by self-reflexively calling attention to the 'textuality' of their text—and the same can happen, of course, in whatever medium a text happens to be in—in a way that also serves to highlight the textuality of the book as a whole. What such texts do, in other words, is draw attention to the simple, brute fact that what is in front of the reader is composed of lifeless ink-marks on paper or the play of liquid crystal patterns on a display that are, in themselves, not simply reducible to or easily captured by the word 'meaning'. In other words, such reflexivity also highlights the text as information: that is, as something that is not just meaning, but that without which meaning cannot function.[166] Such textual moments also mark the intrusion of the brute reality or actuality of the text-environment into the reader's reading model: and the intrusion of the physical text itself—whatever its media—radically deflates any ideological reading built on solipsism or relativism by allowing the brute reality of the text-as-text to 'jam' representation by highlighting the difference between perception (the reader/viewer/gamer's engagement with story, plot, character, etc.) and reality (the book, film, game itself as an object): words and images are revealed to be just that—words and images, not reality. At the same time, reality-as-reality is revealed because the breakdown in representation uncovers the split between 'fact' and 'interpretation', 'observation' and 'theory', 'territory' and 'map', 'self' and 'ideology.' The text-environment reasserts itself beyond interpretation as information.

However, it must be said that the self-reflexive foregrounding of the mechanisms of representation in the texts discussed in this chapter is certainly nothing new; nor is it confined to texts that take posthumanism as their focus. Such self-reflexiveness can be seen in art of all kinds from across the centuries: it can be seen in individual paintings like Jan van Eyck's (c.1390–1441) *The Arnolfini Portrait* (1434), which shows the artist reflected in miniature in a convex mirror; in Ambrosius Bosschaert the Elder's (1573–1621) *Bouquet of Flowers in a Glass Vase* (1621), which shows a bouquet with flowers in bloom that do not bloom at the same time; in Diego Velázquez's (1599–1660) *Las Meninas* (1656), which shows what the subjects sitting for a portrait would have seen while being painted; in Laurence Sterne's (1713–1768) *The Life and Opinions of Tristram Shandy, Gentleman* (1759–1767) and its endless digressions that bring the circularity of writing to the reader's attention. Self-reflexivity also played a large part in the various Modernist movements of the early twentieth century, and can be seen over and over again in the work of the Italian and Russian Futurists, whose experiments with print and paint highlighted the difficulty of capturing the speed of modern life; self-reflexivity also features prominently in the work of James Joyce (1882–1941), whose *Ulysses* (1922) laid bare the powers and limits of language. Indeed, self-reflexiveness became so common in the various abstract and postmodern artistic movements of the late twentieth and early twenty-first centuries, that it has almost become something of a cliché. Obviously, this all-too-brief list is not intended to be exhaustive; it is merely to give an idea of how widespread and persistent self-reflexiveness actually is in art.

But perhaps the most emblematic image illustrating the breakdown of the representational apparatus can be seen in the painting called *La trahison des images* (1928–1929), by the Belgian surrealist artist René Magritte (1898–1967). This painting, which features a beautifully rendered pipe with the words, '*Ceci n'est pas une pipe.*' ('This is not a pipe.') written underneath, explicitly draws the viewer's attention to the simple fact that the 'pipe' in the painting is not—and never will be—a real pipe: it is just a representation of a pipe, and what the viewer is in reality looking at is oil paint marks on a canvas that has been stretched over a frame and hung on a wall in a gallery.

I mentioned above that the questions and problems of representation take on a particular urgency when it comes to science fiction texts like *Frankenstein, Blood Music, Dawn, Naked Lunch, Cloud Atlas, Snow Crash*, etc., which take posthumanism as their focus. This is because such texts are also explicitly concerned with the question of what separates living from non-living, human from nonhuman—machine, cyborg, animal, android, alien, clone, digital simulation, mugwump, and so on. Such texts repeatedly highlight how the 'line' separating human from posthuman is a porous one by teasing out the entanglements of the observer in the observed and posing complex philosophical questions about the 'life', 'sentience' and 'humanity' of nonhuman characters to the reader or viewer. In other words, science fiction texts that take posthumanism as their focus are constantly confronting and succumbing to the problem of anthropomorphism—the belief that the 'behaviour of animals and machines can be interpreted in terms of human folk psychology'.[167] This, perhaps, is to be expected in texts that attempt to extend the concepts of folk-psychology to nonhumans; but the reason the topic of anthropomorphism should be of particular import to anyone interested in a concrete posthumanism comes down to its being the root cause of most of the criticism directed at those who argue that machines or animals can—or could ever—display intelligence and/or subjectivity.[168] Think, for example, of the controversy surrounding whether or not Koko the gorilla is really using language to express herself,[169] or the criticism of the claim that intelligent behaviour exhibited by a machine could ever suggest subjectivity or even real intelligence.[170] The danger, as I suggested in Chapter 2, is that hasty claims of this type are prone to media hype, draw hostile criticism and result in inevitable disappointment, which combine to distort and trivialize actual work being done in animal cognition and AI.

So, when texts such as the ones discussed above disrupt the anthropomorphic suspension of disbelief by foregrounding the mechanisms of representation by simultaneously jamming them, thereby highlighting the difference between reality and perception, they also reveal, on a meta- or extra-textual level, that, for at least some of the questions that posthumanism poses, art overlaps with science and philosophy insofar as it questions the cognitive and folk-psychological mechanisms through which signs of 'life' and 'sentience' are projected by the reader/observer into something 'non-living'. For art, it is a question of the artificial 'life' or 'consciousness' that non-living ink marks, paint daubs, pixels, bits of information, etc., can display; but, for art focused on posthumanism, it is a doubly self-reflexive question about the signs of 'life' or 'sentience' displayed by machines, cyborgs, animals, androids, aliens, clones, etc., which are, in their turn, depicted in non-living ink marks, paint daubs, pixels, bits of information, etc. A critical, self-reflexive art, one that asks if the signs of life and sentience in non-living things are not simply projections from the reader/viewer, is thus central to posthumanism; such an art is always posing questions about what human minds project into what they look at and whether nonhuman artefacts, patterns, figures, systems, etc., should be explained in terms of folk-psychology. And it is to the philosophical register of these questions—and the difficulties of trying to answer them—that I turn in the following chapter.

CHAPTER FIVE

Philosophical Posthumanism

As will be recalled, the concrete posthumanism I've been defining and refining throughout this book so far has two major, but intertwined, aspects: (a) the distributed cognition and distributed embodiment of humans + tools, which obviously includes all manner of technology; and (b) that which blurs the distinction between human, animal and machine. In the previous chapter, I considered concrete posthumanism in conjunction with how science is represented in certain sociocultural theories; I also explored how the representation of posthumanism in science fictional accounts of technologically enhanced humans and non-humans opened up questions about posthumanism in art. In this chapter, I'll continue with my exploration of concrete posthumanism by turning to philosophy, particularly philosophy that is explicitly concerned with AI, robots and animals. In the first major section of this chapter, I'll be focusing on examples from the branch of philosophy known as 'analytic philosophy'; very broadly speaking, analytic philosophy is characterized by making use of the evidence provided by the natural sciences, as well as emphasizing clear and precise argumentation; thus, it often makes use of both formal logic and mathematics. In the second major section, I will be focusing on the branch of philosophy that has come to be known as 'continental philosophy'; again, speaking very broadly, continental philosophy concerns itself with the conditions that it claims underlie all possible experience, including science; thus, it tends to be critical of the view that the natural sciences are the only or most accurate way of understanding natural phenomena.[1] In the third and final major section of this chapter, I'll explore some of the recent—highly speculative and not uncontroversial—philosophical speculations on the impact of technology and AI on the future of humanity.

Animals and robots

We want to know about animal minds because animals are important in our lives. We hunt them, we husband them, and we eat them. Some people think that animals are given to us by nature (or by god) to treat as we like and do with as we will. Other people worry about animal welfare to the extent that their opinions dictate their diet, their lifestyle, and sometimes their hostilities. There is no question that our prejudices about animal minds influence the lives we lead, our laws, and our politics.

We want to know about robot minds, because robots are becoming increasingly important in our lives, and we want to know how to manage them. As robots become more sophisticated, should we aim to control them or trust them? Should we regard them as extensions of our own bodies, extending our control over the environment, or as responsible beings in their own right? Our future policies towards robots and animals will depend largely upon our attitude towards their mentality.[2]

As the above citation from David McFarland's *Guilty Robots, Happy Dogs* makes clear, human lives, politics and ethics are already—and will continue to be—entangled in questions that have to do with animals and robots; and thinking about these entanglements demands situating ourselves on the shifting borders of ethology, biology, psychology, robotics and philosophy— that is, within the shifting, interdisciplinary borders of concrete posthumanism. Animals and robots are central to questions of concrete posthumanism for two major reasons. First, animals and robots are an integral part of posthumanist distributed cognition: animals have long been an integral part of agriculture, industry and transport, while robots and AI are becoming an increasingly integral part of modern life, leisure and industry. Thus, if we are to understand clearly what is at stake in distributed cognition, we need to grapple with how those entities not only help make that type of cognition possible, but also with how evolving distributions of cognition will continue to extend our 'humanness' into 'posthumanness'. Second, concrete posthumanism is concerned with what challenges hard-and-fast distinctions between humans and nonhumans—e.g., animals and machines and so on: thus, posthumanism is concerned with thinking that not only explores what humans, animals, robots and AI do (and don't) share, but also challenges how we might traditionally view and conceive of those entities. As such, concrete posthumanism allows us to see possibilities that might ordinarily be erased or hidden by uncritical, received or fixed ideas about what animals, robots, AI and human beings supposedly 'are'. In the discussion that follows, I'll be focusing on McFarland's wonderfully nuanced and hugely informative consideration of what he calls 'alien minds'—that is, the minds of robots and animals—to guide and inform my exploration of the complex, often dense—and oftentimes overwhelming—tangled web of the stances, concepts, issues and debates that frequently frame philosophical discussions of what links and separates animals, robots and humans. I would also ask the reader to compare and contrast what's explored in this chapter with the discussion in Chapter 2 and, especially, Chapter 3.

Stances

Towards the end of his book, McFarland helpfully sketches the key philosophical 'stances'—pragmatically justified ways of viewing the world[3]—that those who work with and think about animals and robots often adopt, whether consciously or unconsciously:

> *Anthropomorphism*—The behaviour of animals and machines can be interpreted in terms of human folk psychology.
>
> *Materialism*—Everything in the world is material, made up of some combination of matter and energy (alternatives are idealism and dualism).
>
> *The intentional stance*—Anything that behaves in a 'rational' way is behaving 'as if' it had mental states.
>
> *Behaviourism*—Invoking mental states is not necessary in explaining observed behaviour.
>
> *Eliminative materialism*—Explanations in terms of mental states will eventually be eliminated by explanations in physical terms.

Naturalism—Everything in the world is part of nature and will eventually be explained in scientific terms.

Realism—Mental states really do exist and take up space in the brain.

Functionalism—Any state of affairs that plays the role of a mental state is a mental state, whether it be in the brain or not.[4]

Such philosophical stances do a lot of interpretive work since they 'frame' how an object is viewed. For example, someone who adopts a behaviourist stance would try to explain the behaviour of a robot or an animal without invoking concepts like 'mind' or 'subjectivity', while an individual who adopts an eliminative materialist stance would argue that folk psychology—common sense notions of the mind that use concepts like 'beliefs' and 'experiences'—will eventually be explainable in terms of biochemistry or biophysics, and a person who adopts a functionalist stance would argue that animals and robots could be said to have mental states, so long as something that plays a role analogous to a mental state—such as desire—can be observed in those entities.

These different philosophical stances have found their way into fields of study like robotics and ethology—that is, the scientific and objective study of animal (and sometimes robotic) behaviour—because, as McFarland points out, 'philosophers have moved more and more towards a naturalistic viewpoint, looking to science to provide some of the answers', while 'scientists are involving themselves more and more in philosophy'.[5] fields such as robotics and ethology have essentially become interdisciplinary, a circumstance that is itself due in no small part to the nature of the evidence found in those fields: very often, results fit quite well with different—and sometimes mutually contradicting—stances at the same time. For instance, certain experimental evidence might support adopting both a realist and a functionalist stance. This situation, says McFarland, implies that stances are not chosen for purely empirical reasons: 'The stances that [scientists] adopt are consistent with the evidence, but it is clear that they do not adopt their chosen stance for empirical reasons, since the evidence is also fully consistent with the alternative stance.'[6]

To illustrate the slippery nature of evidence, McFarland uses the example of his dog, named Border:

when I see Border entering the kitchen, and heading for the cat's food, I may assume (taking an anthropomorphic stance) that she thinks like a human, and approaches the food with the preformed intent of eating it. If I dismiss this idea as unscientific, I can adopt a behaviourist stance that accounts for the dog's behaviour in terms of associative learning—the cat's dish is associated with food, the kitchen is associated with the cat's dish, etc.—and so there is a chain of stimulus and response that leads the dog to the cat's food. Putting on my philosophical hat, I can suppose that the dog is part of an intentional system and, therefore, has a belief about the cat's food in the sense that the dog has something that functions like a belief. I am now adopting a type of functionalist stance. On the other hand, taking a realist stance, I can suppose that the dog might have brain states that are (in principle) identifiable as beliefs.[7]

But, even for someone as richly experienced in the science of both robotics and animal behaviour as McFarland, drawing a hard-and-fast line between animal, robot and human sometimes appears to be difficult. For example, the various attempts of researchers to demonstrate things like language capacity or reasoning capacity in animals have ended, says McFarland, in 'signal failure'.[8] And yet, when discussing Richard Byrne's *The Thinking Ape*,[9] McFarland raises some doubt about those apparent failures:

After the death of her own baby, Washoe, a chimpanzee taught to sign American Sign Language, was given an infant chimp, which she adopted. The human caretakers did not teach the infant Loulis to sign, and indeed they stopped signing at all in [his] presence. Washoe used both demonstration (with careful attention to Loulis' gaze direction) and moulding of Loulis' hands to teach [him] to sign. Washoe herself had been taught by humans, who sometimes mould her hands into the correct configuration and put the hands through the necessary movement: this is what she did several times with the infant Loulis. The direct effect of Washoe's demonstration and moulding is hard to measure, but certainly Loulis learnt many signs during the years in which [he] saw no human sign and got no human encouragement for doing so: after 5 years [he] reliably used 51 signs, often in two-sign combinations like 'person come'.[10]

Here, McFarland seems to accept not only that Washoe did indeed learn sign language, but also that she managed to teach it to her adopted baby, Loulis. Now, I'm not suggesting that McFarland is contradicting himself here; on the contrary, I'm simply remaking the same point he does elsewhere in his book: the difficulty of drawing a hard-and-fast line between human and animal seems to be a direct consequence of the irreducible ambiguity of the evidence, which permits the simultaneous adoption of multiple stances with respect to the 'same' evidence. In what follows, I'll be considering some more of the research evidence that makes drawing hard-and-fast lines between humans, animals and robots difficult, as well as assess how that evidence can displace some common conceptions of humans, animals, robots and AI. However, I want to be very clear that I won't be arguing in what follows that all the differences between animal, human and machine are somehow 'not real' or are 'merely discursive'; on the contrary, I'll be arguing that some of those differences are perhaps not as decisive as they might at first appear. This, of course, is absolutely not to suggest that there are no differences between these entities; there remain very clear differences between humans and animals: snails or hamsters, for example, do not design aircraft or play *Grand Theft Auto*.

Extended selves: Humans, animals, robots

As I have suggested many times throughout this book, posthumanism is called for by the entanglements of human + tools and technology, which can be seen most obviously in distributed cognition, which is performed by an extended self that incorporates nonhuman and nonbiological components. McFarland, throughout *Guilty Robots, Happy Dogs*, is also interested in the idea of an extended self, which suggests that a 'self' is not 'unified' or 'localizable' in a particular place, like the body or skull:

> When someone dies, parts of their extended self are left behind— their shopping list, for example. The person, when alive, created the shopping list, and did so as an extension of part of themselves, their memory in particular. . . . Of course, we are not always aware of the entirety of our extended selves. I may make a

shopping list and then forget that I have done it. In fact, I am not always aware of things that I know in the ordinary sense.[11]

McFarland's notion of the extended self, then, cuts, just like distributed cognition does, across the categories of biological/ nonbiological, human/nonhuman, natural/artificial, body/non-body, inside/outside, memory/forgetting and so on. As such, the extended self of distributed cognition also overlaps with what Jacques Derrida calls the *pharmakon*, which, as I have suggested in previous chapters, also cannot be contained in neatly opposed categories:

> If the *pharmakon* is 'ambivalent', it is because it constitutes the medium in which opposites are opposed, the movement and the play that links them among themselves, reverses them or makes one side cross over into the other (soul/ body, good/ evil, inside/ outside, memory/ forgetfulness, speech/ writing, etc.). . . . The *pharmakon* is the movement, the locus, and the play: (the production of) difference . . . . even though it 'precedes' the opposition between different effects, even though it preexists differences as effects, does not have the punctual simplicity of a *coincidentia oppositorum*. It is from this fund that dialectics draws its reserves.[12]

Because the pharmakonic extended self cannot, of necessity, simply said to be 'human', then it should not be in the least surprising that there is evidence of the extended self in animals; after all, as I showed in Chapter 2's discussion of neuroplasticity and neuroprosthetics, experiments have repeatedly shown that monkeys in neuroengineering labs routinely incorporate nonbiological apparatuses like robotic arms or wheelchairs into their cognitive maps.

McFarland touches on the notion of an animal's extended self in his discussion of studies of animal metacognition, which use tests to monitor indirectly an animal's awareness of its own knowledge.[13] For instance, the studies reviewed by Shettleworth and Sutton seem to indicate that some dolphins and primates experience stress when given a task that involves matching a symbol to a sample, but do not know which symbol to choose. According to McFarland, however, these metacognition tests 'do not distinguish between memory proper (a representation in the brain) and biochemical prompting that acts as an external "memory" in much the same way that a shopping list does.'[14] And it is not just the bigger-brained 'smarter' animals like humans, dolphins and primates that share in the concept of an extended self; just as humans deposit information in the environment in the form of writing, pictures, structures, etc., so too do other animals in the form of structures, such as nests, or chemical deposits, such as pheromones.[15]

Closely related to the notions of distributed cognition and the extended self is tool-use, which is usually defined as the use of an external object as a functional extension of the body in attaining an immediate goal.[16] Although animal tool use has been studied for many decades, deciding whether or not it actually 'requires cognition remains controversial. Part of the problem is that many people, including some scientists, tend to attribute cognition to an animal when it does something that would require cognition in a human.'[17] In other words, it is too easy to assume that an animal has human mental qualities just because it appears to do something that would ordinarily require human levels of intelligence. The oft-cited example of birds—various species of waders, plovers and doves—that act like they have a broken wing in order to deceive predators and lure them away from their nests, serves as a useful way of showing how difficult it can be to not be lured into the trap of assuming that just because an animal acts in a particular way, it must therefore be endowed with the human levels of cognition required were a human to perform that same act. We might imagine that the bird performing such a distraction display believes 'that the predator will be deceived because it automatically pursues an apparently injured prey', or that the bird believes 'that the predator will be deceived because it believes that the bird is injured'.[18] In such cases, we would be ascribing to the bird what's known as a strong 'theory of mind'—that is, a theory relating to the probable states of mind of another being, which here would be the predator. However, the problem is that we may be simply projecting what amounts to a theory of mind about the mind of another creature onto the bird when it does not in fact have one: it could be the case that 'in reality the bird has no theory about the predator', and that it is just simply reacting 'in a way that is effective, as a result of either instinct or learning, or both. From the evolutionary point of view, it does not matter how the bird deceives the predator, provided that its communication is effective.'[19]

In other words, if a complex distraction display boils down to just simple reflex, then it is also possible that other complex, apparently cognitive behaviour in animals, such as tool use or language use, is also reflexive and thus requires no cognitive ability at all. The assumption that the bird is displaying near human-level cognition to distract a predator is therefore open to the charge of philosophical 'liberalism'—ascribing a mind to something that doesn't have one.

One of the main reasons that McFarland counsels us to be careful about ascribing human-like cognition to animals comes down to the simple fact that robots can easily be programmed to display pretty much all of the behaviour found in animals: for example, there 'are some animals that can recognise themselves in a mirror or film—so can some robots'; there are 'some animals that can imitate vocalisations and behaviour of others—so can some robots'; there are 'some animals that seem to demonstrate reasoning—so can some robots'; there are 'some animals that can perform complex feats of navigation—so can some robots'; some 'animals seem to indicate that they are in pain or feel ill—so can some robots'; and there are 'some animals that can apparently remember whether they know something (metacognition)—so can some robots.'[20] In fact, says McFarland, 'probably all the phenomena that have been cited as evidence that animals have some kind of mentality have also been demonstrated in robots'.[21] Because robots that display such complex behaviour have been 'programmed in a purely procedural way', a purely behaviourist stance with respect to animal behaviour is always possible.[22]

Of qualia and quails

Despite the parsimonious explanatory power afforded by adopting a behaviourist stance, there nevertheless seems to be some evidence suggesting that animals experience what are known as 'qualia'— a philosophical term used to describe subjective qualities or experiences, such as how a marshmallow tastes and feels or what a rumbling stomach or toothache feels like. For example, studies by Rozin and Kalat, which involve rats that avoid certain foods that have made them sick in the past, suggest the existence of animal qualia: the rats seem to avoid foods associated with sickness based on a general sensation of sickness rather than the detection of specific chemicals in the food because they do not need to actually eat the food in order to feel sickened by it.[23] McFarland says that these studies not only imply 'that animals are capable of experiencing general sensations of sickness or health', but also 'that animals, having only once experienced the taste or smell (or sight in the case of pigeons) of a novel food that subsequently made them sick, never touch that food again', which indicates 'that the distinctive novel taste or smell sticks in the memory, just as distinctive taste and smell qualia do in humans. These discoveries do not prove that animals experience qualia but they are suggestive of it, in the sense that having and remembering such experiences is necessary for qualia.'[24] And, although the fact that animals seem to respond to other general states, such as well-being and boredom 'does not prove that animals have subjectivity', they too are 'suggestive' of it.[25] It would seem that qualia are not sufficient grounds for drawing a hard-and-fast line between humans and animals after all.

In addition to qualia, imitation is also something that is tied up in humans with notions of the identity of the self and others: for instance, imitating someone else's actions involves observing them carefully, memorizing the sequence of their movements and then translating those movements into your own body's movements; imitation is also often seen as the root of empathy in that through it we come to understand how another person thinks and feels.[26] When it comes to his discussion of imitation in animals, McFarland is characteristically careful not to conflate all imitative behaviour in animals with human imitation; nevertheless, he does note that 'true imitation'—that is, human-level imitation—has been observed in animals: in a study, a group of quail were allowed to watch other groups of quail obtaining rewards, by either pecking at or stepping on a treadle.[27] It turned out that the birds that watched others receiving food for stepping on the treadle were 'more likely to adopt the same behaviour when it came to their turn to operate the treadle. If they did not see their comrades being rewarded, then they did not copy them.'[28] Imitation, however, is not confined to just biological entities. As McFarland notes, there have also been 'numerous demonstrations of robots imitating people, or other robots'.[29] The robot researchers who built these robots were inspired by imitation and social learning in animals and humans to create controllers for their autonomous robots. To get a robot to imitate another body requires that the robot has information about its own body and the body that it is trying to imitate. This information does not have to be designed in, but can be learned. The robot perceives its own body primarily through propriocention (just like us), and perceives other agents through external senses.[30]

The robot is able to match its own body to what it sees: 'It is a short step from here to a robotic "machine self" [i.e., the 'self' that includes the ability to distinguish between self-made movements and other movements, to imitate others, and to respond to oneself in a mirror] and a further step to a robotic "objective self" [i.e. the 'self' that knows about itself as an object in the world]'.[31]

But an interesting question starts to emerge here: how can it be said for sure that the robots' imitation of each other is any different from the imitation displayed by the quails? If we can never quite shut the door on the possibility that what seems like cognition in animals is simply programmable procedural behaviour because experiments have shown that robots can imitate all the animal behaviour suggestive of mentality, then there would appear to be no fundamental way of distinguishing between a robot's and an animal's behaviour. And the is only further complicated by what appears to be happening when a robot imitates a person: 'When we have a case of a robot imitating a person, we have a primitive sort of reciprocity. . . . Would we ascribe mental qualities to it? Maybe so, maybe not, but note that if we do not ascribe such qualities on the basis of imitation by a robot, it is difficult to argue that we should ascribe such qualities on the basis of imitation by an animal.'[32] In other words, should one simply rule out imitation in animals because a robot can be programmed to do it? And what if we approached this question from another angle, say in a manner similar to Cruse and Schilling in Chapter 3 above? Would it not be possible, if we ascribe 'mentality'—however minimal it may be—to a quail that imitates the behaviour of another, to then also ascribe minimal mentality to the imitative robot? Considered from this perspective, it would seem that qualia and subjectivity are graspable in terms of programmable procedure; and, because these qualities are also qualities of the human mind, does this not also suggest that human subjectivity is—at least to a degree—'procedural' and 'programmable'? Is it at all possible to say that the human mind is not quite as 'mindful' as we might think?

Mostly mindless humans?

So, is there then a case to be made for human mindlessness? How much 'mind' might humans be said to have? As was discussed in Chapters 2 and 3, a stimulus must be of a particular intensity and of a particular duration before it crosses the threshold of human subjective experience. According to the cognitive scientist, David Kirsh, the famous roboticist Rodney Brooks has claimed that some 97 per cent of human activity is non-representational.[33] Some psychological studies have shown that there 'may be little or no direct introspective access to higher order cognitive processes'.[34] That is, when people report 'on the processes mediating the effects of a stimulus on a response, they do not do so on the basis of any true introspection. Instead, their reports are based on a priori, implicit causal theories, or judgments about the extent to which a particular stimulus is a plausible cause of a given response.'[35] This finding is also borne out in, for example, a study examining why people gave money to a street musician.[36] After observing the average rate at which people gave money to a street musician, researchers then had a confederate throw some money into the street musician's hat as people approached; they found that people were eight times more likely to give money if someone else gave money. However, when those who gave money were asked why they had done so, 'they all failed to attribute their action to the fact that they had seen someone else give money. Rather, they claimed that something else had been the cause—"I liked the song he was playing" or "I felt sorry for the guy" or "I had some extra change in my pocket".'[37] However, the clear 'key factor was the action of another person. Yet when our study's subjects thought about the reasons for their choices, not one of them hit upon the true cause. That finding illustrates a general psychological principle: People are often poor at recognizing why they behave as they do.'[38] In other words, even when people seem to be making a conscious, rational decision like giving money to someone, they do not seem to be very conscious of why they are doing it and often come up with rationalizations that simply ignore the true influences on and causes of their actions.

McFarland too documents a lot of human mindlessness in *Guilty Robots, Happy Dogs*. To understand this mindlessness better, I want to dig a little deeper into McFarland's explanation—which follows along the lines of the distinction offered by Gilbert Ryle[39]—of the difference between 'explicit knowledge' and 'procedural knowledge'. Explicit knowledge (also called 'knowledge that') is knowledge that is available for a system—a person or a machine—to use; explicit knowledge is explicit information about a person, place or thing that can be articulated into statements like 'I know that the cat is black' or 'I know that she is an editor.' Procedural knowledge (also called 'knowledge how' or 'know-how') is knowledge that is embedded in a system and is not available for use outside the procedure to which it is tied; an example of procedural knowledge would be riding a bicycle, which you can't really use for anything other than riding a bike or easily trade with another person.[40]

The ability to manipulate explicit knowledge is an important aspect of human mental activity; however, it only forms part of the picture, says McFarland, because many modern machines manipulate explicit representations 'but this does not imply that they have minds'; at the same time, we should also be 'free to recognise that there may be some animals ... that can make use of explicit knowledge', such as in the case of experiments on rats that show they are less willing to work for a reward in one situation that has been devalued in another.[41] And, as McFarland points out, it is difficult to explain these results using a behaviourist stance, even though the same behaviour can be reproduced in a robot.[42] So, it would appear that animals and machines can, like humans, manipulate explicit knowledge; and yet, peculiarly, to do so does not appear to necessarily require a mind.

If it is not possible to say that only a human mind can manipulate explicit knowledge, nor even possible to say for certain that a mind is required to do so, what exactly would be the guarantee of an activity that only a fully conscious human mind can perform? What about rationality? Certainly, mental activity is 'characterised by a certain degree of rationality, and by certain types of feelings'.[43] But, says McFarland, rationality cannot be taken for the mark of a mind, either. To make this point, he adopts Daniel Dennett's famous conception of the intentional stance.[44] According to Dennett, to adopt the intentional stance towards something is to ascribe beliefs, desires, and rationality to it in order to explain or predict its behaviour. And what does Dennett mean by rationality? He means something that has been designed for a purpose; this is why he can say (as he often does) that 'Mother Nature'—the process of evolution—is 'rational'. This does not mean that Dennett believes that 'Mother Nature' or evolution has a mind: Dennett sees it more in terms of a 'free-floating rationale'[45] through which 'Mother Nature' or evolution selects particular adaptations.[46] In other words, the process of evolution produces the same results that a person making rational choices would, even though it has no mind at all: given this, it appears that rationality cannot be the necessary mark of a mind.

So, if manipulating explicit knowledge and rationality do not constitute the true mark of a fully conscious human mind, then what about the kind of human 'know-how' required for doing something like, say, riding a bicycle? Would that be the true mark of a human mind? It would appear not. Explicit knowledge relies on explicit representations, whereas know-how depends upon implicit representations: according to McFarland, in order to

> know how to touch my nose with my eyes closed, I have to know, amongst other things, the length of my forearm. This information is represented implicitly in my kinaesthetic system. Similarly, to ride a bicycle, I must learn to coordinate numerous kinaesthetic systems to do with steering and balance. I can then say that I know how to ride a bicycle, but this type of knowledge is . . . procedural knowledge [which] has to do with accomplishing tasks. However, doing x does not always imply knowing how to do x.[47]

So, it would seem that those hallmarks we might ordinarily think of as guaranteeing a fully present or conscious human mind—the manipulation of explicit representations, rationality and the specific technical know-how needed to do something like riding a bike—aren't as definitive as we may have imagined, since processes, entities or beings that do not seem to have or need minds seem to be perfectly capable of bearing them. In fact, when scrutinized, even mathematics, language and metacognition are perhaps not as solid a marker of solely human cognition as they might have seemed:

computers are very adept at manipulating symbols at speeds and in quantities that cannot be matched by humans; Washoe the chimp seems to have been able to teach the sign language she learned to her adopted baby without human intervention; and studies suggest that metacognition may be present in primates and dolphins. Now, once again, I'm not at all suggesting here that there are no differences between humans and animals—that would simply be stupid; what I am suggesting, however, is that the usual lines of exclusion that are drawn to separate human, animal and robot do not always appear to stand up to scrutiny: instead, such 'lines' seem to be anything but continuous or straight.

Mindless economics and pleasure

Economics further problematizes apparently cut-and-dried differences between human, animal and robot behaviour. The field of 'animal economics' applies 'human economic principles to animal behaviour'.[48] According to McFarland, animal economics treats animals as if they were 'shoppers' that obey the laws of consumer economics: the central idea is that animals spend time and energy in a way that parallels the expenditure of time and money by humans. So, an animal's 'budget' is the time and energy it can expend, which, in turn, put constraints on its behaviour. McFarland continues: 'over the past thirty years it has been shown that many types of animal, when put to the test, obey the laws of consumer economics in very many respects. This is not all that surprising once you realise that the microeconomic laws are basically a way of expressing the logic of choice'.[49] In other words, a person, animal, or even a robot must expend energy (which humans also store as money) to obtain necessary resources; because of this, people, animals and robots must all face the same kind of situations, so they 'all home in on the same (logical) laws governing economic behaviour'.[50] For instance, those who study animal welfare pay close attention to how flexible an animal's 'demand functions' are and what that flexibility says about the relative importance of an animal's various activities—for example, feeding, grooming, and territory defence.[51]

What is important to realize here is that such economic behaviour of animals does not necessarily need to be 'mindful', because animal economics are also robot economics: 'here are some fundamentals that apply to all animals (and self-sufficient robots), whether they have mental abilities or not. All animals depend upon certain resources, and all animals must be able to monitor three aspects of these vital resources.'[52] The three aspects of vital resources that must be attended to are 'state, availability, and accessibility'; in combination, these three aspects create the free-floating logic that influences the decisions not only of mindless animals and robots, but also apparently mindful humans: it is this 'combination that influence[s] your decision. It is much the same for other things that you might decide to do. It is much the same for animals, and it is much the same for autonomous robots.'[53] The point with animal economics is that 'it is possible to design a robot with quite complex behaviour, or to account for quite complex animal behaviour, in terms that require no recourse to mental phenomena'.[54] The issue here is that yet again, human economic behaviour does not necessarily have to be guided by a conscious, rational mindfulness.

According to McFarland, animals and robots are quite adept at trading-off competing pressures and arriving at the best or optimal outcome. McFarland cites the work of Reto Zach, which neatly outlines the trade-off in the foraging behaviour of crows that feed on shellfish on Mandarte Island, British Columbia,[55] not too far from where I am writing this.[56] Zach noted that the crows scoured for whelks at low tide, usually selecting the largest ones, which they then tried to smash by dropping them from a certain height onto the rocks below. When Zach tried dropping whelks of various sizes from different heights, he discovered that the number of times a whelk has to be dropped in order to break it is related to the height from which it was dropped. No surprise there; but the cleverness of the crows revealed itself when Zach worked out that the lowest flying cost of energy to the crow is incurred if the whelks are dropped from about 5 metres, which is what the crows usually did: in other words, the crows were 'calculating' the trade-off between the cost in terms of energy required to lift the whelk and the height of the drop. According to McFarland, 'the crows have somehow been programmed to exploit this particular feature of the foraging situation' because 'an animal cannot devote more energy to an activity than it has available. Nor can it devote more time than is available.'[57] The choices these crows make are 'made in accordance to some maximisation principle (always choose the top option in the ranking)', which 'maximises a quantity, usually called *utility*'.[58]

In expanding his discussion of the economics of utility, McFarland turns to a study conducted by Michel Cabanac and Marta Balaskó on rats.[59] In Cabanac and Balaskó's study, the rats had to make trade-offs between thirst, water palatability and cold discomfort; however, during the study, the rats showed a preference for water flavoured with saccharin, an artificial sweetener which was of no nutritional benefit to them: they simply liked the sweet taste. According to Cabanac and Balaskó, this suggests that the rats were making 'their behavioural choices so as to maximise their sensory pleasure';[60] the experimenters, in other words, are claiming that there is an explicit quantity—'pleasure'—that acts as the 'common currency' of decision-making in animals,[61] which, of course, links us back to the philosophy of utilitarianism, mentioned briefly in Chapter 3.

Cabanac's interpretation of pleasure is informed by somewhat similar studies he performed on humans. In these sessions, young male volunteers were asked to walk on a treadmill in a climatically controlled laboratory for 300 metres.[62] In some sessions, the researchers controlled the speed of the treadmill, while in the others, they controlled the gradient; in the sessions where the researchers controlled the speed, the volunteers could control the gradient, while in the others, the volunteers could control the speed. Both the stride rate and heart rate of the volunteers were measured and the volunteers were asked to rate the 'pleasure or displeasure aroused' in their chest and legs;[63] interestingly, the 'outcome was that the subjects adjusted speed and slope reciprocally, with the result that the duration of sessions was constant'.[64] The subjects, in other words, adjusted whatever variable they had control over to produce a near-constant climbing speed, amount of exertion and their level of pleasure by minimizing their displeasure and maximizing their pleasure.[65] What Cabanac's experiments strongly suggest, according to McFarland, is 'that animals have an internal coherence (of their behaviour and physiology), and that this is also true of humans'.[66] It would seem that the finding that people behave as they do in situations such as the treadmill experiments, lends support to Cabanac's view that animals and humans operate in the same way by trying to maximize explicit pleasure; this further implies that animals experience qualia, are capable of subjectivity, and have a self.[67]

Cabanac's experiments could, however, also be taken to suggest that this 'self' does not have to amount to a 'mind', or even a subjective experience. 'Amongst scientists', according to McFarland, 'there are two basic views as to what is going on here'.[68] The first view—the 'automaton view'—holds that the behavioural and physiological adjustments noted in Cabanac's experiments are automatic, and that the system—the human or rat body— economically produces the best compromise among the competing demands. The body thus acts homeostatically, like a self-adjusting cybernetic machine. The second view—the hedonic view, which is basically Cabanac's position—holds that behavioural adjustments are carried out to maximize the feeling of pleasure and minimize that of displeasure. McFarland notes that the 'fundamental difference between the two views is that in the automaton view the quantity maximized is implicit, while in the hedonic view it is explicit'.[69] Because such compromise adjustments are common to all animals, including humans, it would seem that we are back to the problem noted above: if, on the one hand, animals and humans 'share' pleasure, this suggests that they also share something like qualitative experience; if, on the other hand, these adjustments are entirely automatic, then the feelings of pleasure or displeasure cannot be the cause the adjustments in behaviour. When viewed in this way, the human (or animal) 'experience' of pleasure would appear to be surplus to requirements. If, however, both views are correct, and the behaviour is caused automatically and the pleasure generated also plays a causal role, then we have a case of 'overdetermination', which means that 'some of the properties are causally irrelevant'.[70]

Once again, the difficulty here is perhaps less that animals behave automatically, than the possibility that humans do and that subjective feelings of pleasure amount to an epiphenomenal illusion that just sits atop an automatic response without actually having an influence on that response. This difficulty is connected to what is known as the 'exclusion problem', which concerns the problem of how subjective mental events like qualia seem to be excluded as the causes of the 'realizers'—the physical brain properties and structures such as neurons firing—that give rise to them: in other words, neurons firing cause mental states, not the other way round. The exclusion problem as it relates to humans (and, for that matter, animals), however, can also be understood as a version of a classic problem relating to AI and robots: the 'symbol-grounding problem', which concerns the problem of how an apparently meaningless syntactic string of arbitrary symbols becomes 'grounded' in meaning for an AI or a robot, instead of just remaining parasitical on the meanings in our heads. This parasitism is what leads to the kind of philosophically liberalist assumptions that allow a simple chatbot to pass the Turing test.[71]

The symbol-grounding problem is a version of John Searle's famous 'Chinese room' thought experiment, which is basically a rewriting of Alan Turing's imitation game discussed in Chapter 3: imagine you do not know Chinese and are locked in a room with lots of Chinese characters on cards and a set of rules written in English that tells you how to combine the characters; cards with strings of Chinese characters written on them are passed to you through a slit; you compare them to the characters you already have and, using your rulebook, you assemble your own string of Chinese characters, which you then pass back through the slit.[72] What you are actually doing, unbeknownst to you, is answering questions in Chinese without knowing what any of the characters mean; however, to those outside the room, your answers appear to be perfectly fluent and intelligible. While locked in the room, you are, says Searle, simply doing what a computer does: blindly manipulating symbols that mean nothing to you. But, as McFarland and philosophers such as Andy Clark have pointed out, we don't actually have any direct verifiable knowledge about the true nature of our understanding of a language. As such, our understanding of language might actually simply be—albeit sophisticated one—a look-up table that only appears to involve semantics.[73] Indeed, a very recent study has shown that the brain adds new words to a 'visual dictionary' that stores whole words as pictures, without any apparent regard for their actual meaning.[74] What I would suggest, then, is that the symbol-grounding problem and the exclusion problem can be seen to be related problems insofar as they both revolve on the question of how meaning arises from the 'meaningless syntax' of underlying processes, whether they be empty symbols or neurons firing: humans, it would appear, also suffer from the same type of problem as AIs and robots in that respect. So, how can we get from such 'syntax' to 'semantics'?

Values and teleological functionalism

As I noted above, adopting a functionalist stance is to adopt a strategy that holds that certain entities, such as mental ones, are best described in terms of the functional role that they play within a system. So, for a functionalist philosopher like David Lewis, a certain mental state (M) occupies an M-role and it does not matter what kind of state occupies the M-role, so long as it is a physical state, identifiable in the usual scientific manner.[75] As such, it 'could be a neural state, a chemical state, or a state of a silicon chip. Thus, in theory, an invertebrate, a vertebrate, or a robot could have a mental state M, so long as it occupied the M-role. In other words, the same mental states could be caused in different ways in different agents'.[76] Using the functionalist stance also makes it possible to draw parallels between different species: for example, even though an octopus (an invertebrate) and a cat (a vertebrate) may have very different nervous systems, by adopting the functionalist stance, I can make the argument that they both feel pain despite their significant physical differences. And, as McFarland points out, adopting the functionalist stance 'opens the door to the possibility of robot minds'.[77] In other words, if one wants to talk about subjects like robot or animal minds, one necessarily begins to adopt a functionalist stance. From the point of view of functionalism, animals and robots—even humans!—can be said to have mental states so long as they are possessed of some identifiable mechanism or other that can be said to function like—or play the role of—that state. At the same time, however, one must also be careful about being too liberal in one's functionalism, which results in attributing minds to things that do not have one, like, for example, a temperamental moped; this is why a dose of the behaviourist stance is never a bad thing.

Adopting the functionalist stance also makes it possible to argue that a particular mental state is not reducible to a particular physical state; for example, my physical brain state does not have to be the exact same for me to do something each time, like sit down with my computer and write something: even though I may be in a different mood, or feeling jet-lagged in Italy, or hungry, or drowsy from the anti-histamine I just took, I can, nevertheless, still write. In other words, my underlying brain state does not have to be exactly the same each time for me to be able to do something over and over. In fact, such a scenario would be impossible: as I showed in the discussion of neuroprosthetics in Chapter 2, not every single neuron fires, nor fires in either the same order or the same way every time a particular the action is performed; nevertheless, an overall statistical pattern of information is discernible, which a computer can then use to predict the desired movements of the neuroprosthesis. Because the 'same' mental state can thus arise from 'different' physical states, mental states are said to 'supervene' on physical states, and thus do not seem to be entirely reducible to them, a situation that is also known as the 'multiple realisability of mental states'.[78] Supervenience would seem to suggest, then, that functionalism allows for negotiating a way out of the exclusion problem: for example, a feeling of pleasure, even though it supervenes on a physical base, is not reducible to it; as such, pleasure could still act as a cause—albeit an overdetermining one—of an action in addition to the underlying automatic adjustments. So, if getting better at performing a particular action—like, for instance, playing the piano—produces a subjective feeling of pleasure as one improves, then one could use that mental state to motivate—i.e., cause—oneself to keep getting better at it. In other words, pleasure/displeasure can act like a value-set that puts constraints on behaviour.

Related to all this is the so-called 'frame problem.' For philosophers like Daniel Dennett, the frame problem in AI arises when many of the possible consequences of a planned action are not relevant to the decision to perform that action, and the system trying to perform the action gets bogged down:[79] although partial solutions do exist,[80] the 'frame problem remains a problem for classical AI, and its strictly means-end approach', says McFarland.[81] According to McFarland, it 'is worth noting that animals do not suffer from the frame problem, and this may be because they have a value system' in which 'the costs and risks involved in their decision-making' act as 'constraints on their behaviour'.[82] The lack of such 'value' is also one of the main reasons why 'Good Old-Fashioned AI'—like the 'expert systems' discussed in Chapter 3—remains vulnerable to both the symbol-grounding problem and the frame problem. The frame problem also underlines one of the main reasons why, in the 1980s and 1990s, roboticists like Rodney Brooks, Hans Moravec and Rolf Pfeifer rejected a fundamental part of the classical image of mind as profoundly impractical for robotics: the 'central planner' or 'homunculus' that is privy to all the information available anywhere in the system.[83] Brooks also notes in his famous essay, 'Intelligence without Representation', that representations of the world 'simply get in the way. It turns out to be better to use the world as its own model.'[84] In fact, so successful was Brooks and company's proposed approach that it is now widely accepted in AI and robotics that there is simply no need for symbolic representation in the control of situated activities, such as walking, running and avoiding obstacles.

In other words, it would seem that instead of trying to create 'representations' of the world, taking the world as its own model and adopting an economic approach to behaviour (in which a value-system places constraints on behaviour) offers a way out of both the symbol grounding problem and the frame problem. Thus, in a robot created according to this design philosophy, 'the associations formed between specific sensory inputs and responses are driven by learning criteria provided by a predefined value system, which is a kind of 'teacher' guiding the learning process.'[85] This, of course, will be recognized as a version of 'reinforcement learning' discussed in Chapter 3, in which cost functions are implemented to control the robot's behaviour when chasing certain rewards. This value system is essential; since a robot is created to perform particular tasks, a robot's value-system, says McFarland, must, just like an animal's, 'reflect certain characteristics of the ecological niche, within which the animal or robot is designed to operate'; thus, the robot must be taught the values of 'good' and 'bad'—that is, desirable or undesirable behaviour for that niche.[86] A 'successful self-organising robotic system must be kept within bounds by a value system. Otherwise the robot would not be tailored to its ecological niche, and would not be successful in the marketplace.'[87]

If we accept that a robot must be, just like an animal, 'designed' for a particular purpose, then we must also refine the functionalist stance discussed above: it must become teleological functionalism, in which the functionalist elements are put into an evolutionary or behaviourist context, rather than a logical or mathematical context.[88] (I'll add here that such values can, as I showed in Chapter 3, be implemented through mathematics and algorithms.) An important part of teleological functionalism is that philosophers 'generally understand this notion of function to be what something was selected for, either by ordinary natural selection or by some other design process', which means that such functions are not causes, but selected effects.[89] However, the teleological approach is in danger of the opposite fault to philosophical liberalism, namely, philosophical 'chauvinism, because it is all too easy to relate the functional roles of mental events in humans to their biological utility', which 'may not be applicable to animals and robots'.[90] In other words, even though robots can be designed to behave in the way animals do, their behaviour cannot be simply boiled down to 'biological' utility or 'natural' selection, since they are neither 'biological' nor 'naturally selected' in any simple sense; there are clearly engineering, mathematical and logical elements at play in the functioning of a robot that cannot simply be removed or ignored. At the same time, since a robot designer clearly designs his or her robot by 'selecting' certain desired traits, and she or he may make use of economical principles in getting that robot to behave in a manner that makes it fit for its ecological niche, it is entirely possible that the opposition of liberalism and chauvinism may be a false one.

As is hopefully clear by now, philosophical discussions of animals and robots must remain, for the foreseeable future at least, open, because evidence for the mental abilities of animals and robots, as it currently stands, remains too open to interpretation, which is why multiple, irreconcilable stances can be adopted with respect to it. Indeed, it is possible that debate will never be resolved; it may be the case that the evidence is overdetermined, and the opposition between 'mechanical' and 'subjective' could simply be false. Be that as it may, the ambiguity of evidence explains why it is so difficult to draw straight and continuous lines of exclusion that would neatly separate human from robot, robot from animal, animal from human. Nevertheless, when put alongside each other, the animal and robot studies discussed in this section (as well as the studies on neuroprosthetics and genetics discussed in Chapter 2) also allow us to begin 'unpacking' or 'hollowing out' those traditional, humanist and folk-psychological conceptions of human subjectivity and identity that are defined in opposition to machines or animals, or in terms of embodiment, rationality, and the explicit manipulation of knowledge; at the same time, these studies also allow us to take the stuffing out of traditional or folk-psychology notions about animals and robots. And, since they make it difficult to pin down how exactly 'human', 'animal' and 'robot' are different, these studies highlight the need to redraw the usual lines of separation and connection; in short, they highlight the need for a concrete, cybernetically informed, and scientifically literate posthumanism.

Such a posthumanism is not reducible to a fashionable theory that sees science as just another discourse.

Animal . . . human . . . machine: An auto-affective posthumanism

The certainty of suffering

On December 14, 2014, a report from Reuters stated that Sandra, a 29-year-old orang-utan living at the Buenos Aires Zoo, was the first animal in the world to receive the same legal rights as her captors: an Argentine criminal appeals court had supposedly recognized Sandra as a 'non-human person'.[91] According to the same report, animal rights campaigners had 'filed a *habeas corpus* petition—a document more typically used to challenge the legality of a person's detention or imprisonment' on her behalf. Although it turned out to not be true,[92] the report on Sandra served to highlight that this was not the first— nor would it be the last—attempt by animal rights campaigners to secure the rights of life, liberty and freedom from harm for an animal. According to an April 2015 report in the *Guardian*, Manhattan supreme court justice Barbara Jaffe 'granted two chimpanzees [Hercules and Leo] a petition—through human attorneys—to defend their rights against unlawful imprisonment, allowing a hearing on the status of "legal persons" for the primates.'[93] The writ of *habeas corpus* was again rejected, although this decision was, at the time of writing (August 2015), under appeal.[94] Whatever the eventual outcome of these cases, they illustrate that the *legal* line separating human and animal is coming under ever increasing pressure.

These legal attempts to secure 'nonhuman personhood' for animals are a direct response to what the continental philosopher, Jacques Derrida (1930–2004), points to as the overturning of the more traditional forms of the treatment of animals over the last two centuries. These more traditional forms of treatment says Derrida, were upended by 'joint developments of zoological, ethological, biological, and genetic forms of *knowledge*, which remain inseparable from *techniques* of intervention *into* their object [animal life], from the transformation of the actual object, and from the milieu and world of their object'.[95] These developments, Derrida continues, amount to the unleashing of a seemingly limitless violence: 'Everybody knows what terrifying and intolerable pictures a realist painting could give to the industrial, mechanical, chemical, hormonal, and genetic violence to which man has been submitting animal life for the past two centuries.'[96] In this section, I'll follow Derrida's response to the violent treatment of animals, as it is outlined in *The Animal That Therefore I Am*, in order to sketch how his work can be said to overlap with posthumanism as I've been defining it in this book. Derrida, one of the major figures of post-structuralist philosophy, is perhaps best known for developing deconstruction, which itself owes a great deal to the phenomenology of Edmund Husserl (1859–1938). Husserlian phenomenology is the systematic study of the structures of consciousness and the phenomena or 'content' of consciousness; I'll return to both Husserlian phenomenology and Derrida's relation to it, later in my discussion.

For Derrida, the horrific images of 'suffering among the living', open the 'immense question' of 'suffering, pity and compassion', which in turn opens 'a new experience of compassion' that should 'awaken us to our responsibilities vis-à-vis the living in general, and precisely to this fundamental compassion that, were we to take it seriously, would have to change even the very cornerstone . . . of the philosophical problematic of the animal'.[97] In other words, the violence unleashed on animals in the last two hundred years or so should serve to remind us of our responsibilities towards life—'the living'—in general. The 'question' of animal suffering, not surprisingly, leads Derrida to ruminate on Jeremy Bentham (1748–1832), the British philosopher and founder of utilitarianism, and his famous question about animals:

'Can they suffer?' asks Bentham, simply yet so profoundly.

Once its protocol is established, the form of this question changes everything. It no longer simply concerns the *logos* [an important term in Derrida's philosophy, meaning 'word', 'speech', 'reason'; a principle of order and knowledge] that is, the disposition and whole configuration of the *logos*, having it or not, nor does it concern, more radically, . . . this can-have or the power one possesses (as in the power to reason, to speak, and everything that that implies). The question is disturbed by a certain *passivity*. . . . 'Can they suffer?' amounts to asking 'Can they *not be able?*' And what of this inability [*impouvoir*]? . . .

Being able to suffer is no longer a power; it is a possibility without power, a possibility of the impossible.[98]

What interests Derrida, then, in the question of animals' suffering, is their 'passivity', the 'powerlessness' of their 'not-being-able.' In re-asking Bentham's question in this way, Derrida seeks to get around the 'indisputable rock of certainty' that the French philosopher, René Descartes (1596–1650), neatly summed up in his famous 1637 phrase in Latin, 'cogito ergo sum'—«je pense donc je suis» in French; 'I think therefore I am' in English.[99] For Descartes, certainty and knowledge are guaranteed by the cogito: let's say I'm a sceptic who doubts everything; if I doubt everything, I'm also nevertheless still thinking; and even if I doubt everything that can possibly be doubted, says Descartes, I can't doubt that there exists a 'me' who is doing the doubting. However, instead of following in the tracks of Descartes' certainty, Derrida proposes an alternative radical certainty: 'But from another perspective altogether we are putting our trust in an instance that is just as radical, although essentially different: namely, what is undeniable. No one can deny the suffering, fear, or panic, the terror or fright that can seize certain animals and that we humans can witness.'[100] Thus, Derrida calls for a new founding moment of philosophy, one equivalent but different to Descartes' cogito, one that acknowledges that animals can indeed suffer and that we humans can bear witness to it.

The abyssal limits of human/animal

An important part of what interests Derrida in his exploration of animal suffering is the notion of a limit; specifically, the limit that apparently divides humans and animals:

> The discussion becomes interesting once, instead of asking whether or not there is a limit that produces a discontinuity, one attempts to think what a limit becomes once it is abyssal, once the frontier no longer forms a single indivisible line but more than one internally divided line; once, as a result, it can no longer be traced, objectified, or counted as single and indivisible.[101]

Such an 'abyssal' and paradoxical limit is not, however, easily grasped, since the 'frontier' it marks is really no more than the remainders of a fractured line 'between' humans and nonhuman animals. What Derrida is suggesting, then, is that it is ultimately impossible to separate the one from the other for once and for all; humans are, after all, ultimately animals; and it is to the extent that Derrida is concerned with this so-called 'abyssal limit', that his analyses in *The Animal That Therefore I Am* overlap with posthumanism as I have been defining it in this book: both challenge the notion of making a simple distinction between humans and nonhumans.

However, just because the limit that supposedly separates human and animal is paradoxical and hard-to-grasp, does not mean that one can say that human and animal are somehow simply 'the same'. On the contrary, this paradoxical limit also confronts the philosopher who tries to follow this non-Cartesian 'track' of thinking about animals, with the profound 'otherness' of animals, their nonhumanness: 'That is the track I am following, the track I am ferreting out [*la piste que je dépiste*], following the traces of this "wholly other they *call* 'animal', for example, 'cat' ".'[102] And it is the phrase 'I am following'—in French, *je suis*, which can also mean 'I am'—that allows Derrida to subject the certitude of Descartes' «*je pense donc je suis*» to a dizzying multilingual wordplay wherein animals become inseparable from the question of human existence. In Derrida's hands, the *cogito* transforms into 'I think therefore I am (following)':

> To follow and to be after will not only be the question, and the question of what we call the animal. . . . And by wondering whether one can answer for what 'I am (following)' means when that seems to necessitate an 'I am inasmuch as I am *after* [après] the animal' or 'I am inasmuch as I am *alongside* [*auprès*] the animal.' . . . *Being-after-it* in the sense of the hunt, training, or taming, or *being-after-it* in the sense of a succession or inheritance? In all cases, if I am (following) *after* it, the animal therefore comes before me, earlier than me. . . . The animal is there before me, there next to me, there in front of me—I who am (following) after it. And also, therefore, since it is before me, it is behind me. It surrounds me.[103]

If, according to Derrida, the animal 'surrounds' human existence, then it would appear that human existence—the 'I am'—is unthinkable outside a relation to animals: in other words, 'being-with' or 'being-after' animals would not come to modify a more 'primitive' or original existence or 'I am.' Thus, tracing the philosophical line that apparently separates humans from animals—and this despite their obvious differences—becomes a difficult, if not impossible, task.

Following the other track of thinking about animals that is based on the certitude of their suffering, means that Derrida's analysis of the fractured limit that separates humans from animals has a very complex relationship with philosophy after Descartes, which Derrida attempts to formulate into what he calls a 'thesis': 'thinking concerning the animal, if there is such a thing, derives from poetry. There you have a thesis: it is what philosophy has, essentially, had to deprive itself of. It is the difference between philosophical and poetic thinking.'[104] Poetry and poetic thinking, it would seem, is where the alternative thinking concerning the animal comes from, not philosophy. Some pages later, however, Derrida develops this thesis by invoking prophecy, but, in doing so, he complicates the apparently neat distinction between poetry and philosophy:

> Other than the difference mentioned earlier between poem and philosopheme [that is, philosophical phrase], there would be, at bottom, only two types of discourse, two positions of knowledge, two grand forms of theoretical or philosophical treatise regarding the animal. . . . In the first place there are texts signed by people who have no doubt seen, observed, analyzed, reflected on the animal, but who have never been *seen seen* by the animal. Their gaze has never intersected with that of an animal directed at them. . . . They have taken no account of the fact that what they call 'animal' could *look at* them, and *address* them from down there, from a wholly other origin. That category of discourse, texts, and signatories (those who have never been seen seen by an animal that addressed them) is by far the one that occurs most abundantly. It is probably what brings together *all* philosophers and theoreticians as such. At least those of a certain 'epoch', let's say, from Descartes to the present . . . . the other category of discourse, found among those signatories who are first and foremost poets or prophets, in the situation of poetry or prophecy, those men and women who admit to taking upon themselves the address that an animal addresses to them.[105]

Poetry and prophecy, says Derrida here, constitute the 'other', non-philosophical, 'category of discourse', whose signatories let themselves be '*seen seen*' by animals, let themselves be addressed by the gaze an animal directs at them. At the same time, however, Derrida also says that 'poetic' or 'prophetic' discourse is nonetheless also philosophical/theoretical: poetry and prophecy constitute one of the 'two grand forms of theoretical or philosophical treatise regarding the animal'. It would seem that Derrida is grappling with the distinction between poetry and philosophy: he cannot simply say that the 'other track' of thinking about animals—however poetic it may be—has nothing whatsoever to do with philosophy, especially given the centrality Jeremy Bentham's question about animal suffering enjoys in his analysis. The other track of thinking about animals, would appear to be less simply 'non-philosophical' than 'quasi-philosophical'.

The already puzzling relations between the other track of thinking about animals and poetry and philosophy are complicated further by Derrida's discussion of fables: it is, he says, 'necessary to avoid fables. We know how the history of fabulization and how it remains an anthropomorphic taming, a moralizing subjection, a domestication. Always a discourse *of* man, on man, indeed on the animality of man, but for and in man.'[106] Fables, then, are to be avoided—despite the fact that they come from the stable of poetry and literature—because they are a form of 'anthropomorphic taming' of the animal; that is, they turn animals into a vehicle for the discussion of the animalistic behaviour of humankind. Furthermore, following the 'other track' of thinking is fraught with danger because it too can corral and domesticate animals for man's use: for instance, when Derrida tells us that his own works have, down the years, contained 'a horde of animals' in order to welcome what he calls in French «*les animots*»—which literally means 'animalwords' in English; when said French, however, *les animots* is a homophone for «*les animaux*», the plural, 'animals'—he had to take care to avoid exhaustively parading those *animots* before the reader for fear that such a parade would become 'a circus' where the 'multiple *animot* would still suffer from always having its master on its back. It would have it up to the neck [*en aurait plein le dos*] with being thus domesticated, broken in, trained, docile, disciplined, tamed.'[107] In other words, even poetic thinking can wind up domesticating animals, exploiting them for gain; once again, it seems more accurate to say that the other track of thinking about animals Derrida is pursuing is less 'poetic thinking', than 'quasi-poetic thinking'.

Derrida's reasons for underlining the need for the 'other track' of thinking concerning animals to be cautious when dealing with poetry and philosophy perhaps become even clearer if one turns to his intriguing remarks on a little cat that boldly looks at him while he is naked in his own home. The little cat that regards him, he says, is not poetic or literary: it does not belong to, for example, 'Baudelaire's family of cats, or Rilke's, or Buber's', nor is it—he insists—the 'one who speaks in Alice in Wonderland'.[108] If Derrida insists on it being 'a real cat',[109] instead of a literary-poetic cat, it is because he wants to 'mark its unsubstitutable singularity'.[110] Before identifying the kingdom, species or even sex of the cat, 'it comes to me as this irreplaceable living being that one day enters my space into this place where it can encounter me, see me, even see me naked. Nothing can ever rob me of the certainty that what we have here is an existence that refuses to be conceptualized [rebelle à tout concept].'[111] Philosophy, poetry, fables and literature: all risk effectively erasing the particularity of the actual, concrete, little cat that looks at Derrida, and whose 'singularity' or uniqueness so interests him. There is a conflict, then, between the singular uniqueness of the cat regarding Derrida and its representation (however unavoidable) in language or discourse, a distinction that Derrida wants us to keep in mind.

However, the 'other track' of thinking about animals that involves both thinking about how human and animals existence are entangled as well as coming to grips with this unique living being that looks at me 'would not be a matter of "giving speech back" to animals but perhaps of acceding to a thinking, however fabulous and chimerical it might be, that thinks the absence of the name and the word otherwise, and as something other than a privation'.[112] In other words, the other track of thinking about animals will have to try to think the absence of logos—word, speech, reason—in animals in a different way. The quasi-philosophical, quasi-poetic thinking Derrida is pursuing here is thus not about giving speech back to animals; rather, it tries to think about an animal's 'lack of speech' as something other than a privation. Such a conception of an animal only makes sense, Derrida implies, from the point of view of an animal's unfavourable comparison with a human: an animal 'lacks' the power of speech a human has, which suggests that an animal is something of an 'incomplete' or 'defective' human. Such a position is obviously nonsensical: to illustrate this, you could ask yourself,

'How is a shark like an "incomplete" human?' 'It's not', you likely answered, 'it's simply a different species.' In this way, Derrida dislocates the philosophical limit most often used to separate humans from animals—*logos*; this effectively permits him to consider what humans and animals, despite their radical otherness, share.

Auto-affection

Once he has dislocated *logos* as that which creates the philosophical limit separating animals from humans, Derrida deepens his analysis of what humans and animals share by considering the mechanism of 'auto-affection'. I want to take a few moments here to outline 'auto-affection', which is necessary if the reader is to understand what Derrida says humans and animals share.

'Auto-affection' constitutes a complex and recurrent motif in Derrida's work that goes back to some of his earliest work on Edmund Husserl's *Ideas*.[113] It is especially important, for example, in *Speech and Phenomena*, which explores auto-affection's intimate connection to the problems of subjectivity and time in Husserl's philosophy.[114] As Derrida points out in *Speech and Phenomena*, auto-affection is, for Husserl, the mechanism that maintains 'the actual *now* [which] is necessarily something punctual and remains so' as '*a form that persists through continuous change of matter*';[115] in other words, auto-affection is that which turns a present moment—the ever-departing split-second 'now'—into an enduring *presence*. On Derrida's reading, however, auto-affection is actually the force that disrupts presence even as it makes it possible: this is because the 'presence of the perceived present', says Derrida, 'can only appear as such only inasmuch as it is *continuously compounded* with a nonpresence and nonperception, with primary memory and expectation (retention and protention)'.[116] Memory and expectation are not simply 'presents': they are 'not-nows' and 'nonperceptions', that are 'neither added to, nor do they *occasionally* accompany, the actually perceived now; they are essentially and indispensably involved in its possibility'.[117] In other words, in extending the actual 'now' into the persistent form of presence, perception must be composed of the 'non-perceptual' 'non-presences' of memory and expectation: 'As soon as we admit this continuity of the now and the not-now, perception and non-perception, in the zone of primordiality common to primordial impression and primordial retention, we admit the other into the self-identity of the *Augenblick*; nonpresence and nonevidence are admitted into the *blink of the instant*. There is the duration of the blink, and it closes the eye.'[118]

This 'otherness', Derrida continues, 'is in fact the condition for presence, presentation' in general :[119] thus, memory and expectation compound and fracture the 'now' with 'not-nows' and repetition, without which there could not be 'presence'. For Derrida, these 'not-nows' are connected to the body, which offers itself as a *différantial* [a word Derrida coins to combine the notion of temporal 'deferring' and spatial 'differing'] exterior: 'I see myself, either because I gaze upon a limited region of my body or because it is reflected in a mirror.'[120] In these cases, 'what is outside the sphere of "my own" has already entered the field of this auto-affection, with the result that it is no longer pure.'[121] This means that 'auto-affection supposed that a pure difference comes to divide self-presence. In this pure difference is rooted the possibility of everything we think we can exclude from auto-affection: space, the outside, the world, the body, etc.'[122] auto-affection is thus always already 'hetero-affection'.

It is auto-affection understood thus that Derrida, in *The Animal That Therefore I Am*, explicitly associates not just with the 'life of the living' and animals, but also the word that signifies the singular uniqueness of a human:

> It happens that there exist, between the word *I* and the word *animal*, all sorts of significant connections. They are at the same time functional and referential, grammatical and semantic. Two general singulars to begin with: the 'I' and the 'animal', both preceded by the definite article, designate an indeterminate generality in the singular. The 'I' is anybody at all; 'I' am anybody at all, and anybody at all must be able to say 'I' to refer to herself to his own singularity. Whoever says 'I' or apprehends or poses herself as an 'I' is a living animal. By contrast, animality, the life of the living, at least when one claims to distinguish it from the inorganic, from the purely inert or cadaverous physic-chemical, is generally defined as sensibility, irritability, and *auto-motricity*, a spontaneity that is capable of movement, of organizing itself and affecting itself, marking, tracing, and affecting itself with

traces of itself. This *auto-motricity* as auto-affection and relation to itself is the characteristic recognized as that of the living and of animality in general, even before one comes to consider the discursive thematic of an utterance or of an *ego cogito*, more so of a *cogito ergo sum*. But between this relation to the self (this Self, this ipseity) and the *I* of the 'I think', there is, it would seem, an abyss.[123]

This is a complex passage, but Derrida's discussion of the 'I' here involves underscoring the linguistic notion of deixis. Words are deictic if their semantic meaning is fixed but their denotational meaning varies depending on time and/or place. Thus, words or phrases requiring contextual information to convey any meaning— such as pronouns, spatial markers like 'here' and 'there' or temporal markers like 'now' and 'then'—are deictic. Derrida here notes that despite the similarities between the *words* 'I' and 'animal', there still seems to be an 'abyss' dividing the life of the living (animal) from the thinking *I* of the (human) *cogito*. At the same time, he notes that '*auto-motricity* as auto-affection and relation to itself is the characteristic recognized as that of the living and of animality in general.' In other words, auto-motricity-auto-affection-animality in general pre-exists, and is presupposed by, all the *cogito*'s thinking and thus disrupts any attempt to draw a clear line to separate humans from nonhumans. Derrida's reference here to an 'abyss' separating human from nonhuman is a clear call-back to his comments on the 'abyssal' limit, where 'the frontier no longer forms a single indivisible line but more than one internally divided line' which 'can no longer be traced, objectified, or counted as single and indivisible'.[124] And it is auto-affection that makes the abyss separating human and nonhuman 'abyssal'; auto-affection would thus be the name of a properly concrete posthumanist mechanism. It would thus share a great deal with the autopoiesis of second-order cybernetics.

Later in *The Animal That Therefore I Am*, Derrida notes, in the course of his discussion of Immanuel Kant's *Anthropology from a Pragmatic Point of View*[125]—the text where Kant reworks the Cartesian *cogito* into the 'I think' of the transcendental unity of apperception, the 'I think' that Kant believes accompanies the subject's every representation and gives him/her unity of consciousness and identity)—that there are humans who do not

have the *word* 'I' in their language. Such an awareness necessitates
a shift in how the difference between humans and animals is
conceived: it shifts from a 'linguistic-I' to a 'thought-I' that 'is in
thinking before being in language [and] is nothing other than
thinking itself.'[126] In other words, the discovery of humans who do
not use the pronoun 'I' means that distinction between human and
animal must now be redrawn on the grounds of something *beyond*
language: 'the power to think, the understanding that is lacking in
the animal'.[127] And, since this 'I think' is also the human power to
identify oneself, it turns out that it must be precisely this power that
animals lack:

> This would perhaps be the place or moment to clarify once more
> the both subtle and decisive stakes of the power of the 'I.' No
> doubt it will not simply be a case of the relation to self, not
> even of a certain automotion, an auto-kinetic spontaneity that no
> one, not even the most negative of minds vis-à-vis the animal, not
> even Descartes, disallows in the animal. Let me repeat it, every
> living creature, and thus every animal to the extent that it is living,
> has recognized in it this power to move spontaneously, to feel itself
> and to relate to itself. . . . But what is in dispute—and it is here
> that the functioning and structure of the 'I' count so much, even
> where the word *I* is lacking—is the power to make reference to the
> self in deictic or autodeictic terms, the capability at least virtually
> to turn a finger toward oneself in order to say 'this is I.'[128]

Not only can one clearly see once again Derrida's proximity to
cybernetics in this passage, one can also see how the linguistic
category of deixis has to be extended into thought itself; once
language has to be abandoned as a marker of the subject, there must
instead be a sort of non-linguistic auto-deixis in thought that allows
the subject to have an identity. Thus, animals must be deprived of
the ability to 'say'—even 'virtually'—'this is I'. And yet, this shift
beyond language actually opens up more difficulties for any thinking
that wishes to separate nonhuman animals from humans precisely
because such a shift opens the way for an auto-affection that slips,
as it were, 'behind' language. If language can no longer be said to
offer a cut-and-dried way of separating human from animal, and we
must instead invoke a non-verbal auto-deicticity, it becomes very
difficult indeed to separate humans from animals:

It is not certain that this auto-deicticity, is not at work, in various forms, evidently, in every genetic system in general, where each element of the genetic writing has to identify itself, mark itself according to a certain reflexivity, in order to signify in the genetic chain; nor is it certain that this auto-deicticity doesn't take on highly developed, differentiated, and complex forms in a large number of social forms that can be observed in the *animot*.[129]

Once again, it should be easy to see here what Derrida's 'other track' of thinking about animals shares with the autopoiesis discussed in Chapters 2 and 4.

To point out the *animot*'s auto-deicticity, however, does not simply amount to trying to restore unproblematically an 'I' to the animal in a manner that would amount to the misguided attempt to 'restore' speech to animals; nevertheless, as Derrida makes clear, auto-deicticity is inextricable from auto-motricity as auto-hetero-affection, the hallmark of the life of the living and animality in general:

> it is not just a matter of giving back to the animal whatever it has been refused, in this case the *I* of *automonstration*. It is also a matter of questioning oneself concerning the axiom that permits one to accord purely and simply to the human or to the rational animal that which one holds the just plain animal to be deprived of. If autoposition, the *automonstrative autotely* of the 'I,' even in the human, implies the 'I' to be an other that must welcome within itself some irreducible hetero-affection (as I have tried to demonstrate elsewhere [Derrida's reference here is, of course, to the passages from his *Speech and Phenomena*, discussed above]), then this autonomy of the 'I' can be neither pure nor rigorous; it would not be able to form the basis for a simple and linear differentiation of the human and the animal.[130]

In other words, auto-affection-as-hetero-affection, is reducible to neither the 'linguistic-I' nor the 'thought-I' of humanity: it names the auto-deicticity of a living 'self' that does not need a human 'I.' And, since it cannot be confined to either human thought or human language because it can be seen in animal auto-deicticity, auto-affection once again marks and highlights the abyssal limits of humans and animals; at the same time, once auto-affection begins to slip outside human language, then it is no longer certain that an animal is incapable of either indicating itself or of responding. However, such 'showing' or 'responding'—the scare-quotes are necessary—insofar as they do not unproblematically amount to a human 'I' or a 'self', also remain inseparable from 'hiding' and 'nonresponse'. We are, in other words, at the very limits of language, representation, discourse, etc.

Animal . . . machine

Auto-affection also allows the other track of thinking concerning animals to open onto machines more generally, which, I would suggest, is yet another clear indicator of how much Derrida's auto-affection owes to cybernetics;[131] and it is precisely this entanglement of animals, humans and machines that will occupy the final paragraphs of this section of this chapter. As I will argue below, Derrida's discussion of animals and machines necessarily brings with it a disruption of anthropocentrism and even, to a certain degree, the dislocation of the very concept of 'otherness'.

Given its highlighting of what constantly slips beyond language and its dislocation of *logos* as that which would separate animals from humans, the other track of thinking concerning animals that Derrida follows seeks to tease out a path beyond anthropocentrism; at the same time, however, such thinking also underscores how paying lip-service to 'otherness'—now become a tiresome and disagreeable academic buzzword in the humanities due to its chronic overuse by those who wield it with a censorious piety—will not be enough to displace that anthropocentrism:

> Besides all the differences that are reintroduced and taken into account in this way (among humans, among animals, between humans and animals), the question of the 'I', of 'I am' or 'I think', would have to be displaced toward the prerequisite question of the other: the other, the other me that I am (following) or that is following me. Which other? And how will the determination of the law of the other, of heteronomy, permit the anthropocentrism whose logic we are following to be either displaced or confirmed, its logic or the *logos* (for its logic is an active interpretation of the *logos*, a logocentrism)? That question awaits us still.[132]

It is this doubt over 'the other' that leads Derrida to ask, in relation to the work of the French philosopher Emmanuel Levinas (1906–1995) and that of the French psychoanalyst Jacques Lacan (1901–1981),

> whether a logic of the wholly other and of the unconscious, a primordial reference to the other as is found in Levinas and in Lacan, is sufficient, by itself, to remove the anthropocentric prejudice that comes down from Descartes, that is to say, along the whole Epipromethean-Islamic-Judeo-Christian descendancy. (My response will be 'no,' as you have already understood, both for Levinas and for Lacan.)[133]

Both Levinas and Lacan held that it was 'otherness' that determined human existence. Put simply, for Levinas the 'Other' is the radical alterity of another human being that the self can never know as such, whereas for Lacan the 'Other' represents the language and the law that the human subject cannot identify with as s/he would another human being. Levinas's 'Other', for example, remains dogmatically anthropocentric; for all its apparent otherness, it repeatedly denies the animal a face and skin: 'The animal has neither face nor even skin in the sense that Levinas has taught us to give to those words.'[134]

What Derrida makes clear here is that it is simply not enough to invoke Levinasian 'otherness' to displace the anthropocentrism that gives rise 'to the industrial, mechanical, chemical, hormonal, and genetic violence to which man has been submitting animal life for the past two centuries'.[135] Even such an ethical otherness remains bound by an anthropocentrism that insists on a clear and distinct line being drawn between humans and animals, which must also be displaced if one is to explore the abyssal limits of humans and animals. Indeed, Derrida asserts that the displacement of the anthropocentric border between human and animal has been at work in his 'deconstruction of logocentrism'—the dismantling of those systems of thinking that use *logos* to separate humans from other forms of life and non-life—from the very beginning: the 'very first substitution of the concept of the trace or mark for those of speech, sign, or signifier was destined in advance, and quite deliberately, to cross the frontiers of anthropocentrism, the limits of a language confined to human words and discourse. Mark, *gramma*, trace and *différance* refer differentially to all living things, all the relations between living and nonliving.'[136] Derrida's earliest work thus amounts to an attempt to displace human 'language' and 'speech' through words like 'mark' or 'trace', which designate activities of beings or agents other than humans but which can also designate the activities of humans. For example, an animal might 'mark' its territory with a scent or a robot might leave 'traces' on an object as it manipulates it; nor are marks or traces 'living' things—pixels or ink-marks, as I argued in Chapter 4, are simply not 'alive'. Thus has Derrida's deconstruction, in its concern for the trace or mark, from the outset complicated the borders between living and non-living, human and nonhuman; it has always been concerned with posthumanism.

And, once the borders between the living and the non-living begin to quiver, the abyssal human/animal border becomes even more complicated, fractured by the question of machinery: the question, 'But as for me, who am I (following)?' cannot be separated from citation, mechanical reproduction or textuality:

> I repeat it, I can reproduce it mechanically, it has always been capable of being recorded, it can always be mimed, aped, parroted by these animals, for example, those apes and parrots about which it is said that they can imitate (even though Aristotle denied them mimesis) without any understanding or thinking, and especially without replying to the questions they are asked. According to many philosophers and theoreticians, from Aristotle to Lacan, animals do not respond and they share that irresponsibility with writing, at least in the terms in which Plato interprets the latter in the *Phaedrus*. . . . No matter what question one asks them, writings remain silent, keeping a most majestic silence or else always replying in the same terms, which means not replying.[137]

The crossovers of machines, animals and texts have to do with non-response and what Derrida will later call 'the question of the question and the question of the response'.[138] Machines, animals and texts fail to respond in ways that a human would because they are stuck 'in a system of nonresponse, a language that doesn't respond because it is fixed or stuck in the mechanicity of its programming, and finally lack, defect, deficit or deprivation'.[139] This, in a nutshell, is the defining feature of the anthropocentric discourse that, according to Derrida, stretches from Aristotle to

Levinas. However, as I suggested above, once language can no longer be seen as the mark of the human and one must resort to a thoughtful deicticity, auto-motricity as auto-affection makes it very difficult to separate cleanly humans from 'the living' and 'animality in general', where, as I argued in the previous section of this chapter, the problems and questions of mechanical 'non-responses' seem so common.

Indeed, one can see Descartes himself struggling with just how many responses can be explained in terms of purely mechanical non-responses when Derrida cites his discussion of *homo faber* or *technicus*, the engineer who manufactures

> automatons that resemble humans for some, and animals (a horse, a dog, a bird, says Descartes) for others, resembling them enough to be mistaken for them. They would walk, eat, even *breathe* . . . They would 'imitate' (Descartes' word) 'as much as was possible, all the other actions of the animals they resemble, without excluding even the signs we use in order to witness to . . . our passions, such as crying out when struck, or fleeing when there is a lot of noise about them.'[140]

Descartes' *homo faber* is a 'programmer [*informaticien*] of artificial intelligences who is unable to discern, among his own automatons, between true and false passions, because the signs resemble each other so';[141] he is undone by an auto-affection that criss-crosses the entangled and abyssal borders of humans, animals and machines, thereby entangling further those abyssal borders. What Derrida's *The Animal That Therefore I Am* does, then, is point to a deconstructive analogue of cybernetics and posthumanism, where auto-affection confronts us with the strange entanglements of human, nonhuman, animal and machine, language and non-language, and the living and the non-living.

Transhumanism and singularity

To conclude my discussion of philosophical posthumanism, I want to turn to two entwined strands: transhumanism and what's recently become popularly known as 'the Singularity'. Both these strands are, unlike much of what has been discussed in this book so far, necessarily speculative since they concern unproven or as-yet uninvented theoretical technologies. Thus, a lot of what is usually discussed under the headings of both transhumanism and the Singularity is particularly vulnerable, not only to outright dismissal as the stuff of science fiction, but also to wild and outlandish unscientific and pseudoscientific claims and statements. Transhumanism and the Singularity, in other words, operate in a zone of speculation, which means that a reader must exercise a great deal of caution and scepticism when reviewing the claims made in their name. At the same time, outright cynical dismissal also constitutes an unsatisfactory stance, since the fruits of these theoretical technologies, should they be realized, promise to be quite thrilling; it would thus be a shame to stifle the imagination of future visionaries, researchers and inventors by dismissing these proposed technologies out of hand. That said, however, the promised advancements, like all technological advancements, would not come without considerable costs.

Transhumanism

According to the philosopher Nick Bostrom, transhumanism 'promotes the quest to develop further so that we can explore hitherto inaccessible realms of value. Technological enhancement of human organisms is a means that we ought to pursue to this end.'[142] Thus, transhumanism 'promotes an interdisciplinary approach to understanding and evaluating the opportunities for enhancing the human condition and the human organism opened up by the advancement of technology. Attention is given to both present technologies, like genetic engineering and information technology, and anticipated future ones, such as molecular nanotechnology and artificial intelligence.'[143] For transhumanists, the human body stands in need of technological enhancement because of its relatively short life span, the result of being too vulnerable to death through injury, disease and aging. Humans are also subject to intellectual, emotional and physical shortcomings: for example, a human's limited intellectual capacity makes contemplating 20-dimensional hyperspheres or reading all the books in the Library of Congress with perfect recollection simply impossible. Further, humans can only sense the world within a narrow band of sensory perceptions and are subject to fleeting moods, bad habits and addictions, and so on. Transhumanism, according to Bostrom, seeks solutions to these shortcomings; transhumanists are also interested in space colonization, the possibility of creating superintelligent machines and all 'other potential developments that could profoundly alter the human condition'.[144]

Transhumanism, despite how it might seem, is 'not limited to gadgets and medicine, but encompasses also economic, social, institutional designs, cultural development, and psychological skills and techniques'.[145] Nor does transhumanism seek a simple break with the 'human' past; as Bostrom makes clear in his essay, 'A History of Transhumanist Thought', transhumanism combines Renaissance humanism

> with the influence of Isaac Newton, Thomas Hobbes, John Locke, Immanuel Kant, the Marquis de Condorcet, and others to form the basis for rational humanism, which emphasizes empirical science and critical reason—rather than revelation and religious authority—as ways of learning about the natural world and our place within it, and of providing a grounding for morality. Transhumanism has its roots in rational humanism.[146]

Transhumans, or 'moderately enhanced humans', are transitional entities that mark the beginning of the shift from the limitations of what it is to be a human to what Bostrom calls 'full-blown posthumans'.[147] Thus, for Bostrom, transhumanism points the way from human to posthuman, a change in state that Bostrom compares to the relation between chimpanzees and humans:

> In much the same way as chimpanzees lack the cognitive wherewithal to understand what it is like to be human—the ambitions we humans have, our philosophies, the complexities of human society, or the subtleties of our relationships with one another, so we humans may lack the capacity to form a realistic intuitive understanding of what it would be like to be a radically enhanced human (a 'posthuman') and of the thoughts, concerns, aspirations, and social relations that such humans may have.'[148]

As should be clear, Bostrom's definition of the 'posthuman' differs from the concrete posthumanism I have been examining throughout this book in some important respects. For example, I have defined the unit of analysis of concrete posthumanism as 'human + tool' (which includes techno-science), while Bostrom does not; I have also outlined how posthumanism challenges the neatly drawn lines that separate the categories of human, animal and machine; finally, I have reiterated again and again how concrete posthumanism is rooted in specific examples of currently available technologies, specific artefacts and techniques and have argued that posthumanism is already, as it were, 'here', already underway for us posthuman beings. Bostrom's posthumanism, by contrast, is defined by speculative, future technologies that may or may not come to pass at some point in the future; in many ways, one could argue—but only by taking into account the differences I just outlined—that Bostrom's transhumanism perhaps comes closer to posthumanism as I have defined it throughout previous chapters.

For Bostrom, posthumanism need not amount to a simple break with—or rejection of—all things human: the 'transhumanist view that we ought to explore the realm of posthuman values does not entail that we should forego our current values. The posthuman values can be our current values, albeit ones that we have not yet clearly comprehended.'[149] Transhumanism, then, argues that 'the right way of favoring human beings' is both to realize human ideals better, but also to understand that 'some of our ideals may well be located outside the space of modes of being that are accessible to us with our current biological constitution.'[150] In other words, it is only by becoming posthuman that we will see the value of certain aspects of humanism; at the same time, there may be posthuman values that we simply can't currently see, just as a chimpanzee cannot see, say, how a simple on/off switch could become a computer.

In 'Transhumanist Values', Bostrom also tackles what is perhaps the most common complaint that is made about human enhancement: the loss of identity. For Bostrom, enhancement does not necessarily amount to a loss of identity: a 'person could obtain quite a bit of increased life expectancy, intelligence, health, memory, and emotional sensitivity, without ceasing to exist in the process'.[151] In fact, he argues, 'enhancement' is already an everyday occurrence: for instance, a person's intellectual life can be transformed radically by getting an education, while a person's life can be extended significantly by being cured of a deadly disease. In neither case do these developments spell the end of 'the original person'.[152] Further, diseases (for example, Alzheimer's) and injuries (brain damage) are already everyday occurrences that rob people of their identities; if enhancements could be used to prevent such diseases and injuries, then such modifications would actually strengthen identity, not dissolve it.

According to Bostrom, the opportunities and benefits uncovered by transhumanism should be available to all, not just the 1 per cent elite: it 'is not enough that the posthuman realm be explored by someone. The full realization of the core transhumanist value requires that, ideally, everybody should have the opportunity to become posthuman.'[153] It would, says Bostrom, be 'sub-optimal' if the opportunity to become posthuman were restricted to 'a tiny elite'.[154] If transhumanism is truly about benefitting 'humanity' as a species through technology, then we would be very poorly served by transhumanism if it was only reserved for those who could afford it; such a transhumanism would then only amount to an increase in inequality, lack of opportunity, unfairness, suffering and disrespect.[155] Nevertheless, and this a point that Bostrom does not consider, there is absolutely nothing to guarantee that such advances in technology would be made available to the world's poor.

Whole brain emulation

As was mentioned above, one of the key aspects of transhumanism has to do with its goal of extending the human being's relatively short life span. One form of extension in particular that has received a fair bit of attention recently is what's variously known as 'whole brain emulation' (WBE), 'mind uploading', or 'mind downloading'. In this subsection, I'm going to look in a bit of detail at WBE because it highlights how transhumanists tend to handle the question of the speculative future technologies that they believe might allow them achieve their goals.

The basic idea with WBE, according to Anders Sandberg and Nick Bostrom, is 'to take a particular brain, scan its structure in detail, and construct a software model of it that is so faithful to the original that, when run on appropriate hardware, it will behave in essentially the same way as the original brain'.[156] The feasibility of WBE hinges on what's known as a Turing machine, first devised by Alan Turing in 1936.[157] A Turing machine is a hypothetical, abstract or idealized computing device, which Turing famously described as having:

> [an] infinite memory capacity obtained in the form of an infinite tape marked out into squares on each of which a symbol could be printed. At any moment there is one symbol in the machine; it is called the scanned symbol. The machine can alter the scanned symbol and its behaviour is in part determined by that symbol, but the symbols on the tape elsewhere do not affect the behaviour of the machine. However the tape can be moved back and forth through the machine, this being one of the elementary operations of the machine. Any symbol on the tape may therefore eventually have an innings.[158]

In addition, the head or scanner can be in any one of a certain number of internal 'states', each of which has a bearing on what the machine does next depending on the symbol it reads, and functions like a rudimentary computer program: so if, for example, in state A the machine reads a '0', it might write a '1', move the tape one square right and switch to state B; if in state B it reads a '0', it might write a '1', move the tape to the left and switch to state C, whereas if in state B it read a '1' instead, it might erase it, print a '0' and move the tape left and switch to state A . . . and so on, until it halts. However, by proceeding according to these very rigid, simple steps—scan, print, erase, move and change state—a Turing machine, had it a tape long enough and all the time it needed, could, in principle, carry out *any* particular computation, no matter how complex. This circumstance, Turing noticed, meant that it would in turn be 'possible to invent a single machine which can be used to compute any computable sequence'.[159] This hypothetical machine, a Universal Turing Machine (U), could, if supplied with a tape on the beginning of which is written the rules of operation (program) of a particular computing machine (M), compute the same sequence as M.[160] Now, if Us seem very abstract, that's sort of the point: a U is not an actual computer; rather, it describes how a computer in general would work. That's why, according to Turing, a 'man provided with paper, pencil, and rubber, and subject to strict discipline, is in effect a universal machine'.[161] A U, of course, also basically describes how a modern computer works: shuffling the simplest of bits—1s and 0s—to do extremely complex mathematics.

So, for Sandberg and Bostrom, 'if brain activity is regarded as a function that is physically computed by brains, then it should be possible to compute it on a Turing machine'[162]: so, the theory is that if the brain can be understood as something that functions essentially like a computer (M), then it can be mimicked by U, since such a device can compute anything that any other device can compute.

An emulation is a 1-to-1 model that encapsulates all of a system's relevant properties; so, by

> analogy with a software emulator, we can say that a brain emulator is software (and possibly dedicated non-brain hardware) that models the states and functional dynamics of a brain at a relatively fine-grained level of detail. In particular, a mind emulation is a brain emulator that is detailed and correct enough to produce the phenomenological [i.e., subjective] effects of a mind.[163]

Thus, WBE requires 'three main capabilities: the ability to physically scan brains in order to acquire the necessary information, the ability to interpret the scanned data to build a software model, and the ability to simulate this very large model. These in turn require a number of subcapabilities.'[164] Both Sandberg and Bostrom admit that, as things currently stand, WBE is a theoretical technology, confined to the realms of science fiction and speculation; and, since WBE is 'currently only a theoretical technology. This makes it vulnerable to speculation, "handwaving" and untestable claims.'[165] In an attempt to counter such responses, Sandberg and Bostrom borrow Nick Szabo's notion of 'falsifiable design' to ground their discussion of WBEs.[166] The falsifiable design approach involves sketching a roadmap that identifies the assumptions and uncertainties associated with the technology in question that have not yet been subjected to laboratory testing and proposes experiments designed to reduce those uncertainties. One might wonder here if Sandberg and Bostrom's efforts with falsifiable design, do, at the end of the day distinguish their work on WBEs from so-called 'hard' science fiction.

One of the central assumptions behind WBEs is, as I suggested above, the assumption that the brain behaves like a Turing machine. Another key assumption made by WBE advocates is 'that in order to emulate the brain we do not need to understand the whole system, [. . .] we just need a database containing all necessary low-level information about the brain and knowledge of the local update rules that change brain states from moment to moment. A functional understanding (why is a particular piece of cortex organized in a certain way) is logically separate from detail knowledge (how is it organized, and how does this structure respond to signals)'.[167] The functionalist stance, which was discussed in the first section of this chapter, thus plays an important role in the thinking about WBEs; also crucial is the related notion of supervenience, which can be seen in Sandberg's discussion elsewhere of what he calls 'Scale Separation', which he sees as a key challenge for any WBE project: 'Does there exist a scale in the brain where finer interactions average out, or is each scale strongly linked to larger and smaller scales? If no such scale separation exists, then the feasibility of WBE is much in doubt: no method with a finite size cut-off would achieve emulation.'[168] In other words, for WBEs to be possible, the kind of supervenience discussed in both the first section of this chapter and Chapter 3, where mind and mental states supervene on—or 'emerge' from—the physical system, is necessary. Sandberg and Bostrom also make explicit the importance of such emergence in their joint paper on WBEs: 'the amount of functional understanding needed to achieve a 1-to-1 model is small. Its behaviour is emergent from the low-level properties, and may or may not be understood by the experimenters.'[169]

Sandberg and Bostrom flesh out their roadmap to WBE by looking at current scientific research actually being done on WBE, arguing that it 'appears feasible within the foreseeable future to store the full connectivity or even multistate compartment models of all neurons in the brain within the working memory of a large computing system'.[170] Much of their optimism is based on the 'so far (2006) largest simulation of a full Hodgkin-Huxley neuron network', which was 'performed on the IBM Watson Research Blue Gene supercomputer using the simulator SPLIT'.[171] This brain simulation of part of a rat's neocortex (the part of the brain thought to be responsible for higher functions such as conscious thought), consisted 'of 22 million 6-compartment neurons with 11 billion synapses, with spatial delays corresponding to a 16 cm^2 cortex surface and a simulation length of one second real-time.... Simulating one second of neural activity took 5,942 [seconds].'[172] In other words, even though this project was only a simulation, and not a full emulation of only a part of a rat's brain, it still took the machine just over 99 minutes to simulate just one second of the rat's brain activity. Even though this may seem like very small potatoes indeed, Henry Markram, a Professor at the École Polytechnique Fédérale de Lausanne in Switzerland, director of both the aforementioned rat brain project and the recently announced Human Brain Project—set up in 2013 with the aim of providing a first draft human whole brain model within its 10-year funding period—was confident enough to announce during a TED talk in 2010 that it 'is not impossible to build a human brain and we can do it in 10 years'.[173]

However, even if Markram's very optimistic claims do come to fruition, this does not mean that the brain to be emulated will remain alive; on the contrary, it 'is likely that the scanning methods used to provide raw data for WBE will be, at least in the early days, destructive methods making use of sectioning and scanning'.[174] The price to be paid for WBE is the organic matter of the brain itself. Such an approach 'is the technologically simplest approach. Destructive scanning has greater freedom both in physical effects used, energy levels, and fixating the brain through freezing and/or chemical fixation.'[175]

But a virtual brain, it seems, need not be connected to a full body: this is the assumption of 'brain-centeredness', the assumption that 'in order to produce accurate behaviour only the brain and some parts of the body need to be simulated, not the entire body'.[176] There already exist many simpler 'biomechanical simulations of bodies connected to simulated nervous systems' that have 'been created to study locomotion': for example, there is the simulated roundworm (C. elegans) body, 'a multi-joint rigid link where the joints were controlled by motorneurons in a simulated motor control network'; a simulated lamprey; simulated stick insects; and a simulation of the hind legs of cat, 'where a rigid skeleton is moved by muscles either modeled as springs contracting linearly with neural signals'.[177] All these models include sensory feedback from 'stretch receptors, enabling movements to adapt to environmental forces', since 'locomotion involves an information loop between neural activity, motor response, body dynamics, and sensory feedback.'[178] Sandberg and Bostrom's roadmap also points out how the creation of WBE will help current research in neuroscience and philosophy: they are the 'logical endpoint of computational neuroscience's attempts to accurately model neurons and brain systems' and thus understand the brain better; they would also be an empirical 'test of many ideas in the philosophy of mind and philosophy of identity' and would likely 'provide a novel context for thinking about such ideas'.[179]

However, perhaps some of the more unsettling impacts of how WBE could change humanity will be played out in the spheres of economics and culture: 'the economic impact of copyable brains could be immense, and could have profound societal consequences', not only because it would be theoretically possible to have these emulations perform certain kinds of intellectual work, but also because an entire corporation could be run by just 'one person' and many emulations of themselves; and, once 'emulation of particular brains is possible and affordable', and concerns about maintaining an individual identity can be met, emulation would enable the creation of back-up copies of individuals, thereby ensuring 'digital immortality'.[180]

Singularities?

The anxiety that humans could create an intelligent being that ends up outperforming its creators and eventually wipes them out is not exactly new. As I noted above, the anxiety that Mary Shelley's *Frankenstein* helped create and shape in 1818 has been remarkably resilient; it frequently colours discussions of AI and, mostly recently, has enjoyed something of a resurgence in the work of futurists and philosophers that deals with what has popularly come to be known as 'the technological Singularity'.

The technological Singularity—sometimes called 'superintelligence', or 'the intelligence explosion'—refers to a hypothetical event: the advent of an artificial general superintelligence that far exceeds both human intellectual capacity and human control. And, because the capabilities and motivations of such an intelligence could be so far beyond human comprehension and understanding, predicting the course of events after its advent would be impossible. The notion of a Singularity first emerged in the thinking and work of the Hungarian-American mathematician and physicist, John von Neumann (1903–1957); in the 1960s, the idea of an 'intelligence explosion' appeared in the work of the British mathematician I.J. Good (1916–2009); and, more recently, the idea has been popularized by the American mathematician, computer scientist and sci-fi writer, Vernor Vinge, the philosopher, Nick Bostrom, and the American inventor and futurist, Ray Kurzweil.

The more recent surge of interest in, anxiety about, and popularity of the idea of a 'technological Singularity' was sparked by Vernor Vinge in the 1980s, who brought it to a head in his 1993 essay, 'The Coming Technological Singularity: How to Survive in the Post-Human Era'.[181] In that essay, Vinge gave the name 'Singularity' to the hypothetical occurrence of artificial superintelligence because it marks 'a point where our models must be discarded and a new reality rules. As we move closer and closer to this point, it will loom vaster and vaster over human affairs till the notion becomes a commonplace. Yet when it finally happens it may still be a great surprise and a greater unknown.'[182] Vinge traces the origin of speculation on the Singularity back to the 1950s, and in particular to a conversation that Stanisław Ulam (1909–1984), the Polish-American mathematician, recalled having with John von Neumann: 'One conversation centered on the ever accelerating progress of technology and changes in the mode of human life, which gives the appearance of approaching some essential singularity in the history of the race beyond which human affairs, as we know them, could not continue.'[183] For Vinge, then, the Singularity—which he estimates will occur some time before 2030[184]—will constitute such a radical break with how human affairs have hitherto been conducted that 'the new era is simply too different to fit into the classical frame of good and evil. That frame is based on the idea of isolated, immutable minds connected by tenuous, low-bandwith links.'[185] The Singularity, in other words, promises to be *pharmakonic*.

Vinge's apprehension is shared by Nick Bostrom, who also believes that the Singularity—or, as he prefers to call it, 'superintelligence'—may not be compatible with humanity's future. In his essay, 'How long before Superintelligence?', Bostrom defines 'superintelligence' as 'an intellect that is much smarter than the best human brains in practically every field, including scientific creativity, general wisdom and social skills'.[186] Such a superintelligence says Bostrom, could pose an existential risk to humankind, leading to our annihilation: 'When we create the first superintelligent entity . . ., we might make a mistake and give it goals that lead it to annihilate humankind, assuming its enormous intellectual advantage gives it the power to do so. For example, we could mistakenly elevate a subgoal to the status of a supergoal. We tell it to solve a mathematical problem, and it complies by turning all the matter in the solar system into a giant calculating device, in the process killing the person who asked the question.'[187]

This same anxiety is also apparent in Bostrom's work with Vincent Müller. As I mentioned above, Müller and Bostrom recently sent a survey to experts working in AI to see 'what probability the best experts currently assign to high-level machine intelligence coming up within a particular time-frame, which risks they see with that development, and how fast they see these developing.'[188] The results showed that the

> median estimate of respondents was for a one in two chance that high-level machine intelligence will be developed around 2040–2050, rising to a nine in ten chance by 2075. Experts expect that systems will move on to superintelligence in less than 30 years thereafter. They estimate the chance is about one in three that this development turns out to be 'bad' or 'extremely bad' for humanity.[189]

It would seem, then, that experts actually working in AI at the moment entertain the possibility that a high-level artificial general intelligence will arrive by the middle of the twenty-first century, with 'superintelligence' coming along some thirty years after that. And, although Müller and Bostrom's anxieties about superintelligence being 'extremely bad' for humanity, are given only a 31 per cent chance of occurring by those working in AI, both philosophers still see that chance as being high enough to warrant taking steps now in an effort to reduce those odds: 'We know of no compelling reason to say that progress in AI will grind to a halt (though deep new insights might be needed) and we know of no compelling reason that superintelligent systems will be good for humanity. So, we should better investigate the future of superintelligence and the risks it poses for humanity.'[190]

The kind of artificial intelligence that could be dangerous to humankind, however, need not be an artificial human intelligence, with human intentionality and emotions; it could instead be an intelligence in pursuit of a particular programmed goal. An oft-cited example of such an intelligence is Bostrom's 'paperclip maximizer', an AI that has one goal, and one goal only: to maximize the number of paperclips it has.[191] If the AI has been given sufficient intelligence and connectivity, it might start small by collecting paperclips, then move on to using the stock market, making trades to earn money so as to buy more paperclips; it may even conclude that the best route to the goal of more paperclips is to invest in manufacturing them. At the same time, the paperclip maximizer could also work to improve its own intelligence—understood as an optimization process that would maximize its reward/utility function—if it thought doing so would increase the number of paperclips it could get. In this scenario, its superintelligence (should it attain it) would just be a means to the end of its primary goal—more paperclips. The AI could also come up with ways of preventing itself from ever being switched off, since doing so would stop it amassing paperclips; and so, the AI would keep on amassing paperclips, innovating as it goes, eventually getting to the point where it might start converting its 'nonessential surroundings'—our cars, airplanes, building, cities, us—into paperclips. This scenario, no doubt, sounds outrageously monstrous and monstrously outlandish to us; however, that is the point of the example: what humans value wouldn't matter to such an AI since it doesn't share our goals and values—it just wants more and more paperclips.

No matter how you view it, it seems clear enough that for Bostrom's paperclip maximizer scenario to be at all remotely possible, two conditions are necessary: the first is that superintelligence must occur very quickly—taking, at the very most, a couple of days to 'take off'; the second is that the system must have reached a point where improvements to itself are recursive; that is, the improvements that are made to the system by the system itself and not by others working on it. If both conditions aren't met, humankind would likely see what was occurring and takes steps to deal with it. Nevertheless, as Bostrom argues in his recent book, *Superintelligence*, even the remote possibility of this type of scenario happening means that we should at the very least be taking steps to instil AI with goals that are compatible with human survival.[192]

Other thinkers, such as Ray Kurzweil, diverge sharply from the fear and caution espoused by the likes of Vinge and Bostrom.[193] Whereas Bostrom remains agnostic with regard to a specific date, Kurzweil believes the Singularity will occur by 2045, some 15 years later than Vinge's prediction. And, for Kurzweil, the Singularity is something to be wholeheartedly optimistic about. Indeed, in 2009, both he and the X-Prize founder, Peter Diamandis, announced the establishment of Singularity University, the stated mission of which is 'to educate, inspire and empower leaders to apply exponential technologies to address humanity's grand challenges'.[194] According to Kurzweil in his 2006 book, *The Singularity is Near*, the question, 'What, then, is the Singularity?', is to be answered as follows:

> It's a future period during which the pace of technological change will be so rapid, its impact so deep, that human life will be irreversibly transformed. Although neither utopian nor dystopian, this epoch will transform the concepts that we rely on to give meaning to our lives, from our business models to the cycle of human life, including death itself.... The key idea underlying the impending Singularity is that the pace of our human-created technology is accelerating and its powers are expanding at an exponential pace [that is, an expansion by means of repeatedly *multiplying* by a constant, as opposed to linear, which expands by repeatedly *adding* a constant]. Exponential growth is deceptive. It starts out almost imperceptibly and then explodes with unexpected fury—unexpected, that is, if one does not take care to follow its trajectory.[195]

Kurzweil thus sees the Singularity as being the direct result of explosive exponential growth in human-created technology. This explosion, says Kurzweil, will be neither dystopian nor utopian; however, he says—echoing Vinge—that the Singularity promises to transform all the concepts—from business to death—that humans have hitherto used to give meaning to their lives. These changes, Kurzweil argues, will result from the fusion of humans with technology, leading to the final transcendence of 'our biological roots':

> The Singularity will represent the culmination of the merger of our biological thinking with our technology, resulting in a world that is still human but that transcends our biological roots. There will be no distinction, post Singularity, between human and machine or between physical and virtual reality. If you wonder what will remain unequivocally human in such a world, it's simply this quality: ours is the species that inherently seeks to extend its physical and mental reach beyond current limitations.[196]

Despite his earlier insistence that the Singularity will be neither dystopia not utopia, Kurzweil, unlike Bostrom or Vinge, clearly prefers to see the Singularity in utopian terms: the Singularity is to be welcomed as a sort of Techno-Messiah for 'human' kind:

> The Singularity will allow us to transcend [the] limitations of our biological bodies and brains. We will gain power over our fates. Our mortality will be in our own hands. We will be able to live as long as we want (a subtly different statement from saying we will live forever). We will fully understand human thinking and will vastly extend and expand its reach. By the end of this century, the nonbiological portion of our intelligence will be trillions of trillions of times more powerful than unaided human intelligence.[197]

It should now be possible to see just how steeped Kurzweil's thinking is in actual scientific research being done in the fields of AI, neuroprosthetics and genetics; however, it is also possible to see just how much Kurzweil's thinking has been coloured by the science fiction scenarios painted so vividly by Iain M. Banks in his 'The Culture' series of novels; indeed, one could even argue that the overall trajectory Kurzweil paints for humanity's future seems to be ripped, almost point for point, from the plot of Greg Bear's *Blood Music*. And one is also tempted to wonder if the being that Kurzweil is predicting the existence of could still be referred to as 'human': it can no longer get sick and die; nor can it any longer be understood in terms of organic matter, since it has essentially merged with its technology:

> Before the middle of this century, the growth rates of our technology—which will be indistinguishable from ourselves—will be so steep as to appear essentially vertical. From a strictly mathematical perspective, the growth rates will still be finite but so extreme that the changes they bring about will appear to rupture the fabric of human history. That, at least, will be the perspective of unenhanced biological humanity. [...] If you wonder what will remain unequivocally human in such a world, it's simply this quality: ours is the species that inherently seeks to extend its physical and mental reach beyond current limitations.[198]

All in all, you'd be forgiven for thinking that Kurzweil's vision simply extrapolates from the current state of affairs, where information readily flows across the borders that only appear to separate digital and biological matter, combined with a very heavy dose of science fiction and more than a liberal pinch of evangelical zeal.

There are, however, those who are very critical of the notion of the Singularity.[199] For example, Selmer Bringsjord, Alexander Bringsjord and Paul Bello argue in their paper, 'Belief in The Singularity is Fideistic', that the Singularity corresponds to a 'category of events marked by being at once *weighty, unseen,* and *temporally removed* (*wutr*, for short)'.[200] Because the Singularity is a *wutr* event, and because it fails to 'fit with both rationalist and empiricist argument schemas in support of this belief', the authors conclude 'not that The Singularity won't come to pass, but rather that regardless of what the future holds, believers in the "machine intelligence explosion" are simply fideists'.[201] Belief in the Singularity is, in other words, a matter of faith, not science.

However, perhaps more troubling for believers in the Singularity are the criticisms of Theodore Modis, a strategic business analyst, futurist and physicist, whose work Kurzweil often cites in *The Singularity is Near*. In his essay, 'The Singularity Myth', Modis takes no prisoners, accusing 'Kurzweil and the singularitarians' of 'indulging in some sort of para-science, which differs from real science in matters of methodology and rigor' in that they 'tend to overlook rigorous scientific practices such as focusing on natural laws, giving precise definitions, verifying the data meticulously, and estimating the uncertainties'.[202] As mentioned above, key to Kurzweil's understanding of the Singularity is the explosive exponential growth in human technology; what is particularly contentious for Modis is how Kurzweil time and again imposes an exponential growth curve on everything he makes predictions about. This, according to Modis, is wrongheaded because 'all natural growth processes' tend to follow a smooth, S-shaped curve—our old friend, the logistic curve—instead. So, what might, at first sight, look like an exponential curve could simply be, in reality, a logistic curve 'which indeed can be approximated by an exponential in its early stages. Explosions may seem exponential but even they, at a closer look, display well-defined phases of beginning, maturity, and end.'[203] Modis is also very critical of Kurzweil's attempts to locate 'the "knee" of an exponential curve, the stage at which an exponential begins to become explosive'.[204] For Modis, it is 'impossible to define such a knee in a rigorous way because of the subjective aspect of the word "explosive".... There is no way to single out a particular region on an exponential curve because the pattern has no intricate structure.'[205] This subjective aspect, says Modis, introduces a fatal bias into Kurzweil's graphs.[206] In sum, what Modis's sharp criticisms of Kurzweil boil down to is that Kurzweil repeatedly mistakes part of a logistic curve for a runaway process of exponential growth; and, because natural growth follows a logistic curve, the exponential growth that Kurzweil believes he sees will eventually flatten out; this, in turn, means that many of Kurzweil's predictions—about, for example, the continued growth in the computing power—will never be realized.

So, what does Modis see in humanity's future? Interestingly—terrifyingly—Modis draws on work done by Paul D. Boyer, winner of the Nobel Prize in Chemistry to suggest in the closing paragraphs of his paper that the next 'milestone' on the curve of human history is more likely to be environmental catastrophe, the one following that being human extinction:[207]

> Boyer—whose data Kurzweil uses when he makes his central point—has anticipated two future milestones very different from Kurzweil's. Boyer's 1st future milestone is 'Human activities devastate species and the environment,' and the 2nd is 'Humans disappear; geological forces and evolution continue.' I estimated above that the next milestone should be between 13.4 and 38 years from 1995. I suspect that there are many hard-core scientists who would agree with Boyer's first milestone and my time estimates.[208]

No Singularity, then, says Modis; instead, there's more likely to be a devastating environmental catastrophe round about the year 2033, followed by human extinction. The Earth, apparently, will continue to do her thing.

So, who's right—Modis, Kurzweil or Bostrom? Now, if there's one thing I can say with a degree of confidence, it's that hyped-up predictions of the imminent arrival of artificial general intelligence—never mind artificial superintelligence—have proven to be notoriously inaccurate in the past and repeated disappointments have conditioned people to doubt whether such a thing could even happen at all. Personally, I've no idea if something like a Singularity could come to pass, and only time will tell. But if the Singulartarians are on to something, then there might be no harm in indulging in an AI version of 'Pascal's Wager': Blaise Pascal, in section III of his *Penseés*, argued that humans bet with their lives whether or not God exists.[209] Given even the possibility that God actually does exist and eternal suffering in Hell could be a real possibility, the rational person, says Pascal, should live as though God and Hell exist. If God does not actually exist, then that person will have only a finite loss— some pleasure, some luxuries, etc.—but no real harm will occur to him or her. If, however, God does exist and Hell is real, then you've chosen very well indeed. In light of Pascal, perhaps we should be making what I'd call Bostrom's Wager: let's act rationally and ensure that any AI to be developed is compatible with human values and humankind's continued existence. If superintelligence never comes to pass, then what harm? If superintelligence does come to pass, then we've chosen well.

If, however, Modis is right, then we've been the danger to ourselves all along.

CHAPTER SIX

Conclusion

Some thoughts on digital humanities and 'posthumanities'

Crisis? Maybe

As I've been arguing throughout this book, an actual, concrete posthumanism is that which takes its unit of analysis to be 'humans + tools'. As such, it can be readily grasped using concepts like 'distributed cognition', which describes situations wherein 'cognition' can no longer be understood in purely 'human' or 'organic' terms since it incorporates 'nonhuman' or 'non-organic' elements. Concrete posthumanism is thus concerned with all those situations where the lines that apparently separate 'human' from 'nonhuman' are porous; posthumanism is thus especially concerned with those branches of techno-science, such as neuroprosthetics, artificial intelligence and genetic manipulation, where the hard and fast distinction between human and nonhuman is actively challenged. Concrete posthumanism is also concerned with how second-order cybernetics illuminates how humans, animal and machines can be understood to act alike as cybernetic systems. It is also concerned with folk-psychology projections of 'human' qualities into 'nonhuman' artefacts from robots to animals to artistic creations, as well as in how states, procedures and abilities that originate in organic matter—brains—can be so effectively emulated in non-organic circuitry and systems.

In what follows, I want to consider some of the ways in which such a posthumanism suggests that we should be rethinking both the traditional humanities, as well as what teachers, researchers and writers 'in' the humanities do. I'll also be considering literary-cultural studies in some detail. So, why am I focusing on the humanities and literary-cultural studies? Well, mainly because posthumanism highlights the shortcomings in the humanities and literary-cultural studies particularly sharply: because techno-science is an integral part of posthumanism, any course of study that is not fundamentally transdisciplinary is going to repeatedly fail to grasp it properly. Not only that, but, as I'll argue below, the humanities and literary-cultural studies have much to gain by engaging concrete posthumanism; however, for reasons noted above, the sciences have little to gain from the humanities as they are currently constituted. Now, it would perhaps be too easy to dismiss the critical comments that follow by lumping them into the perennial and perhaps tiresome debate on whether or not the humanities are in 'crisis'. Certainly, some recent reports of the demise of the humanities greatly exaggerate its condition; also, such reports have been a recurrent staple of debate about the humanities for nearly a century.[1] Indeed, something of a cottage industry has sprung up when it comes to publishing stories on 'the crisis in the humanities': stories are published pointing to the steady-but-not-steep decline in enrolments in the humanities in the United States since 2009. These are invariably followed by responses from professors lucky (and networked) enough to have found work in elite universities telling everybody that—and I'm paraphrasing here—'no, actually, there is no real decline in the numbers and any drop in numbers studying the humanities only looks like a drop compared to the 1960s'.[2] There is, nonetheless, evidence that the primary factor in the drop-off in humanities enrolments is young women turning away from humanities degrees, and it seems very unlikely that that trend will reverse any time soon.[3] It is also a little harder to try and spin the global drop in funding for the humanities as a non-crisis. According to a December, 2013, report in *The New York Times,* financing 'for humanities research in the United States has fallen steadily since 2009, and in 2011 was less than half of one percent of the amount dedicated to science and engineering research and development', a trend that is echoed globally: 'international arts and humanities funding has been in constant decline since 2009'.[4] The same report goes on to quote Rosemary G. Feal, the then executive director of the Modern Language Association of America, as saying 'the decline in funding for humanities research in the United States is related both to fiscal emergencies and "the devaluing of the humanities, especially by legislators who themselves have not experienced first-hand the value of studying the humanities"'.

One might be tempted to ask what 'the value of studying the humanities' Feal refers to here might be, and even though I'll be touching on this question below, I won't be arguing for 'the value of studying the humanities' as it currently stands because I have yet to hear a convincing answer to that question. Instead, my primary focus for the remainder of this book will be on how concrete posthumanism necessitates a shift in the way the humanities have traditionally been conceived of and taught. No doubt, what I'll have to say on this matter will be read by some as part and parcel of what is hastening the decline of the humanities:[5] after all, how can the humanities be defended through posthumanism, if it appears to be intent on eroding the very basis of the humanities— humans and humanism? But, as I've pointed out above, concrete posthumanism cannot make a simple 'break' with humanism; nor is posthumanism a simple continuation of humanism. Posthumanism is instead best understood as the natural evolution of humanism, one that takes seriously the premise that humanism has historically defined itself using science and technology; concrete posthumanism simply takes into account how recent developments in science and technology have changed, and will continue to change, how human beings and humanity are and how they are understood. Concrete posthumanism's connection to rationality and evidence, its greatest strength, is thus what ultimately relates it to humanism even as it moves posthumanism beyond humanism. And what I'd be tempted to call 'the posthumanities',[6] simply highlights the need for the humanities to evolve alongside humanism as it has become posthumanism, even if that evolution goes deep into unsettling and uncharted territory. Concrete posthumanism is simply an encounter with contemporary reality that takes the question of where that reality points us to seriously; and, as I've been arguing, it is better to face that reality with eyes open and critical faculties fully engaged. Ideologically driven criticisms of science, along with denials of the existence of nature and reality, for all their supposedly good intentions, will be of no help to anyone who wishes to negotiate that reality in a fully engaged manner. In the sections that follow, I'll consider some elements of digital humanities and how they shed light on the humanities generally; I'll then take a look at how digital technology necessitates becoming familiar with the questions of big data and metadata and how such questions open digital humanities onto concrete posthumanism; I'll then finish by making a few suggestions about what a posthumanities discipline and 'subject' might look like. The discussion that follows, however, should in no way be taken as the final word—nor even my final word—on the relations between the humanities and the posthumanities.

Digital humanities: towards the posthumanities

Given the importance of tools and technologies in concrete posthumanism, the first step towards what I would call 'posthumanities' necessitates a quick exploration of the field of study known as digital humanities. In a nutshell, digital humanities is where the traditional humanities—history, philosophy, linguistics, literature, art, archaeology, music, cultural studies—meets digital technology—computers, programming, data visualization, information retrieval, data mining, statistics, text mining, digital mapping and digital publishing. Alan Liu, a pioneer in digital humanities, argues in his essay, 'Where Is Cultural Criticism in the Digital Humanities?', that the 'core areas' of digital humanities are 'text encoding, text analysis, pattern discovery, the creation of digital archives and resources'.[7] And, as Kathleen Fitzpatrick points out in her essay, 'The humanities, done digitally',[8] in the early days of digital humanities, those working in the field—people like Ray Siemens and John Unsworth—were keen to distance it from 'mere digitizing', passively turning texts and/or archive material into digital files. In a January, 2015 interview, Fitzpatrick defines digital humanities as bringing 'the tools and techniques of digital media to bear on traditional humanistic questions. But it's also bringing humanistic modes of inquiry to bear on digital media.'[9]

But it is already possible to see an anxiety about how digital humanities came to be perceived by the more traditional humanities in Siemens and Unsworth's early attempts to ward off the idea that digital humanities are merely about digitizing the more 'important stuff', like texts and archives. And, as Alan Liu makes clear in his above-mentioned essay, that anxiety has not gone away:

Julia Flanders nicely captures the stigma of servitude that has marked the digital humanities when she writes, 'Representational technologies like XML, or databases, or digital visualization tools appear to stand apart from the humanities research activities they support. [. . .] Humanities scholarship has historically understood this separateness as indicating an ancillary role—that of the handmaiden, the good servant/poor master—in which humanities' insight masters and subsumes what these technologies can offer.'[10]

In other words, technology remains a 'mere' tool in the service of some (unspecified) human 'insight'.

The irony, as Liu goes on to point out, is that being an instrumental 'handmaiden' not only describes how digital humanities are viewed by the humanities 'proper', but also how the humanities 'proper' are viewed within the university as an institution. The humanities 'also struggle against the perception that they are primarily instrumental because their assigned role is to provide students with a skill set needed for future life and work. For example, the rhetoric of university course catalogs . . . speak[s] of the humanities as providers of "skills" in critical analysis, language, and so on', with the clear implication being 'that the main function of the humanities is service: they teach the analytical, communicational, and other abilities needed as means to other ends.' The paradox, of course, is that the view the humanities 'proper' has of digital humanities is the view that university administrators have of the humanities 'proper', which is the very thinking that has overseen the cuts in funding to the humanities globally. Further complicating this situation are the perceptions of those outside the university, like the politicians referred to by Rosemary G. Feal in the article mentioned above, and the parents of students, who see the humanities as being useless for a good career: 'the humanities suffer even more from seeming to be noninstrumental to the point of uselessness. In hard economic times [. . .], parents actually come up to chairs of English departments at graduation to complain that their daughter's humanities degree is only good for working at Starbucks. [. . .] The catch-22 is that the harder the humanities work to become research enterprises equipping students with specialized competencies and vocabularies, the more cut off they seem from practical use.'[11] On top of all this, the increasingly frequent reports of Millennial poverty,[12] as well as the impending automation crunch discussed in Chapter 3, will only serve to sharpen such concerns and questions. Why get so in debt pursuing a humanities degree, when there are no well-paid jobs when you graduate to help pay off debts? And if you really like reading literature, why would you not just join a reading club online or at your local community centre for free?

Liu proposes that digital humanities can avoid being seen as a servant of the humanities 'proper' by taking some lessons from cultural criticism. However, even Liu himself seems somewhat unconvinced by this strategy, as becomes clear when he cites Alex Reid's criticism of an earlier form of his proposal. For Reid, the humanities themselves are largely responsible for their own irrelevance, due, in no small part, to the very cultural studies that Liu proposes as a possible solution: 'I don't think it is unreasonable to argue that cultural critique as it has developed over the past 30–40 years has been a contributing factor to the general cultural decline of the humanities. At the very least, with historical hindsight, it was not the change that we needed if our intention was to remain culturally relevant.'[13] Reid continues: 'Cultural critique has led us to be overspecialized, largely irrelevant, and barely intelligible, even to one another, let alone to the broader society. Yes, digital humanities can help us address that by providing new means to reach new audiences, but that won't help unless we are prepared to shift our discourse.' In other words, part of the crisis in the humanities appears to be due to what is being taught to students in the humanities—'cultural studies' of all stripes.

Reid's criticisms also echo the recent blossoming of distrust in what has come to be known as the 'symptomatic reading' of texts—that is, treating a text as the carrier of 'subtextual ideology' that must be unmasked by the—Marxist, feminist, queer, etc.—critic. As N. Katherine Hayles suggests in her discussion of the work of Stephen Best and Sharon Marcus, 'How We Read: Close, Hyper, Machine',[14] the growth in disenchantment with symptomatic readings is in part due to their being formulaic and predictable. Instead, Best and Marcus advocate for what they call surface reading', which focuses on 'what is evident, perceptible, apprehensible in texts.'[15] But, one might wonder here if trying not to be 'predictable' is at all worthwhile solution to what ails the humanitites since that only opens the humanities up to intellectual 'fashions', which is the origin of the problems the humanities currently faces. One might also wonder if 'surface reading' is the answer to the problems the humanities has in connecting with those outside—and, very often, inside—it. This is because, as Liu points out, the 'expertise' of humanities 'experts' is peculiarly vulnerable to digital media and its ability to bring people together:

> As perhaps best exemplified by Wikipedia, the new networked public is now developing its own faculty of expertise through bottom-up processes of credentialing (e.g., Wikipedia's 'administrators'), refereeing, governance, and so on. It will take at least a generation for the academy (and mediating agencies such as journalism) to create or adapt the institutional protocols, practices, and technologies that can negotiate a new compact of knowledge between expertise and networked public knowledge— for example, between the standards of peer review and crowdsourcing. In the meantime, the humanities are caught in a particularly vicious form of the communicational impasse of expertise. While the networked public still tolerates specialized knowledge from scientists, engineers, doctors, and others, it seems to have ever less patience for specialized humanities knowledge, since in the domain of 'human' experience everyman with his blog is an autodidact. And this is not even to mention the ridiculous mismatch between the forms of humanities knowledge and the new networked public knowledge—for example, between the scale, structure, and cadence of a humanities monograph and those of a blog post or tweet.[16]

In other words, it seems like literature professors face some serious, if not fatal, competition from online literature group discussions.

There have also been some directly 'posthuman' suggestions for revitalizing the humanities, an example of which can be found in Rosi Braidotti's *The Posthuman*. In Chapter 4, I discussed how Braidotti argues that a 'technologically mediated post-anthropocentrism can enlist the resources of biogenetic codes, as well as telecommunication, new media and information technologies to the task of renewing the Humanities'.[17] However, given their reliance on STS science-criticism and thoroughly debunked notions such as 'vitalism', it is difficult to see how Braidotti's contributions could be said to offer a workable, desirable or even realistic model for the humanities going forward. Indeed, such notions could be downright detrimental; one can easily imagine the reaction of a budget-cutting university administrator or politician on hearing that the 'way forward' for the humanities included teaching vitalism as a valid critical approach. How long a future could such a renewed humanities realistically be expected to have? Braidotti also seems to think 'trans-disciplinary discursive fronts', which she sees as having emerged from 'around the edges of the classical Humanities and across the disciplines',[18] are an integral part of the 'posthuman' renewal of the humanities. She sees such fronts—for example, 'disability studies', 'ecological studies', 'animal studies' and so on— as being responsible for producing 'an explosion of scholarship' in the humanities.[19] But, one might wonder, if this 'explosion' is not better understood as the fragmentation of the humanities into ever more narrowly-focused and boutique-y 'niche-studies'. How and when would such fragmentation stop? One might also wonder how such niche studies would bring about a new future for the humanities, especially in a climate where more traditional humanities departments are being either cut, downsized or rolled into larger departments,[20] never mind create the noble goal of greater human 'interconnectedness' on a world-wide scale that Braidotti seems to value elsewhere in her book.[21] And how employable would PhDs from such niche-studies programmes actually be?[22]

What if, instead of pursuing a strain of the 'posthuman' that is anti-science and attempts to resurrect long since debunked notions, the 'future of humanities' lay in the direction of using the digital tools and technology available in digital humanities to transform that which they are supposedly handmaidens in the service of—the 'texts' and 'archives'? Might that not allow for the transformation of, say, literary or cultural studies, into something that the networked public Liu refers to above, would respect? It would certainly mean—in the context of literary studies—dislocating both beliefs about the primacy of written manuscripts or print media and—more generally—the conception of a book, film, game etc. as a historical, sacred, aesthetic artefact that is a carrier of meaning. Indeed, it could be argued that something amounting to the 'dislocation of print' has been underway in 'literary studies' for quite some time, as it has come under the influence of structuralism, poststructuralism, psychoanalysis, cultural studies, semiotics, adaptation studies, etc. Now a 'text' can be a book, or a film, a game, a photograph, a fashion, a hairstyle, a building, a film of a play, a society, and so on. However, unlike, ideological critique, which, in cultural studies, is often uncritically wielded and applied to texts in cookie-cutter fashion to produce politically correct assessments using divisive identity politics, digital humanities is not exhausted by such symptomatic readings, which do little more than catalogue representations and critique them as symptoms of subsurface ideologies, often with a healthy dose of 'outrage'. This is because digital tools and technologies transform—their original media, their aesthetic form or their historical context—and revitalize the texts they are used to explore.

A good example of how a digital tool can change a text can be found in the Hayles essay I mentioned above, which cites work done by students in Alan Liu's innovative 'Literature +' undergraduate and graduate courses at UC Santa Barbara. In one class, Liu's students transformed Shakespeare's *Romeo and Juliet* by transposing it into the *Facebook* platform, which involved mapping characters' social relations, filling out characters' personality profiles, etc.[23] Now, my deep reservations about *Facebook* aside, not only is such a transformation of the text (God forbid!) fun, it also means that students have to make critical decisions about what is important for understanding the characters in the play, plotting the networks of their relations, etc., and finding creative ways of adapting the play to the new medium. This type of digital transformation, in other words, actually makes students pay closer attention to the specificity of the text they are transforming. Reading texts in such a manner thus turns 'literary studies' into a sort of 'imaginative laboratory', where students get to acquire digital skills by experimenting with and eventually mastering cutting-edge digital tools. It is easy to imagine students taking sci-fi novels such as *Frankenstein* or *Blood Music* and, using storyboarding software such as *Storyboard That*, turning the novels into storyboards. Such an exercise would require that the student make critical, aesthetic and creative decisions about what elements of the original novel to play up or down, what plot-points to reveal in what order, what elements work in one medium and what ones don't in another, what media supplements might be needed, etc., as the novel migrates from one medium to another. It is also easy to imagine students plotting and graphing the networks of relations of characters in *Dawn* or *Snow Crash* using Gephi or creating maps of the texts' universes. In taking texts apart thus students learn how they were put together and can bring any other talents they may have to bear on their work. Other possible digital transformations of texts could include, but would not be confined to: audio recordings of a text, that could incorporate sound effects and music; video recordings of re-enactments of the text that could also incorporate dance or other visual materials and techniques; hypertextual annotations of a text's allusions, using video and/or audio files; or even, once the technology becomes cheap and stable enough, creating computer generated virtual worlds of texts: imagine slipping on an Oculus Rift virtual reality headset and being able to take a stroll through Vergil's bathroom as he is transformed by the noocytes or sitting under a pseudotree aboard the living Oankali ship . . .

Now, some might argue that the position outlined above amounts to a radical and undesirable deflation of the 'sanctity' of text and print culture generally that also vastly underestimates a reader's or viewer's susceptibility to the meanings, messages and ideologies that such texts can impose on individuals. Such an objection, of course, amounts to an argument in favour of the need for symptomatic reading. However, there are a number of problems with the assumptions that underlie the argument that symptomatic readings are necessary, which must be highlighted. To do this, let's take the case of the supposed impact that violence in movies and video games has on viewers and players. Christopher J. Ferguson, in a recent essay, 'Does Media Violence Predict Societal Violence? It Depends on What You Look at and When', discusses two studies that were conducted on the apparent relations of media violence rates with societal violence rates. In the first study, Ferguson found that while '[t]hroughout the mid-20th century small-to-moderate correlational relationships can be observed between movie violence and homicide rates in the United States', this 'trend reversed in the early and latter 20th century, with movie violence rates inversely related to homicide rates'.[24] Ferguson's second study examined 'videogame violence consumption' against the background of 'youth violence rates in the previous 2 decades'.[25] Ferguson found that videogame 'consumption is associated with a decline in youth violence rates. Results suggest that societal consumption of media violence is not predictive of increased societal violence rates.'[26] Ferguson's work, then, acts as a sobering counter to so-called 'hypodermic needle' theories of media, which, he argues, 'remove the user from the media experience except as a passive "victim" of a powerful, influential media.'[27] In other words, the assumption that consumers are brainwashed or influenced by the media they consume is not borne out by Ferguson's work. For this reason, Ferguson advocates a 'limited effects approach' to media because 'it can be anticipated that users will understand that the media experience differs from real life and it should not be assumed that ready transfer occurs from media to real-life behavior. . . . That is to say, it should not be assumed that the reward structures of the media experience can override reward and punishment structures from real life.'[28] So, it would seem that those who watch violent movies and/or play violent video games are (a) able to separate fiction from reality and (b) not influenced by the virtual violence they see because they do not behave violently in the real world. If nothing else, Ferguson's findings should at least make us very cautious around arguments for symptomatic readings which rely on the notion that representations of x or y are 'corrupting influences' on people's behaviour and attitudes. Perhaps such arguments are motivated more by a desire for simple censorship than anything else.

Then there is the problem of reliably proving if, and to what extent, language has an 'unconscious' influence on people. Take for example, the now famous difficulties of replicating the results of so-called 'social priming' experiments in psychology. In their July 2014 *Slate* essay on the poor replication of psychology experiment results, Michelle N. Meyer and Christopher Chabris define social priming in the following terms: 'Social priming, the field that is near the center of the replication debate, is like [psychologists Solomon] Asch [1907–1996] and [Stanley] Milgram [1933–1984] on steroids. According to social priming and related "embodiment" theories, overt instructions or demonstrations from others aren't necessary to influence our behavior; subtle environmental cues we aren't even aware of can have large effects on our decisions.'[29] Meyer and Chabris point to a special issue of *Social Psychology*, which attempted to replicate 27 important findings in social psychology;[30] of those 27, 10 could not be replicated; and, of the 7 that were in the area of social priming, only 1 could be replicated. In another replication study, which involved 100 experiments published in high-ranking psychology journals, published in *Science* found similarly unsettling results: only about one-third to a half of the original findings were also observed in the replication study.[31] According to an August, 2015 article published in *Vox*, one of those involved in the *Science* replication study, David Reinhard, a PhD student at the University of Virginia, tried to replicate a German study that 'looked at how "global versus local processing influenced the way participants used priming information in their judgment of others"'.[32] The original researchers were

> studying how people use concepts they are currently thinking about (in this case, aggression) to make judgments about other people's ambiguous behavior when they were in one of two mindsets: a big-picture (global) mindset versus a more detail-oriented (local) mindset. The original study had found that they were more suggestible when thinking big.... In the end, [Reinhard] couldn't reproduce their findings, and he doesn't know why his experiment failed.[33]

Elsewhere in their *Slate* article, Meyer and Chabris report on the failed replication of another famous and oft-cited priming study conducted by Simone Schnall, Jennifer Benton and Sophie Harvey.[34] In Schnall, Benton and Harvey's study, two experiments were conducted to measure 'the effects of people's thoughts or feelings of cleanliness on the harshness of their moral judgments'. In one of the experiments, '40 undergraduates were asked to unscramble sentences, with one-half assigned words related to cleanliness (like pure or pristine) and one-half assigned neutral words'.[35] They were then asked

> to rate the moral wrongness of six hypothetical scenarios, such as falsifying one's résumé and keeping money from a lost wallet. The researchers found that priming subjects to think about cleanliness had a 'substantial' effect on moral judgment: The hand washers and those who unscrambled sentences related to cleanliness judged the scenarios to be less morally wrong than did the other subjects. The implication was that people who feel relatively pure themselves are—without realizing it—less troubled by others' impurities.[36]

However, the replicators of this experiment—David Johnson, Felix Cheung, and Brent Donnellan of Michigan State University—'found no such difference, despite testing about four times more subjects than the original studies'.[37] According to Meyer and Chabris,

> a few years ago, researchers managed to publish a few failures to replicate prominent social priming experiments. Partly in

response, Nobel Prize-winning cognitive psychologist Daniel Kahneman, whose work has had far-reaching influence in law, government, economics, and many other fields, wrote an open letter to social psychologists working in this area. He counted himself a 'general believer' in the effects [of social priming] and noted that he had cited them in his own work. But Kahneman warned of 'a train wreck looming' for social priming research. 'Colleagues who in the past accepted your surprising results as facts when they were published . . . have now attached a question mark to the field,' he said, 'and it is your responsibility to remove it.[38]

All in all, it would seem that if there is an argument to be made that language and texts consciously and unconsciously 'prime' those who read or view them and must therefore be carefully 'parsed' for their hidden ideological baggage by humanities graduates, then those 'studies' making such an argument must first do the actual work of demonstrating that such a process exists in the first place. If such a process does not exist—and the evidence I've cited above suggests that it does not—and if so much of what passes for analysis in the humanities is predicated on such a process, then it would seem that there's some serious trouble ahead for all such studies.

Metadata and network theory: digital reading

To conclude, I'd like to sketch the outlines of a 'posthumanities interdiscipline'—digital reading, which incorporates both metadata and network theory. As I argued above, literary and cultural studies—and many of the assumptions that undergird them—would be tested and transformed by contact with both digital tools and science of concrete posthumanism; and it is hard to see that transformation as a bad thing if it means moving away from dogmatic assumptions about what texts are and what they are doing. Perhaps the time has come to think about texts—which are, after all, only ever really produced as forms of entertainment and are not 'sacred' in any way, shape or form—as resources that would give students, as users of digital tools, interesting material to practise honing their skills on as they transform that material and become co-re-creators of cultural heritage and artefacts. Digital reading in this manner would no longer be concerned with simply 'preserving' such texts; instead, it would be inextricable from repurposing, re-mixing, transforming and mashing-up the print text in surprising—and, for some, no doubt, upsetting—ways. Imagine a traditional literary-cultural studies classroom transformed into a networked digital media lab, with up-to-date recording equipment, a suite of digital tools, including powerful editing software, and excellent visual displays that would allow students to see and interact with each other's projects in real time. Certainly, new guidelines would need to be drawn up for dealing with the issues of rights management—relating to both the material originally worked on by, as well as the material produced by students—and obviously there would also be a need to rethink research methodologies and even grading practices. But such an approach to literature would at least teach a student vital skill with cutting-edge digital tools; and a student's ability to use digital tools effectively would also make him or her digitally literate and thus even more attractive to a prospective employer.

And yet, all that I have so far outlined would still only amount to tapping a small part of the power and potential of digital tools and machine reading: a major strength of digital tools lies in their relation to what's known as metadata. Metadata is defined as the data that provides information about one or more aspects of data. A commonly used example to illustrate metadata is that of a digital photograph: such a photograph includes data describing how large the picture is, the color depth, the resolution, with what, when and where the photo was taken, etc. (known as Exif data, Exchangeable image file format). In other words, metadata may not tell you what the content of the photograph is, but it will tell you all sorts of other interesting things. It is metadata that Alan Liu points to in passing when he seeks to counter the perception that digital humanities is a mere handmaiden to the humanities 'proper': 'To be an equal partner—rather than, again, just a servant—at the table, digital humanists will need to show that thinking critically about metadata, for instance, scales into thinking critically about the power, finance, and other governance protocols of the world.'[39]

I will return to Liu's point about power, finance and governance below; first, however, I want to highlight how metadata gave rise to what has come to be known as 'distant reading'. Metadata is linked to distant reading insofar as both have less to do with the 'content' of a file than with information about the file; as such, distant reading stands in sharp contrast to the more common practice of 'close reading', which pays careful attention to the content and meaning of a text. The evidence used by close reading usually takes the form of block quotations, and it often overlaps with the symptomatic reading discussed above. The origins of distant reading can be traced to Franco Moretti's groundbreaking 2005 book, *Graphs, Maps, Trees: Abstract Models for a Literary History*,[40] in which he attempts to read literary works using quantitative methods adapted from the social sciences. Alan Liu points out that in the wake of Moretti's work

> [s]ophisticated digital humanities methods that require explicit programmatic instructions and metadata schema now take the ground of elemental practice previously occupied by equally sophisticated but tacit close reading methods. Moretti and his collaborators, therefore, explore 'the great unread' of vast quantities of literature (rather than only exceptional literature) through text analysis, topic modeling, data mining, pattern recognition, and visualization methods that have to be practiced at the beginning and not just interpretive or theoretical end of literary study.[41]

Liu continues:

> the contrast between the practices of close reading and the digital humanities is so stark that it is changing the very nature of the ground being fought over: the text. The relevant text is no longer the New Critical [a type of literary analysis that used close reading and defined the literary artifact as a self-contained object] 'poem itself' but instead the digital humanities archive, corpus, or network—a situation aggravated even further because block quotations serving as a middle ground for fluid movement between close and distant reading are disappearing from view.[42]

One can see here the potential for an empirically grounded return to structuralism, which Matthew L. Jocker's work explicitly points in the direction of.[43] Liu goes on to say that in digital humanities, block quotations drop out of perception entirely because text analysis focuses on microlevel linguistic features (e.g., word frequencies) that map directly over macrolevel phenomena (e.g., different genres or nationalities of novels) without need for the middle level of quoted passages; or they exist as what hypertext theorists, originally inspired by Roland Barthes, call 'lexia'—that is, modular chunks in a larger network where the real interest inheres in the global pattern of the network. In either case, one noticeable effect of distant reading in Moretti['s . . .] mode is that data visualizations of large patterns increasingly replace block quotations as the objects of sustained focus.[44]

So, as block quotations—like the ones I am using here—from an individual text slip from view, metadata, patterns, networks and data visualizations hove into view as the objects of digital reading and analysis. And—as Liu mentions in passing—metadata, patterns and networks are entangled with questions of power, finance and governance. However, since Liu doesn't really expand on what he has in mind here, I want to finish by offering a couple of recent real-world examples that serve to illustrate just what's at stake with metadata when it comes to questions of power, finance and governance.

Starting back in June 2013, Edward Snowden, an American computer professional who was working on contract for the National Security Agency (NSA), began leaking classified information which revealed that the NSA was collecting massive amounts of metadata. But it was not the metadata of terrorists or criminals that interested the NSA; on the contrary, it wanted to, as its former director, General Keith Alexander, said, 'Collect It All.'[45] Nobody, in other words, is safe from this sort of governmental spying, which is only made possible in the first place by the very digital communication devices we use so often. A report that appeared in the June 7, 2013 edition of *The Washington Post*, makes the general process clear: a program, 'code-named BLARNEY . . . gathers up "metadata"— technical information about communications traffic and network devices—as it streams past choke points along the backbone of the Internet. [BLARNEY is] "an ongoing collection program that leverages IC [intelligence community] and commercial partnerships to gain access and exploit foreign intelligence obtained from global networks."'[46] Those looking at the metadata need never know the actual content of whatever data is sent, which is appropriate, since

Claude E. Shannon's conception of information sees it as being somewhat distinguishable from the semantic content of a particular message.[47] For example, if I'm tracking your phone calls and I see you first phone your doctor's office, then the fertility clinic and then close family members, I don't actually need to hear what's being said to know what's likely going on. Instead, all I need do is apply a little abductive reasoning, going from an observation to a hypothesis that accounts for the observation, seeking the simplest and most likely explanation: you are finally pregnant.

Metadata relating to, among other things, IP addresses, hardware ID, telephone numbers, frequency and duration of calls, amounts of data transferred, etc., is then examined using social network analysis (which is not the same as an analysis of social media, like *Twitter* and *Facebook*, although traffic on those networks would be examined also). Social network analysis views social relationships in terms of the mathematics of network theory—networks consist of 'nodes', which represent individual actors within the network, and 'ties', which represent relationships between the individual nodes— to establish the likely relations between those under surveillance. A well-known example of the analytical power of social network analysis can be found in Valdis E. Krebs' 2002 paper, 'Mapping Networks of Terrorist Cells'.[48] In this now classic paper, Krebs set about using social network analysis to reconstruct the terrorist cell behind the tragic events of September 11th; using only public data, he was 'able to map a portion of the network centered around the 19 dead hijackers',[49] which coincided—at least in part—with what official intelligence was uncovering. He was then invited to Washington to meet with intelligence contractors.[50]

What metadata actually says about individuals is also neatly illustrated by a 2012 study of phone metadata—call duration and frequency, amount of time used and data downloaded, etc.—which found that it was possible to determine the gender, age, marital status, job and number of people in a household of users to an accuracy that ranged from 45 to 87 per cent, depending upon the particular classification problem.[51] A more recent study published in *Science*, showed that 90 per cent of individuals could be uniquely re-identified from their credit card metadata using just four pieces of spatio-temporal information, such as knowing if the person in question bought a loaf of bread or visited a restaurant.[52] Once identified, that individual's purchases and movements could then be extensively reconstructed; women, the researchers found, were easier to re-identify than men. And it is the metadata of your browsing habits that online behavioural advertising (OBA) companies like Google and AdRoll collect and sell to companies like Amazon.[53] Although this information is not tied to your personal information—they don't, for example, know your name, your home address, or your phone number—these companies can identify you by a random ID number and they use algorithms to make inferences about your age, sex, interests, etc., and predictions about your interests based on your online activity.

I use these real-world examples to illustrate quickly what's at stake in metadata and using digital tools: metadata and digital tools shift us away from reading models where 'print' and 'symptoms' are central and towards objects of study that are perhaps better understood as dynamic networks of behaviour and information about information. I'd suggest that metadata and digital networks are worthy of the attention of those in the humanities and literary-cultural studies in particular because they amount to digital 'texts' that we 'write', and are 'written' about us by governmental and commercial organizations, day in, day out, through our use of digital communications technology and tools. However, the traditional tools of cultural or literary analysis—symptomatic readings, close readings folk-psychology and so on—are wholly insufficient to read these networks and the metadata they produce because they are only really graspable using digital tools and technologies that are in turn shaped by the mathematical relations of social network analysis, probability and information. In other words, reading such digitally generated texts demands true interdisciplinarity, simply because humanities assumptions and competencies alone are not enough; the stances and competencies found in science, technology, engineering and mathematics are essential to becoming digitally literate. And, since the digital networks I've been describing are now the tools that businesses and governments use to construct us as consumers and citizens, then, in my view, those of us who see ourselves as educators are not doing our jobs if we do not teach our students about the tools and techniques that are being used to read them by teaching them to be digitally literate in the use of those same tools and techniques. A perhaps useful way to think about such 'digital citizenry' involves 'subjectivation' in the Foucauldian sense: power may be that which subjects you, but it is also that which simultaneously enables you.[54] Power, in other words, is thus not simply about dominance; nor, however, can it be divorced from it. Maybe there are no 'symptoms' for symptomatic reading to read after all; all that there is comes down to *pharmakonic* technologies and tools. Digital reading would thus be a prime example of a concrete 'posthumanities interdiscipline', a truly interdisciplinary subject, one that is no longer constrained by the old split between the 'humanities' and the 'sciences'. And digital reading would be an interdiscipline that is also a perfect example of concrete posthumanism insofar as it is nothing other than humans working with digital tools.

NOTES

Chapter 1

1   Michel Foucault, 'What is Enlightenment?' in Paul Rabinow (ed.), *The Foucault Reader* (New York: Pantheon Books, 1984).

2   Foucault, 'What is Enlightenment?', 44.

3   Edwin Hutchins, *Cognition in the Wild* (Cambridge, MA: MIT Press, 1995).

4   Bernard Steigler, *Technics and Time, 1: The Fault of Epimetheus* (trans. Richard Beardsworth and George Collins. Stanford: Stanford University Press, 1998).

5   David McFarland, *Guilty Robots, Happy Dogs: The Question of Alien Minds* (Oxford: Oxford University Press, 2009).

6   Andy Clark, *Natural Born Cyborgs: Minds, Technologies, and the Future of Human Intelligence* (Oxford: Oxford University Press, 2003).

7   Cary Wolfe, *What is Posthumanism?* (Minneapolis: University of Minnesota Press, 2010). Notable also is N. Katherine Hayles, *How We Became Posthuman: Virtual Bodies in Cybernetics, Literature and Informatics* (Chicago: University of Chicago Press, 1999).

8   For more discussion of distributed cognition, see Chapter 2, below.

9   For more on neuroprosthetics, genetics, AI (artificial intelligence) and robotics, see Chapters 2 and 3, below.

10 Jean-Francois Lyotard, *The Postmodern Condition: A Report on Knowledge* (Minneapolis: University of Minnesota Press, 1984).

11 Neil Badmington, *Alien Chic: Posthumanism and the Other Within* (London: Routledge, 2004).

12 For more on functionalism, especially in the context of artificial intelligence, the philosophy of mind, robots and animals see Chapters 2 and 5, below.

13 David McFarland, 'Chapter 7: The Material Mind', *Guilty Robots, Happy Dogs: The Question of Alien Minds* (Oxford: Oxford

University Press, 2008). Throughout this book, I will cite from the Kindle version of McFarland's book; because of this, no page references can be given, only chapter titles.

14 Ibid.

15 Ibid.

16 For more on neuroprosthetics, genetics, AI (artificial intelligence) and robotics, see Chapters 2 and 3, below.

17 John Locke, *Two Treatises of Government* (Cambridge: Cambridge University Press, 1960).

18 For more on data gathering and big data, see Chapter 6, below.

19 For more on neuroprosthetics, see Chapter 2, below.

20 'World premiere of muscle and nerve controlled arm prosthesis', *Science Daily* (http://www.sciencedaily.com/releases/2013/02/130222075730.htm). See also 'Thought-controlled prosthesis is changing the lives of amputees', Chalmers University of Technology Press Release (http://www.chalmers.se/en/news/Pages/Thought-controlled-prosthesis-is-changing-the-lives-of-amputees.aspx).

21 See Kevin Warwick, et al., 'Thought Communication and Control: A First Step Using Radiotelegraphy', *IEE Proceedings on Communications*, 151.3 (2004): 185–189.

22 For more on these experiments and their implications, see Chapters 2 and 5, below.

23 Ernest Cline, *Ready Player One* (New York: Broadway Books, 2012). For more on the role of cultural texts in posthumanism, see Chapter 4, below.

24 Guy Debord, *The Society of the Spectacle* (trans. Donald Nicholson-Smith. New York: Zone Books, 2005).

25 Ibid., 12.

26 Ibid.

27 Ibid., 29.

28 J.G. Ballard, *Crash* (London: Picador, 2001).

29 Geoffrey Chaucer, 'The Wife of Bath's Prologue and Tale' in *The Canterbury Tales* (London: Penguin Classics, 2009).

30 'The World in 2014: ICT Facts and Figures', International Telecommunication Union (http://www.itu.int/en/ITU-D/Statistics/Documents/facts/ICTFactsFigures2014-e.pdf.

31 'The FCC Did NOT Make the Internet a Public Utility', *Backchannel* (http://medium.com/backchannel/the-historical-record-of-net-neutrality-747286cbde62).

32 See Mark Graham, 'The Knowledge Based Economy and Digital Divisions of Labour' in Vandana Desai and Rob Potter (eds.), *The Companion to Development Studies* (London: Routledge, 2014), 189–195. Full text available at SSRN: http://ssrn.com/abstract=2363880.

33 See http://www.raspberrypi.org.

34 'Poverty: Overview', The World Bank (http://www.worldbank.org/en/topic/poverty/overview).

35 See, for example, 'Edward Snowden: the whistleblower behind the NSA surveillance revelations', *The Guardian Online* (http://www.theguardian.com/world/2013/jun/09/edward-snowden-nsa-whistleblower-surveillance). For more on this, see Chapter 6, below.

36 'Poverty: Overview', The World Bank (http://www.worldbank.org/en/topic/poverty/overview). See also 'New Data Show 1.4 Billion Live On Less Than US$1.25 A Day, But Progress Against Poverty Remains Strong', The World Bank Press Release (http://www.worldbank.org/en/news/press-release/2008/09/16/new-data-show-14-billion-live-less-us125-day-progress-against-poverty-remains-strong).

37 See Jon Krakauer, *Into the Wild* (New York: Villard, 1996).

38 See, for example, Micah Lee, 'Encryption Works: How to Protect Your Privacy in the Age of NSA Surveillance', Freedom of the Press Foundation (http://freedom.press/encryption-works).

39 See http://www.rethinkrobotics.com/baxter/.

40 'Foxconn's Robot Army Yet to Prove Match for Humans' *WSJ Tech Blog* (http://blogs.wsj.com/digits/2015/05/05/foxconns-robot-army-yet-to-prove-match-for-humans/).

41 'Growing a Nation: The Story of American Agriculture: Historical Timeline' (http://www.agclassroom.org/gan/timeline/).

42 See 'Report: artificial intelligence will cause "structural collapse" of law firms by 2030', *Legal Futures* (http://www.legalfutures.co.uk/latest-news/report-ai-will-transform-legal-world).

43 Mark Walker, 'BIG and Technological Unemployment: Chicken Little Versus the Economists', *Journal of Evolution and Technology*, 24.1 (February 2014). Available online at: http://jetpress.org/v24/walker.htm. For more on universal basic income schemes, see Chapter 3, below.

44 See, for example, 'Stephen Hawking warns artificial intelligence could end mankind', *BBC Technology News* (http://www.bbc.co.uk/news/technology-30290540) and 'Elon Musk: artificial intelligence is our biggest existential threat', *The Guardian Online* (http://www.

theguardian.com/technology/2014/oct/27/elon-musk-artificial-intelligence-ai-biggest-existential-threat). See also, Nick Bostrom, *Superintelligence: Paths, Dangers, Strategies* (Oxford: Oxford University Press, 2014).

45 See, for example, 'The driverless truck is coming, and it's going to automate millions of jobs', *TechCrunch* (http://techcrunch.com/2016/04/25/the-driverless-truck-is-coming-and-its-going-to-automate-millions-of-jobs/).

46 'The onrushing wave', *The Economist* (http://www.economist.com/news/briefing/21594264-previous-technological-innovation-has-always-delivered-more-long-run-employment-not-less).

47 Thomas Piketty, *Capital in the Twenty-First Century* (Cambridge, MA: Harvard University Press, 2014).

48 See, for example, Erik Olin Wright, 'Basic Income as a Socialist Project.' *Rutgers Journal of Law & Urban Policy*, 2.1 (Fall 2005). Available online at: https://www.ssc.wisc.edu/~wright/Basic%20Income%20as%20a%20Socialist%20Project.pdf.

49 Mary Shelley, *Frankenstein* (New York: W. W. Norton, 2012). For a longer discussion about how science fiction has explored techno-scientific knowledge and the threats and benefits it holds for humanity, see Chapter 4, below.

50 Vincent C. Müller and Nick Bostrom, 'Future progress in artificial intelligence: A Survey of Expert Opinion', in Vincent C. Müller (ed.), *Fundamental Issues of Artificial Intelligence* (Berlin: Springer, 2014). Available online at: http://www.nickbostrom.com/papers/survey.pdf.

51 See, for example, Ray Kurzweil, *The Singularity is Near* (London: Penguin, 2006) and Kurzweil, *How to Create a Mind* (London: Penguin, 2013).

52 For a discussion of the history and examples of AI, see Chapter 3, below; for a discussion of superintelligence and the Singularity, see Chapter 5.

53 See 'Google's DeepMind Masters Atari Games', *Forbes Online* (http://www.forbes.com/sites/paulrodgers/2015/02/28/googles-deepmind-masters-atari-games/). For more on deep learning and DQN, see Chapter 3, below.

54 Jacques Derrida, *Dissemination* (trans. Barbara Johnson. London: Athlone Press, 1981).

55 Ibid., 127.

56 Fredric Jameson, *Postmodernism, or, the Cultural Logic of Late Capitalism* (Durham, NC: Duke University Press, 1991).

57   Ibid., 47.

58   For a longer discussion of these issues, see Chapters 4, 5 and 6, below.

59   For a discussion of these authors and their engagement with questions relating to posthumanism and art, see Chapter 4, below.

Chapter 2

1   See Martin Robbins, 'Why I Spoofed Science Journalism, and How to Fix It' (http://www.theguardian.com/science/the-lay-scientist/2010/sep/28/science-journalism-spoof).

2   See Emily Willingham, 'We Need A Recall System For Bad Science Reporting' (http://www.forbes.com/sites/emilywillingham/2013/06/24/rice-lead-and-the-problem-of-untracked-science-reporting/).

3   See 'How Science Goes Wrong' (http://www.economist.com/news/leaders/21588069-scientific-research-has-changed-world-now-it-needs-change-itself-how-science-goes-wrong).

4   http://www.reddit.com/r/Futurology/.

5   See John Letzing, 'Google Hires Famed Futurist Ray Kurzweil' (http://blogs.wsj.com/digits/2012/12/14/google-hires-famed-futurist-ray-kurzweil/?mod=WSJBlog&utm_source=twitterfeed&utm_medium=twitter&source=email_rt_mc_body&ifp=0)

6   See Conner Forrest, 'Google and Robots: The Real Reasons Behind the Shopping Spree' (http://www.techrepublic.com/article/google-and-robots-the-real-reasons-behind-the-shopping-spree/). As I was editing this chapter (March 2016), I discovered that Google has since put Boston Dynamics up for sale. See 'Google Puts Boston Dynamics Up for Sale in Robotics Retreat' (http://www.bloomberg.com/news/articles/2016-03-17/google-is-said-to-put-boston-dynamics-robotics-unit-up-for-sale).

7   Paul R. Gross and Norman Levitt, *Higher Superstition: The Academic Left and Its Quarrels With Science* (Baltimore: Johns Hopkins University Press, 1997); Alan Sokal and Jean Bricmont, *Fashionable Nonsense: Postmodern Intellectuals' Abuse of Science* (New York: Picador, 1998).

8   See Gross and Levitt, *xi* and 251.

9   See, for example, 'What's a "Safe Space"? A Look at the Phrase's 50-year History' (http://fusion.net/story/231089/safe-space-history/).

10   For more on Gamergate, see 'Occupy WWW Street (EN): Internet Activism and Media in the Age of Social Justice' (http://acko.net/blog/occupy-www-street-en/) and 'Blame GamerGate's Bad Rep on Smears and Shoddy Journalism' (http://observer.com/2015/10/blame-gamergates-bad-rep-on-smears-and-shoddy-journalism/).

11   Bruno Latour, *Reassembling the Social. An Introduction to Actor-Network-Theory* (Oxford: Oxford University Press, 2005), 100.

12   Ibid., 144.

13   Norbert Wiener, *Cybernetics Or Control and Communication in the Animal and the Machine* (New York: Wiley, 1948), 19.

14   Francis Heylighen and Cliff Joslyn, 'Cybernetics and Second-Order Cybernetics.' The original article is to be found in R.A. Meyers (ed.), *Encyclopedia of Physical Science and Technology* (New York: Academic Press, 2001). A stand-alone version of Heylighen and Joslyn's article is available online at: pespmc1.vub.ac.be/papers/cybernetics-epst.pdf. This is the version of the article that I will be referring to throughout this book. The above in-text citation is from page 2 of the PDF.

15   Ibid.

16   According to Wiener, the sense of cybernetics that interests him was not used before 'the summer of 1947' (*Cybernetics*, 19).

17   The American Society for Cybernetics, 'The History of Cybernetics: Chapter 2: The Coalescence of Cybernetics' (http://www.asc-cybernetics.org/foundations/history2.htm).

18   In all, there were ten Macy Conferences on cybernetics, and they were attended fairly consistently by a core group that included Gregory Bateson, Margaret Mead, John von Neumann, Norbert Wiener, Warren McCulloch and Walter Pitts among others. Claude Shannon also attended several Macy Conferences over the years. See The American Society for Cybernetics, 'The History of Cybernetics: Chapter 2: The Coalescence of Cybernetics.'

19   Ibid. See also Heinz von Foerster, 'Ethics and Second-Order Cybernetics' in *Understanding Understanding: Essays on Cybernetics and Cognition* (New York: Springer-Verlag, 2003), 288.

20   Ibid. See also Wiener, *Cybernetics*, 19–20.

21   The American Society for Cybernetics, 'The History of Cybernetics: Chapter 2: The Coalescence of Cybernetics.'

22   Ibid.

23   Ibid.

24   The American Society for Cybernetics, 'The ASC Glossary' (http://www.asc-cybernetics.org/foundations/ASCGlossary.htm).

25 Heinz von Foerster, 'Ethics and Second-Order Cybernetics', 287.

26 The American Society for Cybernetics, 'The ASC Glossary' (http://www.asc-cybernetics.org/foundations/ASCGlossary.htm).

27 James Clerk Maxwell, 'On Governors', *Proceedings of the Royal Society of London* (1868), 270–283. Available online at: www.maths.ed.ac.uk/~aar/papers/maxwell1.pdf. A governor basically closes the throttle valve in response to increases in engine speed and opens it if the speed slows; the goal of the governor is thus to keep the engine's speed running at a near constant.

28 Wiener, *Cybernetics*, 19.

29 W.B. Cannon, 'Physiological Regulation of Normal States: Some Tentative Postulates Concerning Biological Homeostatics', in A. Pettit (ed.), *A Charles Richet: ses amis, ses collègues, ses élèves* (Paris: Les Éditions Médicales, 1926), 91.

30 Richard L. Hills, *Power From the Wind* (Cambridge: Cambridge University Press, 1996).

31 Wiener, *Cybernetics*, 18.

32 See David Kahn, *The Codebreakers* (rev. edn, New York: Simon and Schuster, 1996), 743–751. Claude E. Shannon, 'A Mathematical Theory of Communication', *Bell System Technical Journal*, 27 (1948): 379–423; 623–656.

33 'Bell Labs' (https://en.wikipedia.org/wiki/Bell_Labs).

34 For an informative overview of the origins of Morse Code, see Russell W. Burns' excellent *Communications: An International History of the Formative Years* (London: Institution of Electrical Engineers, 2004).

35 Russell W. Burns, *Communications: An International History of the Formative Years*, 84. The linotype machine—first patented in the US in 1884 by Ottmar Morgenthaler—used to set type in newspaper production at the end of the nineteenth and start of the twentieth centuries also made use of the same principle of letter-frequency. The operators of Morse code or linotype equipment were thus immersed in both probability and the binary encoding of language.

36 Ibid.

37 Ibid.

38 Shannon, 'A Mathematical Theory of Communication', 379.

39 Ibid.

40 Ibid., 393.

41 https://en.wikipedia.org/wiki/Bit.

42 Claude E. Shannon, 'Prediction and Entropy of Printed English', *The Bell System Technical Journal*, 30.1 (1951): 50–64.

43 Shannon, 'Prediction and Entropy', 54.

44 The American Society for Cybernetics, The History of Cybernetics, 'Chapter 3: Proliferation of Cybernetics in the 1950's and Beyond' (http://www.asc-cybernetics.org/foundations/history3.htm).

45 Isaac Asimov, *I, Robot* (New York: Bantam Spectra, 1991). *I, Robot* is a collection of Asimov's stories that had already been published throughout the 1940s in magazines like *Super Science Stories* and *Astounding Science Fiction*. I will return to Asimov and *I, Robot* in particular in Chapter 4, below.

46 The American Society for Cybernetics, The History of Cybernetics, 'Chapter 3: Proliferation of Cybernetics in the 1950's and Beyond' (http://www.asc-cybernetics.org/foundations/history3.htm). See also, 'For God's Sake, Margaret: A Conversation with Gregory Bateson and Margaret Mead', *CoEvolutionary Quarterly*, 10.21 (1976): 32–44. For a discussion of how second-order cybernetics overlaps with certain books and films that examine posthumanism, see Chapter 4, below.

47 Heinz von Foerster, 'Ethics and Second-Order Cybernetics' in *Understanding Understanding*, 289 [italics in original].

48 Here, I am following Heylighen and Joslyn's use of the example on page 9 of their 'Cybernetics and Second-Order Cybernetics.'

49 A quick way to visualize state space would be to think of all the possible positions people can take in an orderly queue—{1, 2, 3, 4, 5,. . .}; a more complex state space would be the one constituted by all the possible positions the pieces in a game of chess could potentially occupy in combination with each other.

50 Heylighen and Joslyn, 'Cybernetics and Second-Order Cybernetics,' 10.

51 Ibid. [italics in original].

52 Ibid.

53 Ibid.

54 Ibid. [italics in original].

55 Ibid., 11.

56 The differences between self-organization, closure and autopoiesis will be important for the discussion of fictional texts that focus on posthumanism in Chapter 4.

57 Gordon Pask, 'Heinz von Foerster's Self-Organisation, the Progenitor of Conversation and Interaction Theories', *Systems Research* 13.3 (1996): 349–362 [353].

58 Von Foerster, 'On Self-Organizing Systems and Their Environments', in *Understanding Understanding: Essays on Cybernetics and Cognition*, 3.

59 'On Self-Organizing Systems and Their Environments', in *Understanding Understanding: Essays on Cybernetics and Cognition*, 7.

60 Humberto R. Maturana and Francisco J. Varela, *Autopoiesis and Cognition: The Realization of the Living* (Dordrecht: D Reidel, 1980), 78.

61 Jerome Lettvin, Humberto R. Maturana, Warren McCulloch and Walter Pitts, 'What the Frog's Eye Tells the Frog's Brain', *Proceedings of the Institute for Radio Engineers* 47.11 (1959): 1940–1951 [1950].

62 Maturana and Varela, *Autopoiesis and Cognition*, xv.

63 Heylighen and Joslyn, 'Cybernetics and Second-Order Cybernetics,' 11 [italics in original].

64 Maturana and Francisco J. Varela, *Autopoiesis and Cognition*, 9.

65 Ibid., xxii.

66 Ibid., 121.

67 Heylighen and Joslyn, 'Cybernetics and Second-Order Cybernetics', 21.

68 Heylighen and Joslyn, 'Cybernetics and Second-Order Cybernetics', 22.

69 'On Constructing a Reality' in *Understanding Understanding: Essays on Cybernetics and Cognition*, 226–227. See also 'On Self-Organizing Systems and Their Environments' in the same volume.

70 Heinz von Foerster, 'On Self-Organizing Systems and Their Environments', in *Understanding Understanding: Essays on Cybernetics and Cognition*, 4 [italics in original].

71 Ibid.

72 'Relativism' and 'relativity' are quite different: in relativism, points of view are subjective and irreconcilable, whereas in *relativity*, space-time coordinates can be transformed unambiguously between reference frames.

73 Ibid. It is interesting to note that in a later essay, 'On Constructing a Reality', von Foerster shifts this formulation back in a direction that seems to me to undo the solution to solipsism he proposes in the just-cited essay. In the later essay, he effectively re-exposes second-order cybernetics to all the problems of relativism by suggesting that

shared reality is actually something purely 'social', not physical. See page 227 especially.

74 Ibid.

75 Philip K. Dick, *I Hope I Shall Arrive Soon* (New York: Doubleday, 1985).

76 James Hollan, Ed Hutchins and David Kirsh, 'Distributed Cognition: Toward a New Foundation for Human-Computer Interaction Research.' *ACM Transactions on Computer-Human Interaction (TOCHI)*, 7.2 (2000), 174–196, 175–6.

77 Edwin Hutchins, *Cognition in the Wild* (Cambridge, MA: MIT Press, 1995), 55.

78 Andy Clark, *Natural Born Cyborgs: Minds, Technologies, and the Future of Human Intelligence* (Oxford: Oxford University Press, 2003), 7. The cerebral cortex is the brain's outer layer of neural tissue and it plays a key role in memory, attention, perception, awareness, thought, language, and consciousness; the hippocampi (humans, like other mammals have two) lie under the cortex and appear to consolidate information from short-term memory to long-term memory and spatial navigation.

79 For more on transhumanism, see Chapter 5, below.

80 Kevin Warwick *et al.*, 'The Application of Implant Technology for Cybernetic Systems', *Archives of Neurology* 60.10 (2003): 1369–1373.

81 Ibid., 1370.

82 William Gibson, *Neuromancer* (New York: Ace Books, 1984).

83 Kevin Warwick *et al.*, 'Thought Communication and Control: A First Step Using Radiotelegraphy', *IEE Proceedings—Communications*, 151.3 (2004): 185–189.

84 Ibid., 188.

85 'Performer Gets Third Ear for Art' (http://news.bbc.co.uk/2/hi/health/7039821.stm).

86 http://www.eecg.toronto.edu/~mann/.

87 'The Brave New World of Biohacking' (http://america.aljazeera.com/articles/2013/10/18/the-brave-new-worldofbiohacking.html).

88 Jacqueline Finch, 'The Ancient Origins of Prosthetic Medicine', *The Lancet*, 377.9765 (12 February 2011): 548–549.

89 Eric C. Leuthardt, Jarod L. Roland, and Wilson Z. Ray, 'Neuroprosthetics', *The Scientist* (November 2014) (http://www.the-scientist.com/?articles.view/articleNo/41324/title/Neuroprosthetics/).

90 Jacques J. Vidal, 'Toward Direct Brain Computer Communication', *Annual Review of Biophysics and Bioengineering*, 2 (1973): 157–180 [157].

91 Leuthardt et al., 'Neuroprosthetics', *The Scientist*.

92 Ibid.

93 Ibid.

94 The word 'cyborg' was first coined by Manfred Clynes and Nathan S. Kline in their essay, 'Cyborgs and Space', *Astronautics* (September 1960): 26–27; 74–76. The 'cyborg deliberately incorporates exogenous components [biochemical, physiological, and electronic modifications] extending the self-regulatory control function of the organism in order to adapt it to new environment' (27).

95 Mikhail A. Lebedev and Miguel A.L. Nicolelis, 'Brain-Machine Interfaces: Past, Present and Future', *TRENDS in Neurosciences*, 29.9 (2006): 536–546 [536].

96 Clark, *Natural Born Cyborgs*, 91–92.

97 Jacques Marescaux, J. Leroy, F. Rubino, M. Vix, M. Simone and D. Mutter, 'Transcontinental Robot Assisted Remote Telesurgery: Feasibility and Potential Applications', *Annals of Surgery*, 235 (2002): 487–492.

98 I will be exploring in detail the relations between Derrida's work on presence, technology and posthumanism elsewhere.

99 Steve M. Potter and Thomas B. DeMarse, 'A New Approach to Neural Cell Culture for Long-Term Studies', *Journal of Neuroscience Methods*, 110 (2001): 17–24.

100 Ibid.

101 Ibid.

102 Michael Kositsky, Michela Chiappalone, Simon T. Alford and Ferdinando A. Mussa-Ivaldi, 'Brain-Machine Interactions for Assessing the Dynamics of Neural Systems', *Frontiers in Neurorobotics*, 3 (March 2009): 1–12 [1].

103 Ibid.

104 Clark, *Natural Born Cyborgs*, 34.

105 Lebedev and Nicolelis, 'Brain-Machine Interfaces: Past, Present and Future', *TRENDS in Neurosciences*, 29.9 (2006): 536–546 [536].

106 Ibid., 536–537.

107 Ibid., 537–538.

108 Ibid., 537.

109 Ibid., 536.

110 Ibid.

111 Ibid., 538.

112 Ibid.

113 Ibid.

114 Ibid.

115 Ibid.

116 Ibid., 539.

117 Ibid.

118 Ibid.

119 I will return to machine learning in Chapter 3.

120 Ibid.

121 Mikhail Lebedev *et al.*, 'Cortical Ensemble Adaptation to Represent Velocity of an Artificial Actuator Controlled by a Brain-Machine Interface', *Journal of Neuroscience,* 25.19 (11 May 2005): 4681–4693 [4682].

122 Lebedev and Nicolelis, 'Brain-Machine Interfaces: Past, Present and Future', 539.

123 Ibid.

124 Ibid., 541–542.

125 Ibid.

126 Ibid., 542.

127 Ibid.

128 Ibid., 543.

129 J.E. O'Doherty, *et al.*, 'Active Tactile Exploration Enabled by a Brain-Machine-Brain Interface', *Nature,* 479 (2011): 228–231.

130 Lebedev and Nicolelis, 'Brain-Machine Interfaces: Past, Present and Future', 540.

131 Ibid.

132 Ibid., 539–540.

133 Ibid., 540–541.

134 Ibid., 541.

135 Ibid., 540.

136 Ibid.

137 Ibid.

138 Ibid.

139 Jia Liu *et al.*, 'Syringe-Injectable Electronics', *Nature Nanotechnology* (08 June, 2015) (http://www.nature.com/nnano/journal/vaop/ncurrent/full/nnano.2015.115.html).

140 http://www.sciencedaily.com/releases/2013/02/130222075730.htm.

141 Max Ortiz-Catalan, Bo Håkansson and Rickard Brånemark, 'An Osseointegrated Human-Machine Gateway for Long-Term Sensory Feedback and Motor Control Of Artificial Limbs', *Science Translational Medicine*, 6.257 (8 October 2014): 1–8.

142 http://www.chalmers.se/en/news/Pages/Thought-controlled-prosthesis-is-changing-the-lives-of-amputees.aspx.

143 Ibid.

144 Lynn Margulis and Dorion Sagan, *Microcosmos: Four Billion Years of Evolution from Our Microbial Ancestors* (Berkeley: University of California Press, 1997).

145 Ibid., 14.

146 Ibid., 18.

147 Dorion Sagan (ed.), *Lynn Margulis: The Life and Legacy of a Scientific Rebel* (White River Junction, VT: Chelsea Green, 2012).

148 See, for example, R. Schwartz and M. Dayhoff, 'Origins of Prokaryotes, Eukaryotes, Mitochondria, and Chloroplasts.' *Science* 199.4327 (1978): 395–403.

149 Charles Mann, 'Lynn Margulis: Science's Unruly Earth Mother.' *Science* 252.5004 (1991): 378–381 [380–381].

150 Ibid., 381.

151 Ibid, 379.

152 Ibid, 380–381.

153 Margulis and Sagan, *Microcosmos*, 28–29.

154 Ibid., 29.

155 Ibid., 115.

156 Ibid., 30.

157 J.M.W. Slack, *Genes: A Very Short Introduction* (Oxford: Oxford University Press, 2014). In the following paragraphs I have relied on Slack's text as well as the accessible Wikipedia entries for 'Genes' (https://en.wikipedia.org/wiki/Gene) and 'DNA' (https://en.wikipedia.org/wiki/DNA) and the International Society of Genetic Genealogy (ISOGG) wiki at http://www.isogg.org/wiki/Wiki_Welcome_Page.

158 See Richard Dawkins, 'Replicator Selection and the Extended Phenotype', *Zeitschrift für Tierpsychologie*, 47 (1978): 61–76; see also, Dawkins, *The Extended Phenotype: The Long Reach of the Gene* (Oxford: Oxford University Press, 1982).

159 Margulis and Sagan, *Microcosmos*, 30.

160 Ibid., 93.

161 Ibid., 82.

162 Ibid.

163 'To Share and Share Alike: Bacteria Swap Genes with Their Neighbors More Frequently Than Researchers Have Realized' (http://www.scientificamerican.com/article/to-share-and-share-alike/).

164 Margulis and Sagan, *Microcosmos*, 85.

165 Eduardo O. Melo *et al.*, 'Animal Transgenesis: State of the Art and Applications', *Journal of Applied Genetics* 48.1 (2007): 47–61.

166 This paragraph is indebted to C. Gyles and P. Boerlin 'Horizontally Transferred Genetic Elements and Their Role in Pathogenesis of Bacterial Disease', *Veterinary Pathology* 51.2 (2014): 328–340, 331.

167 I am taking this information from the very informative Wikipedia page on 'Genetic Engineering' (http://en.wikipedia.org/wiki/Genetic_engineering).

168 Margulis and Sagan, *Microcosmos*, 34.

169 Gary Walsh, 'Therapeutic insulins and their large-scale manufacture', *Applied Microbiology and Biotechnology* 67.2 (2005): 151–159.

170 'Knockout rats have arrived' (http://www.the-scientist.com/?articles.view/articleNo/29194/title/Knockout-rats-have-arrived/).

171 'Harvard's US OncoMouse Patents are All Expired (For the Time Being)' (http://patentlyo.com/patent/2012/09/harvards-us-oncomouse-patents-are-all-expired-for-the-time-being.html).

172 'Glowing monkeys "to aid research"' (http://news.bbc.co.uk/2/hi/science/nature/8070252.stm).

173 Margulis and Sagan, *Microcosmos*, 34.

174 Margulis and Sagan, *Microcosmos*, 93.

175 Susan Young Rojahn, 'Genome Surgery', *MIT Technology Review* (http://www.technologyreview.com/review/524451/genome-surgery).

176 Heidi Ledford, 'CRISPR the Disruptor', *Nature*, 522 (4 June, 2015): 20–4, 21.

177 'CRISPR' (http://en.wikipedia.org/wiki/CRISPR). There are several types of CRISPR. Type II is the most studied, so it is the one I will describe here.

178 Dana Carroll, 'A CRISPR Approach to Gene Targeting', *Molecular Therapy*, 20.9 (September 2012): 1658–1660, 1659.

179 Ibid.

180 Ibid.

181 Young Rojahn, 'Genome Surgery'.

182 Ibid. In March 2016, however, a nasty patent dispute over CRISPR started to work its way through US courts. Both Doudna and Zhang are at the heart of the dispute, which centres on credit for key discoveries in the development of CRISPR. See Sharon Begley, 'In the CRISPR patent fight, the Broad Institute gains edge in early rulings' (http://www.statnews.com/2016/03/18/crispr-patent-dispute/). At the time of writing (March 2016), no final decision in the dispute had been made.

183 Ibid.

184 Ibid.

185 'CRISPR/Cas9 and Targeted Genome Editing: A New Era in Molecular Biology' (http://www.neb.com/tools-and-resources/feature-articles/crispr-cas9-and-targeted-genome-editing-a-new-era-in-molecular-biology).

186 Ledford, 'CRISPR the Disruptor', 21.

187 Ibid.

188 Ibid, 21.

189 Ibid.

190 Ibid.

191 Sharon Begley, 'Scientists Unveil the "Most Clever CRISPR Gadget" So Far.' (http://www.statnews.com/2016/04/20/clever-crispr-advance-unveiled/). See Alexis C. Komor *et al.*, 'Programmable Editing of a Target Base in Genomic DNA without Double-Stranded DNA Cleavage.' *Nature* (20 April 2016) (http://www.nature.com/nature/journal/vaop/ncurrent/full/nature17946.html).

192 Begley, 'Scientists Unveil the "Most Clever CRISPR Gadget" So Far.' See also Kelly Rae Chi, 'Red Hot: CRISPR/Cas Is All the Rage—and Getting More Precise and Efficient', *The Scientist* (1 March 2015) (http://www.the-scientist.com/?articles.view/articleNo/42260/title/Red-Hot/).

193 Ibid.

194 See http://www.editasmedicine.com/about-founders.php.

195 Ledford, 'CRISPR the Disruptor', 21.

196 Ibid., 22.

197 Ibid.

198 Ibid, 22.

199 Ibid.

200 Sharon Begley, 'Malaria Kills a Half-million Africans a Year. Gene-edited Mosquitoes Might Stop It' (http://www.statnews.com/2015/12/07/gene-edited-mosquitoes-stop-malaria/).

201 Ledford, 'CRISPR the Disruptor', 24.

202 Sharon Begley, 'Dare We Edit The Human Race? Star Geneticists Wrestle With Their Power' (http://www.statnews.com/2015/12/02/gene-editing-summit-embryos/).

203 Ledford, 'CRISPR the Disruptor', 24.

204 David Baltimore et al., 'A Prudent Path Forward for Genomic Engineering and Germline Gene Modification', Science 348.36 (2015): 36–38.

205 Ibid., 36–37.

206 Ibid., 37.

207 Ibid.

208 P. Liang et al., 'CRISPR/Cas9-Mediated Gene Editing in Human Tripronuclear Zygotes', Protein & Cell 6.5 (2015): 363–372.

209 David Cyranoski and Sara Reardon, 'Embryo Editing Sparks Epic Debate.' Nature 520 (29 April 2015): 593–594 [594].

210 Ibid., 593.

211 Young Rojahn, 'Genome Surgery.'

212 Ibid.

213 Liang et al., 'CRISPR/Cas9-Mediated Gene Editing in Human Tripronuclear Zygotes', 364; 367.

214 See, for example, the geneticist Doug Mortlock's CRISPR blog at http://mortlockcrispr.blogspot.ca/2015/04/the-reported-off-target-effects-in.html.

215 Cyranoski and Reardon, 'Embryo Editing Sparks Epic Debate', 594.

216 Ibid.

217 Begley, 'Dare We Edit the Human Race? Star Geneticists Wrestle With Their Power.'

218 Cyranoski and Reardon, 'Embryo Editing Sparks Epic Debate', 594.

219 Begley, 'Dare We Edit the Human Race? Star Geneticists Wrestle With Their Power.'

220 Jennifer Doudna, 'Perspective: Embryo Editing Needs Scrutiny.' *Nature* 528.S6 (03 December 2015) (http://www.nature.com/nature/journal/v528/n7580_supp/full/528S6a.html).

221 H.P. Lovecraft, 'The Call of Cthulhu' (Full text available at: http://en.wikisource.org/wiki/The_Call_of_Cthulhu/full).

Chapter 3

1   See Ray Kurzweil, *The Singularity is Near* (London: Penguin, 2006), 289–298. Indeed, this list keeps on growing: not long after this book manuscript was completed (March 2016), Google DeepMind's AlphaGo AI had beaten Lee Se-dol, the 18-time world champion Go player, in a human–machine Go tournament, a task many did not expect an AI to accomplish for at least another ten years. See, 'Google's AlphaGo AI beats Lee Se-dol again to win Go series 4-1' (http://www.theverge.com/2016/3/15/11213518/alphago-deepmind-go-match-5-result).

2   Alan Turing, 'Computing Machinery and Intelligence', *Mind*, LIX.236 (1950): 433–460.

3   Ibid., 434.

4   Ibid., 436.

5   Ibid., 442.

6   Ibid., 442.

7   Ibid., 456.

8   'No, A "Supercomputer" Did NOT Pass The Turing Test For The First Time And Everyone Should Know Better' (http://www.techdirt.com/articles/20140609/07284327524/no-supercomputer-did-not-pass-turing-test-first-time-everyone-should-know-better.shtml).

9   Marvin Minsky, 'Logical vs. Analogical or Symbolic vs. Connectionist or Neat vs. Scruffy.' Available online at: (http://web.media.mit.edu/~minsky/papers/SymbolicVs.Connectionist.html).

10   Ibid.

11   Ibid.

12   Ibid.

13   See Michael A. Nielsen, *Neural Networks and Deep Learning* (Determination Press, 2015), Chapter 1 (available online at: http://neuralnetworksanddeeplearning.com/chap1.html).

14   'Computer Crushes the Competition on "Jeopardy!"'. (http://wayback.archive.org/web/20110219023019/http://www.google.com/

hostednews/ap/article/ALeqM5jwVBxDQvVKEwk_czuv8Q4jxdU1S g?docId=2e3e918f552b4599b013b4cc473d96af).

15 http://plus.google.com/+SelfDrivingCar/posts.

16 Chris Urmson, 'The View from the Front Seat of the Google Self-Driving Car' (http://medium.com/backchannel/the-view-from-the-front-seat-of-the-google-self-driving-car-46fc9f3e6088).

17 See Chapter 5, below.

18 Vincent C. Müller and Nick Bostrom, 'Future Progress in Artificial Intelligence: A Survey of Expert Opinion', in Vincent C. Müller (ed.), *Fundamental Issues of Artificial Intelligence* (Berlin: Springer, 2014). Available online at: http://www.nickbostrom.com/papers/survey.pdf.

19 See, for example, Ray Kurzweil, *The Singularity is Near* and *How to Create a Mind* (London: Penguin, 2013).

20 For more on superintelligence and the Singularity, see Chapter 5, below.

21 Turing, 'Computing Machinery and Intelligence', 459–460.

22 'Japan Child Robot Mimicks Infant Learning' (http://phys.org/news/2009-04-japan-child-robot-mimicks-infant.html).

23 'Robot Baby Diego-San Shows Its Expressive Face on Video' (http://spectrum.ieee.org/automaton/robotics/humanoids/robot-baby-diego-san).

24 http://www.icub.org/

25 http://www.roboy.org/.

26 'Are Child Sex-Robots Inevitable?' (http://www.forbes.com/sites/kashmirhill/2014/07/14/are-child-sex-robots-inevitable/).

27 Ibid.

28 See, for example, Wikipedia, 'Artificial neural network' (http://en.wikipedia.org/wiki/Artificial_neural_network). See also Jürgen Schmidhuber's 'Deep Learning in Neural Networks: An Overview' (*Neural Networks*. 61, January 2015, 85–117; full text available at: http://www.idsia.ch/~juergen/DeepLearning8Oct2014.pdf).

29 Warren McCulloch and Walter Pitts, 'A Logical Calculus of Ideas Immanent in Nervous Activity.' *Bulletin of Mathematical Biophysics*, 5 (4) (1943): 115–133. Note, however, that Schmidhuber locates the origins of neural networking much earlier than the work by McCulloch and Pitts: 'early supervised NNs [neural networks] were essentially variants of linear regression methods going back at least to the early 1800s' [9].

30 See Frank Rosenblatt, *Principles of Neurodynamics: Perceptrons and the Theory of Brain Mechanisms* (Washington, DC: Spartan Books, 1962).

31 Marvin Minsky and Seymour Papert, *Perceptrons: An Introduction to Computational Geometry* (2nd edition with corrections. Cambridge, MA: The MIT Press, 1972).

32 Schmidhuber, 'Deep Learning in Neural Networks: An Overview', 16–23. See also L. Deng and D. Yu, 'Deep Learning: Methods and Applications.' *Foundations and Trends in Signal Processing* 7 (2014): 3–4. Full text available at: http://research.microsoft.com/pubs/209355/DeepLearning-NowPublishing-Vol7-SIG-039.pdf.

33 Anyone reading who is familiar with how z-scores, t-scores and p-values work in statistics and hypothesis testing, will see that using mathematics to make a decision is not at all uncommon.

34 If you're not familiar with how different functions graph, a great tool can be found at: http://graph.tk/. I've found it to be an invaluable tool in grasping how the many mathematical functions used in AI look and work.

35 http://mathinsight.org/vectors_arbitrary_dimensions

36 I am keeping the numbers here very simple; but it should be remembered that different values for w and b will change the position and slope of the line the perceptron draws. For example, increasing b pushes the line further away from the origin, while changing the values of w alters slope of the line.

37 Much of what follows here is indebted to Michael A. Nielsen's excellent online book, *Neural Networks and Deep Learning* (Determination Press, 2015). Available online at: http://neuralnetworksanddeeplearning.com/index.html.

38 Tom Mitchell, *Machine Learning* (New York: McGraw Hill, 1997). Much of what follows here is indebted to both Andrew Ng's wonderfully accessible lecture series at Coursera called simply 'Machine Learning' (http://www.coursera.org/learn/machine-learning) and Nielsen's *Neural Networks and Deep Learning* (Determination Press, 2015).

39 'Convolutional Neural Networks' (http://deeplearning.net/tutorial/lenet.html).

40 See David H. Hubel and Torsten N. Wiesel, 'Receptive Fields of Single Neurones in the Cat's Striate Cortex', *Journal of Physiology* 148 (1959): 574–591; 'Receptive Fields, Binocular Interaction and Functional Architecture in the Cat's Visual Cortex', *Journal of Physiology* 160 (1962): 106–154; 'Receptive Fields and Functional Architecture of Monkey Striate Cortex', *Journal of Physiology* 195 (1968), 215–243. See also Jawad Nagi *et al.*, 'Max-Pooling Convolutional Neural Networks for Vision-based Hand Gesture Recognition' in *Proceedings of the 2011 IEEE International Conference on Signal and Image*

Processing Applications. Available online at: http://ieeexplore.ieee.org/xpl/mostRecentIssue.jsp?punumber=6138563.

41 'Convolutional Neural Network', http://en.wikipedia.org/wiki/Convolutional_neural_network.

42 What follows here is indebted to Aysegul Dundar's video introduction to CNNs at: http://www.youtube.com/watch?v=n6hpQwq7Inw

43 Andrew Ng, 'Deep Learning, Self-Taught Learning and Unsupervised Feature Learning.' Ng's lecture was delivered as part of the IPAM Graduate Summer School at UCLA. Available online at: http://helper.ipam.ucla.edu/wowzavideo.aspx?vfn=10595.mp4&vfd=gss2012

44 See, for example, Mriganka Sur, 'Rewiring Cortex: Cross-modal Plasticity and Its Implications for Cortical Development and Function', in G. Calvert, C. Spence, B.E. Stein (eds.), *Handbook of Multisensory Processing* (Cambridge: MIT Press, 2004), 681–694.

45 E. Sampaio, S. Maris and P. Bach-y-Rita, 'Brain Plasticity: "Visual" Acuity of Blind Persons via the Tongue.' *Brain Research* 908 (2001), 204–207.

46 What follows here is indebted to Richard S. Sutton and Andrew G. Barto's wonderfully accessible *Reinforcement Learning: An Introduction* (MIT) (available online at: http://webdocs.cs.ualberta.ca/~sutton/book/ebook/the-book.html). Sutton and Barto's book is an excellent guide to reinforcement learning, Markov Decision Processes (MDPs) and the Markov process. I have also referred to the Wikipedia pages on Q-learning (http://en.wikipedia.org/wiki/Q-learning) and MDPs (http://en.wikipedia.org/wiki/Markov_decision_process). Both Wiki pages are, it has to be said, quite technical; however, with the help of Sutton and Barto, they are useful for grasping more than just the basics of Q-learning.

47 See, for example, Jeremy Bentham, *An Introduction to the Principles of Morals and Legislation* (Oxford: Clarendon Press, 1907) and John Stuart Mill, *Utilitarianism* (ed. Roger Crisp. Oxford: Oxford University Press, 1998). I will return to philosophical utilitarianism in Chapter 5.

48 Alfred Marshall, *Principles of Economics: An Introductory Volume* (London: Macmillan, 1920), Book III, Chapter 3, 'Gradations of Consumers' Demand' (available online at: http://www.marxists.org/reference/subject/economics/marshall/bk3ch03.htm). Full text available at: http://www.marxists.org/reference/subject/economics/marshall/. See also, Paul Anand, *Foundations of Rational Choice Under Risk* (Oxford: Oxford UP, 1993).

49 See, for example, John von Neumann and Oskar Morgenstern, *Theory of Games and Economic Behavior* (Princeton: Princeton University Press, 1944).

50 Sutton and Barto, 'I.1.1 Reinforcement Learning' (http://webdocs. cs.ualberta.ca/~sutton/book/ebook/node7.html).

51 Volodymyr Mnih *et al.*, 'Human-level Control Through Deep Reinforcement Learning', *Nature* 518.26 (February 2015): 529–533.

52 Sutton and Barto, 'I.1.2 Examples' (http://webdocs.cs.ualberta. ca/~sutton/book/ebook/node8.html) [italics in original].

53 Mnih *et al.*, 'Human-level Control Through Deep Reinforcement Learning', 529.

54 Sutton and Barto, 'I.1.1 Reinforcement Learning' (http://webdocs. cs.ualberta.ca/~sutton/book/ebook/the-book.html) [italics in original].

55 Ibid.

56 Sutton and Barto, 'I.1.3 Elements of Reinforcement Learning' (http:// webdocs.cs.ualberta.ca/~sutton/book/ebook/node9.html) [italics in original].

57 Sutton and Barto, 'I.3.6 Markov Decision Processes' (http://webdocs. cs.ualberta.ca/~sutton/book/ebook/node33.html).

58 See Sutton and Barto, 'I.3.5 The Markov Property' (http://webdocs. cs.ualberta.ca/~sutton/book/ebook/node32.html).

59 Sutton and Barto, 'I.3.2 Goals and Rewards' (http://webdocs. cs.ualberta.ca/~sutton/book/ebook/node29.html).

60 This suggests an interesting overlap between reinforcement learning and the discussion of neuroprosthetics in the previous chapter.

61 Sutton and Barto, 'I.3.3 Returns' (http://webdocs.cs.ualberta. ca/~sutton/book/ebook/node30.html).

62 Ibid.

63 Mnih *et al.*, 'Human-level Control Through Deep Reinforcement Learning', 529.

64 Ibid.

65 Ibid.

66 Ibid.

67 Ibid., 531.

68 Ibid., 529–530.

69 Ibid., 532.

70   Ibid., 530–531.

71   Ibid., 532.

72   Ibid.

73   Ibid.

74   Ibid.

75   Holk Cruse and Malte Schilling, 'Mental States as Emergent Properties: From Walking to Consciousness', in T. Metzinger and J.M. Windt (eds.), *Open MIND* (Frankfurt am Main: MIND Group, 2015), 5.

76   Ibid, 6.

77   Ibid.

78   Ibid., 6.

79   Ibid., 9.

80   David McFarland and Tom Bösser, *Intelligent Behavior in Animals and Robots* (Cambridge, MA: MIT Press, 1993), 4. I will return to McFarland's work in detail in Chapter 5.

81   Ibid.

82   Ibid.

83   Ibid., 8.

84   Ibid.

85   Cruse and Schilling, 'Mental States as Emergent Properties', 9.

86   Malte Schilling *et al.*, 'A Hexapod Walker Using a Heterarchical Architecture for Action Selection', *Frontiers in Computational Neuroscience*, 7.126 (2013), 5–6.

87   Cruse and Schilling, 'Mental States as Emergent Properties', 10.

88   Ibid.

89   Ibid.

90   Ibid., 3.

91   Ibid., 1.

92   Ibid., 2.

93   Ibid., 3.

94   Ibid., 1.

95   Ibid.

96   Ibid.

97   Ibid., 14.

98   I will come back to these questions in Chapter 5.

99 Benjamin Libet, W.W. Alberts, E.W. Wright, L.D. Delatre, G. Levin and B. Feinstein, 'Production of Threshold Levels of Conscious Sensation by Electrical Stimulation of Human Somatosensory Cortex', *Journal of Neurophysiology*, 27.4 (1964): 546–578.

100 Odmar Neumann and Werner Klotz, 'Motor Responses to Non-reportable, Masked Stimuli: Where Is the Limit of Direct Parameter Specification?' in C. Umiltà and M. Moscovitch (eds.), *Attention and Performance XV* (Cambridge, MA: MIT Press, 1994), 123–150.

101 Cruse and Schilling, 'Mental States as Emergent Properties', 15–16.

102 Ibid., 16.

103 Ibid., 17.

104 See also Holk Cruse, 'The Evolution of Cognition—A Hypothesis', *Cognitive Science* 27 (2003), 135–155.

105 Cruse and Schilling, 'Mental States as Emergent Properties', 18.

106 Ibid.

107 Albert Mehrabian, 'Pleasure-Arousal-Dominance: A General Framework for Describing and Measuring Individual Differences in Temperament', *Current Psychology* 4 (1996), 261–292.

108 Cruse and Schilling, 'Mental States as Emergent Properties', 20.

109 Ibid.

110 Ibid.

111 Axel Cleeremans, 'Computational Correlates of Consciousness', *Progress in Brain Research*, 150 (2005), 81–98.

112 Cruse and Schilling, 'Mental States as Emergent Properties', 23.

113 Ibid., 32.

114 Ibid., 27.

115 Ibid., 32.

116 Ibid., 32.

117 Ibid., 31.

118 Ibid.

119 Ken Jennings, who holds the record for the longest winning streak on the US syndicated game show *Jeopardy!*, on being beaten by Watson at his own game.

120 David Ferrucci *et al.*, 'Building Watson: An Overview of the DeepQA Project', *Association for the Advancement of Artificial Intelligence* (Fall 2010), 60.

121 Ibid, 59.

122 Ibid., 63.

123 Ibid., 59.

124 Peter Jackson, *Introduction To Expert Systems* (Boston: Addison Wesley, 1998), 2.

125 Stuart Russell and Peter Norvig, *Artificial Intelligence: A Modern Approach* (New York: Simon & Schuster, 1995), 22–23.

126 Marvin Minsky, 'Logical vs. Analogical or Symbolic vs. Connectionist or Neat vs. Scruffy' (available online at: http://web.media.mit. edu/~minsky/papers/SymbolicVs.Connectionist.html).

127 Ferrucci *et al.*, 'Building Watson: An Overview of the DeepQA Project', 69.

128 Ibid., 71.

129 Ferrucci *et al.*, 'Watson: Beyond Jeopardy!', *Artificial Intelligence* 199–200 (2013): 93–105 [95].

130 Michael C. McCord, 'Using Slot Grammar', *IBM Research Division* (2010), 2–3. Available online at: http://domino.research.ibm.com/ library/cyberdig.nsf/papers/FB5445D25B7E3932852576F10047E1C 2/$File/rc23978revised.pdf.

131 Ibid., 3.

132 Ibid., 3–6.

133 D.C. Gondek *et al.*, 'A Framework for Merging and Ranking of Answers in DeepQA', *IBM Research* (2012), 1 (available online at: http://brenocon.com/watson_special_issue/14%20a%20 framework%20for%20merging%20and%20ranking%20answers.pdf.

134 Ibid., 2.

135 Ferrucci *et al.*, 'Building Watson: An Overview of the DeepQA Project', 60.

136 Ferrucci *et al.*, 'Watson: Beyond Jeopardy!', 94.

137 Ibid., 95.

138 Ibid.

139 'IBM's Watson Now A Second-Year Med Student' (http://www. forbes.com/sites/bruceupbin/2011/05/25/ibms-watson-now-a-second- year-med-student/).

140 'Watson Oncology' (http://www.mskcc.org/about/innovative- collaborations/watson-oncology).

141 'IBM's Watson Gets Its First Piece Of Business In Healthcare' (http:// www.forbes.com/sites/bruceupbin/2013/02/08/ibms-watson-gets-its- first-piece-of-business-in-healthcare/).

142 Ibid.

143 'IBM Watson's Startling Cancer Coup' (http://time.com/3208716/ibm-watson-cancer/).

144 'Artificial Intelligence: Can Watson Save IBM?' (http://www.ft.com/cms/s/2/dced8150-b300-11e5-8358-9a82b43f6b2f.html).

145 Ibid.

146 Ibid.

147 'A Computer Made My Lunch' (http://money.cnn.com/2015/05/07/technology/chef-watson-recipes/).

148 'Meet Ross, the IBM Watson-Powered Lawyer' (http://www.psfk.com/2015/01/ross-ibm-watson-powered-lawyer-legal-research.html#articles-pane-close).

149 http://www.rossintelligence.com/.

150 'Report: Artificial Intelligence Will Cause "Structural Collapse" of Law Firms by 2030' (http://www.legalfutures.co.uk/latest-news/report-ai-will-transform-legal-world).

151 Ibid.

152 http://www.rethinkrobotics.com/baxter/

153 'Interview: Paul Allen's Artificial Intelligence Guru on the Future of Robots and Humanity' (http://www.geekwire.com/2016/geekwire-radio-paul-allens-artificial-intelligence-guru-future-robots-humanity/).

154 'Dutch City Plans to Pay Citizens a "Basic Income," and Greens Say It Could Work in the UK' (http://www.theguardian.com/world/2015/dec/26/dutch-city-utrecht-basic-income-uk-greens).

155 'Kela to Prepare Basic Income Proposal' (http://yle.fi/uutiset/kela_to_prepare_basic_income_proposal/8422295).

156 'A Basic Income For Ontario? Province Plans Pilot Project As Part Of Budget' (http://www.huffingtonpost.ca/2016/02/26/ontario-basic-income_n_9328264.html).

Chapter 4

1 I will use the word 'text' to refer to books, films, videogames, etc. throughout this chapter.

2 Mary Shelley, *Frankenstein* (New York: W.W. Norton, 2012).

3 Shelley herself mentions the role 'galvanism' might play in bringing the dead back to life in the Introduction to the 1831

version of *Frankenstein* (full text available at: http://www.gutenberg. org/files/42324/42324-h/42324-h.htm). For a detailed—and hair-raising—account of the spark experiments, see Marco Piccolino, 'Animal Electricity and the Birth of Electrophysiology: The Legacy of Luigi Galvani.' *Brain Research Bulletin* 46.5 (1998): 381–407.

4   Ibid., 389.

5   Mary Shelley, *Frankenstein* (New York: Norton, 2012), 29. Later, when he is working on the creature, Victor says that he 'pursued nature to her hiding places', 33.

6   See Ornella Moscucci, *The Science of Woman: Gynaecology and Gender in England, 1800–1929* (Cambridge: Cambridge University Press, 1990).

7   Out of many possible examples, Sandra Harding and Jean O'Barr (eds.), *Sex and Scientific Inquiry* (Chicago: U. of Chicago P., 1987); Evelyn Fox Keller, *Reflections on Gender and Science* (New Haven: Yale University Press, 1995); Helen Longino, *Science as Social Knowledge* (Princeton: Princeton University Press, 1990); Lynn Hankinson Nelson, *Who Knows: From Quine to a Feminist Empiricism* (Philadelphia: Temple University Press, 1992); Mary M. Gergen (ed.), *Feminist Thought and the Structure of Knowledge* (New York: New York University Press, 1988). Interestingly, more recent studies have appeared that uncritically reproduce the idea of science as rape of nature: see, for example, Sylvia Bowerbank, *Speaking for Nature: Women and Ecologies of Early Modern England* (Baltimore: Johns Hopkins University Press, 2004). Obviously, this strand in feminist analyses of science also owes something to Paul Feyerabend's *Against Method* (London: New Left Books, 1975), in which he promised to free people of the tyranny of truth, reality and objectivity. For an interesting counter to such feminist appropriations of science from a more rigorously scientific perspective, see Noretta Koertge (ed.), *A House Built on Sand: Exposing Postmodernist Myths about Science* (Oxford: Oxford University Press, 2000). For a more philosophical approach, see, for example, Susan Haack, *Defending Science—Within Reason: Between Scientism and Cynicism* (Amherst: Prometheus Books, 2003). It is, however, also important to note that not all analyses of science and technology that claim to be feminist are simply anti-science or anti-technology: of particular note here would be Donna Haraway's work, especially her *Simians, Cyborgs and Women* (London: Routledge, 1991).

8   'Cambridge University Researchers' Breakthrough Paves Way for Same Sex Couple Babies' (http://www.cambridge-news.co.uk/

Cambridge-university-researchers-breakthrough/story-26065812-detail/story.html).

9 For a thorough overview of folk-psychology, see Ian Ravenscroft, 'Folk Psychology as a Theory' (http://plato.stanford.edu/entries/folkpsych-theory/).

10 Alan Sokal and Jean Bricmont, *Fashionable Nonsense: Postmodern Intellectuals' Abuse of Science* (New York: Picador, 1998), 68.

11 Ibid.

12 Ibid, 65.

13 Ibid, 91–92 [italics in original].

14 Ibid, 56.

15 Ibid, 53.

16 Ibid., 54.

17 Ibid, 53; 55.

18 Ibid, 55.

19 Ibid.

20 Ibid.

21 Ibid, 56.

22 Ibid, 57.

23 Ibid, 58.

24 Karl Popper, *The Logic of Scientific Discovery* (London: Routledge, 2002).

25 Sokal and Bricmont, *Fashionable Nonsense*, 61.

26 Ibid.

27 Ibid, 61–62.

28 Ibid, 66.

29 Ibid, 65.

30 Ibid, 63.

31 Of course, the idea of a swan can easily accommodate black swans (even a white swan's cygnets are grey); similarly, even though the sun will most likely rise again tomorrow, in billions of years time it could well have exhausted its fuel supply and thus no longer brighten the Earth.

32 Sokal and Bricmont, *Fashionable Nonsense*, 68.

33 Ibid, 51.

34 Ibid, 52.

35 Ibid, 85.

36 Solipsism and relativism constitute the epistemological engine that drives the belief that any knowledge about reality is 'just' a social construct and that social constructs are always open to reconstruction. Now, in and of itself, the claim that scientific knowledge is, in part, a 'social construct' is not one that many scientists—even very critical ones like Sokal and Bricmont—would object to (see *Fashionable Nonsense*, 93). Clearly, it would be foolish to deny that social factors play a part in science, when they show up in peer-review of scientific work, lively discussions about possible breakthroughs, decisions about what experiments are technologically feasible, and so on; in fact, such a claim is, at best, trivial. However, the 'scientific-knowledge-is-socially-constructed' model shears off from scientists' own understanding of scientific knowledge when it tries to assert the more radical claim that if science is a social construct, then so too is reality. This more radical claim confuses a fact and the representation of that fact: in other words, it assumes—to use an already over-used phrase—the 'territory' is the same thing as the 'map'. As a result of this belief, the more radical social constructionist model of criticism holds that if one displaces science's social construction of reality, then one can then replace reality itself with a 'better', 'truer' 'alternative' one. And, since in this social construction model the final arbiter of the better or truer 'reality' cannot be 'reality', the final arbiter must be the ideological model or framework that sought to displace science in the first place (and there seems to be nothing at all to stop an infinite regress of 'ideology-realities', each trying to get under the 'realities' of the others to its 'reality').

37 Barry Barnes and David Bloor, 'Relativism, Rationalism and the Sociology of Knowledge', in Martin Hollis and Steven Lukes (eds.), *Rationality and Relativism* (Oxford: Blackwell, 1981): 21–47 [21–22].

38 Sokal and Bricmont, *Fashionable Nonsense*, 87.

39 See Bruno Latour, 'For David Bloor and Beyond . . . A Reply to David Bloor's "Anti-Latour,"' *Studies in History and Philosophy of Science*, 30.1 (1999): 113–129.

40 Steve Fuller, *Philosophy, Rhetoric, and the End of Knowledge: The Coming of Science and Technology Studies*. (Madison: University of Wisconsin Press, 1993), xii; cited in Sokal and Bricmont, *Fashionable Nonsense*, 98.

41 Sokal and Bricmont, *Fashionable Nonsense*, 98.

42 Rosi Braidotti, *The Posthuman* (Cambridge: Polity Press, 2013), 145.

43   Ibid., 146.

44   Ibid., 147. Elizabeth Grosz, *Becoming Undone* (Durham, NC: Duke University Press, 2011).

45   Braidotti, *The Posthuman*, 158.

46   Ibid., 147.

47   See, in particular, her discussion at 158 and following.

48   William Bechtel and Robert C. Richardson, 'Vitalism', in E. Craig (ed.), *Routledge Encyclopedia of Philosophy*. (London: Routledge, 1998). Available online at: http://mechanism.ucsd.edu/teaching/philbio/vitalism.htm.

49   Ibid.

50   Bruno Latour, 'Why Has Critique Run out of Steam? From Matters of Fact to Matters of Concern.' *Critical Inquiry*, 30 (2004): 225–248. For a more detailed discussion, see his *Reassembling the Social: An Introduction to Actor-Network-Theory* (Oxford: Oxford University Press, 2005). See also Dennis W.C. Liu, 'Science Denial and the Science Classroom.' *CBE—Life Sciences Education*, 11.2 (2012): 129–134, and Haack, *Defending Science*.

51   Ed Zern, 'Exit Laughing', *Field and Stream*, November (1959): 142 (available online at: http://edzern.com/?p=42).

52   Chapter 2, above

53   I would add here that this list is in no way intended to be exhaustive, and that the reader is encouraged to supplement it with texts of his or her choosing that share the specified traits.

54   David McFarland, *Happy Dogs, Guilty Robots: The question of Alien Minds* (Oxford: Oxford University Press, 2008), 'Chapter 3: Interpreting Behaviour.' I am using the Kindle version of McFarland's text, so all references are given by chapter rather than page. I also will be making extensive use of McFarland's book in the following chapter.

55   Shelley, *Frankenstein*, 90.

56   Ibid., 102.

57   Ibid., 51.

58   Ibid., 59.

59   Ibid., 121.

60   Isaac Asimov, *I, Robot* (New York: Bantam Spectra, 1991).

61   Ibid., 4.

62   Ibid., 74.

63   Ibid., 109.

64   Ibid., 223.

65   Ibid., 235.

66   Ibid., 238.

67   Ibid., 268–270. See also Asimov's *The Naked Sun* (New York: Bantam Spectra, 1991) and *The Robots of Dawn* (New York: Doubleday, 1983).

68   Asimov, *I, Robot*, 265.

69   Ibid., 268.

70   Ibid., 270.

71   See, for example, Banks's *Consider Phlebas* (London: Macmillan, 1987), *The Player of Games* (London: Macmillan, 1988) and *Excession* (London: Orbit, 1996).

72   Philip K. Dick, *Do Androids Dream of Electric Sheep?* (New York: Ballantyne Books, 1996).

73   Ibid., 37.

74   Ibid.

75   Ibid., 5.

76   Ibid., 136.

77   Ibid., 142.

78   Ibid., 141.

79   Ibid., 184.

80   William Gibson, *Neuromancer* (New York: Ace Books, 1984).

81   Ibid., 269.

82   Ibid., 233.

83   Ibid., 236.

84   Ibid., 259.

85   Ibid., 243–244.

86   Ibid., 251.

87   Ibid., 258.

88   Ibid., 259.

89   Iain M. Banks, *Surface Detail* (London: Orbit, 2010); Greg Bear, *Blood Music* (London: Gollancz, 2001).

90   Neal Stephenson, *Snow Crash* (New York: Bantam Books, 1992).

91   Ibid., 89.

92   Ibid., 249.

93   Ibid., 248.

94 Ibid.

95 Ibid., 444.

96 Ibid.

97 Ibid.

98 Ibid., 468.

99 Ibid.

100 David Mitchell, *Cloud Atlas* (Toronto: Vintage, 2004).

101 Kazuo Ishiguro's *Never Let Me Go* (Toronto: Vintage, 2006).

102 Ibid., 187.

103 Ibid.

104 Ibid., 348–349.

105 Ibid., 349.

106 Ibid., 344.

107 For a different approach to this issue, see, for example, Cary Wolfe, 'In Search of Post-Humanist Theory: The Second-Order Cybernetics of Maturana and Varela', *Cultural Critique* (Spring 1995): 33–70.

108 Francis Heylighen and Cliff Joslyn, 'Cybernetics and Second-Order Cybernetics', 2.

109 Heinz von Foerster, 'Ethics and Second-Order Cybernetics' in *Understanding Understanding*, 287.

110 Ibid., 289.

111 *Ex Machina*. Dir. Alex Garland. A24, 2015. Film.

112 William S. Burrough, *Naked Lunch* (New York: Grove Press, 2001).

113 Francis Heylighen and Cliff Joslyn, 'Cybernetics and Second-Order Cybernetics', 9–11.

114 Octavia Butler, *Dawn* (New York: Warner Books, 1987).

115 Heylighen and Joslyn, 'Cybernetics and Second-Order Cybernetics', 10.

116 Ibid. Von Foerster proposes that information is what allows us to measure self-organization in a system, whatever that system may be. See 'On Self-Organizing Systems and Their Environments', in *Understanding Understanding: Essays on Cybernetics and Cognition*, 7.

117 Francis Heylighen, 'Attractors', *Principia Cybernetica Web* (http://pespmc1.vub.ac.be/attracto.html).

118 Ibid.

119 Heylighen and Joslyn, 'Cybernetics and Second-Order Cybernetics', 10.

120 Ibid.

121 Ibid [italics in original].

122 Ibid., 11.

123 Samuel Taylor Coleridge, *Biographia Literaria*, 1817, Chapter XIV. Full text available online at: http://www.gutenberg.org/files/6081/6081-h/6081-h.htm.

124 As discussed in Chapter 2, closure is a key component of autopoiesis. See, for example, Maturana and Varela, *Autopoiesis and Cognition*, xv. Elsewhere in *Autopoiesis and Cognition*, Maturana and Varela make a distinction between the more abstract idea of 'organization' and the more concrete notion of a particular system that is made out of a particular material: 'The organization of a machine (or system) does not specify the properties of the components which realize the machine as a concrete system, it only specifies the relations which these must generate to constitute the machine or system as a unity. Therefore, the organization of a machine is independent of the properties of its components which can be any, and a given machine can be realized in many different manners by many different kinds of components. In other words, although a given machine can be realized by many different structures, for it to constitute a concrete entity in a given space its actual components must be defined in that space, and have the properties which allow them to generate the relations which define it' (77). Organization is thus best understood from the point of view of functionalism (see Chapter 5, below, for more on functionalism); to paraphrase an example they use elsewhere (*The Tree of Knowledge: The Biological Roots of Human Understanding* [Boston: Shambhala, 1987], 47), a toilet is still a toilet if it has the structure or organization of a toilet that allows it to do the job of a toilet, irrespective of the specific materials it is made out of. A functionalist understanding of reading could, for example, be applied to a person reading using prosthetic eyes or optic nerves, or to Watson's ability to read a document and answer a question about it (see Chapter 3, above); however, in such cases, since neither the reader's prosthetic eyes nor Watson's architecture would be physically changed by what is read, the concrete reading situation described here in the main text is just like those situations. If my discussion in the main text highlights the specific biological properties of the components of the reader's visual system, it is because I am saying that there is nothing that happens in reading that alters the specific properties of that system: reading is not like the surgical replacement of an eye, or aural nerve or arm or leg with a prosthesis. Autopoiesis, understood in terms of organization, also readily connects with the discussion of neuroprosthetics in Chapter 2.

125 Heylighen and Joslyn, 'Cybernetics and Second-Order Cybernetics', 21. Again, the constructed nature of knowledge should not simply open the door to solipsism or the idea that all constructions of knowledge or somehow equal. For a discussion of solipsism and relativism, see the first section of the present chapter above. For more discussion of how cybernetics does not dissolve into solipsism and relativism, see Chapter 2, above.

126 'On Self-Organizing Systems and Their Environments', in *Understanding Understanding: Essays on Cybernetics and Cognition*, 6.

127 Heylighen and Joslyn, 'Cybernetics and Second-Order Cybernetics', 15. Disturbances are 'unknown variables' that come from the environment and affect the way the system or organism behaves.

128 I am, unfortunately, familiar with those numerous cases in Humanities departments where 'education' and 'criticism' consists of imposing instructor-approved ideological theories on cultural texts. The discussion that follows above can also, with some tweaks, be easily applied to such cases. I will return to some of these issues, albeit from a different perspective, in the Conclusion.

129 Karl Popper, 'Replies to My Critics', in P.A. Schilpp (ed.), *The Philosophy of Karl Popper, Volume 2* (La Salle, IL: Open Court Publishing, 1974), 961–1167. See also Karl Popper, 'The Demarcation Between Science and Metaphysics', in *Conjectures and Refutations: The Growth of Scientific Knowledge* (New York: Routledge, 2002), 341–394. See Hilary Putnam, 'The "Corroboration" of Theories', in Richard Boyd, Philip Gasper and J.D. Trout (eds.), *The Philosophy of Science* (Cambridge, MA: MIT Press, 1991), 134, for a trenchant critique of Popper's earlier position.

130 Popper, 'Science: Conjectures and Refutations' in *Conjectures and Refutations: The Growth of Scientific Knowledge*, 44.

131 Jerome Lettvin, Humberto R. Maturana, Warren McCulloch and Walter Pitts, 'What the Frog's Eye Tells the Frog's Brain', *Proceedings of the Institute for Radio Engineers* 47.11 (1959): 1940–1951 [1950].

132 Heylighen and Joslyn, 'Cybernetics and Second-Order Cybernetics', 21–22 [italics in original]. See also, for example, von Foerster's memorable postulate, 'The Environment as We Perceive It Is Our Invention' in 'On Constructing a Reality' in *Understanding Understanding*, 212.

133 Heylighen and Joslyn, 'Cybernetics and Second-Order Cybernetics', 22 [italics in original].

134 Ibid.

135 Ibid.

136 Marian David, 'The Correspondence Theory of Truth', in Edward N. Zalta (ed.), *The Stanford Encyclopedia of Philosophy* (Fall 2015 Edition) (http://plato.stanford.edu/archives/fall2015/entries/truth-correspondence/). Needless to say, this is a very bare-bones definition, but it captures the basics of what underlies the correspondence theory. See David's article for an overview of the various flavours of this theory.

137 Sokal and Bricmont, *Fashionable Nonsense*, 96–97.

138 See, for example, Linda Hutcheon, *Narcissistic Narrative: The Metafictional Paradox* (London: Routledge, 1984).

139 Shelley, *Frankenstein*, 34–35.

140 Ibid., 151.

141 Ibid., 36.

142 Ibid., 70.

143 Ibid.

144 Ibid., 17.

145 Butler, *Dawn*, 59.

146 Ibid.

147 Ibid., 59–60.

148 Lynn Margulis and Dorion Sagan, *Microcosmos: Four Billion Years of Evolution from Our Microbial Ancestors* (Berkeley: University of California Press, 1997). See Chapter 2, below. See also, Bruce Clarke, *Posthuman Metamorphosis: Narrative and Systems* (New York: Fordham University Press, 2008).

149 Dick, *Do Androids Dream of Electric Sheep?*, 220–221 [italics in original].

150 Ibid., 221.

151 Stephenson, *Snow Crash*, 278.

152 Ibid.

153 For more on neuroplasticity, see Chapter 2, above.

154 Stephenson, *Snow Crash*, 126.

155 Ibid.

156 Ibid., 276.

157 Ibid., 262–263.

158 William S. Burroughs, *Naked Lunch* (New York: Grove Press, 2001), 192.

159 Ibid., 191.

160 Jonathan Swift, *Gulliver's Travels into Several Remote Nations of the World* (London: Penguin Classics, 2003). Full text available at: http://www.gutenberg.org/ebooks/829.

161 Bear, *Blood Music*, 73.

162 Ibid., 74.

163 Ibid., 160.

164 Ibid., 185.

165 Ibid., 309.

166 For a discussion of information and its relationship with meaning, see Chapter 2, above.

167 McFarland, 'Glossary.' *Happy Dogs, Guilty Robots: The Question of Alien Minds*.

168 This is a much-vexed philosophical and scientific discussion, and I will return to it in some detail in the next chapter.

169 See, for example, H.S. Terrace, L.A. Petitto, R.J. Sanders and T.G. Bever, 'Can an Ape Create a Sentence?' *Science*, 206.4421 (1979): 891–902 and Douglas Keith Candland, *Feral Children and Clever Animals: Reflections on Human Nature* (Oxford: Oxford University Press, 1993).

170 Hubert Dreyfus, *What Computers Still Can't Do* (New York: MIT Press, 1992) and John Searle, *Mind, Language and Society* (New York: Basic Books, 1999).

Chapter 5

1 For a useful overview of the differences between analytic and continental philosophy, see Neil Levy, 'Analytic and Continental Philosophy: Explaining the Differences', *Metaphilosophy*, 34.3 (April 2003): 284–304.

2 David McFarland, '5. Mental Possibilities', *Guilty Robots, Happy Dogs: The Question of Alien Minds* (Oxford: Oxford University Press, 2008). Throughout this chapter, I will be citing the Kindle version of McFarland's book; because of this, no page references can be given, only chapter titles like the one above.

3 Sandy C. Boucher, 'What Is a Philosophical Stance? Paradigms, Policies and Perspectives', *Synthese*, 191.10 (2014): 2315–2332 [2315].

4 McFarland, 'Epilogue: The Alien Mind'.

5 Ibid.

6   Ibid.

7   Ibid., '3. Interpreting Behaviour',

8   Ibid., 'Epilogue: The Alien Mind.

9   Richard Byrne, *The Thinking Ape* (Oxford: Oxford University Press, 1995), 143.

10   McFarland, '5. Mental Possibilities'. I have changed the pronouns relating to Loulis here, to reflect the fact that he is male.

11   Ibid., '8. Mental Autonomy'.

12   Jacques Derrida, *Dissemination* (trans. Barbara Johnson. London: Athlone Press, 1981), 127. See also Chapters 1 and 3, above.

13   See McFarland, '6. The Feeling of Being', and '8. Mental Autonomy'. The studies in question can be found in Sara J. Shettleworth and Jennifer E. Sutton, 'Do Animals Know What They Know?', in Matthew Nudds and Susan Hurley (eds.) *Rational Animals?* (Oxford: Oxford University Press, 2006), 235–246.

14   McFarland, '8. Mental Autonomy'.

15   Ibid. A similar observation is made by Richard Dawkins in his famous definition of the extended phenotype, discussed in Chapter 2, above. See Richard Dawkins, *The Extended Phenotype* (Oxford: Oxford University Press, 1982), 199–200.

16   McFarland, '5. Mental Possibilities'.

17   Ibid., '4. Beyond Automata'.

18   Ibid., '5. Mental Possibilities'.

19   Ibid.

20   Ibid., 'Epilogue: The Alien Mind'.

21   Ibid.

22   Ibid., '4. Beyond Automata'.

23   P. Rozin, 'Specific Aversions as a Component of Specific Hungers.' *Journal of Comparative and Physiological Psychology* 64 (1967): 237–242, and P. Rozin and J.W. Kalat, 'Specific Hungers and Poison Avoidance as Adaptive Specializations of Learning', *Psychological Review* 78 (1971): 459–486.

24   McFarland, '6. The Feeling of Being'.

25   Ibid.

26   See, for example, A.N. Meltzoff, 'Imitation as a Mechanism of Social Cognition: Origins of Empathy, Theory of Mind, and the Representation of Action', in U. Goswami (ed.), *Handbook of Childhood Cognitive Development* (Oxford: Blackwell, 2002), 6–25.

27 See Clive Wynne, *Animal Cognition: The Mental Lives of Animals* (Basingstoke: Palgrave Macmillan, 2001), 23.

28 McFarland, '5. Mental Possibilities'.

29 Ibid. See Kerstin Dautenhahn and Chrystopher L. Nehaniv (eds.), *Imitation in Animals and Artifacts* (Cambridge, MA: MIT Press, 2002).

30 McFarland, '6. The Feeling of Being'.

31 Ibid.

32 Ibid.

33 David Kirsh, 'Today the Earwig, Tomorrow Man', *Artificial Intelligence* 47.1–3 (1991): 161–184, 161. I must admit that I have not been able to find where Brooks actually said this. He does not say it in his famous 'Intelligence Without Representation' (also in *Artificial Intelligence* 47.1–3 [1991]: 139–159; available online at http://www.csail.mit.edu/~brooks/papers/representation.pdf), as Kirsh, Andy Clark, and McFarland (among others) imply.

34 See, for example, Richard E. Nisbett and Thomas D. Wilson, 'Telling More Than We Can Know: Verbal Report on Mental Processes', *Psychological Review* 84, 3 (1977): 231–259.

35 Ibid, 231.

36 Vladas Griskevicius, Robert B. Cialdini and Noah J. Goldstein, 'Applying (and Resisting) Peer Influence.' *MIT Sloan Management Review*. 49.2 (2008): 84–88.

37 Ibid, 87.

38 Ibid.

39 See Gilbert Ryle, *The Concept of Mind* (London: Hutchinson, 1949).

40 McFarland, '4. Beyond Automata'.

41 See Anthony Dickinson *et al.*, 'The Effect of the Instrumental Training Contingency on Susceptibility to Reinforcer Devaluation', *Quarterly Journal of Experimental Psychology* 35B (1983), 35–51; A. Dickinson and Bernard W. Balleine, 'Actions and Responses: The Dual Psychology of Behaviour', in Naomi Eilan, Rosemary McCarthy and Bill Brewer (eds.), *Spatial Representation: Problems in Philosophy and Psychology* (Malden: Blackwell, 1993), 277–293; A. Dickinson, 'Actions and Habits: The Development of Behavioural Autonomy', *Philosophical Transactions of the Royal Society*, Series B, 308 (1985): 67–78; Matias Lopez, B.W. Balleine, and A. Dickinson, 'Incentive Learning and the Motivational Control of Instrumental Performance by Thirst', *Animal Learning and Behavior* 20 (1992): 322–328.

42 McFarland, '4. Beyond Automata'.

43 Ibid.

44 See Daniel Dennett, *The Intentional Stance* (Cambridge, MA: MIT Press, 1987).

45 Daniel Dennett, *Kinds of Minds: Towards an Understanding of Consciousness* (New York: Basic Books, 1996), 122–123.

46 Dennett, *The Intentional Stance*, 259.

47 McFarland, '4. Beyond Automata'.

48 Ibid., '2. Design of Animals and Robots'.

49 Ibid.

50 Ibid.

51 Ibid.

52 Ibid.

53 Ibid.

54 Ibid.

55 Ibid.

56 Reto Zach, 'Shell Dropping: Decision Making and Optimal Foraging in North-western Crows', *Behavior* 68 (1979): 106–117.

57 McFarland, '2. Design of Animals and Robots'.

58 Ibid., '4. Beyond Automata'.

59 Michel Cabanac and Marta Balasko, 'Motivational Conflict Among Water Need, Palatability, and Cold Discomfort in Rats', *Physiology and Behavior* 65 (1998): 35–41.

60 McFarland, '6. The Feeling of Being'.

61 See also, Michel Cabanac, 'Pleasure: The Common Currency', *Journal of Theoretical Biology* 155.2 (1992): 173–200.

62 Michel Cabanac, 'Performance and Perception at Various Combinations of Treadmill Speed and Slope', *Physiology and Behavior* 38 (1986): 839–843.

63 McFarland, '6. The Feeling of Being'.

64 Ibid.

65 Cabanac, 'Pleasure: The Common Currency', 179.

66 McFarland, '6. The Feeling of Being'.

67 Ibid.

68 Ibid.

69 Ibid.

70 Ibid.

71 'No, A 'Supercomputer' Did NOT Pass the Turing Test for the First Time and Everyone Should Know Better' (https://www.techdirt.com/articles/20140609/07284327524/no-supercomputer-did-not-pass-turing-test-first-time-everyone-should-know-better.shtml).

72 John Searle, 'Minds and Brains without Programs', in Colin Blakemore and Susan Greenfield (eds.), *Mindwaves* (Oxford: Blackwell, 1987), 209–233.

73 McFarland, '7. The Material Mind'; Andy Clark, *Mindware* (Oxford: Oxford University Press, 2000).

74 Laurie S. Glezer *et al.*, 'Adding Words to the Brain's Visual Dictionary: Novel Word Learning Selectively Sharpens Orthographic Representations in the VWFA', *The Journal of Neuroscience* 35.12 (2015): 4965–4972.

75 David Lewis, 'Reduction of Mind', in Samuel Guttenplan (ed.), *A Companion to the Philosophy of Mind* (Oxford: Wiley, 1996): 412–431.

76 McFarland, '7. The Material Mind'.

77 Ibid.

78 Ibid.

79 Daniel Dennett, *Kinds of Minds: Towards an Understanding of Consciousness*.

80 Leora Morgenstern, 'The Problems with Solutions to the Frame Problem' (http://www-formal.stanford.edu/leora/fp.pdf).

81 McFarland, '7. The Material Mind'.

82 Ibid.

83 Andy Clark, *Being There: Putting Brain, Body, and World Together Again* (Cambridge, MA: MIT Press, 1997), 21; 191.

84 Rodney A. Brooks, 'Intelligence without Representation', *Artificial Intelligence* 47.1-3 (1991): 139–159 [139]. Available online at: http://www.csail.mit.edu/~brooks/papers/representation.pdf.

85 David McFarland and Tom Bösser. *Intelligent Behavior in Animals and Robots* (Cambridge, MA: MIT Press, 1993), 276.

86 McFarland, '8. Mental Autonomy'.

87 Ibid.

88 McFarland, '7. The Material Mind'.

89 Ibid.

90 Ibid.

91 Richard Lough, 'Captive Orangutan Has Human Right to Freedom, Argentine Court Rules' (http://www.reuters.com/article/2014/12/21/us-argentina-orangutan-idUSKBN0JZ0Q620141221).

92 http://www.nonhumanrightsproject.org/2015/03/06/update-on-the-sandra-orangutan-case-in-argentina/.

93 Alan Yuhas, 'Chimpanzees Granted Petition to Hear "Legal Persons" Status in Court' (http://www.theguardian.com/world/2015/apr/21/chimpanzees-granted-legal-persons-status-unlawful-imprisonment).

94 http://www.nonhumanrightsproject.org/2015/08/20/notice-of-appeal-filed-in-hercules-and-leo-case/.

95 Jacques Derrida, *The Animal That Therefore I Am* (ed. Marie-Louise Maillet; trans. David Wills. New York: Fordham University Press, 2008), 25 [italics in original].

96 Ibid., 26

97 Ibid., 26–27.

98 Ibid., 27–28.

99 René Descartes, *Discourse on the Method, Optics, Geometry and Meteorology* (trans. Paul J. Olscamp. Indianapolis: Hackett, 2001). Available online at: http://www.gutenberg.org/files/59/59-h/59-h.htm. See, especially, Part IV.

100 Derrida, *The Animal That Therefore I Am*, 28.

101 Ibid., 30–31.

102 Ibid., 14 [italics in original].

103 Ibid., 10 [italics in original].

104 Ibid., 7.

105 Ibid., 13–14 [italics in original].

106 Ibid., 37.

107 Ibid., 39.

108 Ibid., 7.

109 Ibid., 8.

110 Ibid., 9.

111 Ibid.

112 Ibid., 48.

113 Edmund Husserl, *Ideas Pertaining to a Pure Phenomenology and to a Phenomenological Philosophy. First Book: General Introduction to a Pure Phenomenology* (trans. F. Kersten. The Hague: Martinus Nijhoff, 1982).

114 Jacques Derrida, *Speech and Phenomena* (trans. David B. Allison. Evanston, IL: Northwest University Press, 1973).

115 Ibid., 63, citing *Ideas*, § 81 [italics in Husserl's original].

116 Ibid., 64 [italics in original].

117 Ibid., 64 [italics in original].

118 Ibid., 65.

119 Ibid.

120 Ibid., 78–79.

121 Ibid., 82.

122 Ibid.

123 Derrida, *The Animal That Therefore I Am*, 49–50 [italics in original].

124 Ibid., 30–31.

125 Immanuel Kant, *Anthropology from a Pragmatic Point of View* (ed. and trans. Robert B. Louden. Cambridge: Cambridge University Press, 2006).

126 Derrida, *The Animal That Therefore I Am*, 94.

127 Ibid.

128 Ibid., 94.

129 Ibid., 95.

130 Ibid., 95 [italics in original].

131 For more on cybernetics, see Chapters 2 and 4 below.

132 Derrida, *The Animal That Therefore I Am*, 95.

133 Ibid., 102.

134 Ibid., 107.

135 Ibid., 26.

136 Ibid., 104.

137 Ibid., 52.

138 Ibid., 86.

139 Ibid., 87.

140 Ibid, 80 [italics in original].

141 Ibid., 82.

142 Nick Bostrom, 'Transhumanist Values', *Review of Contemporary Philosophy* 4 (2005): 3–14. I am citing here from the version available online at: http://www.nickbostrom.com/ethics/values.pdf, page 9. All subsequent page references given for this paper are to the PDF.

143 Ibid., 3.

144 Ibid.

145 Ibid., 3–4.

146 Bostrom, 'A History of Transhumanist Thought' in Michael Rectenwald and Lisa Carl (eds.), *Academic Writing Across the Disciplines* (New York: Pearson Longman, 2011; revised and updated; originally published in *Journal of Evolution and Technology* 14.1 [2005]), 2–3. I am citing from the revised PDF version available online at: http://www.nickbostrom.com/papers/history.pdf.

147 Bostrom, 'Transhumanist Values', 5.

148 Ibid., 4–5.

149 Ibid., 8.

150 Ibid.

151 Ibid., 8–9.

152 Ibid., 9.

153 Ibid., 10.

154 Ibid.

155 Ibid., 10–11.

156 Anders Sandberg and Nick Bostrom, 'Whole Brain Emulation: A Roadmap, Technical Report' (Future of Humanity Institute, Oxford University, 2008), 7. Available online at: www.fhi.ox.ac.uk/reports/2008?3.pdf.

157 Alan Turing, 'On Computable Numbers, with an Application to the Entscheidungsproblem' (1936), in *The Essential Turing: Seminal Writings in Computing, Logic, Philosophy, Artificial Intelligence, and Artificial Life plus The Secrets of Enigma* (Oxford: Oxford University Press, 2004): 58–90.

158 Alan Turing, 'Intelligent Machinery' (1948), in *The Essential Turing: Seminal Writings in Computing, Logic, Philosophy, Artificial Intelligence, and Artificial Life plus The Secrets of Enigma* (Oxford University Press, 2004): 410–432. 413.

159 Turing, 'On Computable Numbers', 68.

160 Ibid.

161 Turing, 'Intelligent Machinery', 416.

162 Sandberg and Bostrom, 'Whole Brain Emulation', 6.

163 Ibid., 7.

164 Ibid., 16.

165 Ibid., 6.

166 Ibid.

167 Ibid., 8.

168 Anders Sandberg, 'Feasibility of whole brain emulation' (original version in Vincent C. Müller, ed., *Theory and Philosophy of Artificial Intelligence* [Berlin: Springer, 2013], 251–64). I am citing here from the version available online at: http://shanghailectures.org/sites/default/files/uploads/2013_Sandberg_Brain-Simulation_34.pdf.

169 Sandberg and Bostrom, 'Whole Brain Emulation', 9.

170 Ibid., 81.

171 Ibid., 71.

172 Ibid.

173 Jonathan Fildes, 'Artificial brain "10 years away"'. (http://news.bbc.co.uk/2/hi/8164060.stm).

174 Sandberg and Bostrom, 'Whole Brain Emulation', 53.

175 Ibid., 40.

176 Ibid., 15.

177 Ibid., 74.

178 Ibid.

179 Ibid., 5.

180 Ibid.

181 Vernor Vinge, 'The Coming Technological Singularity: How to Survive in the Post-Human Era.' Available online at: https://www-rohan.sdsu.edu/faculty/vinge/misc/singularity.html.

182 Ibid.

183 Ibid.

184 Ibid.

185 Ibid.

186 Nick Bostrom, 'How Long Before Superintelligence?', originally published in *International Journal of Future Studies* 2 (1998). I am citing from the revised edition available at: http://www.nickbostrom.com/superintelligence.html. Also notable here is Eliezer Yudkowsky's 'Artificial Intelligence as a Positive and Negative Factor in Global Risk.' in (eds) Nick Bostrom and Milan M. Ćirković, *Global Catastrophic Risks* (New York: Oxford University Press), 308–345.

187 Bostrom, 'Existential Risks: Analyzing Human Extinction Scenarios and Related Hazards', *Journal of Evolution and Technology* 9.1 (2002). I am citing the version available online at: http://www.nickbostrom.com/existential/risks.html, 7.

188 Vincent C. Müller and Nick Bostrom, 'Future Progress in Artificial Intelligence: A Survey of Expert Opinion', in Vincent C. Müller (ed.), *Fundamental Issues of Artificial Intelligence* (Synthese Library; Berlin: Springer, 2014). I am citing here from the version available online at: http://www.nickbostrom.com/papers/survey.pdf, 1.

189 Ibid.

190 Ibid., 15.

191 Nick Bostrom, 'Ethical Issues in Advanced Artificial Intelligence', in I. Smit, W. Wallach, G. Lasker (eds.), *Cognitive, Emotive and Ethical Aspects of Decision Making in Humans and in Artificial Intelligence, Vol. 2* (Windsor, UK: International Institute of Advanced Studies in Systems Research and Cybernetics, 2003), 12–17. Revised version available online at: http://www.nickbostrom.com/ethics/ai.html.

192 Nick Bostrom, *Superintelligence: Paths, Dangers, Strategies* (Oxford: Oxford University Press, 2014).

193 See, for example, Ray Kurzweil, *The Singularity is Near* (London: Penguin, 2006); and *How to Create a Mind* (London: Penguin, 2013).

194 http://singularityu.org/

195 Kurzweil, *The Singularity is Near*, 7–8 [italics in original].

196 Ibid., 9.

197 Ibid.

198 Ibid.

199 For a neat little snapshot of opinions for and against the Singularity from those working in technology, see http://spectrum.ieee.org/computing/hardware/tech-luminaries-address-singularity.

200 Selmer Bringsjord, Alexander Bringsjord and Paul Bello, 'Belief in The Singularity is Fideistic', in Amnon H. Eden, James H. Moor, Johnny H. Søraker and Eric Steinhart (eds.), *Singularity Hypotheses: A Scientific and Philosophical Assessment* (Berlin: Springer, 2012), 395–412. I am citing from the version available online at: http://kryten.mm.rpi.edu/SB_AB_PB_sing_fideism_022412.pdf, 1 [italics in original].

201 Ibid.

202 Theodore Modis, 'The Singularity Myth', *Technological Forecasting and Social Change* 73.2 (2006). I am citing here from the version available online at: http://www.growth-dynamics.com/articles/Kurzweil.htm.

203 Ibid.

204 Ibid.

205 Ibid.

206 Ibid.

207 See also Theodore Modis, 'Forecasting the Growth of Complexity and Change', *Technological Forecasting and Social Change 69.4* (2002). Available at: http://www.growth-dynamics.com/articles/Forecasting_Complexity.pdf.

208 Ibid.

209 The complete text of Pascal's *Pensées* are available online at: http://www.gutenberg.org/files/18269/18269-h/18269-h.htm.

Chapter 6

1 See 'Actually, the Humanities Aren't in Crisis', *The Atlantic* (http://www.theatlantic.com/business/archive/2013/06/actually-the-humanities-arent-in-crisis/277144/), and compare 'The Real Reason the Humanities Are "in Crisis,"' *The Atlantic* (http://www.theatlantic.com/education/archive/2013/12/the-real-reason-the-humanities-are-in-crisis/282441/).

2 See, for example, 'Notes on a Crisis', *Princeton Alumni Weekly* (https://paw.princeton.edu/article/notes-crisis) and 'Humanities Crisis? What Crisis?', *Times Higher Education* (http://www.timeshighereducation.com/news/humanities-crisis-what-crisis).

3 'The Real Reason the Humanities Are "in Crisis,"' *The Atlantic*.

4 'Humanities Studies Under Strain Around the Globe', *The New York Times* (http://www.nytimes.com/2013/12/02/us/humanities-studies-under-strain-around-the-globe.html).

5 'The Humanist Vocation', *The New York Times* (http://www.nytimes.com/2013/06/21/opinion/brooks-the-humanist-vocation.html).

6 'Posthumanities' is also the name of a book series published by the University of Minnesota Press edited by Cary Wolfe (https://www.upress.umn.edu/book-division/series/posthumanities). The series itself is an eclectic one and contains some real food for thought. Some of the books in the series, however, offer anti-digital and anti-science formulations of posthumanism that, for the reasons I have been continually highlighting throughout this book, should not be regarded as effective or even realistic forms of posthumanist analysis.

7 Alan Liu, 'Where Is Cultural Criticism in the Digital Humanities?', in Matthew K. Gold (ed.), *Debates in the Digital Humanities*. Available online at: http://dhdebates.gc.cuny.edu/debates. Throughout this

chapter, I will be citing from this edition, which does not have page references.

8   Kathleen Fitzpatrick, 'The Humanities, Done Digitally.' *The Chronicle of Higher Education* (May 8th, 2011) (http://chronicle. com/article/The-Humanities-Done-Digitally/127382/).

9   'On Scholarly Communication and the Digital Humanities: An Interview with Kathleen Fitzpatrick', *In the Library with the Lead Pipe* (January 14th 2015) (http://www.inthelibrarywiththeleadpipe. org/2015/on-scholarly-communication-and-the-digital-humanities-an-interview-with-kathleen-fitzpatrick/).

10   Liu, 'Where Is Cultural Criticism in the Digital Humanities?' [no page].

11   Ibid.

12   'Let's Talk About Millennial Poverty', *Medium.com* (http://medium. com/@mshannabrooks/but-seriously-lets-talk-about-millennial-poverty-526066ad9adb#.jf93fplh2).

13   Alex Reid, 'Alan Liu, Cultural Criticism, the Digital Humanities, and Problem Solving?' (http://alex-reid.net/2011/01/alan-liu-cultural-criticism-and-the-digital-humanities.html).

14   N. Katherine Hayles, 'How We Read: Close, Hyper, Machine.' *ADE Bulletin* 150 (2010): 62–79, 64–5. Available online at: http:// nkhayles.com/how_we_read.html.

15   Stephen Best and Sharon Marcus, 'Surface Reading: An Introduction.' *Representations* 108.1 (2009): 1–21, 9.

16   Liu, 'Where Is Cultural Criticism in the Digital Humanities?'

17   Rosi Braidotti, *The Posthuman* (Cambridge: Polity Press, 2013), 145.

18   Ibid., 146.

19   Ibid., 146–149.

20   See, for example, 'Social Sciences and Humanities Faculties 'to Close' in Japan after Ministerial Intervention', *Times Higher Education* (http://www.timeshighereducation.com/news/social-sciences-and-humanities-faculties-close-japan-after-ministerial-intervention), 'Where Have All the English Majors Gone?', *Inside Higher Ed* (http://www.insidehighered.com/news/2015/01/26/where-have-all-english-majors-gone) and 'In the Near Future, Only Very Wealthy Colleges Will Have English Departments', *New Republic* (https:// newrepublic.com/article/118025/advent-digital-humanities-will-make-english-departments-pointless).

21   Braidotti, *The Posthuman*, 46.

22 See, for example, 'We Need to Acknowledge the Realities of
    Employment in the Humanities', *The Chronicle of Higher Education*
    (http://chronicle.com/article/We-Need-to-Acknowledge-the/64885/).

23 N. Katherine Hayles, 'How We Read: Close, Hyper, Machine', 75–76.

24 Christopher J. Ferguson, 'Does Media Violence Predict Societal
    Violence? It Depends on What You Look at and When.' *Journal of
    Communication* 65 (2015): E1–E22 [E1].

25 Ibid.

26 Ibid.

27 Ibid., E14.

28 Ibid., E15.

29 Michelle N. Meyer and Christopher Chabris, 'Why Psychologists'
    Food Fight Matters'. (http://www.slate.com/articles/health_and_
    science/science/2014/07/replication_controversy_in_psychology_
    bullying_file_drawer_effect_blog_posts.html).

30 *Social Psychology* 45.3 (2014).

31 Open Science Collaboration, 'Estimating the Reproducibility of
    Psychological Science', *Science* 349.6251 (28 August 2015). http://
    dx.doi.org/10.1126/science.aac4716. In March, 2016, a 'rebuttal' to
    this study was published in *Science* by Dan Gilbert, Gary King,
    Stephen Pettigrew, and Tim Wilson ('Comment on "Estimating the
    Reproducibility of Psychological Science."' *Science* 351.6277 [04
    Mar 2016]: 1037), to which the authors of the original replication
    study replied in the same issue (Christopher J. Anderson *et al.*,
    'Response to Comment on "Estimating the Reproducibility of
    Psychological Science,"' *Science* 351.6277 [04 Mar 2016]: 1037).
    However, as the respondents and a number of other commentators
    pointed out, the authors of the rebuttal made several basic errors in
    their use of statistics as well as making selective interpretations of the
    data. See, for example, Sanjay Srivastava's wonderful analysis,
    'Evaluating a New Critique of the Reproducibility Project', on his
    blog, *The Hardest Science* (http://hardsci.wordpress.com/2016/03/03/
    evaluating-a-new-critique-of-the-reproducibility-project/).

32 Julia Belluz, 'Scientists Replicated 100 Recent Psychology
    Experiments. More Than Half of Them Failed', *Vox* (http://www.vox.
    com/2015/8/27/9216383/irreproducibility-research).

33 Ibid.

34 Simone Schnall, Jennifer Benton and Sophie Harvey, 'With a Clean
    Conscience: Cleanliness Reduces the Severity of Moral Judgments'
    Psychological Science, 19.12 (2008): 1219–1222.

35   Ibid.

36   Ibid.

37   David J. Johnson, Felix Cheung and M. Brent Donnellan, 'Does Cleanliness Influence Moral Judgments?' *Social Psychology* 45.3 (2014): 209–215.

38   Ibid.

39   Liu, 'Where Is Cultural Criticism in the Digital Humanities?'

40   Franco Moretti, *Graphs, Maps, Trees: Abstract Models for a Literary History* (London: Verso, 2005).

41   Liu, 'Where Is Cultural Criticism in the Digital Humanities?'

42   Ibid.

43   Structuralism, in a nutshell, can be understood as a search for the fundamental structures that lie beneath the variations of all the things that human actions, productions, thoughts, etc. Jocker's discussion of his approach is very illuminating. See, for example, 'Revealing Sentiment and Plot Arcs with the Syuzhet Package' (http://www.matthewjockers.net/2015/02/02/syuzhet/) and 'The Rest of the Story' (http://www.matthewjockers.net/2015/02/25/the-rest-of-the-story/).

44   Liu, 'Where Is Cultural Criticism in the Digital Humanities?'

45   Glenn Greenwald, *No Place to Hide: Edward Snowden, the NSA, and the U.S. Surveillance State* (New York: Henry Holt, 2014), 95.

46   Barton Gellman and Laura Poitras, 'U.S., British Intelligence Mining Data from Nine U.S. Internet Companies in Broad Secret Program.' *The Washington Post* (June 7th 2013). (http://www.washingtonpost.com/investigations/us-intelligence-mining-data-from-nine-us-internet-companies-in-broad-secret-program/2013/06/06/3a0c0da8-cebf-11e2-8845-d970ccb04497_story.html.) Despite reports that the NSA 'collect it all' approach ended on June 1st, 2015, bulk collection has not actually stopped at the time of writing (September 2015) and it seems set to continue until at least November 2015. What the spying scandal has made abundantly clear, however, is that it is actually possible to 'collect it all'.

47   Claude E. Shannon, 'A Mathematical Theory of Communication', *Bell System Technical Journal* 27 (1948): 379–423; 623–656. For more on Shannon's formulation of information and its relation to cybernetics, see Chapter 2, above.

48   Valdis E. Krebs, 'Mapping Networks of Terrorist Cells.' *Connections* 24.2 (2002): 43–52. Available online at: http://insna.org/PDF/Connections/v24/2001_I-3-7.pdf.

49 Ibid., 44.

50 'Can Network Theory Thwart Terrorists?' *New York Times* (March 12, 2006) (http://query.nytimes.com/gst/abstract.html?res=9B0CE5D B1531F931A25750C0A9609C8B63).

51 Shahram Mohrehkesh, *et al.*, 'Demographic Prediction of Mobile User from Phone Usage.' *Proceedings of the Nokia Mobile Data Challenge Workshop*. Newcastle, UK, June 2012. Available online at: http://www.researchgate.net/publication/264888907_Demographic_ Prediction_of_Mobile_User_from_Phone_Usage.

52 Yves-Alexandre de Montjoye *et al.*, 'Unique in the Shopping Mall: On the Reidentifiability of Credit Card Metadata.' *Science* 347.6221 (30 January 2015): 536–539.

53 'Advertisers React to Privacy Watchdog's Online Behavioural Advertising Study', *itbusiness.ca* (http://www.itbusiness.ca/news/ advertisers-react-to-privacy-watchdogs-online-behavioural-advertising-study/56314).

54 Michel Foucault, *'Society Must Be Defended': Lectures at the Collège de France, 1975–1976* (trans. David Macey. New York: Picador, 2003), 29; see also Amy Allen, 'Discourse, Power and Subjectivation: The Foucault/Habermas Debate Reconsidered.' *Philosophical Forum* 40.1 (Spring 2009): 1–28.

WORKS CITED

Akst, Jeff. 'Knockout rats have arrived.' *The Scientist* (11 August 2010). (http://www.the-scientist.com/articles.view/articleNo/29194/title/ Knockout-rats-have-arrived/).

Allen, Amy. 'Discourse, power and subjectivation: The Foucault/Habermas debate reconsidered.' *Philosophical Forum*, 40. 1 (Spring 2009): 1–28.

The American Society for Cybernetics. 'Our history of cybernetics.' (http:// www.asc-cybernetics.org/foundations/history.htm).

Anand, Paul. *Foundations of Rational Choice Under Risk* (Oxford: Oxford University Press, 1993).

Arnold, Carrie. 'To share and share alike: Bacteria swap genes with their neighbors more frequently than researchers have realized.' *Scientific American* (1 April 2011). (http://www.scientificamerican.com/article/ to-share-and-share-alike/).

Asimov, Isaac. *I, Robot* (New York: Bantam Spectra, 1991).

Asimov, Isaac. *The Robots of Dawn* (New York: Doubleday, 1983).

Asimov, Isaac. *The Naked Sun* (New York: Bantam Spectra, 1991).

Associated Press. 'Computer crushes the competition on "Jeopardy!"' *CBS News* (15 February 2011). (http://www.cbsnews.com/news/ computer-crushes-the-competition-on-jeopardy/).

BBC News. 'Performer gets third ear for art.' *BBC News* (11 October 2007). (http://news.bbc.co.uk/2/hi/health/7039821.stm).

Badmington, Neil. *Alien Chic: Posthumanism and the Other Within* (London: Routledge, 2004).

Ballard, J.G. *Crash* (London: Picador, 2001).

Baltimore, David, *et al.* 'A prudent path forward for genomic engineering and germline gene modification.' *Science*, 348.36 (2015): 36–38.

Banks, Iain M. *Surface Detail* (London: Orbit, 2010).

Banks, Iain M. *Excession* (London: Orbit, 1996).

Banks, Iain M. *The Player of Games* (London: Macmillan, 1988).

Banks, Iain M. *Consider Phlebas* (London: Macmillan, 1987).

Barnes, Barry, and David Bloor. 'Relativism, rationalism and the sociology of knowledge.' Martin Hollis and Steven Lukes (eds.), *Rationality and Relativism* (Oxford: Blackwell, 1981): 21–47.

Bateson, Gregory and Margaret Mead. 'For God's sake, Margaret: A conversation with Gregory Bateson and Margaret Mead.' *CoEvolutionary Quarterly*, 10.21 (1976): 32–44.

Bear, Greg. *Blood Music* (London: Gollancz, 2001).

Bechtel, William, and Robert C. Richardson. 'Vitalism.' E. Craig (ed.), *Routledge Encyclopedia of Philosophy* (London: Routledge. 1998). (http://mechanism.ucsd.edu/teaching/philbio/vitalism.htm).

Begley, Sharon. 'Scientists unveil the "most clever CRISPR gadget" so far.' *STAT* (20 April 2016). (http://www.statnews.com/2016/04/20/clever-crispr-advance-unveiled/).

Begley, Sharon. 'In the CRISPR patent fight, the Broad Institute gains edge in early rulings.' *STAT* (18 March 2016). (http://www.statnews.com/2016/03/18/crispr-patent-dispute/).

Begley, Sharon. 'Malaria kills a half-million Africans a year. Gene-edited mosquitoes might stop it.' *STAT* (7 December 2015). (http://www.statnews.com/2015/12/07/gene-edited-mosquitoes-stop-malaria/).

Begley, Sharon. 'Dare we edit the human race? Star geneticists wrestle with their power.' *STAT* (2 December 2015). (http://www.statnews.com/2015/12/02/gene-editing-summit-embryos/).

Belluz, Julie. 'Scientists replicated 100 recent psychology experiments: More than half of them failed.' *Vox* (27 August 2015). (http://www.vox.com/2015/8/27/9216383/irreproducibility-research).

Bentham, Jeremy. *An Introduction to the Principles of Morals and Legislation* (Oxford: Clarendon Press, 1907).

Best, Stephen, and Sharon Marcus. 'Surface reading: An introduction.' *Representations* 108.1 (2009): 1–21.

Bindman, Dan. 'Report: Artificial intelligence will cause "structural collapse" of law firms by 2030.' *Legal Futures* (1 December 2014). (http://www.legalfutures.co.uk/latest-news/report-ai-will-transform-legal-world).

Bishop, Todd. 'Interview: Paul Allen's artificial intelligence guru on the future of robots and humanity.' *Geekwire* (1 April 2016). (http://www.geekwire.com/2016/geekwire-radio-paul-allens-artificial-intelligence-guru-future-robots-humanity/).

Boffey, Daniel. 'Dutch city plans to pay citizens a "basic income," and Greens say it could work in the UK.' *Guardian* (26 December 2015). (http://www.theguardian.com/world/2015/dec/26/dutch-city-utrecht-basic-income-uk-greens).

Bostrom, Nick. *Superintelligence: Paths, Dangers, Strategies* (Oxford: Oxford University Press, 2014).

Bostrom, Nick. 'A history of transhumanist thought.' Michael Rectenwald and Lisa Carl (eds.), *Academic Writing Across the Disciplines* (New York: Pearson Longman, 2011). (http://www.nickbostrom.com/papers/history.pdf).

Bostrom, Nick. 'Transhumanist values.' *Review of Contemporary Philosophy*, 4 (2005): 3–14. (http://www.nickbostrom.com/ethics/values.pdf).

Bostrom, Nick. 'Ethical issues in advanced artificial intelligence.' I. Smit, W. Wallach, G. Lasker (eds.), *Cognitive, Emotive and Ethical Aspects of Decision Making in Humans and in Artificial Intelligence, Vol. 2* (Windsor: International Institute of Advanced Studies in Systems Research and Cybernetics, 2003): 12–17. (http://www.nickbostrom.com/ethics/ai.html).

Bostrom, Nick. 'Existential risks: Analyzing human extinction scenarios and related hazards.' *Journal of Evolution and Technology*, 9.1 (2002). (http://www.nickbostrom.com/existential/risks.html).

Bostrom, Nick. 'How long before superintelligence?' *International Journal of Future Studies*, 2 (1998). (http://www.nickbostrom.com/superintelligence.html).

Boucher, Sandy C. 'What is a philosophical stance? Paradigms, policies and perspectives,' *Synthese*, 191.10 (2014): 2315–2332.

Bowerbank, Sylvia. *Speaking for Nature: Women and Ecologies of Early Modern England* (Baltimore: Johns Hopkins University Press, 2004).

Braidotti, Rosi. *The Posthuman* (Cambridge: Polity Press, 2013).

Bringsjord, Selmer, Alexander Bringsjord and Paul Bello. 'Belief in the singularity is fideistic.' Amnon H. Eden, James H. Moor, Johnny H. Søraker and Eric Steinhart (eds.), *Singularity Hypotheses: A Scientific and Philosophical Assessment* (Berlin: Springer, 2012): 395–412.

Brooks, David. 'The humanist vocation.' *The New York Times* (21 June 2013). (http://www.nytimes.com/2013/06/21/opinion/brooks-the-humanist-vocation.html).

Brooks, Rodney A. 'Intelligence without representation.' *Artificial Intelligence*, 47.1–3 (1991): 139–159. (http://www.csail.mit.edu/~brooks/papers/representation.pdf).

Burroughs, William S. *Naked Lunch* (New York: Grove Press, 2001).

Burns, Russell W. *Communications: An International History of the Formative Years* (London: Institution of Electrical Engineers, 2004).

Butler, Octavia. *Dawn* (New York: Warner Books, 1987).

Byford, Sam. 'Google's AlphaGo AI beats Lee Se-dol again to win Go series 4–1.' *The Verge* (15 March 2016). (http://www.theverge.com/2016/3/15/11213518/alphago-deepmind-go-match-5-result).

Byrne, Richard. *The Thinking Ape* (Oxford: Oxford University Press, 1995).

Cabanac, Michel, and Marta Balaskó. 'Motivational conflict among water need, palatability, and cold discomfort in rats.' *Physiology and Behavior*, 65 (1998): 35–41.

Cabanac, Michel, and Marta Balaskó. 'Pleasure: The common currency.' *Journal of Theoretical Biology*, 155.2 (1992): 173–200.

Cabanac, Michel, and Marta Balaskó. 'Performance and perception at various combinations of treadmill speed and slope.' *Physiology and Behavior*, 38 (1986): 839–843.

Cambridge News. 'Cambridge University researchers' breakthrough paves way for same sex couple babies,' *Cambridge News* (22 February 2015). (http://www.cambridge-news.co.uk/Cambridge-university-researchers-breakthrough/story-26065812-detail/story.html).

Candland, Douglas Keith. *Feral Children and Clever Animals: Reflections on Human Nature* (Oxford: Oxford University Press, 1993).

Cannon, W.B. 'Physiological regulation of normal states: some tentative postulates concerning biological homeostatics.' A. Pettit (ed.), *A Charles Richet: ses amis, ses collègues, ses élèves* (Paris: Les Éditions Médicales, 1926).

Carroll, Dana. 'A CRISPR approach to gene targeting,' *Molecular Therapy*, 20.9 (September 2012): 1658–1660.

Cellan-Jones, Rory. 'Stephen Hawking warns artificial intelligence could end mankind.' *BBC News* (2 December 2014). (http://www.bbc.co.uk/news/technology-30290540).

Chalmers University of Technology. 'Thought-controlled prosthesis is changing the lives of amputees.' Press Release (5 December 2012). (http://www.chalmers.se/en/news/Pages/Thought-controlled-prosthesis-is-changing-the-lives-of-amputees.aspx).

Chaucer, Geoffrey. 'The Wife of Bath's Prologue and Tale.' *The Canterbury Tales* (London: Penguin Classics, 2009).

Chi, Kelly Rae. 'Red Hot: CRISPR/Cas is all the rage—and getting more precise and efficient.' *The Scientist* (1 March 2015). (http://www.the-scientist.com/?articles.view/articleNo/42260/title/Red-Hot/).

Clark, Andy. *Natural Born Cyborgs: Minds, Technologies, and the Future of Human Intelligence* (Oxford: Oxford University Press, 2003).

Clark, Andy. *Mindware* (Oxford: Oxford University Press, 2000).

Clark, Andy. *Being There: Putting Brain, Body, and World Together Again* (Cambridge, MA: MIT Press, 1997).

Clarke, Bruce. *Posthuman Metamorphosis: Narrative and Systems* (New York: Fordham University Press, 2008).

Cleeremans, Axel. 'Computational correlates of consciousness.' *Progress in Brain Research*, 150 (2005): 81–98.

Cline, Ernest. *Ready Player One* (New York: Broadway Books, 2012).

Clynes, Manfred, and Nathan S. Kline. 'Cyborgs and space.' *Astronautics* (September 1960): 26–27; 74–76.

Conn, Peter. 'We need to acknowledge the realities of employment in the humanities.' *The Chronicle of Higher Education* (4 April 2010). (http://chronicle.com/article/We-Need-to-Acknowledge-the/64885/).

Coleridge, Samuel Taylor. *Biographia Literaria*. (http://www.gutenberg.org/files/6081/6081-h/6081-h.htm).

Crouch, Dennis. 'Harvard's US OncoMouse patents are all expired (for the time being).' *Patentlyo* (18 September 2012). (http://patentlyo.com/patent/2012/09/harvards-us-oncomouse-patents-are-all-expired-for-the-time-being.html).

Cruse, Holk, and Malte Schilling. 'Mental states as emergent properties: From walking to consciousness.' (eds.) T. Metzinger and J.M. Windt, *Open MIND*: 9T (Frankfurt am Main: MIND Group, 2015): 1–38. (http://open-mind.net/papers/mental-states-as-emergent-properties-from-walking-to-consciousness/at_download/paperPDF).

Cruse, Holk. 'The evolution of cognition: A hypothesis,' *Cognitive Science*, 27 (2003): 135–155.

Cyranoski, David, and Sara Reardon. 'Embryo editing sparks epic debate.' *Nature*, 520 (29 April 2015): 593–594.

Dautenhahn, Kerstin, and Chrystopher L. Nehaniv (eds.). *Imitation in Animals and Artifacts* (Cambridge, MA: MIT Press, 2002).

David, Marian. 'The correspondence theory of truth.' (ed.) Edward N. Zalta, *The Stanford Encyclopedia of Philosophy* (Fall 2015 Edition). (http://plato.stanford.edu/archives/fall2015/entries/truth-correspondence/).

Dawkins, Richard. *The Extended Phenotype* (Oxford: Oxford University Press, 1982).

Dawkins, Richard. 'Replicator selection and the extended phenotype.' *Zeitschrift für Tierpsychologie*, 47 (1978): 61–76.

Debord, Guy. *The Society of the Spectacle* (trans. Donald Nicholson-Smith. New York: Zone Books, 2005).

DeepLearning. 'Convolutional neural networks.' (http://deeplearning.net/tutorial/lenet.html).

Delany, Ella. 'Humanities studies under strain around the globe.' *The New York Times* (1 December 2013). (http://www.nytimes.com/2013/12/02/us/humanities-studies-under-strain-around-the-globe.html).

Deng, L., and D. Yu. 'Deep learning: Methods and applications.' *Foundations and Trends in Signal Processing* 7.3–4 (2014): 197–387. (http://research.microsoft.com/pubs/209355/DeepLearning-NowPublishing-Vol7-SIG-039.pdf).

Dennett, Daniel. *Kinds of Minds: Towards an Understanding of Consciousness*. (New York: Basic Books, 1997).

Dennett, Daniel. *The Intentional Stance* (Cambridge, MA: MIT Press, 1987).

Derrida, Jacques. *The Animal That Therefore I Am* (ed. Marie-Louise Maillet; trans. David Wills. New York: Fordham University Press, 2008).

Derrida, Jacques. *Dissemination* (trans. Barbara Johnson. London: Athlone Press, 1981).

Derrida, Jacques. *Speech and Phenomena* (trans. David B. Allison. Evanston, IL: Northwest University Press, 1973).

Descartes, René. *Discourse on the Method, Optics, Geometry and Meteorology* (trans. Paul J. Olscamp. Indianapolis: Hackett, 2001). (http://www.gutenberg.org/files/59/59-h/59-h.htm).

Dick, Philip K. *Do Androids Dream of Electric Sheep?* (New York: Ballantyne Books, 1996).

Dick, Philip K. *I Hope I Shall Arrive Soon* (New York: Doubleday, 1985).

Dickinson, Anthony, and Bernard W. Balleine. 'Actions and responses: The dual psychology of behaviour.' Naomi Eilan, Rosemary McCarthy and Bill Brewer (eds.), *Spatial Representation: Problems in Philosophy and Psychology* (Malden: Blackwell, 1993), 277–293.

Dickinson, Anthony, and Bernard W. Balleine. 'Actions and habits: The development of behavioural and autonomy.' *Philosophical Transactions of the Royal Society*, Series B, 308 (1985): 67–78.

Dickinson, Anthony, *et al.* 'The effect of the instrumental training contingency on susceptibility to reinforcer devaluation.' *Quarterly Journal of Experimental Psychology*, 35B (1983), 35–51.

Dreyfus, Hubert. *What Computers Still Can't Do* (Cambridge, MA: MIT Press, 1992).

Doudna, Jennifer. 'Perspective: Embryo editing needs scrutiny.' *Nature* 528.S6 (3 December 2015). (http://www.nature.com/nature/journal/v528/n7580_supp/full/528S6a.html).

Dundar, Aysegul. 'Convolutional neural networks.' (http://www.youtube.com/watch?v=n6hpQwq7Inw).

The Economist. 'The onrushing wave.' *The Economist.* Briefing (18 January 2014). (http://www.economist.com/news/briefing/21594264-previous-technological-innovation-has-always-delivered-more-long-run-employment-not-less).

The Economist. 'How science goes wrong.' *The Economist.* Leaders (19 October 2013). (http://www.economist.com/news/leaders/21588069-scientific-research-has-changed-world-now-it-needs-change-itself-how-science-goes-wrong).

Eugenios, Jillian. 'A computer made my lunch.' *CNN Money* (8 May 2015). (http://money.cnn.com/2015/05/07/technology/chef-watson-recipes/).

Ferguson, Christopher J. 'Does media violence predict societal violence? It depends on what you look at and when.' *Journal of Communication*, 65 (2015): E1–E22.

Ferrucci, David, *et al.* 'Watson: Beyond Jeopardy!' *Artificial Intelligence*, 199–200 (2013): 93–105.

Ferrucci, David, *et al.* 'Building Watson: An overview of the DeepQA project.' *Association for the Advancement of Artificial Intelligence* (Fall 2010): 59–79.

Feyerabend, Paul. *Against Method* (London: New Left Books, 1975).

Fildes, Jonathan. 'Artificial brain "10 years away."' *BBC News.* (22 July 2009). (http://news.bbc.co.uk/2/hi/8164060.stm).

Finch, Jacqueline. 'The ancient origins of prosthetic medicine.' *The Lancet*, 377.9765 (12 February 2011): 548–549.

Firger, Jessica. 'The brave new world of biohacking.' *Al Jazeera America* (18 October 2013). (http://america.aljazeera.com/articles/2013/10/18/the-brave-new-worldofbiohacking.html).

Fitzpatrick, Kathleen. 'The humanities, done digitally.' *The Chronicle of Higher Education* (8 May 2011). (http://chronicle.com/article/The-Humanities-Done-Digitally/127382/).

Fitzpatrick, Kathleen. 'On Scholarly communication and the digital humanities: An interview with Kathleen Fitzpatrick.' *In the Library with the Lead Pipe* (14 January 2015). (http://www.inthelibrarywiththeleadpipe.org/2015/on-scholarly-communication-and-the-digital-humanities-an-interview-with-kathleen-fitzpatrick/).

Flaherty, Colleen. 'Where have all the English majors gone?' *Inside Higher Ed* (26 January 2015). (http://www.insidehighered.com/news/2015/01/26/where-have-all-english-majors-gone).

Forrest, Conner. 'Google and robots: The real reasons behind the shopping spree.' *TechRepublic* (5 March 2014). (http://www.techrepublic.com/article/google-and-robots-the-real-reasons-behind-the-shopping-spree/).

Foucault, Michel. *'Society Must Be Defended': Lectures at the Collège de France, 1975–1976* (trans. David Macey. New York: Picador, 2003).

Foucault, Michel. 'What is Enlightenment?' *The Foucault Reader* (ed. Paul Rabinow. New York: Pantheon Books, 1984).

Fuller, Steve. *Philosophy, Rhetoric, and the End of Knowledge: The Coming of Science and Technology Studies.* (Madison: University of Wisconsin Press, 1993).

Garland, Alex (dir.). *Ex Machina.* A24, 2015.

Gellman, Barton, and Laura Poitras. 'U.S., British intelligence mining data from nine U.S. Internet companies in broad secret program.' *The Washington Post* (6 June 2013). (http://www.washingtonpost.com/investigations/us-intelligence-mining-data-from-nine-us-internet-companies-in-broad-secret-program/2013/06/06/3a0c0da8-cebf-11e2-8845-d970ccb04497_story.html).

Gergen. Mary M. (ed.). *Feminist Thought and the Structure of Knowledge* (New York: New York University Press, 1988).

Gibson, William. *Neuromancer* (New York: Ace Books, 1984).

Gibbs, Samuel. 'Elon Musk:Artificial intelligence is our biggest existential threat.' *Guardian* (27 October 2014). (http://www.theguardian.com/technology/2014/oct/27/elon-musk-artificial-intelligence-ai-biggest-existential-threat).

Gilbert, Dan, Gary King, Stephen Pettigrew, and Tim Wilson. 'Comment on "Estimating the reproducibility of psychological science."' *Science*, 351.6277 (4 March 2016): 1037.

Glezer, Laurie S., *et al*. 'Adding words to the brain's visual dictionary: Novel word learning selectively sharpens orthographic representations in the VWFA.' *The Journal of Neuroscience*, 35.12 (2015): 4965–4972.

Gondek, D.C., *et al*. 'A framework for merging and ranking of answers in DeepQA.' *IBM Research* (2012). (http://brenocon.com/watson_special_issue/14%20a%20framework%20for%20merging%20and%20ranking%20answers.pdf).

Graham, Mark. 'The knowledge based economy and digital divisions of labour.' Vandana Desai and Rob Potter (eds.), *The Companion to Development Studies* in (London: Routledge, 2014): 189–195. (http://ssrn.com/abstract=2363880).

Greenwald, Glenn, Ewan MacAskill and Laura Poitras. 'Edward Snowden: The whistleblower behind the NSA surveillance revelations,' *Guardian* (9 June 2013). (http://www.theguardian.com/world/2013/jun/09/edward-snowden-nsa-whistleblower-surveillance).

Greenwald, Glenn. *No Place to Hide: Edward Snowden, the NSA, and the U.S. Surveillance State* (New York: Henry Holt, 2014).

Griskevicius, Vladas, Robert B. Cialdini and Noah J. Goldstein, 'Applying (and resisting) peer influence.' *MIT Sloan Management Review*. 49.2 (2008): 84–88.

Gross, Paul R., and Norman Levitt. *Higher Superstition: The Academic Left and Its Quarrels With Science* (Baltimore: Johns Hopkins University Press, 1997).

Grosz, Elizabeth. *Becoming Undone* (Durham, NC: Duke University Press, 2011).

Grove, Jack. 'Social sciences and humanities faculties 'to close' in Japan after ministerial intervention.' *Times Higher Education* (14 September 2015). (http://www.timeshighereducation.com/news/social-sciences-and-humanities-faculties-close-japan-after-ministerial-intervention).

Guizzo, Erico. 'Robot Baby Diego-San shows its expressive face on video.' *IEEE Spectrum* (9 January 2013). (http://spectrum.ieee.org/automaton/robotics/humanoids/robot-baby-diego-san).

Gyles, C., and P. Boerlin. 'Horizontally transferred genetic elements and their role in pathogenesis of bacterial disease.' *Veterinary Pathology*, 51.2 (2014): 328–340.

Haack, Susan. *Defending Science—Within Reason: Between Scientism and Cynicism* (Amherst: Prometheus Books, 2003).

Haraway, Donna. *Simians, Cyborgs and Women* (London: Routledge, 1991).

Harding, Sandra, and Jean O'Barr (eds.). *Sex and Scientific Inquiry* (Chicago: University of Chicago Press, 1987).

Harris, Malcolm. 'What's a "safe space"? A look at the phrase's 50-year history.' *Fusion* (11 November 2015). (http://fusion.net/story/231089/safe-space-history).

Hayles, N. Katherine. *How We Became Posthuman: Virtual Bodies in Cybernetics, Literature and Informatics* (Chicago: University of Chicago Press, 1999).

Hayles, N. Katherine. 'How we read: Close, hyper, machine.' *ADE Bulletin*, 150 (2010): 62–79. (http://nkhayles.com/how_we_read.html).

Hill, Kashmir. 'Are child sex-robots inevitable?' *Forbes* (14 July 2014). (http://www.forbes.com/sites/kashmirhill/2014/07/14/are-child-sex-robots-inevitable).

Hills, Richard L. *Power From the Wind* (Cambridge: Cambridge University Press, 1996).

Heylighen, Francis. 'Attractors.' *Principia Cybernetica Web*. (http://pespmc1.vub.ac.be/attracto.html).

Heylighen, Francis and Cliff Joslyn. 'Cybernetics and second-order cybernetics.' R.A. Meyers (ed.), *Encyclopedia of Physical Science and Technology* (New York: Academic Press, 2001). (pespmc1.vub.ac.be/papers/cybernetics-epst.pdf).

Hollan, James, Ed Hutchins and David Kirsh, 'Distributed Cognition: Toward a New Foundation for Human-Computer Interaction Research.' *ACM Transactions on Computer-Human Interaction (TOCHI)*, 7.2 (2000), 174–196.

Hubel, David H., and Torsten N. Wiesel. 'Receptive fields and functional architecture of monkey striate cortex.' *Journal of Physiology*, 195 (1968): 215–243.

Hubel, David H., and Torsten N. Wiesel. 'Receptive fields, binocular interaction and functional architecture in the cat's visual cortex.' *Journal of Physiology*, 160 (1962): 106–154.

Hubel, David H., and Torsten N. Wiesel. 'Receptive fields of single neurones in the cat's striate cortex.' *Journal of Physiology*, 148 (1959): 574–591.

Husserl, Edmund. *Ideas Pertaining to a Pure Phenomenology and to a Phenomenological Philosophy. First Book: General Introduction to a Pure Phenomenology* (trans. F. Kersten. The Hague: Martinus Nijhoff, 1982).

Hutcheon, Linda. *Narcissistic Narrative: The Metafictional Paradox* (London: Routledge, 1984).

Hutchins, Edwin. *Cognition in the Wild* (Cambridge, MA: MIT Press, 1995).

International Society of Genetic Genealogy (ISOGG). 'Wiki.' (http://www.isogg.org/wiki/Wiki_Welcome_Page).

International Telecommunication Union. 'The World in 2014: ICT Facts and Figures.' (http://www.itu.int/en/ITU-D/Statistics/Documents/facts/ICTFactsFigures2014-e.pdf).

Ishiguro, Kazuo. *Never Let Me Go* (Toronto: Vintage, 2006).

Jackson, Peter. *Introduction To Expert Systems* (Boston: Addison Wesley, 1998).

Jameson, Fredric. *Postmodernism, or, the Cultural Logic of Late Capitalism* (Durham, NC: Duke University Press, 1991).

Jockers, Matthew L. 'Revealing sentiment and plot arcs with the Syuzhet Package.' (http://www.matthewjockers.net/2015/02/02/syuzhet/).

Jockers, Matthew L. 'The rest of the story.' (http://www.matthewjockers.net/2015/02/25/the-rest-of-the-story/).

Johnson, David J., Felix Cheung and M. Brent Donnellan, 'Does cleanliness influence moral judgments?' *Social Psychology*, 45.3 (2014): 209–215.

Kahn, David. *The Codebreakers* (rev. ed., New York: Simon and Schuster, 1996).

Kant, Immanuel. *Anthropology from a Pragmatic Point of View* (ed. and trans. Robert B. Louden. Cambridge: Cambridge University Press, 2006).

Keefe, Patrick Radden, 'Can network theory thwart terrorists?' *New York Times* (March 12, 2006). (http://query.nytimes.com/gst/abstract.html?res=9B0CE5DB1531F931A25750C0A9609C8B63).

Keller, Evelyn Fox. *Reflections on Gender and Science* (New Haven: Yale University Press, 1995).

Kirsh, David. 'Today the earwig, tomorrow man.' *Artificial Intelligence* 47.1-3 (1991): 161–184.

Koepke, Logan. 'The FCC Did NOT Make the Internet a Public Utility.' *Backchannel* (26 February 2015). (http:// https://backchannel.com/the-historical-record-of-net-neutrality-747286cbde62).

Koertge, Noretta (ed.). *A House Built on Sand: Exposing Postmodernist Myths about Science* (Oxford: Oxford University Press, 2000).

Komor, Alexis C., *et al.* 'Programmable editing of a target base in genomic DNA without double-stranded DNA cleavage.' *Nature* (20 April 2016). (http://www.nature.com/nature/journal/vaop/ncurrent/full/nature17946.html).

Kositsky, Michael, Michela Chiappalone, Simon T. Alford and Ferdinando A. Mussa-Ivaldi. 'Brain-machine interactions for assessing the dynamics of neural systems.' *Frontiers in Neurorobotics*, 3 (March 2009): 1–12.

Krasniansky, Adriana. 'Meet Ross, the IBM Watson-powered lawyer.' *PSFK* (29 January 2015). (http://www.psfk.com/2015/01/ross-ibm-watson-powered-lawyer-legal-research.html).

Krakauer, Jon. *Into the Wild* (New York: Villard, 1996).

Krebs, Valdis E. 'Mapping networks of terrorist cells.' *Connections*, 24.2 (2002): 43–52.

Kurzweil, Ray. *The Singularity is Near* (London: Penguin, 2006).

Kurzweil, Ray. *How to Create a Mind* (London: Penguin, 2013).

Latour, Bruno. *Reassembling the Social: An Introduction to Actor-Network-Theory* (Oxford: Oxford University Press, 2005).

Latour, Bruno. 'Why has critique run out of steam? From matters of fact to matters of concern.' *Critical Inquiry*, 30 (2004): 225–248.

Latour, Bruno. 'For David Bloor and beyond . . . a reply to David Bloor's "Anti-Latour."' *Studies in History and Philosophy of Science*, 30.1 (1999): 113–129.

Lebedev, Mikhail A., *et al.* 'Cortical ensemble adaptation to represent velocity of an artificial actuator controlled by a brain-machine interface.' *Journal of Neuroscience*, 25.19 (11 May 2005): 4681–4693.

Lebedev, Mikhail A., *et al.* and Miguel A.L. Nicolelis. 'Brain-machine interfaces: Past, present and future.' *TRENDS in Neurosciences*, 29.9 (2006): 536–546.

Ledford, Heidi. 'CRISPR the Disruptor.' *Nature*, 522 (4 June, 2015): 20–24.

Lee, Micah. 'Encryption works: How to protect your privacy in the age of NSA surveillance.' Freedom of the Press Foundation. (http://freedom. press/encryption-works).

Lettvin, Jerome, Humberto R. Maturana, Warren McCulloch and Walter Pitts. 'What the frog's eye tells the frog's brain.' *Proceedings of the Institute for Radio Engineers*, 47.11 (1959): 1940–1951.

Letzing, John. 'Google hires famed futurist Ray Kurzweil.' *Wall Street Journal* (14 December 2012). (http://blogs.wsj.com/digits/2012/12/14/ google-hires-famed-futurist-ray-kurzweil/?mod=WSJBlog&utm_ source=twitterfeed&utm_medium&=twitter&source&=email_rt_mc_ body&i&fp&=0).

Leuthardt, Eric C., Jarod L. Roland, and Wilson Z. Ray. 'Neuroprosthetics.' *The Scientist* (1 November 2014). (http://www.the-scientist. com/?articles.view/articleNo/41324/title/Neuroprosthetics/).

Levy, Neil. 'Analytic and continental philosophy: Explaining the differences.' *Metaphilosophy*, 34.3 (April 2003): 284–304.

Lewis, David. 'Reduction of mind.' Samuel Guttenplan (ed.), *A Companion to the Philosophy of Mind* (Oxford: Wiley, 1996): 412–431.

Liang, P., *et al.* 'CRISPR/Cas9-mediated gene editing in human tripronuclear zygotes.' *Protein & Cell*, 6.5 (2015): 363–372.

Libet, Benjamin, W.W. Alberts, E.W. Wright, L.D. Delatre, G. Levin and B. Feinstein. 'Production of threshold levels of conscious sensation by electrical stimulation of human somatosensory cortex.' *Journal of Neurophysiology*, 27.4 (1964): 546–578.

Liu, Alan. 'Where is cultural criticism in the digital humanities?' Matthew K. Gold (ed.), *Debates in the Digital Humanities* (Minneapolis: University of Minnesota Press, 2012). (http://dhdebates.gc.cuny.edu/debates).

Liu, Dennis W. C. 'Science denial and the science classroom.' *CBE—Life Sciences Education*, 11.2 (2012): 129–134.

Liu, Jia, *et al.* 'Syringe-injectable electronics.' *Nature Nanotechnology* (8 June, 2015). (http://www.nature.com/nnano/journal/vaop/ncurrent/full/ nnano.2015.115.html).

Locke, John. *Two Treatises of Government* (Cambridge: Cambridge University Press, 1960).

Longino, Helen. *Science as Social Knowledge* (Princeton: Princeton University Press, 1990).

Lopez. Matias, B.W. Balleine, and A. Dickinson, 'Incentive learning and the motivational control of instrumental performance by thirst.' *Animal Learning and Behavior*, 20 (1992): 322–328.

Lough, Richard. 'Captive orangutan has human right to freedom, Argentine court rules.' *Reuters* (21 December 2014). (http://www.reuters.com/article/2014/12/21/us-argentina-orangutan-idUSKBN0JZ0Q620141221).

Lovecraft, H.P. 'The Call of Cthulhu.' (http://en.wikisource.org/wiki/The_Call_of_Cthulhu/full).

Luk, Lorraine. 'Foxconn's Robot Army Yet to Prove Match for Humans.' *Wall Street Journal* (5 May 2015). (http://blogs.wsj.com/digits/2015/05/05/foxconns-robot-army-yet-to-prove-match-for-humans/).

Lyotard, Jean-Francois. *The Postmodern Condition: A Report on Knowledge* (Minneapolis: University of Minnesota Press, 1984).

Mann, Charles. 'Lynn Margulis: Science's unruly earth mother.' *Science* 252.5004 (1991): 378–381.

Marescaux, Jacques, J. Leroy, F. Rubino, M. Vix, M. Simone and D. Mutter, 'Transcontinental robot assisted remote telesurgery: Feasibility and potential applications.' *Annals of Surgery*, 235 (2002): 487–492.

Margulis, Lynn, and Dorion Sagan, *Microcosmos: Four Billion Years of Evolution from Our Microbial Ancestors* (Berkeley: University of California Press, 1997).

Marshall, Alfred. *Principles of Economics: An Introductory Volume* (London: Macmillan, 1920).

Masnick, Mike. 'No, a "supercomputer" did NOT pass The Turing Test for the first time and everyone should know better,' *TechDirt* (9 June 2014). (http://www.techdirt.com/articles/20140609/07284327524/no-supercomputer-did-not-pass-turing-test-first-time-everyone-should-know-better.shtml).

Math Insight. 'Vectors in arbitrary dimensions.' (http://mathinsight.org/vectors_arbitrary_dimensions).

Maturana, Humberto R., and Francisco J. Varela, *Autopoiesis and Cognition: The Realization of the Living* (Dordrecht: D Reidel, 1980).

Maturana, Humberto R., and Francisco J. Varela, *The Tree of Knowledge: The Biological Roots of Human Understanding* (Boston: Shambhala, 1987).

Maxwell, James Clerk. 'On governors.' *Proceedings of the Royal Society of London*, 270–283. (www.maths.ed.ac.uk/~aar/papers/maxwell1.pdf).

McCulloch, Warren, and Walter Pitts, 'A logical calculus of ideas immanent in nervous activity.' *Bulletin of Mathematical Biophysics*, 5.4 (1943): 115–133.

McFarland, David. *Guilty Robots, Happy Dogs: The Question of Alien Minds* (Oxford: Oxford University Press, 2008).

McFarland, David and Tom Bösser. *Intelligent Behavior in Animals and Robots* (Cambridge, MA: MIT Press, 1993).

McCord, Michael C. 'Using slot grammar.' *IBM Research Division* (2010). (http://domino.research.ibm.com/library/cyberdig.nsf/papers/ FB5445D25B7E3932852576F10047E1C2/$File/rc23978revised. pdf).

Mehrabian, Albert. 'Pleasure-arousal-dominance: A general framework for describing and measuring individual differences in temperament.' *Current Psychology*, 4 (1996): 261–292.

Meltzoff, A.N., 'Imitation as a mechanism of social cognition: Origins of empathy, theory of mind, and the representation of action.' U. Goswami (ed.), *Handbook of Childhood Cognitive Development* (Oxford: Blackwell, 2002): 6–25.

Memorial Sloan Kettering. 'Watson oncology.' (http://www.mskcc.org/ about/innovative-collaborations/watson-oncology).

Melo, Eduardo O., *et al.* 'Animal transgenesis: State of the art and applications.' *Journal of Applied Genetics*, 48.1 (2007): 47–61.

Meyer, Michelle N., and Christopher Chabris. 'Why psychologists' food fight matters.' *Slate* (31 July 2014). (http://www.slate.com/articles/ health_and_science/science/2014/07/replication_controversy_in_ psychology_bullying_file_drawer_effect_blog_posts.html).

Mill, John Stuart. *Utilitarianism* (Roger Crisp (ed.). Oxford: Oxford University Press, 1998).

Minsky, Marvin. 'Logical vs. analogical or symbolic vs. connectionist or neat vs. scruffy.' (http://web.media.mit.edu/~minsky/papers/ SymbolicVs.Connectionist.html).

Minsky, Marvin and Seymour Papert, *Perceptrons: An Introduction to Computational Geometry* (2nd edition with corrections. Cambridge, MA: The MIT Press, 1972).

Mitchell, David. *Cloud Atlas* (Toronto: Vintage, 2004).

Mitchell, Tom. *Machine Learning* (New York: McGraw Hill, 1997).

Mnih, Volodymyr, *et al.* 'Human-level control through deep reinforcement learning.' *Nature*, 518.26 (February 2015): 529–533.

Modis, Theodore. 'Forecasting the growth of complexity and change.' *Technological Forecasting and Social Change*, 69.4 (2002). (http:// www.growth-dynamics.com/articles/Forecasting_Complexity.pdf).

Modis, Theodore. 'The Singularity Myth.' *Technological Forecasting and Social Change*, 73.2 (2006). (http://www.growth-dynamics.com/ articles/Kurzweil.htm).

Mohrehkesh, Shahram, *et al.* 'Demographic Prediction of Mobile User from Phone Usage.' *Proceedings of the Nokia Mobile Data Challenge Workshop*. Newcastle, UK, June 2012. (http://www.researchgate.net/

publication/264888907_Demographic_Prediction_of_Mobile_User_
from_Phone_Usage).

Moretti, Franco. *Graphs, Maps, Trees: Abstract Models for a Literary History* (London: Verso, 2005).

Morgenstern, Leora. 'The problems with solutions to the frame problem.' (http://www-formal.stanford.edu/leora/fp.pdf).

Mortlock, Doug. 'The reported off-target effects in the recent Liang et al human embryo #CRISPR paper are partly incorrect.' *A CRISPR Blog/ Bibliography* (29 April 2015). (http://mortlockcrispr.blogspot. ca/2015/04/the-reported-off-target-effects-in.html).

Moscucci, Ornella. *The Science of Woman: Gynaecology and Gender in England, 1800–1929* (Cambridge: Cambridge University Press, 1990).

Müller, Vincent C., and Nick Bostrom. 'Future progress in artificial intelligence: A survey of expert opinion.' Vincent C. Müller (ed.), *Fundamental Issues of Artificial Intelligence* (Synthese Library; Berlin: Springer, 2014). (http://www.nickbostrom.com/papers/survey.pdf).

Nagi, Jawad, *et al.* 'Max-pooling convolutional neural networks for vision-based hand gesture recognition.' *Proceedings of the 2011* IEEE *International Conference on Signal and Image Processing Applications* (November 2011). (http://ieeexplore.ieee.org/xpl/mostRecentIssue. jsp?punumber=6138563)

Nelson, Lynn Hankinson. *Who Knows: From Quine to a Feminist Empiricism* (Philadelphia: Temple University Press, 1992).

Neumann, Odmar, and Werner Klotz. 'Motor responses to non-reportable, masked stimuli: Where is the limit of direct parameter specification? C. Umiltà and M. Moscovitch (eds.), *Attention and Performance XV* (Cambridge, MA: MIT Press, 1994): 123–150.

New England Labs. 'CRISPR/Cas9 and targeted genome editing: A new era in molecular biology.' (http://www.neb.com/tools-and-resources/ feature-articles/crispr-cas9-and-targeted-genome-editing-a-new-era-in- molecular-biology).

Ng, Andrew. 'Deep learning, self-taught learning and unsupervised feature learning.' IPAM Graduate Summer School. UCLA (2012). (http:// helper.ipam.ucla.edu/wowzavideo.aspx?vfn=10595. mp4&vfd=gss2012)

Ng, Andrew. 'Machine learning.' *Coursera.* (http://www.coursera.org/ learn/machine-learning).

Nielsen, Michael A., *Neural Networks and Deep Learning* (Determination Press, 2015). (http://neuralnetworksanddeeplearning.com/index.html).

Nisbett, Richard E., and Thomas D. Wilson. 'Telling more than we can know: Verbal report on mental processes.' *Psychological Review*, 84.3 (1977): 231–259.

Nonhuman Rights Project. 'Notice of appeal filed in Hercules and Leo Case.' *Nonhuman Rights Project.* (20 August 2015). (http://

www.nonhumanrightsproject.org/2015/08/20/notice-of-appeal-filed-in-hercules-and-leo-case/).

O'Doherty, J.E., *et al.* 'Active tactile exploration enabled by a brain-machine-brain interface.' *Nature*, 479.7372 (10 November 2011): 228–231.

Olsen, Hanna Brooks. 'Let's talk about millennial poverty.' *Medium* (9 January 2015). (http://medium.com/@mshannabrooks/but-seriously-lets-talk-about-millennial-poverty-526066ad9adb#.jf93fplh2).

Open Science Collaboration. 'Estimating the reproducibility of psychological science.' *Science*, 349.6251 (28 August 2015). (http://dx.doi.org/10.1126/science.aac4716).

Ortiz-Catalan, Max, Bo Håkansson and Rickard Brånemark. 'An osseointegrated human-machine gateway for long-term sensory feedback and motor control of artificial limbs.' *Science Translational Medicine*, 6.257 (8 October 2014): 1–8.

Palmer, Jason. 'Glowing monkeys "to aid research."' *BBC News* (27 May 2009). (http://news.bbc.co.uk/2/hi/science/nature/8070252.stm).

Pascal, Blaise. *Pensées* (New York: E. P. Dutton, 1958). (http://www.gutenberg.org/files/18269/18269-h/18269-h.htm).

Pask, Gordon. 'Heinz von Foerster's self-organisation, the progenitor of conversation and interaction theories.' *Systems Research*, 13.3 (1996): 349–362.

Petersen, Ryan. 'The driverless truck is coming, and it's going to automate millions of jobs.' *TechCrunch* (25 April 2016). (http://techcrunch.com/2016/04/25/the-driverless-truck-is-coming-and-its-going-to-automate-millions-of-jobs/).

Piccolino, Marco. 'Animal electricity and the birth of electrophysiology: The legacy of Luigi Galvani.' *Brain Research Bulletin*, 46.5 (1998): 381–407.

Piketty, Thomas. *Capital in the Twenty-First Century* (Cambridge, MA: Harvard University Press, 2014).

Popper, Karl. *The Logic of Scientific Discovery* (London: Routledge, 2002).

Popper, Karl. 'The demarcation between science and metaphysics.' *Conjectures and Refutations: The Growth of Scientific Knowledge* (New York: Routledge, 2002): 341–394.

Popper, Karl. 'Replies to my critics.' P.A. Schilpp (ed.), *The Philosophy of Karl Popper, Volume 2* (La Salle: Open Court Publishing, 1974): 961–1167.

Potter, Steve M., and Thomas B. DeMarse. 'A new approach to neural cell culture for long-term studies.' *Journal of Neuroscience Methods*, 110 (2001): 17–24.

Pulizzi, James. 'In the near future, only very wealthy colleges will have English departments.' *New Republic* (9 June 2014). (https://newrepublic.com/article/118025/advent-digital-humanities-will-make-english-departments-pointless).

Putnam, Hilary. 'The "corroboration" of theories.' Richard Boyd, Philip Gasper and J.D. Trout (eds.), *The Philosophy of Science* (Cambridge, MA: MIT Press, 1991).

Ravenscroft, Ian. 'Folk psychology as a theory.' Edward N. Zalta (ed.), *The Stanford Encyclopedia of Philosophy* (Fall 2015 Edition). (http://plato.stanford.edu/entries/folkpsych-theory/).

Reid, Alex. 'Alan Liu, cultural criticism, the digital humanities, and problem solving?' *Digital Digs* (17 January 2011). (http://alex-reid.net/2011/01/alan-liu-cultural-criticism-and-the-digital-humanities.html).

Robbins, Martin. 'Why I spoofed science journalism, and how to fix it.' *Guardian* (28 September 2010). (http://www.theguardian.com/science/the-lay-scientist/2010/sep/28/science-journalism-spoof).

Rodgers, Paul. 'Google's DeepMind masters Atari games.' *Forbes* (28 February 2015). (http://www.forbes.com/sites/paulrodgers/2015/02/28/googles-deepmind-masters-atari-games/).

Rojahn, Susan Young. 'Genome surgery.' *MIT Technology Review* (11 February 2014). (http://www.technologyreview.com/review/524451/genome-surgery).

Rosen, Gideon. 'Notes on a crisis.' *Princeton Alumni Weekly* (21 January 2016). (https://paw.princeton.edu/article/notes-crisis).

Rosenblatt, Frank. *Principles of Neurodynamics: Perceptrons and the Theory of Brain Mechanisms* (Washington, DC: Spartan Books, 1962).

Rozin, P. 'Specific aversions as a component of specific hungers.' *Journal of Comparative and Physiological Psychology*, 64 (1967): 237–242.

Rozin, P., and J.W. Kalat. 'Specific hungers and poison avoidance as adaptive specializations of learning.' *Psychological Review*, 78 (1971): 459–486.

Russell, Stuart, and Peter Norvig, *Artificial Intelligence: A Modern Approach* (New York: Simon & Schuster, 1995).

Ryle, Gilbert. *The Concept of Mind* (London: Hutchinson, 1949).

Sagan, Dorion (ed.). *Lynn Margulis: The Life and Legacy of a Scientific Rebel* (White River Junction: Chelsea Green, 2012).

Sampaio, E., S. Maris and P. Bach-y-Rita. 'Brain plasticity: "Visual" acuity of blind persons via the tongue.' *Brain Research*, 908 (2001): 204–207.

Sandberg, Anders. 'Feasibility of whole brain emulation.' Vincent C. Müller (ed.), *Theory and Philosophy of Artificial Intelligence* (Berlin: Springer, 2013): 251–264. (http://shanghailectures.org/sites/default/files/uploads/2013_Sandberg_Brain-Simulation_34.pdf).

Sandberg, Anders and Nick Bostrom. 'Whole brain emulation: A roadmap, technical report.' (Future of Humanity Institute, Oxford University, 2008). (http://www.fhi.ox.ac.uk/reports/2008-3.pdf).

Saporito, Bill. 'IBM Watson's startling cancer coup.' *Time* (28 August 2014). (http://time.com/3208716/ibm-watson-cancer/).

Schilling, Malte, *et al.* 'A hexapod walker using a heterarchical architecture for action selection.' *Frontiers in Computational Neuroscience*, 7.126 (2013): 1–17.

Schmidhuber, Jürgen. 'Deep learning in neural networks: An overview.' *Neural Networks*, 61 (January 2015): 85–117. (http://www.idsia. ch/~juergen/DeepLearning8Oct2014.pdf).

Schnall, Simone, Jennifer Benton and Sophie Harvey. 'With a clean conscience: Cleanliness reduces the severity of moral judgments.' *Psychological Science*, 19.12 (2008): 1219–1222.

Schwartz R., and M. Dayhoff. 'Origins of prokaryotes, eukaryotes, mitochondria, and chloroplasts.' *Science*, 199.4327 (1978): 395–403.

Science Daily. 'World premiere of muscle and nerve controlled arm prosthesis.' *Science Daily* (22 February 2013). (http://www. sciencedaily.com/releases/2013/02/130222075730.htm).

Searle, John. *Mind, Language and Society* (New York: Basic Books, 1999).

Searle, John. 'Minds and brains without programs.' Colin Blakemore and Susan Greenfield (eds.) *Mindwaves* (Oxford: Blackwell, 1987): 209–233.

Shannon, Claude E. 'Prediction and entropy of printed English.' *The Bell System Technical Journal*, 30.1 (1951): 50–64.

Shannon, Claude E. 'A mathematical theory of communication.' *The Bell System Technical Journal*, 27 (1948): 379–423; 623–656.

Shelley, Mary. *Frankenstein* (New York: Norton, 2012).

Shettleworth, Sara J., and Jennifer E. Sutton. 'Do animals know what they know?' Matthew Nudds and Susan Hurley (eds.), *Rational Animals?* (Oxford: Oxford University Press, 2006): 235–246.

Slack, J.M.W., *Genes—A Very Short Introduction* (Oxford: Oxford University Press, 2014).

Sokal, Alan, and Jean Bricmont. *Fashionable Nonsense: Postmodern Intellectuals' Abuse of Science* (New York: Picador, 1998).

Srivastava, Sanjay. 'Evaluating a new critique of the Reproducibility Project.' *The Hardest Science* (3 March 2016). (http://hardsci. wordpress.com/2016/03/03/evaluating-a-new-critique-of-the-reproducibility-project/).

Steigler, Bernard. *Technics and Time, 1: The Fault of Epimetheus* (trans. Richard Beardsworth and George Collins. Stanford, Stanford University Press, 1998).

Stephenson, Neal. *Snow Crash* (New York: Bantam Books, 1992).

Stone, Brad and Jack Clark. 'Google puts Boston Dynamics up for sale in robotics retreat.' *Bloomberg* (17 March 2016). (http://www. bloomberg.com/news/articles/2016-03-17/google-is-said-to-put-boston-dynamics-robotics-unit-up-for-sale).

Sur, Mriganka. 'Rewiring cortex: Cross-modal plasticity and its implications for cortical development and function.' G. Calvert, C. Spence, B. E. Stein (eds.), *Handbook of Multisensory Processing* (Cambridge, MA: MIT Press, 2004): 681–694.

Sutton, Richard S., and Andrew G. Barto. *Reinforcement Learning: An Introduction* (Cambridge: MIT Press, 1998). (http://webdocs.cs. ualberta.ca/~sutton/book/ebook/the-book.html).

Suzuki, Miwa. 'Japan child robot mimicks infant learning.' *Phys.org* (5 April 2009). (http://phys.org/news/2009-04-japan-child-robot-mimicks-infant.html).

Swift, Jonathan. *Gulliver's Travels into Several Remote Nations of the World* (London: Penguin Classics, 2003).

Tencer, Daniel. 'A basic income for Ontario? Province plans pilot project as part of budget.' *Huffington Post* (26 February 2016). (http://www.huffingtonpost.ca/2016/02/26/ontario-basic-income_n_9328264.html).

Terrace, H.S., L. A. Petitto, R. J. Sanders and T. G. Bever. 'Can an ape create a sentence?' *Science*, 206.4421 (1979): 891–902.

Turing, Alan. 'Computing Machinery and Intelligence.' *Mind*, LIX.236 (1950): 433–460.

Turing, Alan. 'On computable numbers, with an application to the Entscheidungsproblem (1936).' B. Jack Copeland (ed.), *The Essential Turing: Seminal Writings in Computing, Logic, Philosophy, Artificial Intelligence, and Artificial Life plus The Secrets of Enigma* (Oxford: Clarendon, 2004): 58–90.

Turing, Alan. 'Intelligent machinery (1948).' B. Jack Copeland (ed.), *The Essential Turing: Seminal Writings in Computing, Logic, Philosophy, Artificial Intelligence, and Artificial Life plus The Secrets of Enigma* (Oxford: Clarendon, 2004): 410–432.

Tworek, Heidi. 'The real reason the humanities are "in crisis."' *The Atlantic* (18 December 2013). (http://www.theatlantic.com/education/archive/2013/12/the-real-reason-the-humanities-are-in-crisis/282441/).

Upbin, Bruce. 'IBM's Watson gets its first piece of business in healthcare.' *Forbes* (8 February 2013). (http://www.forbes.com/sites/bruceupbin/2013/02/08/ibms-watson-gets-its-first-piece-of-business-in-healthcare/).

Upbin, Bruce. 'IBM's Watson now a second-year med student.' *Forbes* (25 May 2011). (http://www.forbes.com/sites/bruceupbin/2011/05/25/ibms-watson-now-a-second-year-med-student).

Urmson, Chris. 'The view from the front seat of the Google self-driving car.' *Medium* (11 May 2015). (http://medium.com/backchannel/the-view-from-the-front-seat-of-the-google-self-driving-car-46fc9f3e6088).

Vidal, Jacques J. 'Toward direct brain computer communication.' *Annual Review of Biophysics and Bioengineering*, 2 (1973): 157–180.

von Foerster, Heinz. *Understanding Understanding: Essays on Cybernetics and Cognition* (New York: Springer-Verlag, 2003).

von Neumann, John, and Oskar Morgenstern. *Theory of Games and Economic Behavior* (Princeton: Princeton University Press, 1944).

Vinge, Vernor. 'The coming technological Singularity: How to survive in the post-human era.' (http://www-rohan.sdsu.edu/faculty/vinge/misc/singularity.html).

Walker, Mark. 'BIG and technological unemployment: Chicken Little versus the economists.' *Journal of Evolution and Technology*, 24.1 (February 2014). (http://jetpress.org/v24/walker.htm).

Walsh, Gary. 'Therapeutic insulins and their large-scale manufacture.' *Applied Microbiology and Biotechnology*, 67.2 (2005): 151–159.

Waters, Richard. 'Artificial intelligence: Can Watson save IBM?' *Financial Times* (5 January 2016). (http://www.ft.com/cms/s/2/dced8150-b300-11e5-8358-9a82b43f6b2f.html).

Warwick, Kevin, *et al.* 'Thought communication and control: A first step using radiotelegraphy.' *IEE Proceedings—Communications*, 151.3 (2004): 185–189.

Warwick, Kevin, *et al.* 'The application of implant technology for cybernetic systems.' *Archives of Neurology* 60.10 (2003): 1369–1373.

Weissmann, Jordan. 'Actually, the humanities aren't in crisis.' *Atlantic* (24 June 2013). (http://www.theatlantic.com/business/archive/2013/06/actually-the-humanities-arent-in-crisis/277144/).

Wiener, Norbert. *Cybernetics Or Control and Communication in the Animal and the Machine* (New York: Wiley, 1948).

Wikipedia. 'Artificial neural network.' (http://en.wikipedia.org/wiki/Artificial_neural_network).

Wikipedia. 'Bell Labs.' (http://en.wikipedia.org/wiki/Bell_Labs).

Wikipedia. 'Bit.' (http://en.wikipedia.org/wiki/Bit).

Wikipedia. 'Convolutional neural network.' (http://en.wikipedia.org/wiki/Convolutional_neural_network).

Wikipedia. 'CRISPR.' (http://en.wikipedia.org/wiki/CRISPR).

Wikipedia. 'DNA.' (https://en.wikipedia.org/wiki/DNA).

Wikipedia. 'Genes.' (http://en.wikipedia.org/wiki/Gene).

Wikipedia. 'Genetic engineering.' (http://en.wikipedia.org/wiki/Genetic_engineering).

Wikipedia. 'Markov Decision Process.' (http://en.wikipedia.org/wiki/Markov_decision_process).

Wikipedia. 'Q-learning.' (http://en.wikipedia.org/wiki/Q-learning).

Willingham, Emily. 'We need a recall system for bad science reporting.' *Forbes* (24 June 2013). (http://www.forbes.com/sites/emilywillingham/2013/06/24/rice-lead-and-the-problem-of-untracked-science-reporting/).

Wittens, Steven. 'Occupy WWW Street (EN): Internet activism and media in the age of social justice.' *ACKO* (30 November 2015). (http://acko.net/blog/occupy-www-street-en/).

The World Bank. 'Poverty: Overview.' (http://www.worldbank.org/en/topic/poverty/overview).

The World Bank. 'New data show 1.4 billion live on less than US$1.25 a day, but progress against poverty remains strong.' Press Release (16 September 2008). (http://www.worldbank.org/en/news/press-release/2008/09/16/new-data-show-14-billion-live-less-us125-day-progress-against-poverty-remains-strong).

Wolfe, Cary. *What is Posthumanism?* (Minneapolis: University of Minnesota Press, 2010).

Wolfe, Cary. 'In search of post-humanist theory: The second-order cybernetics of Maturana and Varela.' *Cultural Critique*, 30 (Spring 1995): 33–70.

Wong, Christine. 'Advertisers react to privacy watchdog's online behavioural advertising study.' *itbusiness.ca*. (http://www.itbusiness.ca/news/advertisers-react-to-privacy-watchdogs-online-behavioural-advertising-study/56314).

Wright, Erik Olin. 'Basic income as a socialist project.' *Rutgers Journal of Law & Urban Policy*, 2.1 (Fall 2005). (https://www.ssc.wisc.edu/~wright/Basic%20Income%20as%20a%20Socialist%20Project.pdf).

Wynne, Clive. *Animal Cognition: The Mental Lives of Animals* (Basingstoke: Palgrave Macmillan, 2001).

YLE. 'Kela to prepare basic income proposal.' *YLE* (31 October 2015). (http://yle.fi/uutiset/kela_to_prepare_basic_income_proposal/8422295).

Young, Cathy. 'Blame GamerGate's Bad Rep on Smears and Shoddy Journalism.' *Observer* (13 October 2015). (http://observer.com/2015/10/blame-gamergates-bad-rep-on-smears-and-shoddy-journalism/).

Yudkowsky, Eliezer. 'Artificial Intelligence as a Positive and Negative Factor in Global Risk.' in (eds) Nick Bostrom and Milan M. Ćirković, *Global Catastrophic Risks* (New York: Oxford University Press), 308–345.

Yuhas, Alan. 'Chimpanzees granted petition to hear "legal persons" status in court.' *Guardian* (21 April 2015). (http://www.theguardian.com/world/2015/apr/21/chimpanzees-granted-legal-persons-status-unlawful-imprisonment).

Zach, Reto. 'Shell dropping: Decision making and optimal foraging in north-western crows.' *Behavior*, 68 (1979): 106–117.

Zern, Ed. 'Exit laughing.' *Field and Stream*, November (1959): 142. (http://edzern.com/?p=42).

INDEX